HUMAN
RIGHTS
WATCH

WORLD REPORT

2011

EVENTS OF 2010

ISBN-13: 978-1-58322-921-7

Front cover photo: *Aung Myo Thein, 42, spent more than six years in prison in Burma for his activism as a student union leader. More than 2,200 political prisoners—including artists, journalists, students, monks, and political activists—remain locked up in Burma's squalid prisons.* © 2010 Platon for Human Rights Watch

Back cover photo: *A child migrant worker from Kyrgyzstan picks tobacco leaves in Kazakhstan. Every year thousands of Kyrgyz migrant workers, often together with their children, find work in tobacco farming, where many are subjected to abuse and exploitation by employers.* © 2009 Moises Saman/Magnum for Human Rights Watch

Cover and book design by Rafael Jiménez

350 Fifth Avenue, 34th floor
New York, NY 10118-3299 USA
Tel: +1 212 290 4700
Fax: +1 212 736 1300
hrwnyc@hrw.org

51 Avenue Blanc, Floor 6,
1202 Geneva, Switzerland
Tel: +41 22 738 0481
Fax: +41 22 738 1791
hrwgva@hrw.org

1630 Connecticut Avenue, N.W., Suite 500
Washington, DC 20009 USA
Tel: +1 202 612 4321
Fax: +1 202 612 4333
hrwdc@hrw.org

Poststraße 4-5
10178 Berlin, Germany
Tel: +49 30 2593 06-10
Fax: +49 30 2593 06-29
berlin@hrw.org

2-12 Pentonville Road, 2nd Floor
London N1 9HF, UK
Tel: +44 20 7713 1995
Fax: +44 20 7713 1800
hrwuk@hrw.org

1st fl, Wilds View
Isle of Houghton
Boundary Road (at Carse O'Gowrie)
Parktown, 2198 South Africa
Tel: +27-11-484-2640, Fax: +27-11-484-2641

27 Rue de Lisbonne
75008 Paris, France
Tel: +33 (0) 1 41 92 07 34
Fax: +33 (0) 1 47 22 08 61
paris@hrw.org

#4A, Meiji University Academy Common bldg. 7F, 1-1,
Kanda-Surugadai, Chiyoda-ku
Tokyo 101-8301 Japan
Tel: +81-3-5282-5160, Fax: +81-3-5282-5161
tokyo@hrw.org

Avenue des Gaulois, 7
1040 Brussels, Belgium
Tel: + 32 (2) 732 2009
Fax: + 32 (2) 732 0471
hrwbe@hrw.org

Mansour Building 4th Floor, Apt. 26
Nicholas Turk Street
Medawar, Beirut, Lebanon 20753909
Tel: +961-1-447833, Fax +961-1-446497

www.hrw.org

Human Rights Watch is dedicated to protecting the human rights of people around the world.

We stand with victims and activists to prevent discrimination, to uphold political freedom, to protect people from inhumane conduct in wartime, and to bring offenders to justice.

We investigate and expose human rights violations and hold abusers accountable.

We challenge governments and those who hold power to end abusive practices and respect international human rights law.

We enlist the public and the international community to support the cause of human rights for all.

HUMAN RIGHTS WATCH

Human Rights Watch is one of the world's leading independent organizations dedicated to defending and protecting human rights. By focusing international attention where human rights are violated, we give voice to the oppressed and hold oppressors accountable for their crimes. Our rigorous, objective investigations and strategic, targeted advocacy build intense pressure for action and raise the cost of human rights abuse. For over 30 years, Human Rights Watch has worked tenaciously to lay the legal and moral groundwork for deep-rooted change and has fought to bring greater justice and security to people around the world.

Human Rights Watch began in 1978 with the founding of its Europe and Central Asia division (then known as Helsinki Watch). Today, it also includes divisions covering Africa, the Americas, Asia, and the Middle East and North Africa; a United States program; thematic divisions or programs on arms, business and human rights, children's rights, health and human rights, international justice, lesbian, gay, bisexual and transgender rights, refugees, terrorism/counterterrorism, and women's rights; and an emergencies program. It maintains offices in Amsterdam, Beirut, Berlin, Brussels, Cairo, Chicago, Geneva, Johannesburg, London, Los Angeles, Moscow, New York, Paris, San Francisco, Tokyo, Toronto, Washington DC, and Zurich, and field presences in 20 other locations globally. Human Rights Watch is an independent, nongovernmental organization, supported by contributions from private individuals and foundations worldwide. It accepts no government funds, directly or indirectly.

Acknowledgments

A compilation of this magnitude requires contribution from a large number of people, including most of the Human Rights Watch staff. The contributors were:

Pema Abrahams, Brad Adams, Maria Aissa de Figueredo, Setenay Akdag, Brahim Alansari, Chris Albin-Lackey, Yousif al-Timimi, Joseph Amon, Amy Auguston, Leeam Azulay, Clive Baldwin, Neela Banerjee, Shantha Barriga, Jo Becker, Fatima-Zahra Benfkira, Nicholas Bequelin, Andrea Berg, Carroll Bogert, Philippe Bolopion, Tess Borden, Amy Braunschweiger, Sebastian Brett, Reed Brody, Christen Broecker, Jane Buchanan, Wolfgang Buettner, Maria Burnett, Elizabeth Calvin, Haleh Chahrokh, Anna Chaplin, Grace Choi, Sara Colm, Jon Connolly, Adam Coogle, Kaitlin Cordes, Zama Coursen-Neff, Emma Daly, Philippe Dam, Kiran D'Amico, Sara Darehshori, Juliette de Rivero, Kristina DeMain, Rachel Denber, Richard Dicker, Boris Dittrich, Kanae Doi, Corinne Dufka, Andrej Dynko, Jessica Evans, Elizabeth Evenson, Jean-Marie Fardeau, Guillermo Farias, Jamie Fellner, Bill Frelick, Arvind Ganesan, Meenakshi Ganguly, Liesl Gerntholtz, Alex Gertner, Neela Ghoshal, Thomas Gilchrist, Allison Gill, Antonio Ginatta, Giorgi Gogia, Eric Goldstein, Steve Goose, Yulia Gorbunova, Ian Gorvin, Jessie Graham, Laura Graham, Eric Guttschuss, Danielle Haas, Andreas Harsono, Ali Dayan Hasan, Leslie Haskell, Jehanne Henry, Eleanor Hevey, Peggy Hicks, Saleh Hijazi, Nadim Houry, Lindsey Hutchison, Peter Huvos, Claire Ivers, Balkees Jarrah, Rafael Jiménez, Preeti Kannan, Tiseke Kasambala, Aruna Kashyap, Nick Kemming, Elise Keppler, Amr Khairy, Nadya Khalife, Viktoria Kim, Carolyn Kindelan, Juliane Kippenberg, Amanda Klasing, Kyle Knight, Soo Ryun Kwon, Erica Lally, Mignon Lamia, Adrianne Lapar, Leslie Lefkow, Lotte Leicht, Iain Levine, Diederik Lohman, Tanya Lokshina, Jiaying Long, Anna Lopriore, Linda Louie, Drake Lucas, Lena Miriam Macke, Tom Malinowski, Noga Malkin, Ahmed Mansour, Joanne Mariner Edmon Marukyan, Dave Mathieson, Géraldine Mattioli-Zeltner, Veronica Matushaj, Maria McFarland, Megan McLemore, Amanda McRae, Wenzel Michalski, Kathy Mills, Lisa Misol, Marianne Mollmann, Ella Moran, Heba Morayef, Mani Mostofi, Priyanka Motaparthy, Rasha Moumneh, Siphokazi Mthathi, Jim Murphy, Samer Muscati, Dipika Nath, Stephanie Neider, Rachel Nicholson, Agnes Ndige Muriungi Odhiambo, Jessica Ognian, Erin O'Leary, Alison Parker, Sarah Parkes, Elaine Pearson, Rona Peligal, Sasha Petrov, Sunai Phasuk, Enrique Piraces, Laura Pitter,

Dinah PoKempner, Tom Porteous, Jyotsna Poudyal, Andrea Prasow, Marina Pravdic, Mustafa Qadri, Daniela Ramirez, Ben Rawlence, Rachel Reid, Aisling Reidy, Meghan Rhoad, Sophie Richardson, Lisa Rimli, Mihra Rittmann, Phil Robertson, Kathy Rose, James Ross, Kenneth Roth, Faraz Sanei, Joe Saunders, Ida Sawyer, Max Schoening, Jake Scobey-Thal, David Segall, Kathryn Semogas, Kay Seok, Jose Serralvo, Anna Sevortian Vikram Shah, Bede Sheppard, Robin Shulman, Gerry Simpson, Emma Sinclair-Webb, Peter Slezkine, Daniel W. Smith, Ole Solvang, Mickey Spiegel, Xabay Spinka, Nik Steinberg, Joe Stork, Judith Sunderland, Steve Swerdlow, Veronika Szente Goldston, Maya Taal, Tamara Taraciuk, Letta Tayler, Carina Tertsakian, Elena Testi, Tej Thapa, Laura Thomas, Katherine Todrys, Simone Troller, Wanda Troszczynska-van Genderen, Farid Tukhbatullin, Bill Van Esveld, Gauri Van Gulik, Anneke Van Woudenberg, Elena Vanko, Nisha Varia, Rezarta Veizaj, Jamie Vernaelde, José Miguel Vivanco, Florentine Vos, Janet Walsh, Ben Ward, Matthew Wells, Lois Whitman, Sarah Leah Whitson, Christoph Wilcke, Daniel Wilkinson, Minky Worden, Riyo Yoshioka.

Joe Saunders edited the report with assistance from Ian Gorvin, Danielle Haas, Iain Levine, and Robin Shulman. Brittany Mitchell coordinated the editing process. Layout and production were coordinated by Grace Choi and Rafael Jiménez, with assistance from Anna Lopriore, Veronica Matushaj, Jim Murphy, Enrique Piraces, and Kathy Mills.

Leeam Azulay, Adam Coogle, Guillermo Farias, Alex Gertner, Thomas Gilchrist, Lindsey Hutchison, Carolyn Kindelan, Kyle Knight, Erica Lally, Adrianne Lapar, Linda Louie, Stephanie Neider, Erin O'Leary, Jessica Ognian, Marina Pravdic, Daniela Ramirez, Jake Scobey-Thal, David Segall, and Vikram Shah proofread the report.

For a full list of Human Rights Watch staff, please go to our website:
www.hrw.org/about/info/staff.html.

This 21st annual World Report is dedicated to the memory of our beloved colleague Ian Gorvin, who died of cancer on November 15, 2010, at age 48. Ian, senior program officer at Human Rights Watch, edited the World Report for most of the past decade, was an expert on human rights issues in Europe and around the world, and made lasting contributions to the human rights movement through his work with Amnesty International and the Organization for Security and Co-operation in Europe as well as Human Rights Watch. An experienced activist, Ian brought good judgment as well as linguistic savvy and an unerring eye for detail to his editing. And he never lost sight of our mission: to tell the stories of victims of human rights violations with dignity and compassion and to press for justice to ensure that others do not suffer the same fate. He was ever the voice of calm, sensible advice, with an understated but potent sense of humor. We miss him enormously.

Table of Contents

A Facade of Action

Whose News?

Schools as Battlegrounds

Photo Essays

A Facade of Action:
The Misuse of Dialogue and Cooperation with Rights Abusers

By Kenneth Roth

In last year's World Report, Human Rights Watch highlighted the intensifying attacks by abusive governments on human rights defenders, organizations, and institutions. This year we address the flip side of the problem—the failure of the expected champions of human rights to respond to the problem, defend those people and organizations struggling for human rights, and stand up firmly against abusive governments.

There is often a degree of rationality in a government's decision to violate human rights. The government might fear that permitting greater freedom would encourage people to join together in voicing discontent and thus jeopardize its grip on power. Or abusive leaders might worry that devoting resources to the impoverished would compromise their ability to enrich themselves and their cronies.

International pressure can change that calculus. Whether exposing or condemning abuses, conditioning access to military aid or budgetary support on ending them, imposing targeted sanctions on individual abusers, or even calling for prosecution and punishment of those responsible, public pressure raises the cost of violating human rights. It discourages further oppression, signaling that violations cannot continue cost-free.

All governments have a duty to exert such pressure. A commitment to human rights requires not only upholding them at home but also using available and appropriate tools to convince other governments to respect them as well.

1

No repressive government likes facing such pressure. Today many are fighting back, hoping to dissuade others from adopting or continuing such measures. That reaction is hardly surprising. What is disappointing is the number of governments that, in the face of that reaction, are abandoning public pressure. With disturbing frequency, governments that might have been counted on to generate such pressure for human rights are accepting the rationalizations and subterfuges of repressive governments and giving up. In place of a commitment to exerting public pressure for human rights, they profess a preference for softer approaches such as private "dialogue" and "cooperation."

There is nothing inherently wrong with dialogue and cooperation to promote human rights. Persuading a government through dialogue to genuinely cooperate with efforts to improve its human rights record is a key goal of human rights advocacy. A cooperative approach makes sense for a government that demonstrably wants to respect human rights but lacks the resources or technical know-how to implement its commitment. It can also be useful for face-saving reasons—if a government is willing to end violations but wants to appear to act on its own initiative. Indeed, Human Rights Watch often engages quietly with governments for such reasons.

But when the problem is a lack of political will to respect rights, public pressure is needed to change the cost-benefit analysis that leads to the choice of repression over rights. In such cases, the quest for dialogue and cooperation becomes a charade designed more to appease critics of complacency than to secure change, a calculated diversion from the fact that nothing of consequence is being done. Moreover, the refusal to use pressure makes dialogue and cooperation less effective because governments know there is nothing to fear from simply feigning serious participation.

Recent illustrations of this misguided approach include ASEAN's tepid response to Burmese repression, the United Nations' deferential attitude toward Sri Lankan atrocities, the European Union's obsequious approach to Uzbekistan and Turkmenistan, the soft Western reaction to certain favored repressive African leaders such as Paul Kagame of Rwanda and Meles Zenawi of Ethiopia, the weak United States policy toward Saudi Arabia, India's pliant posture toward Burma and Sri Lanka, and the near-universal cowardice in confronting China's deepening crackdown on basic liberties. In all of these cases, governments, by abandoning public pressure, effectively close their eyes to repression.

Even those that shy away from using pressure in most cases are sometimes willing to apply it toward pariah governments, such as North Korea, Iran, Sudan, and Zimbabwe, whose behavior, whether on human rights or other matters, is so outrageous that it overshadows other interests. But in too many cases, governments these days are disappointingly disinclined to use public pressure to alter the calculus of repression.

When governments stop exerting public pressure to address human rights violations, they leave domestic advocates–rights activists, sympathetic parliamentarians, concerned journalists–without crucial support. Pressure from abroad can help create the political space for local actors to push their government to respect rights. It also can let domestic advocates know that they are not alone, that others stand with them. But when there is little or no such pressure, repressive governments have a freer hand to restrict domestic advocates, as has occurred in recent years in Russia, Ethiopia, Rwanda, Cambodia, and elsewhere. And because dialogue and cooperation look too much like acquiescence and acceptance, domestic advocates sense indifference rather than solidarity.

A Timid Response to Repression

In recent years the use of dialogue and cooperation in lieu of public pressure has emerged with a vengeance at the UN, from Secretary-General Ban Ki-moon to many members of the Human Rights Council. In addition, the EU seems to have become particularly infatuated with the idea of dialogue and coopera-tion, with the EU's first high representative for foreign affairs and security poli-cy, Catherine Ashton, repeatedly expressing a preference for "quiet diploma-cy" regardless of the circumstances. Leading democracies of the global South, such as South Africa, India, and Brazil, have promoted quiet demarches as a preferred response to repression. The famed eloquence of US President Barack Obama has sometimes eluded him when it comes to defending human rights, especially in bilateral contexts with, for example, China, India, and Indonesia. Obama has also not insisted that the various agencies of the US government, such as the Defense Department and various embassies, convey strong human rights messages consistently–a problem, for example, in Egypt, Indonesia, and Bahrain.

This is a particularly inopportune time for proponents of human rights to lose their public voice, because various governments that want to prevent the vig-orous enforcement of human rights have had no qualms about raising theirs. Many are challenging first principles, such as the universality of human rights. For example, some African governments complain that the International Criminal Court's current focus on Africa is selective and imperialist, as if the fate of a few African despots were more important than the suffering of count-less African victims. China's economic rise is often cited as reason to believe that authoritarian government is more effective for guiding economic develop-ment in low-income countries, even though unaccountable governments are more likely to succumb to corruption and less likely to respond to or invest in people's most urgent needs (as demonstrated by the rising number of protests in China–some 90,000 annually by the government's own count–fueled by growing discontent over the corruption and arbitrariness of local officials). Some governments, eager to abandon long-established rules for protecting civilians in time of war or threatened security, justify their own violations of the laws of war by citing Sri Lanka's indiscriminate attacks in its victory over the rebel Tamil Tigers, or Western (and especially US) tolerance of torture and arbitrary detention in combating terrorism. Governments that lose their voice on human rights effectively abandon these crucial debates to the opponents of universal human rights enforcement.

Part of this reticence is due to a crisis of confidence. The shifting global balance of power (particularly the rise of China), an intensified competition for markets and natural resources at a time of economic turmoil, and the decline in moral standing of Western powers occasioned by their use with impunity of abusive counterterrorism techniques have made many governments less willing to take a strong public stand in favor of human rights.

Ironically, some of the governments most opposed to using pressure to promote human rights have no qualms about using pressure to deflect human rights criticism. China, for example, pulled out all stops in an ultimately unsuccessful effort to suppress a report to the UN Security Council on the discovery of Chinese weaponry in Darfur despite an arms embargo. Sri Lanka did the same in an unsuccessful effort to quash a UN advisory panel on accountability for war crimes committed during its armed conflict with the Tamil Tigers. China also mounted a major lobbying effort to prevent the awarding of the Nobel Peace Prize to imprisoned Chinese writer and human rights activist Liu Xiaobo, and when that failed, it tried unsuccessfully to discourage governments from attending the award ceremony in Norway. China made a similar effort to block a proposed UN commission of inquiry into war crimes committed in Burma.

The United Nations and Its Member States

The obsession with dialogue and cooperation is particularly intense at the UN Human Rights Council in Geneva, where many of the members insist that the Council should practice "cooperation, not condemnation." A key form of pressure at the Council is the ability to send fact-finders to expose what abuses were committed and to hold governments accountable for not curtailing abuses. One important medium for these tools is a resolution aimed at a particular country or situation. Yet many governments on the Council eschew any country resolution designed to generate pressure (except in the case of the Council's perennial pariah, Israel). As China explained (in the similar context of the UN General Assembly), "[s]ubmitting [a] country specific resolution...will make the issue of human rights politicized and is not conducive to genuine cooperation on human rights issues." The African Group at the UN has said it will support country resolutions only with the consent of the target government, in other words, only when the resolution exerts no pressure at all. This approach was taken to an extreme after Sri Lanka launched indiscriminate attacks on civilians in the final months of its war with the Tamil Tigers—rather than condemn these atrocities, a majority of Council members overcame a minority's objections and voted to congratulate Sri Lanka on its military victory without mentioning government atrocities.

If members of the Council want dialogue and cooperation to be effective in upholding human rights, they should limit use of these tools to governments that have demonstrated a political will to improve. But whether out of calculation or cowardice, many Council members promote dialogue and cooperation as a universal prescription without regard to whether a government has the political will to curtail its abusive behavior. They thus resist tests for determining whether a government's asserted interest in cooperation is a ploy to avoid pressure or a genuine commitment to improvement—tests that might look to the government's willingness to acknowledge its human rights failings, welcome UN investigators to examine the nature of the problem, prescribe solutions, and embark upon reforms. The enemies of human rights enforcement oppose critical resolutions even on governments that clearly fail these tests, such as Burma, Iran, North Korea, Sri Lanka, and Sudan.

Similar problems arise at the UN General Assembly. As the Burmese military reinforced its decades-long rule with sham elections designed to give it a civilian facade, a campaign got under way to intensify pressure by launching an international commission of inquiry to examine the many war crimes committed in the country's long-running armed conflict. A commission of inquiry would be an excellent tool for showing that such atrocities could no longer be committed with impunity. It would also create an incentive for newer members of the military-dominated government to avoid the worst abuses of the past. The idea of a commission of inquiry, originally proposed by the independent UN special rapporteur on Burma, has received support from, among others, the US, the United Kingdom, France, Netherlands, Canada, Australia, and New Zealand.

Yet some have refused to endorse a commission of inquiry on the spurious grounds that it would not work without the cooperation of the Burmese junta. EU High Representative Ashton, in failing to embrace this tool, said: "Ideally, we should aim at ensuring a measure of cooperation from the national authorities." Similarly, a German Foreign Ministry spokeswoman said that, to help advance human rights in the country, it is "crucial to find some co-operation mechanism with the [Burmese] national authorities." Yet obtaining such cooperation from the Burmese military in the absence of further pressure is a pipe dream.

One favorite form of cooperation is a formal intergovernmental dialogue on human rights, such as those that many governments conduct with China and the EU maintains with a range of repressive countries, including the former-

Soviet republics of Central Asia. Authoritarian governments understandably welcome these dialogues because they remove the spotlight from human rights discussions. The public, including domestic activists, is left in the dark, as are most government officials outside the foreign ministry. But Western governments also often cite the existence of such dialogues as justification for not speaking concretely about human rights violations and remedies in more meaningful settings—as Sweden did, for example, during its EU presidency when asked why human rights had not featured more prominently at the EU-Central Asia ministerial conference.

Human Rights Watch's own experience shows that outspoken commentary on human rights practices need not preclude meaningful private dialogue with governments. Human Rights Watch routinely reports on abuses and generates pressure for them to end, but that has not stood in the way of active engagement with many governments that are the subject of these reports. Indeed, governments are often *more* likely to engage with Human Rights Watch, because the sting of public reporting, and a desire to influence it, spurs them to dialogue. If a nongovernmental organization can engage with governments while speaking out about their abuses, certainly governments should be able to do so as well.

The Need for Benchmarks

Dialogues would have a far greater impact if they were tied to concrete and publicly articulated benchmarks. Such benchmarks would give clear direction to the dialogue and make participants accountable for concrete results. But that is often exactly what dialogue participants want to avoid. The failure to set clear, public benchmarks is itself evidence of a lack of seriousness, an unwillingness to deploy even the minimum pressure needed to make dialogue meaningful. The EU, for example, has argued that publicly articulated benchmarks would introduce tension into a dialogue and undermine its role as a "confidence-building exercise," as if the purpose of the dialogue were to promote warm and fuzzy feelings rather than to improve respect for human rights.

Moreover, repressive governments have become so adept at manipulating these dialogues, and purported promoters of human rights so dependent on them as a sign that they are "doing something," that the repressors have managed to treat the mere commencement or resumption of dialogue as a sign of "progress." Even supposed rights-promoters have fallen into this trap. For example, a 2008 progress report by the EU on the implementation of its Central Asia strategy concluded that things were going well but gave no specifics beyond "intensified political dialogue" as a measurement of "progress."

Even when benchmarks exist, Western governments' willingness to ignore them when they prove inconvenient undermines their usefulness. For example, the EU's bilateral agreements with other countries are routinely conditioned on basic respect for human rights, but the EU nonetheless concluded a significant trade agreement and pursued a full partnership and cooperation agreement with Turkmenistan, a severely repressive government that cannot conceivably be said to comply with the agreements' human rights conditions. It is as if the EU announced in advance that its human rights conditions were mere window-dressing, not to be taken seriously. The EU justified this step in the name of "deeper engagement" and a new "framework for dialogue and cooperation."

Similarly, despite Serbia's failure to apprehend and surrender for trial indicted war crimes suspect Ratko Mladic (the former Bosnian Serb military leader)—a litmus test for the war-crimes cooperation that the EU has repeatedly insisted is a requirement for beginning discussions with Serbia about its accession to the EU—the EU agreed to start discussions anyway. The EU also gradually lifted sanctions imposed on Uzbekistan after security forces massacred hundreds in

2005 in the city of Andijan, even though no steps had been taken toward per-mitting an independent investigation—originally the chief condition for lifting sanctions—let alone prosecuting those responsible or doing anything else that the EU had called for, such as releasing all wrongfully imprisoned human rights activists.

By the same token, the Obama administration in its first year simply ignored the human rights conditions on the transfer of military aid to Mexico, under the Merida Initiative, even though Mexico had done nothing as required toward prosecuting abusive military officials in civilian courts. While in its sec-ond year the administration did withhold a small fraction of funding, it once again certified—despite clear evidence to the contrary—that Mexico was meet-ing Merida's human rights requirements. The US also signed a funding com-pact with Jordan under the Millennium Challenge Corporation even though Jordan had failed to improve its failing grades on the MCC's benchmarks for political rights and civil liberties.

Weak Leadership

UN Secretary-General Ban Ki-moon has been notably reluctant to put pressure on abusive governments. As secretary-general, he has two main tools at his disposal to promote human rights—private diplomacy and his public voice. He can nudge governments to change through his good offices, or he can use the stature of his office to expose those who are unwilling to change. Ban's disin-clination to speak out about serious human rights violators means he is often choosing to fight with one hand tied behind his back. He did make strong public comments on human rights when visiting Turkmenistan and Uzbekistan, but he was much more reticent when visiting a powerful country like China. And he has placed undue faith in his professed ability to convince by private persuasion the likes of Sudanese President Omar al-Bashir,

Burmese military leader Than Shwe, and Sri Lankan President Mahinda Rajapaksa.

Worse, far from condemning repression, Ban sometimes went out of his way to portray oppressive governments in a positive light. For example, in the days before Burma's sham elections in November, Ban contended that it was "not too late" to "make this election more inclusive and participatory" by releasing political detainees—an unlikely eventuality that, even if realized, would not have leveled the severely uneven electoral playing field. Even after the travesty was complete, Ban said only that the elections had been "insufficiently inclusive, participatory and transparent"—a serious understatement.

When he visited China the same month, Ban made no mention of human rights in his meeting with Chinese President Hu Jintao, leaving the topic for lesser officials. That omission left the impression that, for the secretary-general, human rights were at best a second-tier priority. In commenting on the awarding of the Nobel Peace Prize to Liu Xiaobo, the imprisoned Chinese human rights activist, Ban never congratulated Liu or called for his release from prison but instead praised Beijing by saying: "China has achieved remarkable economic advances, lifted millions out of poverty, broadened political participation and steadily joined the international mainstream in its adherence to recognized human rights instruments and practices."

The new British prime minister, David Cameron, did only marginally better during his visit to China. He did not mention Liu in his formal meeting with Chinese Prime Minister Wen Jiabao, saving the matter for informal talks over dinner. And his public remarks stayed at the level of generality with which the Chinese governments itself is comfortable—the need for "greater political opening" and the rule of law—rather than mention specific cases of imprisoned government critics or other concrete rights restrictions.

The government of German Chancellor Angela Merkel showed a similar lack of courage in its dealings with China. "Dialogue" is the German government's widely mentioned guiding principle, and Merkel in public remarks during her latest visit to China made only the slightest passing reference to human rights, although she claimed to have mentioned the issue privately. At the "China Meets Europe" summit in Hamburg, German Foreign Minister Guido Westerwelle, without mentioning concrete abuses, cited an "intensive rule of law dialogue" and a "human rights dialogue" as "build[ing] a solid foundation for a real partnership between Germany and China." In France, President Nicolas Sarkozy, as he was about to welcome Chinese President Hu Jintao in Paris in November, did not even congratulate Liu Xiaobo for having been awarded the Nobel Peace Prize.

With respect to Saudi Arabia, the US government in 2005 established a "strategic dialogue" which, because of Saudi objections, did not mention human rights as a formal subject but relegated the topic to the "Partnership, Education, Exchange, and Human Development Working Group." Even that dialogue then gradually disappeared. While the US government contributed to keeping Iran off the board of the new UN Women agency in 2010 because of its mistreatment of women, it made no such effort with Saudi Arabia, which has an abysmal record on women but was given a seat by virtue of its financial contribution. Similarly, the UK has maintained a quiet "two kingdoms" dialogue with Saudi Arabia since 2005. Its launching included only oblique references to human rights, and it has exerted no discernible pressure on the Saudi government to improve its rights record.

Other Interests at Stake

Sometimes those who promote quiet dialogue over public pressure argue efficacy, although often other interests seem to be at play. In Uzbekistan, which provides an important route for resupplying NATO troops in Afghanistan, the

EU argued that targeted sanctions against those responsible for the Andijan massacre were "alienating" the government and "standing in the way of a constructive relationship," as if making nice to a government that aggressively denied any responsibility for killing hundreds of its citizens would be more successful at changing it than sustained pressure. In making the case for why human rights concerns should not stand in the way of a new partnership and cooperation agreement with severely repressive Turkmenistan, a country with large gas reserves, the EU resorts to similar stated fears of alienation. To avoid public indignation if it were to openly abandon human rights in favor of these other interests, the EU feigns ongoing concern through the medium of private dialogue.

A similar dynamic is at play in China, where Western governments seek economic opportunity as well as cooperation on a range of global and regional issues. For example, in its first year in office, the Obama administration seemed determined to downplay any issue, such as human rights, that might raise tensions in the US-China relationship. President Obama deferred meeting with the Dalai Lama until after his trip to China and refused to meet with Chinese civil society groups during the trip, and Secretary of State Hillary Clinton announced that human rights "can't interfere" with other US interests in China. Obama's efforts to ingratiate himself with Chinese President Hu Jintao gained nothing discernible while it reinforced China's view of the US as a declining power. That weakness only heightened tension when, in Obama's second year in office, he and Secretary Clinton rediscovered their human rights voice on the case of Liu Xiaobo, although it remains to be seen whether they will be outspoken on rights during the January 2011 US-China summit.

Western governments also have been reluctant to exert pressure for human rights on governments that they count as counterterrorism allies. For example, the Obama administration and the Friends of Yemen, a group of states and intergovernmental organizations established in January 2010, have not conditioned military or development assistance to Yemen on human rights improvements, despite a worsening record of abusive conduct by Yemeni security forces and continuing government crackdowns on independent journalists and largely peaceful southern separatists.

US policy toward Egypt shows that pressure can work. In recent years, the US government has maintained a quiet dialogue with Egypt. Beginning in 2010, however, the White House and State Department repeatedly condemned abuses, urged repeal of Egypt's emergency law, and called for free elections. These public calls helped to secure the release of several hundred political detainees held under the emergency law. Egypt also responded with anger–for example, waging a lobbying campaign to stop a US Senate resolution condemning its human rights record. The reaction was designed to scare US diplomats into resuming a quieter approach, but in fact it showed that Egypt is profoundly affected by public pressure from Washington.

Defending Rights by Osmosis

One common rationalization offered for engagement without pressure is that rubbing shoulders with outsiders will somehow help to convert abusive agents of repressive governments. The Pentagon makes that argument in the case of Uzbekistan and Sri Lanka, and the US government adopted that line to justify resuming military aid to Indonesia's elite special forces (Kopassus), a unit with a long history of severe abuse, including massacres in East Timor and "disappearances" of student leaders in Jakarta. With respect to Kopassus, while the Indonesian government's human rights record has improved dramatically in recent years, a serious gap remains its failure to hold senior military officers accountable for human rights violations, even in the most high-profile cases. In 2010 the US relinquished the strongest lever it had by agreeing to lift a decade-old ban on direct military ties with Kopassus. The Indonesian military made some rhetorical concessions–promising to discharge convicted offenders and to take action against future offenders–but the US did not condition resumption of aid on such changes. Convicted offenders today remain in the military, and there is little reason to credit the military's future pledge given its poor record to date. Notably, the US did not insist that Indonesian President Susilo Bambang Yudhoyono authorize a special court to investigate Kopassus officers implicated in the abduction and presumed killing of student leaders in 1997-98, a step already recommended by Indonesia's own parliament. And the US did not insist on ending the military's exclusive jurisdiction over crimes committed by soldiers.

Trivializing the significance of pressure, US Defense Secretary Robert Gates justified resuming direct ties with Kopassus: "Working with them further will produce greater gains in human rights for people than simply standing back and shouting at people." Yet even as the US was finalizing terms with Indonesia on resumption of aid to Kopassus, an Indonesian general implicated in abductions of student leaders was promoted to deputy defense minister and a colonel implicated in other serious abuses was named deputy commander of Kopassus.

A similarly misplaced faith in rubbing shoulders with abusive forces rather than applying pressure on them informed President Obama's decision to continue military aid to a series of governments that use child soldiers–Chad, Sudan, Yemen, and the Democratic Republic of Congo–despite a new US law prohibiting such aid. In the case of Congo, for example, the military has had children in its ranks since at least 2002, and a 2010 UN report found a "dramatic increase" in the number of such children in the prior year. Instead of using a cutoff of military assistance to pressure these governments to stop using child soldiers, the Obama administration waived the law to give the US time to "work with" the offending militaries.

Another favorite rationale for a quiet approach, heard often in dealings with China, is that economic liberalization will lead on its own to greater political freedoms—a position maintained even after three decades in which that has not happened. Indeed, in 2010 the opposite occurred—in its regulation of the internet, China began using its economic clout to try to strengthen *restrictions* on speech, pressing businesses to become censors on its behalf. In the end, it was a business—Google—that fought back, in part because censorship threatened its business model. GoDaddy.com, the world's largest web registrar, also announced that it would no longer register domains in China because onerous government requirements forcing disclosure of customer identities made censorship easier.

Despite these efforts, China still leveraged access to its lucrative market to gain the upper hand because others in the internet industry, such as Microsoft, did not follow Google's lead. Conversely, the one time that China backed off was when it faced concerted pressure—it apparently abandoned its "Green Dam" censoring software when the industry, civil society, governments, and China's own internet users all loudly protested. And even Google's license to operate a search engine in China was renewed, casting further doubt on the idea that a public critique of China's human rights practices would inevitably hurt business.

Humanitarian Excuses

Some governments and intergovernmental organizations contend that promoting human rights must take a back seat to relieving humanitarian suffering. Humanitarian emergencies often require an urgent response, but this argument becomes yet another excuse to avoid pressure even when human rights abuses are the cause of the humanitarian crisis. That occurred in Zimbabwe during Operation Murambatsvina (Clean the Filth), when the government destroyed the homes of tens of thousands of people, and in Sri Lanka during the final stages of the civil war, when the army disregarded the plight of hundreds of thousands of Tamil civilians who were trapped in a deadly war zone.

In Zimbabwe, the UN country team never publicly condemned the destruction and displacement caused by Operation Murambatsvina, and almost never spoke out publicly about the extremely serious human rights abuses committed by Robert Mugabe's government and the ruling Zimbabwe African National Union- Patriotic Front (ZANU-PF). In fact, during his four-year tenure in Zimbabwe, the UN resident representative rarely met with Zimbabwean human rights activists, never attended any of their unfair trials, and almost never spoke publicly about the widespread and severe human rights abuses being committed. Such silence did not translate into better access to the displaced civilian population–the Zimbabwean authorities and ZANU-PF officials continued to restrict and manipulate humanitarian operations in Zimbabwe, and frequently prevented humanitarian organizations from reaching vulnerable populations suspected of being pro-opposition. But by failing to publicly condemn the abuses in Zimbabwe, the UN country team lost key opportunities to use its substantial influence as the most important implementer of humanitarian and development assistance in the country. It also left itself addressing the symptoms of repression rather than their source.

By contrast, the special envoy appointed by then Secretary-General Kofi Annan to investigate Operation Murambatsvina issued a strongly worded report in 2005 citing the indiscriminate and unjustified evictions and urging that those responsible be brought to justice. The report led to widespread international condemnation of Mugabe's government–pressure that forced the government to allow greater humanitarian access to the displaced population.

Similarly in Sri Lanka, in the final months of the war with the Tamil Tigers, UN personnel were virtually the only independent observers, giving them a unique capacity to alert the world to ongoing war crimes and to generate pressure to spare civilians. Instead, the UN covered up its own information about civilian casualties, stopped the release of satellite imagery showing how dire the situation was, and even stayed silent when local UN staff members were arbitrarily arrested. UN officials were concerned that by speaking out they would lose access required to assist a population in need, but given Sri Lanka's complete dependence on international assistance to run camps that ultimately housed 300,000 internally displaced persons, the UN arguably overestimated the risk of being barred from the country. In addition, the government's use of an expensive Washington public-relations firm to counter criticism of its war conduct showed its concern with its international image. By not speaking out, the UN lost an opportunity to influence the way the Sri Lankan army was conducting the war and thus to prevent civilian suffering rather than simply alleviate it after the fact. By contrast, after the conflict, when the independent UN special rapporteur on the rights of the internally displaced spoke out about the lack of freedom of movement for the internally displaced, the government promptly began releasing civilians from the camps.

A comparable pattern could be found in the role played by Western development-assistance bureaucracies in dealing with Rwanda and Ethiopia. Both countries are seen as efficient, relatively uncorrupt recipients of development assistance. Western donor agencies, often finding it difficult to productively invest the funds that they are charged with disbursing, thus have a strong interest in maintaining warm relationships with the governments. (Ethiopia's role in combating the terrorist threat emanating from Somalia reinforces this interest.) Indeed, economic assistance to both countries has grown as their repression has intensified. Because it would be too callous to say that economic development justifies ignoring repression, the European Commission, the UK, several other EU states, and the US have offered various excuses, from the claim that public pressure will backfire in the face of national pride to the assertion that donor governments have less leverage than one might think.

The result is a lack of meaningful pressure—nothing to change the cost-benefit analysis that makes repression an attractive option. Quiet entreaties are least likely to be effective when they are drowned out by parallel delivery of massive quantities of aid.

Dated Policies

Brazil, India, and South Africa, strong and vibrant democracies at home, remain unsupportive of many human rights initiatives abroad, even though each benefitted from international solidarity in its struggle to end, respectively, dictatorship, colonization, and apartheid. Their foreign policies are often based on building South-South political and economic ties and are bolstered by reference to Western double standards, but these rationales do not justify these emerging powers turning their backs on people who have not yet won the rights that their own citizens enjoy. With all three countries occupying seats on the UN Security Council, it would be timely for them to adopt a more responsible position toward protecting people from the predation of less progressive governments.

Japan traditionally has resisted a strong human rights policy in part because Japanese foreign policy has tended to center around promoting exports and building good will, in part because the setting of foreign policy has been dominated by bureaucrats who faced little public outcry over their inclination to maintain smooth relations with all governments, and in part because Japan still has not come to terms with its own abusive record in World War II. However, in recent years, partly due to a change in government and partly due to growing pressure from the small but emerging Japanese civil society, the Japanese government has begun to be more outspoken on human rights with regard to such places as North Korea and Burma.

The Chinese government is naturally reluctant to promote human rights because it maintains such a repressive climate at home and does not want to bolster any international system for the protection of human rights that might come back to haunt it. But even China should not see turning its back on mass atrocities—a practice that, one would hope, China has moved beyond—as advancing its self-interest.

Conclusion

Whatever the rationalization, the quest for dialogue and cooperation is simply not a universal substitute for public pressure as a tool to promote human rights. Dialogue and cooperation have their place, but the burden should be on the abusive government to show a genuine willingness to improve. In the absence of demonstrated political will, public pressure should be the default response to repression. It is understandable when governments that them-selves are serious human rights violators want to undermine the option of public pressure out of fear that it will be applied to them in turn. But it is shameful when governments that purportedly promote human rights fall for, or endorse, the same ploy.

Defending human rights is rarely convenient. It may sometimes interfere with other governmental interests. But if governments want to pursue those inter-ests instead of human rights, they should at least have the courage to admit it, instead of hiding behind meaningless dialogues and fruitless quests for cooperation.

This Report

This report is Human Rights Watch's twenty-first annual review of human rights practices around the globe. It summarizes key human rights issues in more than 90 countries and territories worldwide, drawing on events through November 2010.

Each country entry identifies significant human rights issues, examines the freedom of local human rights defenders to conduct their work, and surveys the response of key international actors, such as the United Nations, European Union, Japan, the United States, and various regional and international organizations and institutions.

This report reflects extensive investigative work undertaken in 2010 by the Human Rights Watch research staff, usually in close partnership with human rights activists in the country in question. It also reflects the work of our advocacy team, which monitors policy developments and strives to persuade governments and international institutions to curb abuses and promote human rights. Human Rights Watch publications, issued throughout the year, contain more detailed accounts of many of the issues addressed in the brief summaries collected in this volume. They can be found on the Human Rights Watch website, www.hrw.org.

As in past years, this report does not include a chapter on every country where Human Rights Watch works, nor does it discuss every issue of importance. The failure to include a particular country or issue often reflects no more than staffing limitations and should not be taken as commentary on the significance of the problem. There are many serious human rights violations that Human Rights Watch simply lacks the capacity to address.

The factors we considered in determining the focus of our work in 2010 (and hence the content of this volume) include the number of people affected and the severity of abuse, access to the country and the availability of information about it, the susceptibility of abusive forces to influence, and the importance of addressing certain thematic concerns and of reinforcing the work of local rights organizations.

The World Report does not have separate chapters addressing our thematic work but instead incorporates such material directly into the country entries.

Please consult the Human Rights Watch website for more detailed treatment of our work on children's rights, women's rights, arms and military issues, business and human rights, health and human rights, international justice, terrorism and counterterrorism, refugees and displaced people, and lesbian, gay, bisexual, and transgender people's rights, and for information about our international film festivals.

Kenneth Roth is executive director of Human Rights Watch.

WHOSE NEWS?:
THE CHANGING MEDIA LANDSCAPE AND NGOS

By Carroll Bogert

These are tough times for foreign correspondents. A combination of rapid technological change and economic recession has caused deep cuts in the budget for foreign reporting at many Western news organizations. Plenty of ex-foreign correspondents have lost their jobs, and many others fear for their jobs and their futures. Consumers of news, meanwhile, are watching international coverage shrink in the pages of major papers. One recent study estimated that the number of foreign news stories published prominently in newspapers in the United Kingdom fell by 80 percent from 1979 to 2009.[1] The Organization for Economic Co-operation and Development estimates that 20 out of its 31 member states face declining newspaper readerships;[2] since foreign reporting is expensive, it is often the first to be cut.

While changes in the media world may be hard on journalists and unsettling for news consumers, they also have very significant implications for international NGOs such as Human Rights Watch. Foreign correspondents have always been an important channel for international NGOs to get the word out, and a decline in global news coverage constitutes a threat to their effectiveness. At the same time, not all the implications of this change are bad. These are also days of opportunity for those in the business of spreading the word. This essay attempts to examine the perils and possibilities for international NGOs[3] in these tectonic shifts in media.

Of course NGOs of all kinds accomplish a great deal without any recourse to the media at all. Human rights activists pursue much of their mission outside the public eye: private meetings with diplomats; closed-door policy discussions with government officials; strategy sessions with other NGOs; and, of course, interviews with victims and eyewitnesses whose identity and safety must be protected from the glare of publicity. NGOs that do research in the field may share a close bond with journalists, but research is only part of their overall mission of effecting social change.

Not all NGOs deal regularly with foreign correspondents; in fact, quite the opposite. Most NGO activists are working inside their own national borders. If the local media are at least somewhat free, they are likely to be more focused on national coverage. The international or regional media may serve as an additional form of pressure on the activists' own government, but changes in the funding and composition of foreign correspondents will not always have a significant impact on their work.

NGOs have a complex and ambivalent relationship with journalists. They work at a different pace from the media, take a considerably longer time to publish their findings, and feel far removed from the feeding frenzies and 15-minute celebrities that often dominate commercial media. They frequently feel that in the rush of the news cycle, key facts may get forgotten or taken out of context, and the headline-grabbing aspects of the story may not be the most meaningful or important angles for their own advocacy.

At the same time, with a few exceptions, NGOs are constantly seeking greater media attention for their work. The changing media landscape presents new challenges and possibilities for such groups, particularly those that view international media as an important channel for getting their message out.

NGOs and Foreign Correspondents: A Symbiosis

One of the most potent tools of international human rights NGOs has always been "naming and shaming," or publicizing specific human rights violations and identifying those responsible. Its usefulness can be measured in part by the resources governments mobilize to combat it. At the United Nations

Human Rights Council in Geneva, for example, government delegations conduct extensive diplomatic campaigns to avoid being publicly censured.

Bad publicity can help spark government action. When a video surfaced in October 2010 showing two Papuan farmers being tortured by Indonesian soldiers, the Indonesian government clearly felt pressure to act. United States President Barack Obama was scheduled for a visit that month and neither government wanted the torture issue to dominate the headlines. The Indonesian government, which has been notoriously reluctant to punish its soldiers for human rights abuses, promptly tried and convicted four soldiers of torture.[4] It was clearly responding to media pressure in doing so.

For groups that do not enjoy extensive grass-roots support or mass membership, media coverage may act as a kind of stand-in for public pressure. In very few countries, and relatively rare circumstances, does the public become seriously mobilized over an issue of foreign policy. To be sure, the Israeli-Palestinian conflict has the capacity to rally global publics outside the region—on both sides—and so does the use of US military power abroad. The Save Darfur campaign brought hundreds of thousands of students and other supporters to street demonstrations. But those are exceptions. In general, foreign affairs pique the interest of a narrow subsection in any society. Extensive media coverage of an issue may help to affect policy even when the public remains silent on the issue. Serbian atrocities in Kosovo at the end of the 1990's comes to mind; significant public debate, in the media and elsewhere, helped generate pressure on NATO policymakers to take action.

Media coverage can also act as an informal "stamp of approval" for international advocacy groups. When a prominent publication cites an NGO official in a story, it signifies that the reporter, who is supposed to be knowledgeable about the issue, has determined the NGO to be credible. When an NGO spokesperson appears on a well-regarded television show, she may thereafter carry greater weight with the policymakers she is trying to reach. Her very access to the media megaphone makes her a bigger threat, and a person to be reckoned with.

If advocacy groups need the media, it is clear that media need them, too. In many countries where the press corps is not fully free, journalists rely on international groups to say things that they cannot. In Bahrain, for example, the ruling family promotes itself as reformist but it would have been very difficult for the one independent local newspaper there to report extensively on renewed use of torture during police interrogations. The fact of this resurgence was widely alleged by activists and detainees, but considered too sensitive to publicize locally.[5] When Human Rights Watch published a report on the issue,[5] the local independent newspaper covered the issue extensively, reproducing much of the report in its pages without major fear of retribution.

Foreign correspondents working in repressive countries do not face the same consequences that local journalists do when they report on human rights or social justice issues. But they, too, may pull their punches in order to avoid problems with their visas or accreditation. Quoting an NGO making critical comments is safer than doing so oneself.

Some journalists feel a strong bond of kinship with NGOs that work on political repression and abuse of power. Whether it was *Washington Post* correspondents Bob Woodward and Carl Bernstein bringing the Watergate crimes to light, or the international press corps covering the wars in the former Yugoslavia, journalists are often driven by the desire to expose the crimes of political leaders and see justice done.

Whose Sky is Falling?

Paradoxically, it is precisely in wealthier countries where the media are sickest today. In the United States, the triple blow of the internet, the economic recession, and the poor management of a few major newspapers has dramatically shrunk the cadre of foreign correspondents. Several daily papers, such as the *Boston Globe* and *Newsday*, have shut down their foreign bureaus entirely. Television networks have closed almost all of their full-fledged bureaus, leaving local representatives in a handful of capitals. *The New York Times* and *The Washington Post*, the reigning monarchs of international coverage, appear to maintain their foreign bureaus more out of the personal commitment of the families who still own them. In the United States, at least, the commercial model for international fact-gathering and distribution is evidently broken.

No one is more vocal about the dire consequences of these cutbacks than the newspapers' foreign correspondents themselves. Pamela Constable, a respected foreign correspondent for *The Washington Post*, wrote in 2007: "If newspapers stop covering the world, I fear we will end up with a microscopic elite reading *Foreign Affairs* and a numbed nation watching terrorist bombings flash briefly among a barrage of commentary, crawls, and celebrity gossip."[6] As *The New York Times*' chief foreign correspondent said: "When young men ask me for advice on how to become a foreign correspondent, I tell them: 'Don't.' It is like becoming a blacksmith in 1919–still an honorable and skilled profession; but the horse is doomed."[7]

But the correspondent, C.L. Sulzberger, made that comment in 1969. Every age laments its own passing, and old foreign correspondents are no exception. It is not entirely clear that the American public, or the public in any of the countries where foreign correspondents are in decline, is less well-informed than it used to be. At least one study has shown, in fact, that the American public is roughly as informed about international affairs as it was 20 years ago, before the big declines in traditional sources of foreign reporting.[8] And overall, even among Western publics, media consumption is increasing.[9]

Meanwhile, in countries such as Malaysia, Singapore, Vietnam, and others, the internet is allowing the public to get foreign news without government filters—an important advance in their knowledge of the world.[10] And the OECD has estimated that, while readership of newspapers is declining among most of its members, that decline is more than offset by the overall growth in the newspaper industry globally.[11]

A number of media outlets from the global South have greatly enhanced their international presence in recent years. Al-Jazeera and al-Jazeera English, financed by the emir of Qatar, report on a wide range of global news, although the network has recently cut back one of its four international broadcasting centers. Others are not so free-wheeling. Xinhua, the state-run news agency of China, and other Chinese media organizations such as CCTV, are loathe to run much human rights news—and are positively allergic to such news out of China or its allies.

A Peril and a Boon

The information revolution made possible by the internet represents both a peril and a boon to international NGOs grappling with the decline in Western media reporting on foreign news. On the one hand, the plethora of online publications, blogs, Facebook, and Twitter feeds, cable and satellite television stations, and other forms of new media is clamorous and confusing. How are advocacy groups to know which media are important? If one purpose of getting media coverage, as laid out above, is to reach policymakers, how does one ascertain which media they are consuming? Previously, in most countries, a couple of daily papers, a weekly magazine or two, and a few radio and television broadcasts constituted the core of what critical decision-makers in government were likely to get their news from. Nowadays their reading habits are not so easy to guess. The audience for international news has fractured.

A 2008 study by graduate students at Columbia University asked a range of officials associated with the UN in New York what media they read, listened to, and watched. Unsurprisingly, nearly three-quarters of those surveyed said they read *The New York Times* every day. Fifty percent read *The Economist*–also no surprise. But a significant number of respondents said they were also reading the frequent postings of a blogger at the *Inner City Press*, who covers UN affairs closely but is virtually unknown outside the UN community.[12]

The internet poses the challenge of the glut. Advocacy groups, after all, not only seek media coverage but also respond to media queries. Which questioners are worthy of the scarce attentions of an NGO? Which bloggers are merely cranks who will waste an inordinate amount of staff time while offering little impact? And how does one tell the difference? And how much time should an NGO spend poring through the latest data-dump from Wikileaks?

But then there is the boon. The same internet that has blown a gaping hole in media budgets is also allowing NGOs to reach their audiences directly. Technologies that were once the exclusive preserve of a professional class are now widely available. Taking a photograph of a policeman beating up a demonstrator and transmitting the image to a global audience used to involve expensive equipment and access to scarce transmission technology. Only a handful of trained journalists could do it. Now the same picture can be taken and transmitted with a US$35 mobile phone. During Egypt's parliamentary elections in late November 2010, for example, the government rejected international observers and drastically restricted local monitors. But NGO activists managed to film a local mayor affiliated with the ruling party filling out multiple ballots and, in another place, plainclothes men with sticks disrupting a polling station.

Picking Up the Slack?

For NGOs with large field presences—and even for those with only an occasional investigator or representative overseas—the ability to generate and distribute content is potentially revolutionary. But it requires more than taking a cell-phone photograph of a news event and posting it to Facebook. The question is whether NGOs will operate systematically in the vacuum left by the commercial media. To do so will require re-purposing the information they are already gathering, and acquiring the skills to reach the public directly with features capable of attracting public attention. At present not many NGOs have the resources to reconfigure their research and information into user-friendly content. Most of them operate on the written word. Often they are addressing other experts rather than the public at large. Importantly, they generally have precious little visual information to illustrate their findings.

That is beginning to change. Human Rights Watch assigns professional photographers, videographers, and radio producers to work in the field alongside its researchers, documenting in multimedia features what the researchers are documenting in words.[13]

Amnesty International is creating an autonomous "news unit," staffed with five professional journalists, to generate human rights news. Medecins Sans Frontieres also uses photography and video extensively, while the Natural Resources Defense Council is assigning journalists to write about environmental issues.

Even if NGOs are able to produce user-friendly content, the question remains of how to distribute it. An NGO can post content on its website, and reach a few thousand people, perhaps tens of thousands. Distributing via Facebook, Twitter, YouTube, and other social media might garner a few thousand more. Content that "goes viral" and reaches millions of people remains the rare exception. Sooner or later the question of distribution returns to the mainstream media, whose audiences still dwarf those of the non-profit sector. Will they distribute content produced by NGOs?

With budgets for foreign news in decline, one might expect editors and producers to be grateful for the offer of material from non-profit sources. But that is not always the case, and the answer depends on the country, the media outlet, and the NGO. The BBC, for example, rarely takes material from advocacy groups for broadcast. CBS, in the US, recently tightened up its regulations for taking content from outside sources.[14] *Time* magazine will not accept images from a photographer whose assignment was underwritten by an NGO.

And many media commentators, writing on the rising importance of NGOs as information producers, are wary of the trend. "While journalists–if sometimes imperfectly–work on the principle of impartiality, the aid agency is usually there to get a message across: to raise money, to raise awareness, to change a situation."[15]

Issues of Objectivity and Neutrality

NGOs like Human Rights Watch do not present facts for the sake of reporting the news but to inform the public and advocate on behalf of victims of abuse. That sets their work apart from traditional journalism and raises the very important question of whether the information being gathered and conveyed by these NGOs is less trustworthy. Unless the NGO is transparent about its aims, about the provenance of the material it is distributing, and about the standards it uses in its own information-gathering, the consumer–whether a journalist or a visitor to the website–will be justifiably wary.

The best media professionals spend their entire careers trying, as hard as they can, to rid their own reporting of bias and to be fair to all sides. They believe, and they are correct, that unbiased information is a genuine public good and that biased information can mislead readers, including policymakers, into bad decisions—even social strife and violence. Many media training organizations in conflict zones around the world are struggling to instill the notion of unbiased reporting in media environments where the lack of it has proved disastrous. At the same time few people believe that the American media, where the culture of neutral and apolitical reporting has been most fiercely propagated, are in fact unbiased.

Research-driven NGOs put a premium on rigorous, factual reporting. If they play fast and loose with the facts, they lose credibility and so lose traction with policymakers. Their reputations depend on objective reporting from the field. At the same time, they work in service of a cause, advocating on behalf of victims and seeking accountability for perpetrators. While different NGOs have different standards for gathering, checking, and vetting information, the entire purpose of that information is to act to protect human dignity. Those who gather information must do so impartially, from all sides, but they are not neutral towards atrocity.

Media organizations and advocacy groups stay independent of each other for good reason. They are pursuing different objectives. Journalists' refusal to distribute content produced by others protects against the partisan abuse of the media space. Meanwhile, international advocacy groups are wary of drifting from their core mission into the media business. But changes in technology and commerce, at least in some countries, are pushing them closer together.

To the extent that NGOs do produce more user-friendly content, they must keep in mind a few principles for establishing their credibility: first, transparency in the methods of collecting the information; second, a proven track record and a reputation, over many years, for reliable research; and third, complete openness about the aims of the organization and the fact of its authorship.

NGOs still face the question of how far they want to go in creating user-friendly content. Few seem inclined to reorient their identities as information producers in the new information age. Filling the vacuum in international news takes money, and most NGOs struggle to meet their existing budgets, let alone expand into areas that seem tangential to their central mission. But if they turn their backs on the trend, they will miss a critical opportunity to be heard.

This information revolution has big implications for more than just a handful of advocacy groups. Any entity that produces denser material written for a more specialist audience must now realize that the legions of those who will transform it into something the layperson can understand—in other words, a work of journalism—are now much diminished. To have maximum impact in the world today, information must be repurposed and refashioned for multiple audiences and platforms, like a seed sprouting in every direction. That is a trend that no one who cares about influencing public opinion can afford to ignore.

Carroll Bogert is the deputy executive director, external relations, of Human Rights Watch.

[1] Martin Moore, *Shrinking World: The decline of international reporting in the British press* (London: Media Standards Trust, November 2010), p 17. The study looked at foreign stories appearing in the first ten pages of four major daily newspapers.

[2] Organisation for Economic Co-operation and Development: Directorate for Science, Technology and Industry Committee for Information, Computer, and Communications Policy, "The Evolution of News and the Internet," June 11, 2010 http://www.oecd.org/dataoecd/30/24/45559596.pdf (accessed November 20, 2010), p.7. The steepest declines were registered in the United States, the United Kingdom, Greece, Italy, Canada, and Spain.

[3] This essay focuses primarily on NGOs that do research and advocacy in multiple countries and therefore interact regularly with journalists who cover one country for audiences in another. Most of these remarks concern NGOs working on human rights and other social justice issues, rather than, for example, global warming and the environment, although they face some of the same challenges.

[4] The four were actually convicted of torture that was revealed in another, unrelated video. See "Indonesia: Investigate Torture Video From Papua," Human Rights Watch news release, October 20, 2010, http://www.hrw.org/en/news/2010/10/20/indonesia-investigate-torture-video-papua.

[5] Human Rights Watch, *Torture Redux: The Rivival of Physical Coercion during Interrogations in Bahrain*, February 8, 2010, http://www.hrw.org/en/reports/2010/02/08/torture-redux

[6] Pamela Constable, "Demise of the Foreign Correspondent," The Washington Post, February 18, 2007.

[7] John Maxwell Hamilton, *Journalism's roving eye: a history of American foreign reporting* (Lousiana State University Press, 2010), p. 457.

[8] "Public Knowledge of Current Affairs Little Changed by News and Information Revolutions: What Americans Know: 1989-2007," The Pew Research Center for the People & the Press, April 15, 2007 http://people-press.org/report/319/public-knowledge-of-current-affairs-little-changed-by-news-and-information-revolutions (accessed November 29, 2010).

[9] Richard Wray, "Media Consumption on the Increase," The Guardian, April 19, 2010 http://www.guardian.co.uk/business/2010/apr/19/media-consumption-survey (accessed November 21, 2010).

[10] See, for example, the Temasek Review in Singapore; Malaysiakini and other online portals in Malaysia; numerous Vietnamese bloggers; and the Democratic Voice of Burma and Mizzima, among others.

[11] OECD, 2010

[12] "Mass Media and the UN: What the Advocacy Community Can Do to Shape Decision Making," Columbia University School of International Public Affairs, May 2009, on file at Human Rights Watch. The respondents came from the UN Secretariat, various UN departments whose work touches on human rights, and diplomats representing 12 of the 15 UN Security Council members.

[13] Many photographers now raise money from foundations to partner with NGOs. Among the most active donors, for example, is the Open Society Institute's Documentary Photography Project: http://www.soros.org/initiatives/photography (accessed November 20, 2010); photographers at Magnum are increasingly willing to "partner… with select charitable organizations and provid[e] free or reduced rate access to the Magnum Photos archive," http://magnumfoundation.org/core-programs.html (accessed November 20, 2010).

[14] Private conversation with CBS producer, October 2010.

[15] Glenda Cooper, "When lines between NGO and news organization blur," *Nieman Journalism Lab*, December 21, 2009, http://www.niemanlab.org/2009/12/glenda-cooper-when-lines-between-ngo-and-news-organization-blur/ (accessed November 20, 2010).

Schools as Battlegrounds:
Protecting Students, Teachers, and Schools from Attack

By Zama Coursen-Neff and Bede Sheppard

Of the 72 million primary school-age children not currently attending school worldwide, more than half—39 million—live in countries afflicted by armed conflict. In many of these countries, armed groups threaten and kill students and teachers and bomb and burn schools as tactics of the conflict.[1] Government security forces use schools as bases for military operations, putting students at risk and further undermining education.

In southern Thailand, separatist insurgents have set fire to schools at least 327 times since 2004, and government security forces occupied at least 79 schools in 2010. In Colombia, hundreds of teachers active in trade unions have been killed in the last decade, the perpetrators often pro-government paramilitaries and other parties to the ongoing conflict between the government and rebel forces. In northern Democratic Republic of Congo (DRC), the rebel Lord's Resistance Army (LRA) has abducted large numbers of children from schools and taken revenge on villages believed to be aiding LRA defectors by, among other things, looting and burning schools.

"We warn you to leave your job as a teacher as soon as possible otherwise we will cut the heads off your children and shall set fire to your daughter," read a threatening letter from Taliban insurgents in Afghanistan, where between March and October 2010 20 schools were attacked using explosives or arson, and insurgents killed 126 students.

While attacks on schools, teachers, and students in Afghanistan have perhaps been most vivid in the public eye—men on motorbikes spraying pupils with gunfire, girls doused with acid—intentional targeting of education is a far-reaching if underreported phenomenon. It is not limited to a few countries but a broader problem in the world's armed conflicts. Human Rights Watch researchers have documented attacks on students, teachers, and schools— and their consequences for education—in Afghanistan, Colombia, the DRC, India, Nepal, Burma, Pakistan, the Philippines, and Thailand. The United Nation's Education, Science, and Cultural Organization (UNESCO) reports that attacks occurred in at least 31 countries from 2007 to 2009.[2]

While only a few non-state armed groups openly endorse such attacks, too little is being done to document, publicize, and take steps to end them. Nor is the negative impact of long-term occupation of schools by military forces fully appreciated. Access to education is increasingly recognized as an important part of emergency humanitarian response, particularly during mass displacement and natural disasters. But protecting schools, teachers, and students from deliberate attack in areas of conflict is only now receiving greater attention. Humanitarian aid groups increasingly are alert to the harm and lasting costs of such attacks and human rights groups have begun to address them in the context of protecting civilians in armed conflict and promoting economic and social rights, including the right to education.

An effective response to attacks on education will require more focused policies and action by concerned governments and a much stronger international effort. Making students, teachers, and schools genuinely off limits to non-state armed groups and regular armies will require governments, opposition groups, and other organizations to implement strong measures that are enforced by rigorous monitoring, preventive interventions, rapid response to violations, and accountability for violators of domestic and international law.

Why Schools, Teachers, and Students Are Attacked

Non-state armed groups target schools, teachers, and students for a variety of reasons. Rebel groups often see schools and teachers as symbols of the state. Indeed in rural areas, they may be the only structures and government employees in the vicinity, serving multiple purposes. In India, Pakistan, and Afghanistan, for example, armed opposition groups have attacked schools used as polling places around elections.

Teachers and schools make high-visibility "soft" targets: they are more easily attacked than the government security forces, and attacks are likely to garner media attention to the assailants and their political agenda, and undermine confidence in government control. Opposition groups may also view schools and teachers as symbols of an oppressive educational system. A teacher in southern Thailand told Human Rights Watch how he became a target of both sides of the separatist conflict there. Muslim insurgents warned him that, as a Muslim, he should not be teaching at a government school. Later, local government paramilitary troops also threatened him for allegedly supporting the insurgents. Soon after, unidentified assailants shot him on his way home from daily prayers at his mosque, seriously wounding him.

Sometimes schools are attacked because armed groups are hostile to the content of the education being delivered or because of the students they educate. In some countries, schools have been targeted because their curriculum is perceived to be secular or "Western," others simply because the schools educate girls. Not all the violence is ideological: criminal elements may want to drive out competing sources of authority; some attacks are simply local disputes that may or may not have to do with education.

Schools and the routes students take to reach them can also be preyed upon by rebels, paramilitaries, and others seeking children for their armies, for indoctrination, or for coerced sex. During the prolonged civil war in Nepal, for example, Human Rights Watch documented how Maoist rebels used a variety of techniques for recruiting children, including the abduction of large groups of children, often from schools, for indoctrination.

The Consequences of Attacks

The impact of attacks can be devastating. Large numbers of teachers and pupils may be injured or traumatized, in some cases killed. And attacks often lead to dramatic decreases in school attendance rates. When attendance remains low over the long term there are negative knock-on effects on the economy and on key development indices such as measures of maternal and child health.

In the worst cases, hundreds of schools are closed. For example, Afghanistan's Ministry of Education reported in March 2009 that roughly 570 schools remained closed following attacks by the Taliban and other insurgent groups, with hundreds of thousands of students denied an education.

Attacks can also damage facilities and teaching materials, requiring extensive repairs and costly new materials before schools can reopen. If not shut down entirely, classes may be suspended for days, weeks, or even longer and, when resumed, held in dangerous, partially destroyed structures or even outside. Other valuable services provided to communities in school buildings, such as adult education and community health and other services, may also be lost.

When governments fail to rebuild after an attack, the impact is even greater. For example, in India, none of the schools attacked by Maoist rebels (known as Naxalites) that Human Rights Watch visited in 2009 had received any government assistance to repair or rebuild. The attacks had occurred between two and six months earlier, and state governments had stated that they had the funding to rebuild.

Attacks on schools and teachers traumatize students and affects teachers' work performance. Even where school buildings remain intact or the physical infrastructure is restored, teachers and students may be too fearful to return. Qualified teachers may refuse to work in the area, leaving those who remain stretched thin.

For example, in rural Bihar state in India, local residents described to Human Rights Watch how a large Maoist force blew up the middle school building in their town. In response, local paramilitary police established a camp inside the remaining structures. School classes were being held in a travelers' shelter partially exposed to the elements, without toilets or the government-mandated midday meal. As one parent told Human Rights Watch, "When people hear about these problems, parents take their children out [of the school]."

Attacks can also have a ripple effect on surrounding schools and affect the overall calculation that parents and students make in assessing the costs and benefits of attending school. In conflict areas, the quality of education is often already weak and families may be highly sensitive to violence. When two teachers were assassinated on their way to a local market in southern Thailand in September 2010, for example, the local teachers' federation suspended classes in all government schools in the province for three days.

Threats alone can be very effective in shutting down schools in environments where violence is widespread and perpetrators go unpunished. A teacher in rural Laghman province, Afghanistan, told Human Rights Watch that a third of her students dropped out after a so-called "night letter" was left at the mosque, which stated: "We warn you to stop sending your girls to these classes or you cannot imagine the consequences. Your classes will be blown up by a bomb, or if any of your daughters is raped or kidnapped, you cannot complain later on."

Use of Schools for Military Purposes

Closely related to targeted attacks on schools is the use of school facilities by national armed forces or other armed groups. Attracted by schools' central locations, solid structures, and electrical and sanitation facilities, some security forces take over schools for weeks or months, and sometimes years. In Bihar and Jharkhand states in India, for example, where government security forces took over dozens of schools as outposts in conflicts with Maoist rebels, all of the 21 school occupations Human Rights Watch investigated in 2009 and 2010 had lasted between six months and three years. Military use of schools not only disrupts students' education, it may itself provoke attacks from opposing forces.

Even when schools are not being used for classes, military use is problematic because attacks by opposing forces can destroy school infrastructure and blur the lines between civilian and military installations, potentially exposing schools to attack when students return. When security forces take over a school, they frequently fortify and militarize the school buildings and grounds—for example, by establishing reinforced sentry boxes, digging trenches, and constructing protective walls of barbed wire and sand bags. When security forces leave, they often leave these fortifications behind. This places the school in ongoing danger by giving the appearance of a military presence long after the forces have left.

In some instances, security forces entirely displace students. In none of the cases investigated by Human Rights Watch had governments taken steps to provide alternative educational facilities of comparable quality to children displaced by military occupations of school facilities.

In other cases, militaries occupy only certain areas within schools, with classes continuing to be held in the unoccupied parts. Such partial occupation of schools is also problematic. In partially occupied schools visited by Human Rights Watch in India and southern Thailand, students, teachers, and parents

41

variously complained about problems as diverse as overcrowding of class-rooms, loss of kitchens that had provided mid-day meals, and inability to use school latrines. (Lack of access to toilets is a globally recognized factor contributing to lowered school attendance by girls.) Students try to continue their studies alongside armed men whose often poor behavior—ranging from beating criminal suspects in front of students to gambling, drinking, and using drugs—are all counter to a safe and positive learning environment for children.

When security forces move in, there is typically an immediate exodus of students. And long-term occupations deter new enrollments. Girls appear more likely to drop out or fail to enroll, motivated in part by fear of harassment by occupying soldiers or police. Students and teachers in Jharkhand and Bihar in India, for example, complained that security force personnel bathed in their underwear in front of girls. Girls in southern Thailand told us that paramilitary Rangers had asked them for their older sisters' phone numbers. This kind of behavior obviously has no place on school grounds.

International Standards Protecting Education

Under international human rights law—namely the widely-ratified Convention on the Rights of the Child and the International Covenant on Economic, Social, and Cultural Rights—states are obligated to make primary education compulsory and available free to all, and secondary education available and accessible. They must work to progressively improve regular attendance at schools and to reduce drop-out rates for both boys and girls. In order to ensure the right to education, states have an obligation to prevent and respond to attacks by non-state armed groups so that the schools function and children receive an education. Attacks on students, teachers, and schools will violate various provisions of domestic criminal law.

In situations that rise to the level of armed conflict, international humanitarian law—the laws of war—also applies. International humanitarian law is binding on all parties to a conflict, both the government and opposition armed groups. Applicable law includes the Geneva Conventions of 1949 and its two additional protocols and customary international law. Under international humanitarian law, schools and educational institutions are civilian objects that are protected from deliberate attack unless and only for such time as they are being used by belligerent forces for a military purpose. Thus a school that serves as a headquarters or an ammunition depot becomes a military objective subject to attack.

International humanitarian law also forbids acts or threats of violence with the primary purpose of spreading terror among the civilian population.

When government forces or non-state armed groups take over schools during an armed conflict, they have an obligation to take all feasible precautions to protect civilians from attack and to remove them from the vicinity: it is unlawful to use a school simultaneously as an armed stronghold and as an educational center. The longer a school cannot be used for educational purposes, the greater the obligation on the state to ensure the affected students' right to education by other means. When a structure ceases being used as a school, the authorities must relocate the school's teachers and students to a safe locale where education can continue or they are denying children the right to an education under international human rights law.

* * *

Putting an end to attacks on schools, teachers, and students requires action at national and international levels on three fronts:

- Stronger monitoring systems;

- Targeted preventive measures, and more decisive and timely response when incidents do occur; and

- Effective justice mechanisms that hold violators of domestic and international law accountable.

Monitoring

A more effective deterrence to attacks on education needs to begin with acknowledgment of the problem, including clear public statements by officials and, wherever possible, rebel group commanders, that attacks on students and teachers are prohibited and the use of schools for military purposes should be off limits. Too often, government policies and regulations on use of schools for military operations in conflict zones are ambiguous or nonexistent. A notable positive model is the Philippines, which specifically criminalizes attacks against education buildings, and prohibits the use of school buildings by government forces as command posts, detachments, depots, or other types of military facility.[3]

Information is also critical. Officials need to put in place monitoring systems that ensure that attacks on schools, teachers, and students are tracked: it is impossible to devise an effective response if the scope of the problem is not known. Too often attacks on education have fallen between the cracks of pro-tection and education agencies and thus have not been addressed as a sys-tematic problem requiring monitoring and a coordinated response. And while governments are in the best position to monitor attacks, some lack the capaci-ty or will to do so, or are themselves implicated. Here, the UN and other inter-national actors have an important role to play.

International monitoring is especially important for overlooked conflicts, including low level conflicts that have not produced widespread displacement but which involve attacks on education. Militaries, embassies, political affairs offices, and other peace and security institutions should also be encouraged to view—and thus monitor—access to and attacks on education at all levels as a critical measurement of security.

The UN Security Council's Monitoring and Reporting Mechanism (MRM) on Children and Armed Conflict provides a vehicle that, if more focused on such attacks, could have particularly far-reaching impact. The MRM was established in 2005 and now operates in 13 countries, feeding information on abuses against children in conflict from the field to the Security Council. The Security Council in turn has the power to take strong action against parties who commit abuses against children during armed conflicts, including imposing sanctions and arms embargoes and referring perpetrators of war crimes and crimes against humanity to the International Criminal Court.

At present the MRM is only "triggered" by evidence of the war crimes of recruitment and use of children as soldiers, sexual violence against children in conflict, and killing and maiming of children. Once it is operational in a country, however, the mechanism is required to monitor other abuses, including attacks on education. The Security Council has rightly urged parties to conflicts to refrain from "attacks or threats of attacks on school children or teachers as such, the use of schools for military operations, and attacks on schools that are prohibited by applicable international law."[4] It has, however, made far fewer recommendations on education via the MRM than on higher profile issues such as child soldiers. The MRM is also not present in some places, such as southern Thailand and India, that continue to suffer repeated attacks on school facilities and personnel.

Supported by the MRM, the UN has achieved substantial successes reducing the use of child soldiers by negotiating action plans with both governments and armed groups to demobilize children from their forces and end new recruitment of children. To achieve similar success in ending attacks on education, the UN-led country teams that monitor violations against children in armed conflict should improve their monitoring of attacks on education, providing the Security Council with more information and recommendations for action. Additionally, the Security Council should include attacks on education as a "trigger" to start up the MRM.

Preventive Measures and Timely Response

When attacks occur or even loom as a possibility, officials need to take immediate measures to protect teachers and students from further harm. For example, by enhancing community participation in school construction and management, education providers may draw on local information about how to
best deter threats and increase incentives among community members to support their schools. Other steps may include providing private guards or escorts
for school buildings and transport; exploring alternative schools sites and
schedules; prohibiting the use of schools for any military or police purpose;
and negotiating with all parties the status of schools as protected or demilita-
rized zones as provided for under international humanitarian law. In some
contexts, opposition groups may be influenced by statements from influential
religious leaders or even those leaders' active participation in schools, by
interaction with community leaders, and other steps that would discourage
rebel attacks on education.

For example, in Nepal the Schools as Zones of Peace initiative and the
Partnerships for Protecting Children in Armed Conflict (PPCC) are often cited as
effective partnerships of non-governmental organizations and international
agencies that, among other things, have helped keep armed groups out of
schools. In contrast, in Afghanistan in the lead up to the 2009 elections, a
group of humanitarian agencies and the Minister of Education used data on
attacks to call for schools to be used as polling places only as a last resort.
Their call was unheeded, and according to the ministry, 26 of the 2,742
schools used as polling places were attacked on election day.[5]

The government's immediate response to an attack, including repairing buildings and replacing materials, is important for mitigating its effects and getting
students back to school as quickly as possible. As governments and education

agencies try out responses, a "tool kit" of proven preventive measures and responses would be useful to assist their efforts.

Justice

Finally, accountability for attacks on education—including prosecuting perpetrators—is critical. Countries that have not done so should explicitly criminalize within domestic law and military codes attacks on schools and place greater restrictions on the military use and occupation of schools. The United Kingdom's Ministry of Defense Manual of the Law of Armed Conflict, for example, includes specific references to the protection of education buildings.[6] In addition to stating that attacks on schools are unlawful unless being used for military purposes, the manual notes that the "use of a privileged building for an improper purpose" is a "war crime traditionally recognized by the customary law of armed conflict."[7] In another example, the Indian Supreme Court and various Indian state courts have ordered police and paramilitary forces engaged in military operations to vacate occupied schools; however, security forces have often ignored these orders.

Domestic prosecutions for attacks, including of non-state actors, are indispensible. For example, in the DRC, an Ituri Military Tribunal in August 2006 convicted Ives Kahwa Panga Mandro ("Chief Kahwa"), founder of the Party for Unity and Safeguarding of the Integrity of Congo, on six charges, including the war crime of intentionally directing attacks against a primary school, a church, and a medical center. Citing the DRC constitution's provision allowing courts and military tribunals to apply international treaties, the tribunal directly applied the crime under the International Criminal Court's Rome Statute of intentionally directing attacks against institutions of education. Kahwa received a 20-year sentence.[8] In a decision light on both legal and factual reasoning, however, an appeals court cancelled the verdict,[9] and the case remains in legal limbo at this writing.

Where governments are unwilling or unable to prosecute, international courts can play an important role in punishing perpetrators and deterring future violations. The International Criminal Court, for example, has explicit jurisdiction over intentional attacks against buildings dedicated to education in both international and internal armed conflicts, provided they are not military objectives. The court has yet to include attacks on education in its charges and should give specific consideration to the issue during relevant investigations and pursue cases where the evidence indicates that such attacks are among the most serious crimes of concern to the international community and which are of sufficient gravity to warrant ICC prosecution.

Outside of formal justice mechanisms, commissions of inquiry and truth and reconciliation commissions should address attacks on education. The 1998 final report of South Africa's Truth and Reconciliation Commission, for example, recognized that a variety of state and non-state actors had bombed, burned, and occupied schools, and assaulted and killed teachers. Many individual perpetrators came before the commission to admit to their own involvement in attacks against schools, students, and teachers.[10]

The Committee on the Rights of the Child, which monitors the implementation of the Convention on the Rights of the Child, is also well-placed to highlight how attacks and occupations violate the right to education. It has already commented on the problem in at least four countries: Burundi, Ethiopia, Israel, and Moldova.[11] As a next step, the Committee could issue a "General Comment", a statement that expands upon and clarifies provisions within the Convention. In 2008 it held a day of discussion on education in emergency situations, collecting information and recommendations that could be turned into a General Comment. Such an interpretation of the Convention on this issue could assist states to protect students, teachers, and schools during times of emergencies, as well as give the Committee and other international and domestic bodies a set of standards by which to judge government action.

Conclusion

In too many conflict-afflicted countries, combatants are able to target schools, teachers, and students with few if any consequences for the perpetrators. The consequences instead fall heavily on the affected teachers, students, and families, with long-term negative consequences for the affected society as a whole.

The formation in 2010 of a new international coalition of UN agencies, humanitarian organizations and other civil society groups on protection of education signals renewed attention to the issue.[12] The coalition's experience to date already suggests concrete steps governments can take to minimize attacks on education. Lasting improvements in the protection of schools, teachers, and students from attack, however, will require far more focused and coordinated national and international action.

As a tribal elder from northern Helmand province in Afghanistan noted: "The people want schools, even for girls. We are losing a golden opportunity now to lift our children."

Zama Coursen-Neff is deputy director of the Children's Rights Division at Human Rights Watch; Bede Sheppard is senior researcher in the division.

---

[1] Save The Children, "The Future is Now: Education for Children in Countries Affected by Conflict", 2010, pg viii.

[2] Brendan O'Malley, Education under Attack 2010, (Paris: UNESCO, 2010).

[3] An Act Defining and Penalizing Crimes Against International Humanitarian Law, Genocide and Other Crimes Against Humanity, Organizing Jurisdictions, Designating Special Courts, and for Other Related Purposes, Republic Act No. 9851, 2009- criminalizes attacks on school facilities; An Act Providing for Stronger Deterrence and Special Protection Against Child Abuse, Exploitation and Discrimination, Providing Penalties for

its Violation, and for Other Purposes, Republic Act No. 7610, 1992- prohibits use of such facilities for military operations.

4 United Nations Security Council, "Presidential Statement on Children and Armed Conflict", UN Doc. S/PRST/2009/9, April 29, 2009.

5 "Afghanistan: Over 20 Schools Attacked on Election Day," IRIN News, August 24, 2009, http://www.irinnews.org/Report.aspx?ReportId=85831 (accessed October 8, 2009).

6 UK Ministry of Defence, Manual of the Law of Armed Conflict (Oxford: Oxford University Press, 2004).

7 Ibid.,16.16.1, 16.29(c), pp. 428-29, n. 122.

8 Tribunal Militaire de Garnison de l'Ituri, Jugement Contre Kahwa Panga Mandro, RPA No. 039/2006, RMP No. 227/ PEN/2006 (August 2, 2006).

9 Cour Militaire de la Province Orientale, Arrêt Contre Kahwa Panga Mandro, RPA No. 023/2007, RMP 227/PEN/2006 (July 28, 2007).

10 Truth and Reconciliation Commission of South Africa, Report of the Truth and Reconciliation Commission of South Africa (1998), vol. I, p. 34, vol. II, pp. 154, 150, 380, 387, 431, 436, and 661-662, vol. III, pp. 59-60, 236, 311, 370, 408, and 617; vol. IV, p. 266; and vol. V, pp. 255 and 355.

11 United Nations Committee on the Rights of the Child (CRC), UN Committee on the Rights of the Child: Concluding Observations, Burundi, CRC/C/15/Add.133 (October 16, 2000), paras. 64-65; CRC, UN Committee on the Rights of the Child: Concluding Observations, Ethiopia, CRC/C/ETH/CO/3 (November 1, 2006), paras. 27-28; CRC, UN Committee on the Rights of the Child: Concluding Observations, Israel, CRC/C/15/Add.195 (October 9, 2002), para. 52; CRC, Consideration of Reports Submitted by States Parties Under Article 44 of the Convention: Convention on the Rights of the Child: 2nd and 3rd Periodic Reports of States Parties Due in 2005: Republic of Moldova, CRC/C/MDA/3 (July 10, 2008), paras. 423 and 435.

12 The Global Coalition for Protecting Education from Attack (GCPEA) includes the Council for Assisting Refugee Academics, Education Above All, Education International, Human Rights Watch, Save the Children International, UNESCO, and UNICEF, the UN Children's Fund. The coalition is dedicated to raising awareness about the scope of attacks on education and their consequences, and mobilizing a more effective international response.

HUMAN
RIGHTS
WATCH

WORLD REPORT

2011

PHOTO ESSAYS

BURMA, KYRGYZSTAN, KUWAIT, KAZAKHSTAN,
AND THE LORD'S RESISTANCE ARMY

EXILED
BURMA'S DEFENDERS
by Platon

Burma is one of the most repressive and closed societies in the world, run by generals since 1962. Longstanding human rights abuses by the government include silencing of most of civil society, torture in prison, use of child soldiers, forced labor, trafficking of women, and attacks targeting civilians in ethnic minority areas. In May 2010, Human Rights Watch took leading portrait photographer Platon to the Thai-Burma border to photograph former political prisoners, civil society leaders, ethnic minority group members, journalists and other people in exile from their country, Burma.

(left) A group of mine victims: Kio Say, 43; Hsa Ka Twe, 15; Par Taw, 45. Burma is one of the top remaining users of landmines as part of long-running armed conflicts with ethnic minority groups.

(opposite) Left to right: Ashin Sopaka, Ashin Issariya, known as "King Zero," and U Teza. September 2007 saw the largest popular protests against military rule in Burma in nearly 20 years. Burmese government security forces killed, beat, tortured, and violently dispersed peaceful protesters, including monks.

Democratic Voice of Burma broadcast journalists Thiri Htet San, 30, and Moe Myint Zin, 34. The DVB is a satellite radio and television news service, with highly professional reporters who risk their lives to report and record events inside Burma, and then to broadcast the news back into Burma and to distribute it worldwide.

A medical student at the time, Win Min became a leader of the 1988 pro-democracy demonstrations in Burma. He is now one of the driving forces behind an innovative collective called the Vahu (in Burmese: Plural) Development Institute, which trains Burmese civil society workers to work for development and peaceful change.

"WHERE IS THE JUSTICE?"

INTERETHNIC VIOLENCE
IN SOUTHERN KYRGYZSTAN

by Moises Saman/Magnum Photos

Zhura Payzulaeva cries as she
recounts how seven members of
her family were killed in the first
two days of ethnic clashes in Osh.

22-year-old Eliza Makeeve holds a photograph of her late husband, 23-year-old Ulan Dzhoroev, an ethnic Kyrgyz man killed by gunmen during clashes that started June 10 in the city of Osh.

Violence erupted on June 10 when hundreds of Uzbeks gathered near a dormitory in the center of Osh, Kyrgyzstan, allegedly in response to recent scuffles between Uzbeks and Kyrgyz. Human Rights Watch researchers working in southern Kyrgyzstan from June 10 to 22 documented the subsequent massive looting and destruction of civilian property and widespread acts of violence by Kyrgyz and Uzbek mobs in the city of Osh and the towns of Jalal-Abad and Bazar-Kurgan. While both ethnic Kyrgyz and Uzbeks fell victim to the violence, Uzbek neighborhoods were particularly affected as mobs of ethnic Kyrgyz, many of them reportedly from villages surrounding the city of Osh, repeatedly attacked Uzbek areas.

(above) An ethnic Uzbek man walks past the burned remains of a house burned by mobs during ethnic clashes in the southern Kyrgyz city of Osh.

(left) An ethnic Uzbek Kyrgyz woman displays the burned remains of her Kyrgyz passport and her and her son's identity papers after Kyrgyz security forces destroyed them during a security operation in the village of Nariman.

Workers continue to spend long periods waiting at embassy shelters, including the Philippines safe house, shown here. Workers reported spending weeks or months in official custody, moving from embassy shelters to police stations, and from there to criminal investigation facilities, before they were sent to deportation detention.

WALLS AT EVERY TURN

ABUSE OF MIGRANT
DOMESTIC WORKERS IN KUWAIT

by Moises Saman/Magnum Photos

Kuwait has the highest ratio of domestic workers to citizens in the
Middle East. The country's more than 660,000 migrant domestic
workers constitute nearly a third of the work force in this small Gulf
country of only 1.3 million citizens. But domestic workers are
excluded from the labor laws that protect other workers. They have
minimal protection against employers who withhold salaries, force
employees to work long hours with no days off, deprive them of
adequate food, or abuse them physically or sexually.

A recruitment agent stands with a group of Ethiopian
domestic workers as they waited for potential clients at an
agency office in the basement of a shopping center in the
Hawalli neighborhood of Kuwait. Women who leave
employers and return to recruitment agencies—either as
a result of their employer's decision or their request—are
called "returns."

(above) More than 200 women are packed in a sweltering room in the Philippines Embassy, where they sleep on their luggage. Other labor-sending countries, including Sri Lanka, Indonesia, Nepal, Ethiopia, and India, maintain shelters in Kuwait. Most are equally, if not more, crowded.

(left) Gyanu, 21, came from Nepal to work as a domestic worker in Kuwait. After leaving her employers, she sought refuge inside a makeshift shelter operated from a private house on the outskirts of Kuwait City.

63

"HELLISH WORK"

EXPLOITATION OF MIGRANT TOBACCO WORKERS IN KAZAKHSTAN

by Moises Saman/Magnum Photos

Every year, tens of thousands of migrant workers from Kyrgyzstan travel to the Central Asian economic powerhouse of Kazakhstan in search of employment. Thousands of these migrant workers, often together with their children, find work in tobacco farming, where many are subjected to abuse and exploitation by employers supplying tobacco to Philip Morris Kazakhstan, a subsidiary of Philip Morris International, one of the world's largest tobacco companies.

(above) A migrant worker from Kyrgyzstan sits inside her makeshift house in the village of Koram, Kazakhstan.

(opposite) A child migrant worker's hands are covered in tobacco residue after picking leaves on a tobacco farm near Koram, Kazakhstan.

A migrant worker from Kyrgyzstan picks tobacco leaves near the village of Malybai, Kazakhstan.

LORD'S RESISTANCE ARMY

Since September 2008, at least 2,000 civilians have been killed and nearly 3,000 others have been abducted during attacks by the Lord's Resistance Army (LRA). The LRA, a Ugandan rebel group, operates in the border region between northern Congo, the Central African Republic and south Sudan. Many of the victims, including children, were beaten to death, had their skulls crushed or their heads sliced with machetes. Abducted children are forced to kill their family members. Three of the LRA's leaders – Joseph Kony, Okot Odhiambo, and Dominic Ongwen – are sought by the International Criminal Court under arrest warrants issued in July 2005 for war crimes committed in northern Uganda. All three remain at large and continue to commit atrocities.

Boniface, 14, spent six months as a rebel fighter with the Lord's Resistance Army and was released after the government Uganda Peoples' Defense Forces (UPDF) attacked their camp.

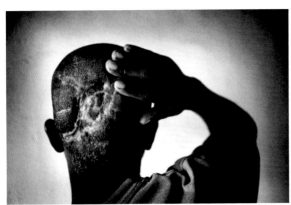

(above) Marcelline, 15, was forced to be the "wife" of an Lord's Resistance Army (LRA) commander. She spent over a year with the LRA.

(left) Masua, 22, is a fisherman and father of three children. He was abducted by the Lord's Resistance Army (LRA) and used as a porter. When he became too tired to continue, LRA commanders forced children to hit him with sticks until he was left for dead.

(above) Olivier, 16, was abducted in October 2009. He was forced to witness and participate in brutal attacks by the Lord's Resistance Army.

(right) Yoris was shot by the Lord's Resistance Army in August 2010 while returning from the market on his bicycle.

An abandoned school lies on the outskirts of Ango, northeastern Congo. People have fled because of recent abductions and killings by the Lord's Resistance Army.

"Off the Backs of the Children"

Forced Begging and Other Abuses against Talibés in Senegal

HUMAN
RIGHTS
WATCH

WORLD REPORT

2011

AFRICA

ANGOLA

On February 5, after minimal public discussion, Angola's new constitution entered into force. It was approved in late January by parliament, which has been dominated by the ruling Popular Movement for the Liberation of Angola (MPLA) since 2008. The constitution consolidates the president's de facto powers over state institutions and prescribes a parliament-based model of electing the president, rather than separate elections.

In April parliament passed a law to curb Angola's endemic corruption, following the president's new "zero-tolerance" anti-corruption discourse. The law has not yet been implemented.

Fundamental rights such as freedom of expression and information became more curtailed in 2010, despite strong guarantees in the new constitution. The environment for human rights defenders remains restricted. Several human rights organizations have continued to struggle with unresolved lawsuits against banning orders, administrative registration obstacles, threats, and intimidation. In Cabinda province, two prominent human rights defenders were sentenced to prison on trumped-up charges following politically motivated proceedings.

Arbitrary Detentions in Cabinda

An intermittent armed conflict with a separatist movement has persisted in Cabinda since 1975, despite a peace agreement signed in 2006. The authorities have long used the conflict to justify restrictions on the rights to freedom of expression, assembly, and association in this oil-rich enclave. The government has not responded to calls for an independent investigation into allegations of torture and other serious human rights violations committed by the Angolan Armed Forces in Cabinda for many years. Perpetrators of torture there have not been prosecuted.

In 2010 the authorities used an armed attack on the Togolese football team on January 8, which killed two Togolese and injured nine others, as a pretext to arrest and convict prominent Cabindan intellectuals and government critics. The Front for the Liberation of the Enclave of Cabinda, a separatist guerrilla group,

ANGOLA

"Transparency and Accountability in Angola"

An Update

HUMAN RIGHTS WATCH

claimed responsibility for the attack. The government has not carried out a credible investigation into the incident.

Only two of the nine men arrested between January 8 and April 11 were formally charged with direct involvement in the attack, and at this writing they are awaiting trial. Six others were formally charged and tried between June and September for unspecified "other crimes" against the security of the state, under article 26 of the 1978 law on crimes against the security of the state. This legal provision contradicts international human rights law because it is overbroad and does not specify the crimes for which the authorities may impose prison penalties.

Those convicted include: a Chevron worker who was arrested on January 8 and sentenced to three years of imprisonment in June; two prominent human rights defenders—Raúl Tati, a Catholic priest, and Francisco Luemba, a lawyer—who were arrested in January and sentenced to five years' imprisonment in August; and civic activist and university professor Belchior Lanso Tati and a former policeman who were also arrested in January and sentenced to six and three years, respectively, of imprisonment in the same trial. In September a former activist of the civic association Mpalabanda, arrested in January 2010, was tried and acquitted.

Another former Mpalabanda activist, António Paca Panzo Pemba, was arbitrarily arrested in April on suspicion of having organized a public demonstration in solidarity with these political detainees, together with two Angolan human rights organizations. In November, charges against him were dropped for lack of evidence. Five other activists were briefly detained and released provisionally in April for wearing and allegedly distributing t-shirts with the faces of political detainees printed on them. In November, two teachers were arrested and convicted to prison sentences for "inciting to civil disobedience." They had authored and distributed leaflets calling on the population to abstain from Angola's independence celebration on November 11.

Defense lawyers in August appealed to the Constitutional Court seeking revocation of article 26 of the 1978 state crime law. In September the Angolan Bar Association also filed a request regarding the same legal provision at the Constitutional Court. At this writing the Constitutional Court's decision is pending, and despite the approval of a revised law on crimes against the security of the state, the convicted persons remain in prison.

Media Freedom

The media environment in Angola remains restrictive, and the government continues to limit access to information, despite the emergence of a number of new media outlets over the past two years. The ruling party imposes a strong political bias in the state media. Authorities routinely limit the access of private media to official information and have curtailed space for open political debate on state and private radio stations, particularly in the provinces. They have also obstructed media coverage of politically sensitive events such as forced evictions. On November 4 the parliament passed a revised law on crimes against the security of the state, which contains provisions that restrict freedom of expression, for example by declaring "insult" of the president a criminal offense.

In September and October two journalists of the Luanda-based Radio Despertar, a radio station close to the opposition party UNITA, were attacked by unknown men. On September 5 the Radio Despertar journalist Alberto Tchakussanga was shot dead in his home. On October 22 the radio satirist António Manuel Jojó was stabbed in the street but survived. Both ran popular programs critical of the government and had previously received anonymous death threats. At this writing police investigations remain inconclusive.

Defamation remains a criminal offense in the new press law. Other offenses, such as "abuse of press freedom," are vague and thus open to political manipulation. No new defamation charges against journalists were reported in 2010, but a number of previous proceedings against journalists of the weekly newspapers *Folha 8*, *A Capital*, and *Novo Jornal* remain pending at this writing. Such litigation, in an increasingly difficult economic environment for the private media, perpetuates a widespread culture of self-censorship that restricts the public's access to independent information.

A new press law was enacted in May 2006 but the additional legislation required to implement crucial parts of the law, which would improve the legal protection of freedom of expression and access to information, have still not passed at this writing. Independent private radio stations cannot broadcast nationwide, while the government's licensing practices have favored new radio and television stations linked with the ruling MPLA and the presidency. The 2006 press law contains provisions that prevent the establishment of media monopolies and require disclosure of shareholders of media corporations. Yet, the real shareholders of companies registered as owners of several media corporations established since 2008, which are reportedly linked to the presidential entourage, have not been disclosed. In June a company reportedly linked to the president bought three of the most popular weekly newspapers known for their government criticism, *Semánario Angolense, A Capital,* and 40 percent of *Novo Jornal.*

Freedom of Assembly and Demonstration

The new constitution guarantees freedom of assembly and peaceful demonstration, and Angolan laws explicitly allow public demonstrations without the need to obtain government authorization. However, in 2010 the authorities arbitrarily banned two public demonstrations organized by civil society organizations, publicly threatened demonstrators, and deployed security forces to prevent the demonstrations. In November the police also temporarily detained peaceful demonstrators and opposition party activists in Luanda who were peacefully distributing leaflets.

In March a demonstration against mass forced evictions and demolition of houses in Huila, organized by the human rights organization Omunga, was banned by the governor of Benguela province. The governor deployed hundreds of police agents and publicly rejected "any responsibility" for the resulting physical damage or harm to the protesters. The demonstration later took place on April 10 following local and international pressure. In May the governor of Cabinda banned a public demonstration organized by civil society groups in solidarity with civilians jailed on suspicion of state security crimes after the January 8 guerilla attack. The governor deployed police and military to prevent the demonstration from taking place on May 22. The military and police also surrounded the organizers' houses on the day of the demonstration, despite the demonstration being called off by its organizers.

Housing Rights and Forced Evictions

Angola's laws do not give adequate protection against forced eviction, nor do they enshrine the right to adequate housing. In 2010 the government continued to carry out mass forced evictions and house demolitions in areas that it claims to be reserved for public construction in Luanda and increasingly also in provincial towns. This has occurred without adequate prior notice or compensation in several documented cases.

Between March and October an estimated 25,000 residents were forcibly evicted from their homes in Huila, without compensation or adequate prior notice, and resettled in peripheral areas without any infrastructure, driving many of the evicted into extreme poverty. In March the government ordered the destruction of at least 3,000 residences in Lubango, Huila province to clear railway lines. Demolitions have proceeded despite massive public criticism of the evictions by civil society organizations, the Catholic Church, opposition parties, the parliament, and a public apology by the Minister of Territorial Administration. In September and October the government has demolished at least 1,500 houses and annexes at the riverside in Lubango to make way for an urban beautification project.

Key International Actors

Angola remains one of Africa's largest oil producers and is China's second most important source of oil and most important commercial partner in Africa. This oil wealth, and Angola's regional military power, has greatly limited leverage of other governments and international organizations pushing for good governance and human rights. Trade partners remain reluctant to criticize the government, to protect their economic interests. Since 2009 falling oil and diamond prices and the global economic crisis have forced the government to invest more efforts to seek support from international partners, including the International Monetary Fund with which Angola signed a Stand-by-Arangement in November 2009.

In February Angola underwent the Universal Periodic Review at the United Nations Human Rights Council. Angola adopted a number of important recommendations from member states. However, it did not issue a standing invitation to all UN special rapporteurs, as requested by a number of member states as well as local and international human rights organizations. In May Angola was re-elected as a member of the Council and reiterated its pledge to sign or ratify all major international human rights instruments. However, none of the pending signings or ratifications has taken place despite a previous pledge in 2007.

Burundi

Burundi held local and national elections between May and September 2010. Following communal elections on May 24, the electoral commission announced an overwhelming majority for the ruling party, the National Council for the Defense of Democracy–Forces for the Defense of Democracy (CNDD-FDD). Opposition parties cried fraud and boycotted subsequent elections. Government officials banned opposition meetings and tortured political opponents. Both CNDD-FDD and opposition supporters carried out acts of political violence. International observers, relieved that Burundi had not descended into mass violence, described the elections as "calm."

The government facilitated the illegal takeover of the main opposition party, the National Liberation Forces (FNL), by a dissident wing friendly to the ruling party. Some FNL and other opposition members retreated to the bush and took up arms. Police apprehended and killed several FNL members who were attempting to join the armed groups.

The government cracked down on journalists, civil society organizations, and international organizations that denounced abuses.

Elections and the Breakdown of Democratic Progress

CNDD-FDD's election campaign relied on bribery and use of state resources, along with intimidation. Police shut down the meetings of some opposition parties and arrested some activists.

The May communal election results gave 64 percent of the vote to CNDD-FDD. Opposition parties claimed that there had been massive fraud and formed a coalition, ADC-Ikibiri, which called for a boycott of subsequent elections. They did not present concrete evidence of massive fraud, but the failure of the National Independent Electoral Commission (CENI) to publicize written vote tallies from each voting station—in violation of the electoral law—raised doubts about the integrity of the process.

All six opposition candidates dropped out of the presidential elections in June, leaving incumbent President Pierre Nkurunziza as the sole candidate. One opposition party, UPRONA, participated in legislative elections in July. Still, CNDD-FDD won over 80 percent of parliament seats.

Political Violence and Return to Armed Conflict

Before and throughout the elections most major parties used intimidation tactics, including violence. These parties included the FNL and, to a lesser degree, the Front for Democracy in Burundi (FRODEBU), the Movement for Solidarity and Democracy (MSD), the Union for Peace and Development (UPD), and the Union for National Progress (UPRONA), but the majority of incidents were attributed to CNDD-FDD. Partisan youth groups, including the CNDD-FDD's Imbonerakure, played a significant role in the violence. The Imbonerakure were also involved in carrying out illegal arrests before, during, and after the elections.

In the two weeks before communal elections at least five politically-motivated killings took place. During the presidential and legislative elections at least 128 grenade attacks – many of them targeting political activists on all sides – took place throughout Burundi, killing 11 and injuring at least 69. At least 33 CNDD-FDD meeting places were set on fire during this period.

Throughout July and August FNL members fled their homes to avoid arrest, many returning to the forests where they had fought during Burundi's 16-year civil war. FNL leader Agathon Rwasa went into hiding, as did ADC-Ikibiri spokesperson Leonard Nyangoma. A new armed movement was formed. In September seven workers employed by a prominent CNDD-FDD member were killed; evidence suggested that the perpetrators were FNL members in the Rukoko forest. At least 18 bodies, many mutilated, washed up in the Rusizi River; some were recognized as FNL members. The United Nations mission in Burundi (BINUB) and a Burundian human rights group presented the authorities with evidence that police carried out some of the killings.

BURUNDI

Mob Justice in Burundi

Official Complicity and Impunity

HUMAN
RIGHTS
WATCH

BURUNDI

"We'll Tie You Up and Shoot You"

Lack of Accountability for Political Violence in Burundi

HUMAN
RIGHTS
WATCH

Repression of the Political Opposition and Resurgence of Torture

Over 250 opposition members were arrested in June and July. Charges included "inciting the population not to vote," which is not a crime in Burundi. Others were suspected of serious crimes, including throwing grenades.

At least 12 opposition activists were tortured or ill-treated in June and July by the National Intelligence Service (SNR). Dozens were ill-treated by the police. SNR agents cut off part of the ear of one UPD member and forced him to eat it. Other activists were kicked in the genitals or imprisoned in toilets.

Three opposition leaders were illegally prevented from leaving the country in June. On June 8 Interior Minister Edouard Nduwimana banned all opposition activities. He rescinded the ban in late July, but police still shut down some opposition activities, including a September 17 ADC-Ikibiri press conference.

On August 4 Interior Minister Nduwimana recognized the results of an "extraordinary congress," organized by former FNL members with support of the ruling party, in which FNL president Rwasa was voted out and replaced by more compliant leaders. After years of effort by government officials and the international community to bring Rwasa and the FNL into the political process, the congress violated FNL internal rules and left Rwasa and his supporters with no political voice.

On September 27 MSD spokesperson François Nyamoya was arrested on defamation charges after stating in a radio interview that President Nkurunziza should dismiss SNR chief Adolphe Nshimirimana and Deputy Police Director Gervais Ndirakobuca due to abuses committed by both services. He was released on bail on October 14. In addition to his political activity, Nyamoya is a prominent lawyer who has defended government critics in court. His client Jackson Ndikuriyo, a former police officer who had filed a complaint for unlawful dismissal, was killed on August 26 in what Burundian rights organizations denounced as an extrajudicial execution by police. Ndikuriyo had been fired for denouncing police corruption and had told Nyamoya before his death that he was being threatened by Deputy Police Director Ndirakobuca.

Human Rights Defenders and Journalists

The year 2010 represented a low point for the rights of human rights defenders and journalists, with repression reaching a level not seen since 2006.

On May 18 Foreign Minister Augustin Nsanze revoked the work permit of Human Rights Watch's Burundi researcher, claiming that the organization's May report on political violence in Burundi was "biased" and that the researcher demonstrated "attitudes that are harmful to government institutions." The government did not contest any specific information in the report and as of November Nsanze had not responded to a series of requests from Human Rights Watch for dialogue.

Four journalists were arrested in 2010. Jean Claude Kavumbagu, editor of the online service Net Press, was detained in July on treason charges—by law only applicable "in times of war"—after questioning the army's ability to respond to an attack by al-Shabaab. Prosecutors insinuated that threats from al-Shabaab against Burundi constituted "war." As of October Kavumbagu had been held illegally in pretrial detention for three months. Thierry Ndayishimiye, editor of the newspaper *Arc-en-Ciel*, was detained in August for denouncing corruption at the state energy company. He was released on bail. Two journalists from the private newspaper *Iwacu* were detained for two days in November, with no explanation and no charges.

On July 29 Gabriel Rufyiri, president of the anti-corruption organization OLUCOME, was questioned by a magistrate subsequent to a defamation complaint. Bujumbura prosecutor Renovat Tabu ordered Rufyiri's arrest. The magistrate refused, for lack of evidence, and was transferred the next day to a post in a jurisdiction in rural Burundi.

Eric Manirakiza and Bob Rugurika, the director and editor-in-chief of the private radio station RPA, received death threats. Pacifique Nininahazwe, delegate general of the Forum for the Strengthening of Civil Society (FORSC), was subjected to surveillance by vehicles associated with the SNR.

Hearings were held in the trial of suspects in the April 2009 murder of Ernest Manirumva, OLUCOME vice president. Civil society groups expressed concern that prosecutors have neglected to arrest or question several high-ranking police and

BURUNDI

Closing Doors?

The Narrowing of Democratic Space in Burundi

HUMAN
RIGHTS
WATCH

SNR officials who have been cited by witnesses. They have also presented evidence suggesting that some witnesses have disappeared or have been killed. Prosecutors lost the witnesses' confidence by sharing information on witnesses with the SNR.

Transitional Justice and Criminal Justice

A committee representing the government, the UN, and civil society completed a series of "national consultations" on establishing a Truth and Reconciliation Commission and a Special Tribunal to address past war crimes. The committee presented President Nkurunziza with a report in April, but it still is not public at this writing, preventing progress on establishing the proposed mechanisms.

The Burundian justice system was plagued by backlogs in 2010. Sixty-five percent of prisoners were in pretrial detention. A September court decision upholding the pretrial detention of journalist Kavumbagu held that pretrial detention is always the best means to maintain a suspect "at the disposition of the justice system," in violation of international human rights principles.

Key International Actors

International diplomats in Bujumbura closely followed proceedings in cases affecting human rights defenders and journalists, many personally attended hearings. Belgium's foreign minister condemned the arrests of Kavumbagu and Nyamoya and called for investigations into the allegations of torture of political opponents. The United States, which offered technical assistance from its FBI in investigations into Manirumva's death, pressed the government to pursue high-ranking officials suspected of involvement in the killing.

Many foreign governments failed to denounce restrictions on the rights of the political opposition during the election period. They downplayed the lack of an equal playing field and exerted heavy pressure on the opposition to end its boycott, which resulted in alienating opposition parties.

The UN mission in Burundi systematically documented cases of torture, arbitrary arrests, and extrajudicial executions, and pressed the government to end these practices.

The UN-appointed Independent Expert on the Situation of Human Rights in Burundi has not been able to present any report on the situation in Burundi since September 2008, in a deviation from standard practice at the UN Human Rights Council. Burundi lobbied the Council to postpone the presentation of the independent expert's report during the council's September 2010 session.

Rwandan pressure on Burundi resulted in the illegal repatriation of 103 Rwandan asylum seekers in November 2009. Tanzania took the positive step of naturalizing 162,000 Burundian refugees who had been in Tanzania since 1972.

CHAD

A rapprochement agreement between Chad and Sudan, signed January 15, 2010, marked the end of a five-year proxy war. The normalization of relations led to the repatriation of Chadian rebels from Sudan, the opening of the border between the two countries in April after seven years of closure, and the deployment of a joint force to secure the border, though attacks on civilians in the area continue. President Idriss Déby visited Khartoum, Sudan's capital, in February for the first time in six years; and in July Chad, a state party to the International Criminal Court, hosted Sudanese President Omar al-Bashir, earning the dubious distinction of being the first ICC member state to harbor a suspect from the court. The Chadian government clashed with rebel forces in eastern Chad in January and April. Criminality, banditry, kidnappings, carjackings, and armed robbery targeting humanitarian agencies led to the withdrawal and temporary suspension of some humanitarian operations.

In January the government of Chad requested that the United Nations begin the process of withdrawing the peacekeeping mission in eastern Chad. The government cited the mission's slow deployment, uneven record of success, and improvements in the security situation as reasons for its decision. In May the UN revised the mission's mandate and authorized its gradual drawdown and closure by the end of the year, and effectively shifted full responsibility for the protection of civilians, including displaced populations and refugees from Darfur, to the Chadian security forces.

The implementation of the reforms promised in an August 2007 agreement with opposition parties has been slow and uneven. President Déby, one of Africa's longest-serving heads of state, has failed to make adequate funding available and has instead tightened his grip on power. Despite a new media law passed in August, the government continues to suppress free speech.

Throughout the country, government forces continue to arbitrarily arrest and detain civilians and suspected rebels, often on the basis of ethnicity, and subject them to ill-treatment and torture, sometimes in unofficial places of detention. Chad's prison conditions are among the harshest on the African continent.

Weak institutions of justice contributed to a culture of impunity. The government has not investigated or prosecuted serious abuses against civilians, such as killings and rapes by government security forces and rebels following clashes at Am Dam in May 2009. The disappearance of opposition leader Ibni Oumar Mahamat Saleh during the February 2008 attack on N'Djamena, the capital, remains unresolved.

Drawdown of the United Nations Mission in Chad

Peacekeepers from the UN Mission in the Central African Republic and Chad (MIN-URCAT) have been in eastern Chad and northeastern Central African Republic since mid-2008 with a mandate to protect refugees and displaced populations, facilitate humanitarian assistance, and promote human rights.

Following the UN decision to draw down the mission by the end of 2010, representatives of UN agencies formed a working group with the Chadian government to improve security for humanitarian groups in eastern Chad. The plan includes consolidation of the Chadian Integrated Security Detachment (DIS), a component of MINURCAT comprised of Chadian police forces trained by the UN, which provide security in and around the refugee camps. However, the plans do not clearly address the security concerns of refugees, internally displaced persons (IDPs), or the local population.

Refugees and Internally Displaced Persons

More than 250,000 Sudanese refugees and 168,000 Chadian displaced people live in camps and elsewhere in eastern Chad. In April approximately 5,000 new Sudanese refugees arrived from West Darfur, following renewed fighting there between the Sudanese rebel group Justice and Equality Movement (JEM) and Sudanese government forces.

The security situation of refugees and IDPs in camps remains precarious, with continued reports of human rights abuses and other crimes. The militarization of camps, unexploded landmines, and the proliferation of arms in eastern Chad continue to put civilians at risk. Humanitarian needs were greatly exacerbated by food shortages and pockets of famine. Severe flooding destroyed the infrastructure of some refugee camps and left 4,000 refugees completely without shelter.

In May the prime minister encouraged IDPs to return to their areas of origin. An estimated 20,000 people returned in the Dar Sila and Ouaddai regions between April and July, but the sustainability of these movements is uncertain. Returnees continue to report cases of unlawful killings, attacks, and theft. The lack of basic infrastructure, such as access to drinking water, health centers, or schools also stops many IDPs from returning home. Inequity in the justice system and violations perpetrated by the Chadian Armed Forces further add to this climate of fear.

Sexual Violence

Sexual and gender-based violence, including rape, early and forced marriages, and female genital mutilation, was reported frequently to UN human rights monitors in eastern Chad; in the first half of 2010 DIS registered over 250 complaints in this area. Most victims are children. The high levels of violence are exacerbated by an entrenched culture of impunity and structural gender inequality. Rapes occur in domestic settings, near victims' residences, and outside villages, refugee camps, and IDP sites; perpetrators include members of the Chadian National Army (ANT). Women and girls do not have adequate access to health and legal services.

Child Soldiers

Various Chadian security forces, including the ANT and JEM, continued to recruit and employ children in eastern Chad. In January and February six children recruited to JEM between 2007 and 2008 deserted and returned to the Iridimi refugee camp. In September the special representative of the secretary-general for children and armed conflict presented a report to the UN Human Rights Council listing both the ANT and JEM as parties that recruit and use children. In 2007 the Chadian government signed an agreement with the UN Children's Fund (UNICEF) to release all children from its armed forces.

On September 14, 2010, the Chadian government arrested four Sudanese rebels who were allegedly recruiting child soldiers in the Goz Amir refugee camp. UNICEF has demobilized over 800 child soldiers in Chad over the past three years; more than 90 percent of these children were affiliated with Chadian armed opposition groups.

In June the government hosted a regional conference on child soldiers with five other Central African nations, leading to the adoption of the "N'Djamena Declaration," which pledges to stop the use of children in armed conflict and to release and reintegrate child soldiers.

Hissène Habré Trial

The Senegalese government continues to delay judicial proceedings against former Chadian president Hissène Habré, who stands accused of crimes against humanity and torture during his 1982-1990 rule. In 2006 Senegal accepted an African Union "mandate" to prosecute Habré "on behalf of Africa," but then stated that the prosecution would not move forward unless international donors assumed the full expense of organizing a trial, which Senegal estimated at US$40 million.

In July 2010 a joint African Union-European Union team, with the support of the United States, presented Senegal with a proposed budget of $9 million for the trial. Senegal has accepted the proposed budget and a donors' conference is scheduled to take place in Dakar, the Senegalese capital, by the end of 2010.

Meanwhile thousands of victims of torture and killings under Habré's rule have never received compensation or recognition from Chad's current government, and many of Habré's henchmen still hold key positions of power, including state security jobs.

International Actors

Despite solid evidence of widespread and serious human rights abuses in Chad, the country's key international partners have refrained from pressing the Chadian government on its human rights commitments. By lodging a formal request to the UN for the non-renewal of the mission's mandate, Chad succeeded in diverting international attention from its election and domestic human rights problems.

The government of Chad received ongoing military support from both France and the US. France has had troops stationed in Chad since 1986; currently they number 1,000 soldiers. Yet the Chadian government has started to question the justification of the French deployment and, during celebrations of Chad's 50th anniversary of independence, President Déby said that France must "pay a price" if it "wants to stay in Chad, to use its airplanes, and train its soldiers there." It is not clear yet how France's stated plan to reorganize troops stationed in its former colonies and negotiate new defense agreements will affect its military cooperation with Chad.

As one of the key US allies on the African continent, Chad received US military assistance under the Trans-Saharan Counterterrorism Partnership, a scheme through which the US sends Special Forces instructors to train antiterrorist commandos in Chad. US President Barak Obama issued a waiver allowing US military assistance to continue to flow to Chad, the Democratic Republic of Congo, Sudan, and Yemen, despite State Department findings that these countries violate the US Child Soldiers Prevention Act.

China is becoming an increasingly important international player in Chad. Attracted by the growing petroleum industry in the Sahel region of Africa, Chinese companies have increased their presence there. In June 2010 the China National Petroleum Corporation—one of China's largest oil and gas companies, which is also present in Sudan—began working on an oil pipeline in southwestern Chad. The pipeline is expected to be operational in 2011 and will facilitate the transport of crude oil from the Koudalwa field (300 kilometers, or 186 miles, south of N'Djamena) to the Djarmaya refinery (north of N'Djamena).

In early February 2010 Chad won reelection onto the Peace and Security Council of the AU, the AU's most important organ in charge of the day-to-day management of peace and security issues on the continent.

CÔTE D'IVOIRE

A long-delayed presidential vote on October 31 left President Laurent Gbagbo and former prime minister Alassane Ouattara in a run-off scheduled for November 28. Optimism among Ivorians and international partners that the country was moving toward reunification after a calm first round was tempered by the ethnic-regional split among voters, as well as concerns that incendiary rhetoric by the candidates' supporters could lead to incidents of communal and political violence. A successful election would signal an end to the political uncertainty that has beleaguered the country for more than five years.

Meanwhile the almost singular focus on elections by the Ivorian government and its international partners resulted in grossly insufficient efforts to address disarmament, human rights abuses, and deficiencies within rule of law institutions. Ivorians continue to suffer high levels of sexual violence, banditry, and land conflict with little recourse in a justice system plagued by corruption, lack of independence, and insufficient resources. The state institutions mandated to protect the population and investigate and hold accountable perpetrators of serious crimes continue to engage in unprofessional and predatory conduct, including the open extortion of citizens at checkpoints throughout the country.

Elections and a Continuing Political-Military Stalemate

In the first round of presidential elections, almost 80 percent of eligible Ivorians cast their votes in a process that international observers deemed to be free and fair. However, none of the candidates received 50 percent of the vote, resulting in a run-off between Gbagbo and Ouattara. Votes were cast sharply along ethnic and regional lines during the first round, with Gbagbo controlling the south and west and Ouattara the north. There were widespread concerns that a contested second round would fail to end the country's long-term political uncertainty.

Ivorian authorities made minimal effort to disarm former combatants in 2010, allowing for the continued abundance of arms, particularly in the rebel-held north and the formerly pro-government militia stronghold in the far west of the country. As of August the United Nations Operation in Côte d'Ivoire (UNOCI) had collected only 715 arms during their disarmament programs for rebel and militia forces combined, despite the government's census of 70,000 combatants and claims that around 30,000 combatants had already been demobilized. Rebel forces were increasingly unwilling to cooperate with inspectors from the UN Group of Experts tasked with monitoring compliance of a 2004 arms embargo. The government's Republican Guard has refused outright to cooperate since the embargo was imposed.

Rule of Law

The judicial system remains marked by corruption and lack of independence. The planned redeployment of judicial officials to the north progressed slowly in 2010, although several tribunals and correctional facilities were able to reopen after being in rebel hands for seven years. However, *Forces Nouvelles* rebels' refusal to relinquish de facto control of much of the north, including prisons and security, hampered the judiciary's ability to be effective and independent.

Land Rights

Violent conflicts over land rights remain a persistent problem in southern and western Côte d'Ivoire, exacerbated by the chronic failure of the judicial system to resolve disputes. Many such conflicts pit indigenous populations against immigrant communities. In May at least 10 people were killed in a clash around Mont Peko, one of many protected forest regions where land is illegally sold and turned into cocoa fields, while more than 20 people were seriously injured during a September confrontation in Fresco. In the far west, almost 900 ethnic Burkinabé internally displaced persons remain within a camp outside Guiglo due to fear of retribution from the indigenous population should they return to their land.

Extortion and Racketeering

As in past years the government took no meaningful steps to address widespread extortion and racketeering by government security forces and rebels. In the government-controlled south, police, gendarmes, and customs officials routinely demand bribes at checkpoints. Individuals who refuse to pay bribes to corrupt officials are refused passage, intimidated, and often beaten or arbitrarily

CÔTE D'IVOIRE

Afraid and Forgotten

Lawlessness, Rape, and Impunity in Western Côte d'Ivoire

HUMAN
RIGHTS
WATCH

detained. Immigrant populations and other perceived outsiders are targeted for particularly severe treatment.

Extortion remains even more problematic in the north, where *Forces Nouvelles* rebels continue to exert almost complete economic control over the population. The rebels reap the equivalent of hundreds of millions of dollars annually at checkpoints and through rackets on businesses, particularly the lucrative cocoa and timber trade. In late August rebel leaders promised that forces would stay in their barracks during the two months preceding the elections. However, at this writing, many are still illegally manning checkpoints.

Political Violence

The first round of presidential voting occurred with few reported incidents of violence or intimidation. However, in the prelude to the run-off between Gbagbo and Ouattara, inflammatory rhetoric by party media organs and incidents of intimidation by party youth wings intensified. At this writing there were increasing fears that intimidation and violence might mar the second round and the announcement of results.

Tensions flared in early February as a result of disputes over the voter list. Following reports that judicial authorities were controversially removing names from the voter list, protests turned violent in several towns across Côte d'Ivoire, leaving several persons dead or seriously injured. Government buildings were sacked in Man, Bouaké, and Vavoua. President Gbagbo dissolved the government and electoral commission on February 12, citing the protests and accusations that the electoral commission's head committed fraud, leading to additional protests throughout the country. Law enforcement officials fired on demonstrators in Gagnoa on February 19, killing five. An investigation by UNOCI's human rights division found that Ivorian security and defense forces committed serious violations in suppressing these protests and riots, including extrajudicial killings, physical violence, and illegal arrests and detentions.

Sexual Violence

Sexual violence remained pervasive throughout the country. Problems are partic-ularly acute in the far west of Côte d'Ivoire, where armed men sexually assault women and girls in their homes, as they tend to their fields, as they walk to or from the market, and after hauling them from transport vehicles. Victims are typi-cally attacked during a robbery. The attacks are especially common during the cocoa harvest and on market days. Victims' access to health and legal services remains extremely limited. Attempts to investigate and prosecute cases of sexual violence are hampered by lack of political will among police and court officials, and aggravated by severe deficiencies in the justice system, particularly in the north and west.

Accountability for Past Abuses

Impunity for serious crimes committed in Côte d'Ivoire remains a major concern. The UN Security Council has still not made public the findings of the UN Commission of Inquiry into serious violations of human rights and international humanitarian law since September 2002, delivered to the UN secretary-general in November 2004. In 2003 the Ivorian government accepted the jurisdiction of the International Criminal Court over serious crimes committed in violation of interna-tional law. However, it has since repeatedly failed to facilitate ICC initiatives to assess national efforts on accountability for such crimes, including to determine whether the ICC should open an investigation there.

The National Human Rights Commission, which began work in July 2008, submit-ted its second annual report in August 2010. The commission still failed to meet the standards laid out in the Paris Principles because it remained politicized, not effectively independent from the executive, and inadequately funded.

Key International Actors

Côte d'Ivoire's key partners – including the UN, the Economic Community of West African States, the European Union, and France – grew increasingly frustrated with election delays, and throughout the year exerted considerable pressure on the Ivorian government to hold elections in 2010. They also provided significant financial support for election preparations. However, these international partners remained reluctant to publicly criticize the government for its human rights record, or to push for accountability for those responsible for war crimes, political violence, or rampant crime.

With the notable exception of the August report on human rights violations during the February demonstrations, UNOCI continued to fail to make its statistics and reporting on human rights abuses in the country publicly available.

UN Security Council Resolution 1933, adopted in June, extended UNOCI's mandate through December, authorizing over 8,400 military and police personnel. In advance of elections the Security Council agreed to deploy 500 additional peacekeeping troops, and UNOCI was given a clearer mandate regarding the protection of civilians. However, proactive efforts to stem rampant violence, including sexual violence, remained nominal. France maintained 900 troops in Côte d'Ivoire to support UNOCI.

The Security Council extended a sanctions regime through April 30, 2011, including an arms embargo, a ban on the import of Ivorian diamonds, and travel bans and asset freezes on three individuals, two of whom were implicated in attacks against UN personnel in 2006. In its August report, UNOCI recommended an exception allowing the Ivorian government to import anti-riot equipment, citing the lack of such equipment as a contributing factor to the February abuses by security forces.

In January 2010 the UN Human Rights Council published a report on Côte d'Ivoire under its Universal Periodic Review mechanism. Côte d'Ivoire committed to implement recommendations on the rule of law and to end impunity for sexual violence by bringing perpetrators to justice. However, virtually no efforts were made during the year to achieve these goals.

Democratic Republic of Congo

Attacks on civilians and other human rights abuses continued with disturbing frequency in 2010. The Congolese army sustained its military campaigns against foreign and national armed groups in the east and north, and launched a new campaign in the west to quell a local insurgency. As in the past, all sides targeted civilians, who were killed, raped, arbitrarily arrested, pressed into forced labor, and looted. The ongoing violence left nearly 2 million people displaced and a further 145,000 as refugees in neighboring countries.

The United Nations peacekeeping mission was renamed the UN Organization Stabilization Mission in Congo (MONUSCO) following calls for its withdrawal by the Congolese government, which was eager to claim security improvements ahead of the 50th anniversary of Congo's independence. The new name made little difference in the struggle to protect civilians. Some perpetrators were arrested on war crimes charges, but many others remained in positions of power, most notably Bosco Ntaganda, a general sought on an arrest warrant from the International Criminal Court (ICC). Violent attacks on journalists and human rights defenders increased.

Attacks by the Lord's Resistance Army in Northern Congo

Attacks against civilians were the most severe in northern Congo, where the Lord's Resistance Army (LRA), a Ugandan rebel group, continued its brutal campaign. A further 604 people were killed and 473 abducted, bringing the death toll in Congo to over 2,000 and the number of abducted to 2,600 since the LRA began its latest campaign of violence in 2008. The LRA also attacked civilians across the border in the Central African Republic and Southern Sudan. The largest attack in Congo was in the remote Makombo area of Haut Uele District, where in December 2009 LRA combatants clubbed to death at least 345 civilians and abducted 250 others. The attack was one of the worst ever perpetrated by the rebel group in its bloody 24-year history. The LRA also carried out widespread abductions in Bas Uele District, deliberately targeting children whom the group forced to serve as soldiers.

The Ugandan army—in coordination with the Congolese, Central African, and Southern Sudanese armed forces—continued its military campaign against the LRA. The operation had some success in weakening the rebel group, but the LRA's ability to attack civilians remained undiminished. No progress was made on apprehending three of the LRA's top leaders sought by the ICC for crimes committed in northern Uganda. Congolese army and MONUSCO efforts to protect civilians in LRA-affected areas remained inadequate, with limited resources directed to address the threat.

Military Operations in the East and West

The Congolese army continued military operations in North and South Kivu provinces of eastern Congo against the Democratic Forces for the Liberation of Rwanda (FDLR), a predominantly Rwandan Hutu rebel group, some of whose leaders participated in the 1994 genocide. At the same time the army sought to integrate nearly two dozen former armed groups into its ranks, a condition of the peace accords signed in March 2009. The integration process was fraught with problems. A number of the armed groups dropped out, angry that their enemies received higher ranks or more lucrative posts. Other groups, such as the National Congress for the Defense of the People (CNDP), conducted their own military operations under the guise of the Congolese army, but without approval from the military hierarchy. The confusion affected chains of command and control of the troops.

Attacks on civilians by the army and armed groups were rampant. Hundreds were killed and raped as each warring party accused local populations of supporting its enemies. For example, at least 105 civilians were killed in western Masisi territory when former CNDP troops newly integrated into the army conducted unilateral operations against the FDLR and their allies. In another incident in Walikale territory in early August, FDLR combatants and a local armed group, the Mai Mai Cheka, systematically gang raped at least 303 civilians in 13 villages. The attackers accused their victims of supporting the Congolese army.

As in 2009, UN peacekeepers provided logistical and operational support to the Congolese military operations against the FDLR. Following earlier criticisms that peacekeepers had failed to put in place adequate conditions to ensure respect for

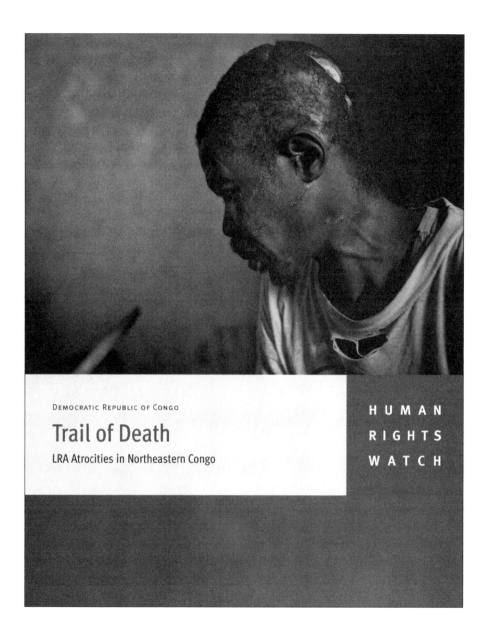

DEMOCRATIC REPUBLIC OF CONGO

Trail of Death

LRA Atrocities in Northeastern Congo

HUMAN
RIGHTS
WATCH

DEMOCRATIC REPUBLIC OF CONGO

Always on the Run

The Vicious Cycle of Displacement in Eastern Congo

HUMAN
RIGHTS
WATCH

human rights, MONUSCO strengthened its conditionality policy and sought to support only battalions it had previously screened. But the confused chains of command made the policy's application exceedingly difficult. Many officers with a known track record of human rights abuses remained in command positions. The most blatant example was General Bosco Ntaganda, sought on an arrest warrant from the ICC, who continued to play the de facto role as deputy commander of the joint military operations. Ntaganda also continued to perpetrate human rights abuses and was implicated in assassinations and arbitrary arrests of individuals opposed to him.

In addition to problems in the east, the Congolese army also deployed to western Equateur Province to counter an insurgency led by the Enyele ethnic group, after a local fishing dispute spun out of control. The insurgents attacked opponents from other ethnic groups, as well as policemen and soldiers. While quelling the insurgency, Congolese security forces were themselves responsible for numerous human rights violations. The UN estimated that 100 civilians were killed in the clashes.

Sexual Violence and Sexual Orientation and Gender Identity

The level of sexual violence in Congo continued at an alarming rate. Over 15,000 cases of sexual violence were reported in 2009. In 2010 there were no signs that the trend was decreasing. For the first six months of the year 7,685 cases were reported. More than half of the victims were under 18 years of age.

In October a private member's bill was introduced in the National Assembly proposing a punishment of three to five years' imprisonment for "homosexual relations" and to outlaw all publications and films that highlight "sexual practices against nature." The bill also seeks to criminalize members and financers of associations that promote or defend "sexual relations against nature" with six months to one year in prison.

Threats to Journalists and Human Rights Defenders

Congolese human rights defenders and journalists were increasingly targeted in 2010. A prominent human rights defender, Floribert Chebeya Bahizire, executive director of Voice of the Voiceless, was found dead on June 1, following a visit to police headquarters in Kinshasa, the capital. His driver, Fidele Bazana Edadi, remains missing at the time of writing. The national police chief was suspended and other senior police officers were detained following the murder, though none was charged at the time of writing. In eastern Congo, on June 30, a human rights defender working for Le Bon Samaritain was killed by armed men in uniform near Beni, North Kivu. Sylvestre Bwira Kyahi, civil society president of Masisi territory, was abducted by army soldiers on August 24 and held for a week in an underground prison, where he was repeatedly beaten for writing a public letter denouncing abuses by soldiers under Ntaganda's command and calling for his arrest.

Freelance cameraman Patient Chebeya Bankome was shot dead by soldiers outside his home in Beni on April 5. *Radio France Internationale* (RFI) began broadcasting again in Congo on October 12, after being off the air since June 2009. Other radio stations, including in Bandundu and Kisangani, were shut down or interrupted by authorities when they criticized government policy.

Justice and Accountability

The vast majority of crimes committed in Congo have gone unpunished and, in many cases, perpetrators are rewarded rather than brought to justice.

Despite the somber trend, there were some positive developments. On November 17, 2009, the FDLR president, Ignace Murwanashyaka, and his deputy, Straton Musoni, were arrested in Germany by the German police for war crimes and crimes against humanity committed by FDLR troops under their command in eastern Congo. Another FDLR leader, Callixte Mbarushimana, was arrested in France by French police on October 11, 2010, under an arrest warrant issued by the ICC for similar crimes.

In Congo the government increased military prosecutions against soldiers accused of human rights violations, including crimes of sexual violence, although the majority of those prosecuted held junior ranks. In one notable exception, following pressure from the UN Security Council and human rights organizations, judicial authorities in Kinshasa arrested General Jerome Kakwavu in April 2010 on

DEMOCRATIC REPUBLIC OF CONGO

"You Will Be Punished"

Attacks on Civilians in Eastern Congo

HUMAN
RIGHTS
WATCH

war crimes charges for rape and torture. Kakwavu is the first general arrested on rape charges in Congo's history.

In another important landmark, the Office of the UN High Commissioner for Human Rights published on October 1 its report of a human rights mapping exercise in Congo, which documented 617 incidents of serious violations of international humanitarian law between 1993 and 2003. The report described the role of the main Congolese and foreign parties responsible—including military or armed groups from Rwanda, Uganda, Burundi, and Angola—and suggested options to pursue justice for the crimes, including the proposed establishment of a mixed chamber in Congo with Congolese and international judges. Rwanda and Uganda, among others, rejected the report. In an important statement, the Congolese government welcomed it and said it would support the option of a mixed chamber.

Key International Actors

At the insistence of the government, the UN withdrew some 1,500 peacekeepers and pledged to conduct a joint security assessment with the government to determine future drawdown.

Following the mass rape in Walikale, the UN dispatched its assistant secretary-general for peacekeeping operations, Atul Khare, to Congo to assess the challenges for protecting civilians and recommend improvements. The UN secretary-general's special representative on sexual violence in conflict, Margot Wallström, also visited Congo twice to strengthen UN action to address sexual violence and hold perpetrators accountable.

On May 24 United States President Barack Obama signed legislation committing the US to developing a comprehensive strategy to protect civilians from LRA attacks and to end the group's violence.

Equatorial Guinea

Equatorial Guinea remains mired in corruption, poverty, and repression under the leadership of Teodoro Obiang Nguema Mbasogo, the country's president for over 30 years. Vast oil revenues fund lavish lifestyles for the small elite surrounding the president, while the majority of the population lives in dire poverty. The government regularly engages in torture and arbitrary detention. It also continues a practice of abducting perceived opponents abroad and holding them in secret detention. Journalists, civil society, and members of the political opposition face heavy government repression.

President Obiang, who overwhelmingly won re-election in November 2009 in a deeply flawed vote, unsuccessfully sought to enhance his international image by announcing purported human rights reforms. Several prominent Obiang initiatives, including a the United Nations Educational, Scientific and Cultural Organization (UNESCO) prize in his honor, were blocked due to widespread concern over well-documented corruption and abuse in his administration.

Economic and Social Rights

Significant oil revenues and the country's small population make Equatorial Guinea's per capita gross domestic product among the highest in the world, and the highest in sub-Saharan Africa. Nevertheless, socioeconomic conditions for the country's population of approximately 600,000 remain dismal. One study published in *The Lancet* found that the country had the world's highest child mortality rate, though a second study in the same publication found that the country did see progress in reducing maternal mortality.

The government has failed to utilize available resources to progressively realize the social and economic rights of the population. Given its high oil revenues, it has invested only paltry sums in health, education, and other social services. As reported by the International Monetary Fund in May, after a four-year delay, Equatorial Guinea in 2010 began to disburse "small" amounts for those purposes through its Social Development Fund. The government, instead, has prioritized investments in projects, such as an ultra-modern hospital, that have little benefit for the poor who lack access to basic health services. An anti-malaria campaign largely funded by Western oil companies has lowered the incidence of malaria.

In February a United States Senate investigation revealed that President Obiang's eldest son and presumed successor—known by the nickname Teodorín—who serves as minister of agriculture and forestry, bypassed money-laundering controls and used suspect funds to finance expensive purchases in the US. The son's spending on luxury goods from 2004-2007 was nearly double the Equatoguinean government's 2005 budget for education. The US Senate also reported that Teodorín is under criminal investigation in the US. In response to this negative publicity, he hired a Washington communications firm to polish his image, selecting the same firm used by his father. President Obiang also hired a new US lobbyist, replacing the firm he retained after a 2004 US Senate investigation exposed his improper personal spending from national oil accounts.

Freedom of Expression and Association

Equatorial Guinea remains notorious for its lack of press freedom; its ranking by Reporters Without Borders fell to 167th out of 178 countries in 2010. A few non-state-controlled media outlets publish erratically and are tightly restrained. Journalists from the state media are not permitted to criticize the government.

According to international press freedom groups, in January the government fired four reporters from the state radio and television broadcaster for "lack of enthusiasm." In February a journalist with state-run radio was arrested and held for three days after he reported on-air that seven bodies were found at a trash dump in Bata, the largest city on the country's mainland. In April the sole foreign correspondent in Equatorial Guinea, an Agence France-Presse reporter, was detained and held for several hours when he attempted to cover the arrival of foreign dignitaries at the airport in Malabo, the capital.

Freedom of association and assembly are also severely curtailed, infringing on the development of civil society. The government imposes restrictive conditions on the registration and operation of nongovernmental groups. As a result, there is not one legally registered independent human rights organization in the country. The few local activists who openly promote needed reforms are vulnerable to intimidation, harassment, and reprisals. The government is also intolerant of critical views from abroad, frequently characterizing those who expose President Obiang's autocratic and corrupt rule as racist and colonialist. It also regularly denies visas to foreign journalists.

Political Parties and Political Opposition

Contrary to President Obiang's claims that "my country is democratic," free and fair elections are denied to its people. In the lead-up to the November 2009 presidential vote, which President Obiang won with 95.4 percent of the ballot, the government stifled and harassed the country's beleaguered political opposition, denied the opposition equal access to the media, and imposed serious constraints on international observers.

The ruling Democratic Party (PDGE) maintains a monopoly over political life. Only two of the four other political parties with candidates running in the election—the Convergence for Social Democracy (CPDS) and the People's Union (UP)—actively oppose the ruling party and Obiang. Opposition parties are silenced through the use of criminal prosecution, arbitrary arrest, and harassment. Freedom House named Equatorial Guinea as one of the "worst of the worst" countries for the harsh repression of political rights and civil liberties, as it has for several previous years.

In July Teodorín was elected to head the ruling party's youth wing. That role automatically confers on the younger Mr. Obiang the vice-presidency of the PDGE and presumably ensures that he is next in line to replace his father.

Abduction, Arbitrary Detention, Torture, and Unfair Trials

There is no independent judiciary in Equatorial Guinea. The government commonly employs arbitrary detention and arrests without due process. Detainees continued to be held indefinitely without knowing the charges against them. Basic fair trial standards are disregarded. Torture remains a serious problem despite a national law prohibiting it. Equatorial Guinea's security services have kidnapped more than a dozen perceived opponents abroad, including at least four in 2010.

Amnesty International reported that Equatorial Guinea abducted four nationals living in exile in Benin in January 2010, held them in secret detention where they were tortured and forced to confess to participating in a February 2009 attack on the presidential palace, and then executed them in August following a military trial that violated international human rights standards and the country's own laws.

The government had earlier arbitrarily detained and accused 10 opposition politicians and scores of Nigerian citizens, including fisherman and traders, of involvement in the same attack on the presidential palace. In March, after more than a year in detention, seven of the Nigerian citizens were prosecuted in an unfair civilian trial and each sentenced to 12 years in prison, while two Equatoguinean opposition members were first acquitted by the civilian court and then retried in August by a military court, receiving sentences of 20 years.

Key International Actors

At its review under the Universal Periodic Review mechanism of the UN Human Rights Council in December 2009, and during a follow-up session in March 2010, Equatorial Guinea accepted over 100 recommendations to improve its human rights record, including commitments to end torture and arbitrary and secret detentions. In June President Obiang announced a reform plan at the Global Forum in Cape Town, South Africa, pledging that he would make his country's oil revenues fully transparent, increase social spending, institute legal reforms, protect human rights, and preserve the environment. Although President Obiang hired a "reform adviser" to help promote these purported improvements, the various pledges were consistently belied by his government's action.

In April the Extractive Industries Transparency Initiative, a global initiative promoting openness on petroleum and mining revenues, expelled Equatorial Guinea for failing to meet its most basic criteria. In July, the Community of Portuguese-Speaking Countries deferred Equatorial Guinea's application to join, also in the wake of controversy over President Obiang's record. (Although Portuguese is not spoken in the former Spanish colony, President Obiang declared it Equatorial Guinea's newest national language.) In August the US government, as well as a UN working group and others, sharply criticized the unfair trial and executions that took place that month in Equatorial Guinea. In October, after stalling a decision several times, UNESCO indefinitely suspended an award named after—and funded by—President Obiang. UNESCO's executive board acted after a global civil society campaign generated an international uproar over the planned "dictator prize" that threatened to seriously taint the organization.

The US is Equatorial Guinea's main trading partner and US companies dominate the country's oil sector. The US government took some steps to hold Equatorial Guinea to global standards, notably taking a strong stance at UNESCO against the Obiang prize.

Spain could play an important role as the former colonial power, but it generally has declined to apply pressure on Equatorial Guinea regarding human rights issues. The Spanish government, however, also opposed the UNESCO prize.

In addition to the reported criminal inquiry against Teodorín Obiang in the US, legal challenges are proceeding in France, Spain, and before the African Commission on Human and Peoples' Rights alleging misuse of Equatorial Guinea's oil funds.

Eritrea

By any measure, the unelected government of President Isayas Afewerki is oppressive. It allows no space for individual autonomy in any sphere—political, economic, or religious. Arbitrary arrests, torture, and forced labor are rampant. Rule by fiat is the norm. The Eritrean government refuses to implement a constitution approved in 1997 containing civil and human rights provisions. Many Eritreans conclude that they can avoid oppression only by fleeing the country at risk to their lives.

Arbitrary Detention, "Enforced Disappearances," and Deaths in Custody

Thousands of Eritreans are incarcerated without charge, trial, or opportunity to appeal. They are denied access to lawyers or family. The government releases no information about numbers of prisoners, their places of confinement, whether they remain alive, or why they are being held. Many detainees simply "disappear."

Prisoners include high-ranking government officials arrested in September 2001 after they publicly criticized President Isayas's leadership, as well as editors and publishers of all private newspapers. None have been charged or brought to trial. There have been persistent reports from former prison guards that over half the officials and journalists arrested in 2001 are dead. Among those still held is a journalist with dual Eritrean-Swedish citizenship, Dawit Isaac. In 2010 President Isayas's principal political advisor told Swedish interviewers the journalist was jailed for conspiring to "facilitate" an Ethiopian invasion of Eritrea during the 1998-2000 war. The advisor refused to provide substantiation and reiterated the "conspirators" would never be brought to trial or released.

Despite government secrecy, information about arrests leaks out. In May and June 2010 the government arrested several hundred citizens, most belonging to the Afar ethnic group, according to external opposition websites. (An Afar insurgent group has been active along Eritrea's southeast Red Sea coast). About 30 women members of an "unregistered" Christian church were arrested in December 2009. Although members of such churches are frequently arrested, Eritrea's information minister said that "religion had nothing to do with" their arrests. "I'm sure they were committing a crime," he added. Their crime has never been disclosed. A prominent former government journalist was arrested in March 2010 with no explanation for the arrest. A government journalist arrested in 2009 along with 11 of her colleagues, also without explanation, was reported to have been placed in solitary confinement in 2010.

Death in custody is common from ill-treatment, torture, starvation, and denial of medical care. In April 2010 a woman held for over two years in a shipping container because she would not renounce her unregistered religious faith died at the Sawa military training center from maltreatment.

Torture and Cruel, Inhuman, and Degrading Treatment

Torture and other forms of cruel, inhuman, and degrading treatment in detention are routine. Former detainees report that detention almost always includes severe beatings, often leading to permanent bodily harm. Punishments also entail mock drowning, being hung by the arms from trees, and being tied up in the sun in contorted positions for hours or days.

Poor detention conditions often amount to torture. Many prisoners are held in unlit underground bunkers and in shipping containers with broiling daytime and freezing nighttime temperatures. A woman with deep visible scars from beatings in detention told a BBC reporter in 2010 she had been held 23 hours a day in an underground cell in "unbearable" heat and made to walk on sharp rocks and thorns for an hour each day.

Restrictions on Freedom of Expression and Association

The government has monopolized all information media since 2001. No private newspapers have been allowed since then and no political organization other than the ruling People's Front for Democracy and Justice (PFDJ) is permitted. All unions are government-run. Nongovernmental public gatherings are prohibited. Asking a critical question at a government-convened forum constitutes grounds for arrest. No NGOs exist.

Homosexuality is illegal. In March 2010 a government minister told the United Nations Human Rights Council that homosexuality is in "direct contradiction" to Eritrean values and will not be legalized.

Restrictions on Religious Freedom

It is unlawful to practice a faith unless it is one of four "registered" religions: Eritrean Orthodox, Muslim, Catholic, or Lutheran. Security forces arrest members of "unregistered" religions, often during religious services. A religious-freedom monitoring group reported that scores were arrested in 2010. Persons arrested for this reason are subject to the same torture and abuse as other prisoners, but can often obtain their release by renouncing their faith. Those who refuse sometimes pay with their lives. Jehovah's Witnesses are especially targeted; three have been detained since 1994 for refusing to submit to military service. The patriarch of the Orthodox Church, deposed by the government in 2006, remains under house arrest without access to communication.

Indefinite Conscription and Forced Labor

By law, all able-bodied adult Eritreans must perform 18 months of national service. In practice, national service is routinely prolonged indefinitely. National service conscripts are paid a pittance and often used as cheap, involuntary labor on projects personally benefiting ranking civilian and military leaders. They have been used as forced labor to implement development projects. A former gold-mine employee reported that national service recruits were involuntarily assigned to his gold-prospecting team, receiving only national service pay. Abuse of conscripts, including torture, is common.

Prolonged service, harsh treatment, and starvation wages are principal reasons for the hundreds of monthly desertions. President Isayas said in 2010 that most deserters left for economic reasons or were "going on a picnic."

Indefinite conscription also forces many Eritreans to flee the country. Despite a "shoot-to-kill" policy for anyone caught trying to cross the country's borders, thousands of refugees pour out of Eritrea to Sudan and Ethiopia. In March 2010 the UN High Commissioner for Refugees reported that 50,000 Eritrean refugees were housed in camps in Ethiopia, a third of them military deserters, with 1,800 Eritreans escaping monthly. The most prominent defections occurred in December 2009 when 12 Eritrean football players defected in Kenya and later obtained asylum in Australia. Some escapees never make it. Border guards reportedly killed 12 refugees in March 2010 during an escape attempt, according to an unconfirmed Sudanese press report.

United Nations Sanctions and Horn of Africa Relations

In December 2009 the UN Security Council imposed sanctions on Eritrea for defying the council's demands that it remove troops from territory in neighboring Djibouti and stop providing political, financial, and logistical support to armed insurgents in Somalia. Sanctions include an arms embargo, travel restrictions on Eritrean officials and organizations designated by a UN sanctions committee, and a freeze of their assets.

In June 2010, two years after Eritrea invaded Djibouti, it withdrew its troops and agreed to binding demarcation of the border following Qatari mediation. During the two years, President Isayas repeatedly called allegations that Eritrea had invaded Djibouti "fabrications" and refused to meet with UN and African Union investigators. About 230 Eritrean troops deserted to Djibouti in the months following the June 2008 battle and received refugee status. Eritrean government media have never informed the Eritrean public about the invasion, withdrawal, or desertions.

A UN monitoring committee reported in March 2010 that "the scale and nature of Eritrean government support [of Somali insurgent groups] had either diminished or become less visible, but had not altogether ceased." While detectable military assistance had declined, Eritrea continued to provide political and, possibly, financial support, according to the UN report. At year's end, UN sanctions remained in place.

Eritrea's relations with Ethiopia remain strained. Ethiopia occupies Eritrean territory, having reneged on a commitment, made in an agreement ending a two-year war between the countries, to accept as final a border demarcated by a neutral Border Commission. A Claims Commission in 2005 found Eritrea had violated international law by attacking Ethiopia in 1998. Eritrea continues to try to destabilize Ethiopia by funding and arming insurrection groups in that country.

Key International Actors

At least 14 mining companies from Canada, China, Australia, the United Kingdom, India, and Libya are prospecting for gold and other minerals in Eritrea. A Canadian mining company, Nevsun, Inc., is to begin commercial operations in early 2011 at Bisha, 150 kilometers west of Asmara, the capital. The Eritrean government owns 40 percent of the Bisha project. Mining income is unaffected by United Nations sanctions for now.

Eritrea receives a modest amount of foreign aid. China was the largest contributor in 2010, largely as a lender of soft loans. It announced a US$60 million loan for mining activities, apparently used by Eritrea to buy a 30 percent stake in the Bisha project (Eritrea already owned 10 percent by law). China also lent US$6 million for food security programs. The African Development Bank donated US$20 million for higher education. Eritrea is in the second year of a five-year €122-million European Commission grant for food production and infrastructure projects. Little of the grant has been disbursed because of Eritrea's failure to improve human rights conditions. Other ongoing lenders and donors include the United Arab Emirates, Iran, Qatar, and Libya; none announced new assistance programs in 2010.

During the 2010 Universal Periodic Review (UPR) of human rights practices at the UN Human Rights Council, Eritrea committed to acceding to the Convention Against Torture. At year's end it hadn't done so, and there was no evidence that its practices changed.

ETHIOPIA

The ruling Ethiopian People's Revolutionary Democratic Front (EPRDF) consolidated political control with a striking 99.6 percent victory in the May 2010 parliamentary elections. The polls were peaceful, but were preceded by months of intimidation of opposition party supporters and an extensive government campaign aimed at increasing support for the ruling party, including by reserving access to government services and resources to ruling party members.

Although the government released prominent opposition leader Birtukan Midekssa from her most recent two-year stint in detention in October 2010, hundreds of other political prisoners remain in jail and at risk of torture and ill-treatment. The government's crackdown on independent civil society and media did not diminish by year's end, dashing hopes that political repression would ease following the May polls.

The 2010 Elections

Although the sweeping margin of the 2010 victory came as a surprise to many observers, the ruling party's win was predictable and echoed the results of local elections in 2008. The 99.6 percent result was the culmination of the government's five-year strategy of systematically closing down space for political dissent and independent criticism. European election observers said that the election fell short of international standards.

In the run-up to the 2010 elections there were a few incidents of violent assaults, including the March 1 killing of Aregawi Gebreyohannes, an opposition candidate in Tigray. More often, voters were influenced by harassment, threats, and coercion. The Ethiopian government's grassroots-level surveillance machine extends into almost every community in this country of 80 million people through an elaborate system of *kebele* (village or neighborhood) and sub-*kebele* administrations, through which the government exerts pressure on Ethiopia's largely rural population.

Voters were pressured to join or support the ruling party through a combination of incentives—including access to seeds, fertilizers, tools, and loans—and discriminatory penalties if they support the opposition, such as denial of access to public sector jobs, educational opportunities, and even food assistance. During April and May officials and militia from local administrations went house to house telling residents to register to vote and to vote for the ruling party or face reprisals from local party officials, such as bureaucratic harassment or losing their homes or jobs.

Political Repression, Pretrial Detention, and Torture

In one of Ethiopia's few positive human rights developments in 2010, in October the government released Birtukan Midekssa, the leader of the opposition Unity for Democracy and Justice Party, after she spent 22 months in detention. Along with many other opposition leaders, Birtukan was initially arrested in 2005 and then pardoned in 2007 after spending almost two years in jail. She was rearrested in December 2008. In December 2009 United Nations experts determined that her detention was arbitrary and in violation of international law.

Hundreds of other Ethiopians have been arbitrarily arrested and detained and sometimes subjected to torture and other ill-treatment. No independent domestic or international organizations have access to all of Ethiopia's detention facilities, so it is impossible to determine the number of political prisoners and others who have been arbitrarily detained.

Torture and ill-treatment have been used by Ethiopia's police, military, and other members of the security forces to punish a spectrum of perceived dissenters, including university students, members of the political opposition, and alleged supporters of insurgent groups, as well as alleged terrorist suspects. Secret detention facilities and military barracks are most often used by Ethiopian security forces for such activities. Although Ethiopia's criminal code and other laws contain provisions to protect fundamental human rights, they frequently go unenforced. Very few incidents of torture have been investigated promptly and impartially, much less prosecuted.

Torture and ill-treatment of detainees arrested on suspicion of involvement with armed insurgent groups such as the Oromo Liberation Front and the Ogaden National Liberation Front in Somali region remains a serious concern. The

ETHIOPIA

Development without Freedom

How Aid Underwrites Repression in Ethiopia

HUMAN
RIGHTS
WATCH

Ethiopian military and other security forces are responsible for serious crimes in the Somali region, including war crimes, but at this writing no credible efforts have been taken by the government to investigate or prosecute those responsible for the crimes.

Freedom of Expression and Association

The government intensified its campaign against independent voices and organizations, as well as its efforts to limit Ethiopians' access to information in late 2009 and 2010. By May, when the parliamentary elections took place, many of Ethiopia's leading independent journalists and human rights activists had fled the country due to implicit and sometimes explicit threats. While a few independent newspapers continue to publish, they exercise self-censorship.

In December 2009 government threats to invoke the 2009 Anti-Terrorism Proclamation against the largest circulation independent newspaper, *Addis Neger*, forced its editors to close the paper and flee the country. A few days later, police beat an *Addis Neger* administrator responsible for winding down the newspaper's affairs.

Other newspapers were also threatened or attacked. The Committee to Protect Journalists reported that 15 journalists fled the country between late 2009 and May 2010. An official of the government's media licensing office accused the *Awramba Times* of "intentionally inciting and misguiding the public." In August unknown assailants smashed windows and doors of its office. In September police interrogated the editor of *Sendek* after it published interviews with an opposition party leader; the police purportedly were investigating whether the newspaper was licensed.

In March a panel of the Supreme Court reinstated large fines against the owners of four publishing companies convicted in 2007 for "outrages against the constitution" solely for their coverage of the 2005 parliamentary elections. In February a judge sentenced the editor of *Al Quds* to one year in prison for an article he wrote two years earlier challenging Prime Minister Meles Zenawi's characterization of Ethiopia as an Orthodox Christian country.

Foreign media did not face much better. The government began jamming the Voice of America language programs in Amharic, Oromo, and Tigrinya in February 2010 and followed by jamming Deutsche Welle; the jamming ended in August. Prime Minister Meles personally justified the jamming on the grounds that the broadcasters were "engaging in destabilizing propaganda" reminiscent of Rwandan radio broadcasts advocating genocide.

The assault on independent institutions extends to nongovernmental organizations, particularly those engaged in human rights work. The repressive Charities and Societies Proclamation, enacted in 2009, forbids Ethiopian nongovernmental organizations from doing work on human rights or governance if they receive more than 10 percent of their funding from foreign sources.

The effects of the law on Ethiopia's slowly growing civil society have been predictable and devastating. The leading Ethiopian human rights groups have been crippled by the law and many of their senior staff have fled the country due to the sometimes blatant hostility toward independent activists.

All organizations were forced to re-register with the newly created Charities and Societies Agency in late 2009. Some organizations have changed their mandates to exclude reference to human rights work. Others, including the Ethiopian Human Rights Council (EHRCO), Ethiopia's oldest human rights monitoring organization, and the Ethiopian Women's Lawyers Association (EWLA), which engaged in groundbreaking work on domestic violence and women's rights, slashed their budgets, staff, and operations. The government froze both groups' bank accounts in December 2009, allowing them access to only 10 percent of their funds. Meanwhile, the government is encouraging a variety of ruling party-affiliated organizations to fill the vacuum, including the Ethiopian Human Rights Commission, a national human rights institution with no semblance of independence.

Key International Actors

Regional security concerns—particularly regarding Sudan's upcoming referendum and the increasing reach of Somalia's Islamist armed groups—have thus far insulated Ethiopia from increased human rights pressure from Western donors.

Ethiopia's African neighbors have been mute in the face of Ethiopia's deteriorating human rights situation, while China, South Korea, and Japan have increased engagement in 2010, although their contributions remain small compared to Western aid. Chinese money largely flows into infrastructure, although trade also increased 27 percent to more than US$800 million in the first six months of 2010, according to *The Economist*.

Few governments commented publicly on the increasing political repression gripping the country in the months before and after the May elections. In a rare exception, the United States noted in late May that "an environment conducive to free and fair elections was not in place even before Election Day." The European Union's election observers also raised multiple concerns with the unlevel playing field and constraints on freedom of assembly and expression. Yet even after the election result proved the EPRDF's consolidation of a single-party state, Ethiopia's donors continued to channel enormous sums of development assistance through the government. The government received more than $3 billion in development assistance in 2008 alone.

The final report of the UN Human Rights Council's Universal Periodic Review of Ethiopia's human rights record was adopted in March 2010. Ethiopia committed to ratifying the Convention on the Rights of Persons with Disabilities. It rejected recommendations that it repeal or amend the Charities and Societies Proclamation and that it end the impunity of Ethiopia's security forces.

GUINEA

The June and November 2010 presidential elections marked a major step forward in Guinea's transition from military to civilian rule. While some irregularities and a leadership crisis within the electoral commission marred the credibility of the polls, they were nevertheless considered to be the first free and fair elections since independence in 1958. However, serious bouts of intercommunal violence and clashes between supporters of the two parties, and the excessive use of lethal force by the security forces in responding to them, highlighted the fragility of the security situation and pressing rule of law challenges.

At year's end there was considerable optimism that the new government would begin to address Guinea's deeply entrenched human rights problems, notably a longstanding culture of impunity, a bloated and poorly managed army, criminal acts in the face of inadequate policing, striking deficiencies within the judicial system, weak rule of law, and endemic corruption that deprives Guineans of key economic rights.

Some of the officers who assumed control of the security forces in late 2009 made a concerted effort to instill discipline within the ranks. However, violations against demonstrators and ordinary Guineans continued, and there was only limited progress in ensuring accountability for past atrocities, notably the 2007 and 2009 massacres of unarmed demonstrators by members of the security forces.

International actors—including France, the United States, the European Union, the Economic Community of West African States (ECOWAS), and the African Union—intervened proactively to keep the transition to democratic rule on track, but remained virtually silent on the need for justice for past crimes.

Political Developments

The elections brought to an end a period of profound political instability beginning in December 2008, when Captain Moussa Dadis Camara took power in a coup after the death of Lansana Conté, Guinea's authoritarian president for 24 years. Throughout 2009 the military violently suppressed the opposition, culminating in a large-scale massacre of some 150 demonstrators in September 2009 in the capital, Conakry. In December 2009 Camara was removed following an assassination attempt against him, and his deputy, the more moderate General Sékouba Konaté, took over, committing to move the country toward democratic elections.

In January Dadis Camara formally handed over power to General Konaté, under considerable pressure from international actors, by way of an agreement signed in the Burkinabé capital Ouagadougou, which called for the formation of a transitional government of national unity; an ad hoc parliamentary body comprised of members of civil society, political parties, the security forces, and religious bodies; and democratic elections within six months.

In the run-up to elections, there were few allegations of violations of freedom of expression, peaceful assembly, association for political parties and movements, and protection from political violence. However, clashes between supporters of opposing candidates and violent protests against the electoral commission resulted in at least six deaths.

Both rounds of elections were marred by procedural flaws including the late or non-delivery of voting materials and vote tampering. Candidates mounted numerous legal challenges to the election result. Despite the many problems, both domestic and international election observers concluded that the elections were generally free and fair.

Legislative Developments

The new constitution, adopted in April by the ad hoc parliamentary body, the National Transition Council, includes several provisions which, if implemented, could increase respect for human rights and good governance. These include establishing Guinea's first independent national human rights institution, requiring public asset declarations by the president and his ministers, and creating a Court of Audit mandated to conduct yearly financial audits of public institutions. The constitution also strengthened the independence of the High Council of Judges, responsible for the discipline, selection, and promotion of judges.

Conduct of the Security Forces

In October and November, members of the security forces used excessive lethal force in responding to bouts of electoral and intercommunal violence; at least eight protesters and passersby died, and scores of others were wounded as a result. During the violence, the security forces also engaged in theft, robbery, and assault. There were few attempts to investigate, discipline, or prosecute the soldiers and policemen implicated in these criminal acts. The military hierarchy also failed to put on administrative leave, pending investigation, soldiers and officers known to have taken part in the September 2009 violence.

Numerous soldiers and civilians allegedly involved in the December 2009 assassination attempt against Dadis Camara were beaten, assaulted and in the case of at least seven soldiers, tortured to death, inside the Alpha Yaya Diallo military camp in Conakry. Some 30 soldiers, detained in April after being accused of trying to sabotage the transition to civilian rule, remain in arbitrary detention within a gendarme camp at this writing.

The military hierarchy's efforts to instill greater discipline included the creation of a Military Police force, banning off-duty soldiers from wearing uniforms or carrying guns in public places, and adopting a Use of Force Policy committing Guinean security forces to internationally recognized best practices.

Meanwhile police were repeatedly implicated in extortion, solicitation of bribes, and, in a few cases, sexual abuse of female detainees. Crime victims are frequently required to pay for investigations, while authorities commonly fail to conduct adequate investigations and, in some cases, free alleged criminals. Police leadership made no effort to address these problems.

Detention Conditions

Severe shortages of judicial personnel, unprofessional conduct, poor record-keeping, and insufficient infrastructure and resources, continue to lead to widespread detention-related abuses, notably prolonged pretrial detention and dreadfully poor prison conditions. Prison and detention centers are severely overcrowded and lack adequate nutrition, health care, and sanitation. The population of the country's largest detention facility—designed for 300 detainees—stands at over

900. Between 80-90 percent of prisoners in Guinea were held in prolonged pretrial detention. Prison officials consistently fail to separate convicted and untried prisoners and, in some centers, children from adults. Unpaid prison guards regularly extort money from prisoners and their families, exacerbating problems of hunger and malnutrition.

Progress included the late December 2009 release of some 15 military personnel held for over one year by the coup government, and the May 15 release of some 100 prisoners held in extended pretrial detention for minor offenses.

Accountability for the September 28, 2009 Massacre and Other Crimes

In December 2009 the International Commission of Inquiry led by the United Nations issued its report confirming the killing of at least 156 people and the rape of over 100, and concluding that the crimes perpetrated in Conakry on September 28, 2009, rose to the level of crimes against humanity. The inquiry identified several military officers, including former coup leader Dadis Camara, as bearing direct individual criminal responsibility for the crimes. This contradicted the government's investigation, published in February, which absolved Dadis Camara, laid blame solely on his then-aide de camp Lieutenant Abubakar Diakité and the soldiers he commanded, and set the number of dead at 63.

The then-government committed to bringing to justice the perpetrators of the September 2009 violence, and in early 2010 appointed three investigating judges to the case. However, there has been scant information on the investigation's progress, and no evidence of government efforts to locate the more than 100 bodies believed to have been disposed of secretly by the security forces.

Meanwhile, there were no attempts to investigate, much less hold accountable, members of the security forces responsible for the 2007 killing of some 130 demonstrators, or the several alleged crimes committed by the security forces in 2010.

GUINEA

Bloody Monday

The September 28 Massacre and Rapes
by Security Forces in Guinea

HUMAN
RIGHTS
WATCH

The International Criminal Court, which in October 2009 confirmed that Guinea was under preliminary examination, visited the country in February, May, and November to assess progress made in national investigations.

Key International Actors

Efforts to undermine and delay the electoral process were met with consistent interventions by ECOWAS, the UN, the AU, France, the US, and the EU. The international response was organized through an International Contact Group for Guinea (known as the Contact Group). High-level visits by the UN Security Council's special representative for West Africa, the presidents of Burkina Faso and Mali, and the AU chairman, helped keep the electoral process on track. After the intervention of the Contact Group, Malian General Siaka Toumani Sangaré was appointed as head of the electoral commission. Some 70 EU and 200 ECOWAS observers monitored the elections. However, Guinea's partners remained largely silent on the need for those responsible for the September 2009 violence to be held accountable for their crimes.

With few exceptions, the sanctions, arms embargos, travel bans, and asset freezes against former government members imposed in response to the 2009 violence remained in place. The US funded a private security company to train a unit of the Presidential Guard. Israeli authorities fined an Israeli security firm for negotiating a deal to provide weapons and military training to the former military government in violation of Israeli rules governing such contracts.

The UN Security Council held several formal and informal consultations on Guinea. In July the Office of the United Nations High Commissioner for Human Rights established a mission in Guinea following a recommendation contained in the report by the International Commission of Inquiry. The office is tasked with helping establish a national human rights institution, undertaking judicial reforms, and combating impunity. In May 2010 Guinea underwent the UN Human Rights Council's Universal Periodic Review during which Guinea committed to reform the judiciary and security services, and address rampant impunity.

KENYA

In a historic move, Kenya's citizens voted overwhelmingly in favor of accountability and reform when they supported a new constitution by a two-thirds majority in August 2010. Constitutional reform was among the steps to which the coalition government agreed after the 2007 post-election violence. It paves the way for restructuring the government, establishing a land commission, and carrying out sweeping changes to the police and judiciary. The year also saw the prosecutor of the International Criminal Court open an investigation into the post-election violence. Kenya continues to suffer the regional effects of Somalia's crisis, with a steady flow of refugees entering the country; some suffered serious abuses at the hands of Kenyan police as they tried to find safety.

A New Constitution

The new constitution, supported by 67 percent of Kenyan voters on August 4, was the culmination of four decades of effort. The new coalition government committed to a new constitution, among other reforms, after post-election violence in 2007 in which 1,300 people died and hundreds of thousands were displaced.

The new constitution addresses several longstanding concerns, namely the concentration of power in the executive, the absence of checks and balances, and the use of land as a tool of political patronage. It creates a smaller cabinet of ministers who do not have to be parliament members; reforms the legislature by creating an upper house, the Senate; and devolves considerable power to a new tier of county governments and governors. In an effort to address the judiciary's lack of independence, the new constitution creates a new judiciary service commission to nominate judges, creates a new post of director of public prosecutions, and requires parliamentary approval for appointing the attorney general. It also enshrines in law a land commission, which removes the president's ability to allocate land, review existing land holdings, and set minimum and maximum holdings of land.

Celebration of the constitution was marred by the presence of Sudanese President Omar al-Bashir, who is wanted on ICC arrest warrants for genocide, crimes against humanity, and war crimes. The government's invitation to al-

Bashir and its failure to cooperate with the ICC to arrest him call into question its commitment to cooperate with the court's investigation.

Impunity and Accountability for Post-Election Violence

Impunity remains a pervasive problem in Kenya. In 2008 the coalition government promised to establish a national tribunal to investigate and prosecute those most responsible for the post-election violence, or refer the crimes to the ICC. It failed to do either, and in November 2009 the ICC prosecutor sought authority from an ICC pre-trial chamber to begin investigations in Kenya. On March 31, 2010, the chamber granted permission by a vote of two judges to one, after which the ICC prosecutor announced an ambitious agenda to bring at least two cases against four to six individuals by the end of 2010.

While a limited number of cases are being investigated by the ICC, Kenya has not credibly and effectively investigated and prosecuted other perpetrators of the post-election violence.

Witness protection emerged as a key challenge to investigations. Threats against individuals who witnessed post-election violence, including some who testified before the Commission to Investigate the Post-Election Violence, increased after the prosecutor announced that he would seek to open a Kenya investigation. In May the president signed into law amendments to the Witness Protection Act, a key step in reforming Kenya's witness protection system. The amendments create a new witness protection agency with increased independence, but resources and time are needed to implement changes.

There have been no investigations or forthcoming prosecutions for war crimes committed by the insurgent Sabaot Land Defence Force or Kenyan security forces during the 2006-2008 Mount Elgon conflict; abuses by Kenyan army and police units implicated in using excessive force in disarmament operations in Mandera and Samburu districts; or extrajudicial killings and enforced disappearances of suspected Mungiki gang members by police officers. There were no developments in finding the killers of Oscar Kamau Kingara and John Paul Oulu, human rights defenders from the Oscar Foundation Free Legal Aid Clinic who were gunned down in Nairobi in 2009.

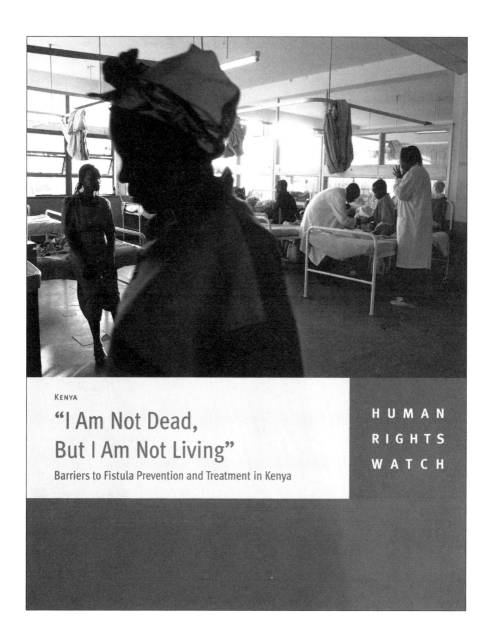

KENYA

"I Am Not Dead, But I Am Not Living"

Barriers to Fistula Prevention and Treatment in Kenya

HUMAN RIGHTS WATCH

KENYA

"Welcome to Kenya"

Police Abuse of Somali Refugees

HUMAN
RIGHTS
WATCH

There were two achievements in the efforts against impunity during 2010.

In a landmark ruling on February 4, 2010, the African Commission on Human and Peoples' Rights condemned Kenya's government for expelling the Endorois people from their traditional land for tourism. It ruled the eviction—with minimal compensation—violated the Endorois' right as an indigenous people to property, health, culture, religion, and natural resources. It ordered Kenya to compensate and restore them to their historic land. It was the first international tribunal ruling to find a violation of the right to development.

In another unprecedented judgment, Kenya's constitutional court awarded US$500,000 compensation to 21 political prisoners who were tortured during the government of former president Daniel Arap Moi, who left office in 2002. The court had previously ruled that the case, from the period when Moi was in office, could not be heard.

Police Reform

In January 2010 President Mwai Kibaki set up the Police Reforms Implementation Committee to monitor the progress of reforms. The committee included members of civil society. Key aspects of the reforms, such as establishing an independent police oversight board, are provided for in the new constitution, but other recommendations, such as merging the administration police with the regular force, are not.

Eight Kenyans were transferred illegally to Uganda following the bombings in Kampala, Uganda's capital, in July and were allegedly mistreated in detention.

Refugees

The overstretched refugee camps in Dadaab, northeastern Kenya, continued to receive thousands of new arrivals during the year, including some 34,000 people between January and September.

Many of the new refugees from Somalia endured serious abuses at the hands of Kenyan police when they crossed the officially closed border. These included violence, arbitrary arrest, unlawful detention in inhuman and degrading conditions, threats of deportation, and wrongful prosecution for "unlawful presence" to extort money from the new arrivals—men, women, and children alike. In some cases, police raped women. Police also failed to diligently investigate and prosecute rapes within the refugee community.

In early 2010 hundreds, and possibly thousands, of Somalis unable to pay extortion demands were sent back to Somalia in flagrant violation of Kenyan and international law. The Kenyan government announced an internal investigation into the allegations. In October the government promised to reconstruct the screening center at Liboi on the Somali border "soon." However, Kenya continued to deny almost 400,000 camp-based refugees the right to free movement in the country, in violation of international law.

Women's and Children's Right to Health

Partly due to health care system failures, tens of thousands of Kenyan women and girls die each year in childbirth and pregnancy, while more suffer preventable injuries, serious infections, and disabilities. Maternal deaths represent 15 percent of all deaths for women of reproductive age—one in 39 women in Kenya die during childbirth according to the United Nations—while an estimated 300,000 women and girls are living with untreated fistula. Kenya's restrictive abortion laws, which criminalize abortion generally, contribute to maternal death and disability. Unsafe abortions cause about 30 percent of maternal deaths.

The Kenyan government fails to provide adequate pain treatment and palliative care for hundreds of thousands of children with diseases such as cancer or HIV/AIDS. Oral morphine, an essential medicine for pain treatment, is currently out of stock. Kenya's few palliative care services, which provide pain treatment but also counseling and support to families of chronically ill patients, lack programs for children.

Sexual Orientation and Gender Identity

Kenya continues to punish consensual adult sexual conduct with up to 14 years imprisonment. On February 11, following unsubstantiated rumors of a "gay wedding" in the coastal town of Mtwapa, influential Muslim and Christian religious

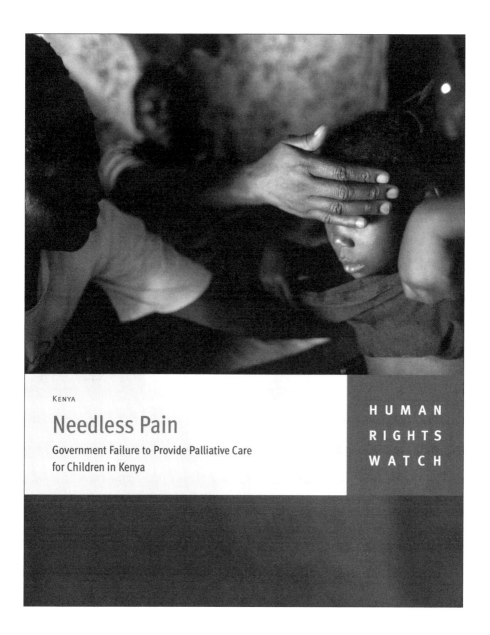

KENYA

Needless Pain

Government Failure to Provide Palliative Care
for Children in Kenya

HUMAN
RIGHTS
WATCH

leaders demanded the closure of the Mtwapa office of the Kenya Medical Research Institute (KEMRI), which conducts research on HIV/AIDS with men who have sex with men. The religious leaders issued a statement promising to "flush out gays" in Mtwapa.

On February 12, a group of over 200 individuals—armed with sticks, stones, and other makeshift weapons—surrounded KEMRI. Smaller mobs went to the homes of people suspected of being gay. The police attempted to protect the individuals targeted by the mob by taking them into custody. Another mob severely beat up a KEMRI volunteer on February 13. Two individuals were beaten up in Mombasa on suspicion of being gay, on February 13 and 16 respectively.

In Mtwapa, Mombasa, and elsewhere, lesbian, gay, bisexual, and transgender people went into hiding in fear for their lives, and HIV/AIDS outreach, testing, and treatment among men who have sex with men remains compromised by the attacks and the continuing climate of homophobia.

Key International Actors

Kenya's partners in Europe and North America are united in pushing for accountability for the election violence and an end to impunity, key conditions of the reform agenda that Kofi Annan brokered in early 2008. The United States and the European Union continued to threaten travel bans against key suspects and government members to encourage Kenya to pursue reform. The US continues to support Kenya's military and police, particularly their counterterrorism efforts, and thus has some influence over the conduct of those forces.

Kenya cited a July 2009 decision by the African Union not to cooperate with the ICC in arresting al-Bashir to justify its failure to do so during his August visit. In the face of criticism over al-Bashir's visit, including from many of Kenya's international partners, officials repeated their commitment to work with the ICC in its Kenya investigation. Kenya also concluded an agreement in September with the ICC to facilitate the court's work within its territory. Nonetheless, concerns over Kenya's willingness to fulfill its commitments to cooperate with the ICC persist in the wake of al-Bashir's visit.

Regionally, the conflict in Somalia where the al-Shabaab militia continues to strengthen and the fragility of Somalia's transitional government remain pressing security concerns for Kenya. The 2011 referendum on the status of neighboring Southern Sudan is a key issue that could have major implications for Kenya as a frontline state and host to refugees.

LIBERIA

During 2010 the Liberian government made some gains in consolidating the rule of law, ensuring sound fiscal management, and improving access to key economic rights, including health care and primary education.

However, inadequate police response to persistent violent incidents, continued deficiencies in the judiciary and criminal justice sectors, and the failure to prosecute civil servants implicated in large-scale embezzlement resulted in increased domestic and , to a lesser extent, international criticism of the government of President Ellen Johnson-Sirleaf. Concern about these weaknesses was heightened by several risk factors, notably high unemployment, communal tensions, and the upcoming 2011 presidential and parliamentary elections.

Meanwhile, there was little progress in ensuring justice for victims of war crimes committed during Liberia's years of armed conflict, or in implementing the recommendations of the 2009 report of Liberia's Truth and Reconciliation Commission (TRC).

Insecurity and Police Conduct

High rates of crime, including armed robbery and rape, as well as violent protests over layoffs and land disputes, including one in Lofa county that left four dead, continued to be of major concern in 2010.

The undisciplined, poorly managed, and ill-equipped Liberian police were challenged to maintain law and order. On several occasions, their failure to do so necessitated the intervention of United Nations peacekeepers, deployed to Liberia since 2003. Lack of public confidence in the police and criminal justice systems led people to take justice into their own hands, resulting in mob attacks on alleged criminals and others, causing several deaths.

Liberian police continue to engage in unprofessional and sometimes abusive and criminal behavior, including frequent absenteeism, extortion, bribery, assault, and rape. They frequently fail to adequately investigate alleged criminals, and when they make arrests, suspects are often freed. Lack of funding for transportation and communications equipment further undermines the effectiveness of the national police, especially in rural areas.

However, the police demonstrated some improvement in 2010. Crime levels in Monrovia, the capital, dropped somewhat as a result of more proactive patrolling. The actions of two new elite squads – the Emergency Response Unit and the Police Support Unit – led to multiple arrests and showed promise in responding to unrest. The police leadership showed an increased willingness and ability to respond to complaints of misconduct within the force, and implemented a performance appraisal system to monitor individual officers, and a database to track cases of misconduct.

Judiciary Weaknesses

Persistent deficiencies in Liberia's judiciary led to widespread abuses of the right to due process and undermined efforts to address impunity for the perpetrators of crimes. The problems include insufficient judicial personnel, including prosecutors, public defenders, and clerks; an inadequate number of courtrooms; logistical constraints, including insufficient computers, photocopiers, and vehicles to transport prisoners and witnesses to court; archaic rules of procedure; and poor case management. Witnesses' refusal to testify, jurors' willingness to accept bribes, and unprofessional and corrupt practices by judicial staff also undermined progress.

Because of the courts' inability to adequately process cases, hundreds of prisoners were held in extended pretrial detention in overcrowded jails and detention centers that lack basic sanitation, nutrition, and health care; in 2010 just over 10 percent of the roughly 1,700 individuals detained in Liberia's prisons had been convicted of a crime. The number of jailbreaks—at least 12 in 2010—illuminated continuing weaknesses in the criminal justice system. Improvements included the deployment of over 20 public defenders throughout Liberia and a mobile "fast track" court operating out of the Monrovia Central Prison, which helped to clear the backlog of pretrial detainees.

Harmful Traditional Practices

Serious abuses and some deaths resulting from harmful traditional practices continued to occur in 2010, in part because of distrust of the judicial system and the
absence of law enforcement and judicial authorities. These included ritual
killings, including one case in which alleged perpetrators were local government
officials; killings of alleged witches; and "trials by ordeal" in which suspects of
crimes are forced to swallow the poisonous sap of a tree or endure burning, their
guilt or innocence determined by whether they survive. The government condemned these practices and on several occasions the police and judiciary took
action against alleged perpetrators.

Sexual Violence

The incidence of rape of women and girls continued to be alarmingly high in
2010, despite the establishment in 2009 of a dedicated court for sexual violence.
The majority of victims were under the age of 16. While public reporting and the
police response to reports of rape improved, deficiencies in the justice system
and the reluctance of witnesses to testify hampered efforts to prosecute cases.

Corruption

While authorities made progress in conducting regular audits and putting programs in place to improve public finance management, these efforts made little
headway in curbing official malfeasance. Corruption scandals—including allegations involving the ministers of information, interior, and gender; the inspector
general of police and police deputy commissioner for administration; the head of
the Telecommunications Authority and high-level members of the Finance
Ministry and Central Bank—resulted in few investigations and only two convictions, with a third case pending. The work of the Anti-Corruption Commission, created in 2008, was hampered by insufficient funds, personnel, and authority to
independently prosecute cases. The government's refusal to prosecute some
high-ranking civil servants and to take action against individuals cited in a controversial financial audit led to the perception that the president lacks the will to
address the problem. Corrupt practices in large part gave rise to the armed con-

flicts that wracked Liberia in the 1990s and ended in 2003, and have long under-mined the provision of basic education and health care to the most vulnerable.

The Liberia Extractive Industries Transparency Initiative, in effect since 2009, was implemented over the course of the year, but the lack of government control over some mining areas undermined adherence to the Kimberley Process Certification Scheme, the global effort to end the trade in conflict minerals.

Legislative Developments

In September the parliament passed the Freedom of Information Bill, and also finally constituted the Independent National Commission on Human Rights, seven years after it was mandated by the Comprehensive Peace Agreement to protect human rights and oversee the implementation of the TRC's recommendations. Problems marred the selection of the commission's members—including a flawed vetting procedure, inadequate involvement of civil society groups, and the initial selection of a member with close ties to the president, and of other members who lacked relevant experience—generating concerns about the president's com-mitment to the commission and its potential for independence.

Truth and Reconciliation Commission and Accountability

The Liberian government made no progress in ensuring the prosecution of those responsible for war crimes committed during the armed conflicts, and made little effort to implement the recommendations of the TRC.

The TRC, mandated to investigate human rights violations committed between 1979 and 2003, presented its final report to the government in December 2009, and concluded its four-year mandate in June 2010. Its key recommendations included dispensing reparations; establishing a criminal tribunal to prosecute the most notorious perpetrators; barring from public office scores of former support-ers of the warring factions, including the current president; and instituting an informal village-based reconciliation mechanism. Implementing the recommenda-tions was slowed by disagreement about whether the executive, legislature, or the Independent National Commission on Human Rights should take the lead, as well as legitimate questions about the constitutionality of some recommendations. The poor quality of sections of the report, notably the lack of solid factual evidence about those recommended for prosecution and bans from public office, further undermined its findings. During the year the president asked the Justice Ministry, the Law Reform Commission, and the Liberian National Bar Association to study the legal and constitutional implications of the recommendations. However, the slow pace of this consultation process raised questions about the president's will to move things forward.

Liberian Army

The program funded and led by the United States to recruit and train a new 2,000-member Liberian army completed its work in December 2009. Continued training and mentoring of the officer corps was conducted throughout the year by some 60 US military personnel. Soldiers nonetheless committed numerous criminal acts, which were mostly addressed by the judiciary. The new army has yet to put in place a court martial board or military tribunal.

Key International Actors

Persistent weaknesses in security and rule of law institutions despite considerable foreign aid generated concern among Liberia's key international and development partners, most notably the UN and US.

In July Liberia reached the completion point under the Heavily Indebted Poor Countries Initiative, bringing the total external debt cancelled since 2007 to US$4.6 billion. The US is Liberia's largest donor, and in fiscal year 2009-2010 contributed more than $450 million to support democratization, security sector reform, girls' education, and reconstruction efforts, including some $250 million in support of the UN Mission in Liberia (UNMIL).

In December 2009 the UN Security Council renewed for one year the travel ban on persons deemed a threat to peace in Liberia, as well as asset freezes on those sanctioned. The council also renewed the mandate for the panel of experts monitoring the implementation of sanctions and resource exploitation, but lifted an arms embargo in place since 2003. In September 2010, the council renewed UNMIL's mandate for one year. The UN Peacebuilding Commission will provide a

$25 million grant to support programs in justice and rule of law, as well as to combat high youth unemployment.

NIGERIA

The May inauguration of President Goodluck Jonathan, following the death from natural causes of President Umaru Yar'Adua, brought hope for improvements in Nigeria's deeply entrenched human rights problems. Jonathan's removal of the attorney general, under whose watch impunity flourished, and his appointment of a respected academic to replace the discredited head of the electoral commission, who presided over phenomenally flawed elections, were widely viewed as positive first steps. Yet major challenges remain.

During the year, episodes of intercommunal violence claimed hundreds of lives, while widespread police abuses and the mismanagement and embezzlement of Nigeria's vast oil wealth continued unabated. Perpetrators of all classes of human rights violations enjoyed near-total impunity. A spate of politically motivated killings by Islamist militants in the north, and continued kidnappings and violence by Niger Delta militants – including the brazen Independence Day bombing in Abuja, the capital, for which they claimed responsibility –raised concern about stability in the run-up to planned 2011 general elections.

The National Assembly again failed to pass legislation to improve transparency, notably the Freedom of Information bill, but approved a watered-down version of an electoral reform bill. Nigeria's judiciary continues to exercise a degree of independence in electoral matters and has, since 2007, overturned more than one-third of the ruling People's Democratic Party (PDP) gubernatorial election victories on grounds of electoral malpractices and other irregularities. Meanwhile free speech and the independent press remained fairly robust. Foreign partners took some important steps to confront endemic corruption in Nigeria, but appeared reluctant to exert meaningful pressure on the government over its poor human rights record.

Intercommunal and Political Violence

Intercommunal, political, and sectarian violence has claimed the lives of more than 14,500 people since the end of military rule in 1999. During 2010, episodes of intercommunal violence in Plateau State, in central Nigeria, left over 900 dead. In January several hundred were killed in sectarian clashes in and around the state capital of Jos, including a massacre on January 19 that claimed the lives of more than 150 Muslims in the nearby town of Kuru Karama. Shortly thereafter, on March 7, at least 200 Christians were massacred in Dogo Nahawa and several other nearby villages. In the months that followed more than 100 people died in smaller-scale attacks and reprisal killings in Jos and surrounding communities. Meanwhile intercommunal clashes in Nassarawa, Niger, Adamawa, Gombe, Taraba, Ogun, Akwa Ibom, and Cross River states left more than 110 dead and hundreds more displaced. State and local government policies that discriminate against "non-indigenes"—people who cannot trace their ancestry to what are said to be the original inhabitants of an area—exacerbate intercommunal tensions.

Widespread poverty and poor governance in Nigeria have created an environment where militant groups thrive. In Bauchi State in December 2009, violent clashes between government security forces and rival factions of a militant Islamist group known as Kala Kato left several dozen dead, including more than 20 children. Between July and October 2010, suspected members of the Boko Haram Islamist group killed eight police officers, an Islamic cleric, a prominent politician, and several community leaders in the northern city of Maiduguri, and in September attacked a prison in Bauchi, freeing nearly 800 prisoners, including more than 100 suspected Boko Haram members.

Targeted killings and political violence increased ahead of the 2011 elections. In January 2010 Dipo Dina, an opposition candidate in the 2007 gubernatorial elections in Ogun State, was gunned down. In a series of attacks in Bauchi State in August, gunmen killed two of the state governor's aides and a security guard for an opposition candidate for governor, and injured several others. Meanwhile, the Nigerian government has still not held accountable those responsible for the 2007 election violence that left at least 300 dead.

Conduct of Security Forces

Again in 2010, members of the Nigeria Police Force were widely implicated in the extortion of money and the arbitrary arrest and torture of criminal suspects and others. They solicited bribes from victims of crimes to initiate investigations, and from suspects to drop investigations. They were also implicated in numerous extrajudicial killings of persons in custody. Meanwhile senior police officials embezzle and mismanage funds intended for basic police operations. They also enforce a perverse system of "returns," in which rank-and-file officers pay a share of the money extorted from the public up the chain of command.

The government lacked the will to reform the police force and hold officers accountable for these and other serious abuses. At this writing, none of the police officers responsible for the brazen execution of the Boko Haram leader, Mohammed Yusuf, and dozens of his suspected supporters in Maiduguri in July 2009 have been prosecuted. Similarly, the government has still not held members of the police and military accountable for their unlawful 2008 killing of more than 130 people during sectarian violence in Jos, or for the 2001 massacre by the military of more than 200 people in Benue State, and the military's complete destruction of the town of Odi, Bayelsa State, in 1999.

Government Corruption

Nigeria made limited progress with its anti-corruption campaign in 2010. The national Economic and Financial Crimes Commission (EFCC) indicted more than a dozen politicians and senior government officials on corruption charges, including a former federal government minister, a former state governor, and a handful of state officials. However, the EFCC failed to indict other senior politicians implicated in the massive looting of the state treasury, including former Rivers State governor Peter Odili.

Key convictions included that of a powerful banker, sentenced to six months in prison in October, and a former head of the national anti-drug agency, sentenced to four years in prison in April for taking bribes from a criminal suspect, the longest sentence handed down to a government official to date. Meanwhile, the governing elite continues to squander and siphon off the country's tremendous oil wealth, leaving poverty, malnutrition, and mortality rates among the world's highest.

Targeted attacks against anti-corruption officials increased significantly in 2010. Gunmen in three separate incidents shot and killed anti-corruption personnel, including the head of the forensic unit and a former senior investigator. Still,

Nuhu Ribadu, the former EFCC head, returned to Nigeria in June, after fleeing the country in 2009 following what he believed to be an assassination attempt.

Violence and Poverty in the Niger Delta

Following a lull in violence in the oil-rich Niger Delta, attacks increased, including kidnappings of schoolchildren, wealthy individuals, and oil workers, and car bombings in Delta State, Bayelsa State, and Abuja. The 2009 amnesty – in which a few thousand people, including top militant commanders, surrendered weapons in exchange for cash stipends – led to a reduction of attacks on oil facil-ities in 2010, but their disarmament, demobilization, and reintegration have been poorly planned and executed. The amnesty has further entrenched impunity, and the government has made little effort to address environmental degradation, endemic state and local government corruption, or political sponsorship of armed groups, which drive and underlie violence and poverty in the region.

Human Rights Concerns in the Context of Sharia

In northern Nigeria 12 state governments apply Sharia law as part of their criminal justice systems, which include sentences such as the death penalty, amputa-tions, and floggings that amount to cruel, inhuman, and degrading punishment. Serious due process concerns also exist in Sharia proceedings, and evidentiary standards in the Sharia codes discriminate against women, particularly in adul-tery cases.

Death Penalty

There are about 870 inmates, including over 30 juvenile offenders, on death row in Nigeria. Although Nigeria has an informal moratorium on the use of the death penalty, state governors in 2010 announced plans to consider resuming execu-tions to ease prison congestion.

Freedom of Expression and the Media

Civil society and the independent press openly criticize the government and its policies, allowing for robust public debate. Yet journalists are subject to intimidation and violence when reporting on issues implicating the political and economic elite. Edo Ugbagwu, a journalist with *The Nation*, one of Nigeria's largest newspapers, was gunned down at his Lagos home in April. In Jos two journalists with a local Christian newspaper were killed in sectarian clashes in April, while a Muslim journalist from Radio Nigeria was badly beaten in March, in an attack the journalist said was incited by a state government official.

Key International Actors

Because of Nigeria's role as a regional power, leading oil exporter, and major contributor of troops to United Nations peacekeeping missions, foreign governments—including the United States and the United Kingdom—have been reluctant to publicly criticize Nigeria's human rights record.

US government officials did speak out forcefully against the country's endemic government corruption and took an important first step to back up these words by revoking the visa of former attorney general Michael Aondoakaa. The UK government continued to play a leading role in international efforts to combat money laundering by corrupt Nigerian officials, demonstrated by the May arrest in Dubai of the powerful former Delta State governor, James Ibori, on an Interpol warrant from the UK, and the conviction of two of his associates in an English court in June for laundering his funds. However, in fiscal year 2010, the UK increased funding to £140 million (US$225 million) in aid to Nigeria, including security sector aid, without demanding accountability for Nigerian officials and members of the security forces implicated in corrupt practices and serious human rights abuses.

The UN secretary-general expressed his concern about the intercommunal violence in Jos, but at this writing a mission by his special adviser on the prevention of genocide is stalled due to resistance from the Nigerian government.

RWANDA

Rwanda's development and economic growth continued in 2010, but there were numerous violations of civil and political rights, and the government failed to fulfill its professed commitment to democracy. The year was marked by political repression and restrictions on freedom of expression and association in the run-up to the presidential election. In August President Paul Kagame was re-elected with 93.8 percent of the vote in an election in which he faced no meaningful challenge. None of the new opposition parties were able to participate in the elections. Opposition party members, independent journalists, and other government critics were subjected to persistent intimidation and harassment, including arrests, detention, ill-treatment, death threats, and at least two extrajudicial killings. A prominent government opponent in exile narrowly escaped an attempt on his life. Human rights organizations encountered hostility and numerous obstacles to their work.

Trials in the *gacaca* courts—community-based courts trying cases related to the 1994 genocide—began to wind down, though the deadline for their closure was postponed several times. The imminent completion of the *gacaca* process opened the way for further justice reforms. However, continuing concerns about fair trials prevented other states, as well as the Tanzania-based International Criminal Tribunal for Rwanda (ICTR), from transferring genocide suspects to Rwanda.

The report of the mapping exercise on the Democratic Republic of Congo (DRC) by the Office of the United Nations High Commissioner for Human Rights documented grave crimes allegedly committed by the Rwandan army in 1996 and 1997.

Attacks on Government Opponents

None of the three new opposition parties were able to nominate candidates in the presidential election. Local authorities prevented the FDU-Inkingi and the Democratic Green Party from registering as parties. Meetings of the PS-Imberakuri were disrupted, sometimes violently, by dissident members and other individuals.

The PS-Imberakuri, registered in 2009, was taken over in March 2010 by dissident members believed to have been manipulated by the ruling Rwandan Patriotic Front (RPF). In late 2009 the Senate summoned the party's president, Bernard Ntaganda, on accusations of "genocide ideology." In June the police arrested Ntaganda and raided his house and the party office. The charges against him included endangering national security, inciting ethnic divisions, and organizing demonstrations without authorization. By November he was still in prison awaiting trial.

Victoire Ingabire, president of the FDU-Inkingi, who returned to Rwanda in January after 16 years in exile, was arrested in April on charges of "genocide ideology," "divisionism," and collaboration with the Democratic Forces for the Liberation of Rwanda (FDLR), an armed group active in eastern DRC and composed in part by individuals who participated in the 1994 Rwanda genocide. Ingabire was released on bail with travel restrictions, but in October was re-arrested following allegations of involvement in forming an armed group. In November she remained in detention awaiting trial.

Members of the three new opposition parties received threats related to their party activities. Several members of the PS-Imberakuri and the FDU-Inkingi were arrested for attempting to hold a demonstration in June. Some were released, but others were arrested in July. Several were ill-treated by police in detention. In July the Green Party's vice-president, André Kagwa Rwisereka, was found dead, his body mutilated, outside the town of Butare. The circumstances of his death remain unclear.

Peter Erlinder, an American and one of Victoire Ingabire's defense lawyers, was arrested in May on charges of "genocide denial and minimization," and "spreading malicious rumors that could endanger national security." He was released on bail three weeks later. The charges against Erlinder, who is also a defense lawyer at the ICTR, related primarily to articles published in previous years in which he questioned key events surrounding the genocide.

On June 19 Faustin Kayumba Nyamwasa, a Rwandan general in exile in South Africa since February, was seriously injured in a murder attempt in Johannesburg. Once a close ally of President Kagame and former chief-of-staff of the Rwandan army, Nyamwasa has become an outspoken government critic since early 2010. South African authorities arrested several suspects. Rwanda has requested Nyamwasa's extradition, alleging he was behind a series of grenade attacks in Kigali earlier in the year.

Deogratias Mushayidi, a former journalist and outspoken government opponent in exile, was arrested in Burundi in March and handed over to Rwandan authorities. In September Mushayidi was found guilty and sentenced to life imprisonment on three charges: spreading rumors inciting civil disobedience, recruiting an armed group to overthrow the government, and using forged documents. He was also charged with four other offenses, including "genocide ideology" and "divisionism."

The government continued to use a law on "genocide ideology"—a broad and ill-defined offense—as a tool to silence independent opinion and criticism. In a welcome development, the minister of justice announced that the law was being reviewed.

Clampdown on Independent Media

In April the government-affiliated Media High Council suspended the independent newspapers *Umuseso* and *Umuvugizi* for six months, then called for their definitive closure, alleging, among other things, that some of their articles threatened national security. The editors of both newspapers fled into exile after receiving threats. Copies of the first edition of *The Newsline*, an English-language newspaper produced by exiled *Umuseso* journalists, were seized at the Uganda-Rwanda border in July.

In February *Umuseso* editor Didas Gasana, former editor Charles Kabonero, and journalist Richard Kayigamba were found guilty of defamation; they received sentences of between six months' and a year's imprisonment and were ordered to pay a large fine. In April *Umuvugizi* editor Jean-Bosco Gasasira was also found guilty of defamation and fined.

Umuvugizi journalist Jean-Léonard Rugambage, who had been investigating sensitive cases including the attempted murder of Nyamwasa, was shot dead in June outside his home in Kigali. He had reported being under increased surveillance in the days before his death.

Three journalists with the *Umurabyo* newspaper were arrested in July in connection with articles published in their newspaper; two remain in detention at this writing, while the other was only held for one day.

Obstructions to the Work of Human Rights Organizations

Human rights organizations operated in a difficult and hostile climate. Rwandan human rights groups, weakened by years of intimidation, received threats and were publicly accused by government officials of supporting the government's overthrow and armed groups linked to the genocide. Civil society itself was divided: organizations close to the government publicly denounced those who were more critical, such as the LDGL and LIPRODHOR, two of the few independent human rights groups left in the country. Under pressure from individuals close to the government, several organizations disowned a joint civil society submission on Rwanda for the Universal Periodic Review at the UN Human Rights Council.

International nongovernmental organizations, including Human Rights Watch, were repeatedly criticized and discredited by senior government officials and the pro-government media. Immigration authorities cancelled the work visa in March of Human Rights Watch's senior researcher in Kigali, rejected her second visa application, and forced her to leave the country in April.

Sexual Orientation and Gender Identity

In December 2009 the parliament took a positive initiative by voting against criminalizing homosexuality. However, continuing negative comments on homosexuality by some public officials and newspapers reinforced the stigma faced by sexual minorities.

Gacaca Trials

Gacaca courts were due to end their genocide trials in 2010, but the definitive completion of the process was repeatedly delayed. The government is developing mechanisms to handle outstanding genocide cases and to adjudicate alleged miscarriages of justice by *gacaca* jurisdictions.

Gacaca courts have prosecuted around 1.5 million cases with involvement from local communities across the country. The conduct of trials before *gacaca* courts has been mixed. Some judges delivered fair and objective judgments. Others handed down heavy sentences, including life imprisonment in isolation, on the basis of very little evidence. A number of witnesses and judges proved vulnerable to corruption and outside influence, affecting the outcome of trials and undermining confidence in the courts. Some defense witnesses were afraid to testify for fear of being accused of genocide themselves, and there were numerous allegations that *gacaca* courts sacrificed the truth to satisfy political interests.

Cases Related to the Democratic Republic of Congo

Laurent Nkunda, former leader of the Congolese rebel group the National Congress for the Defense of the People (CNDP), remaied illegally detained under house arrest, without charge or trial, since January 2009. Repeated attempts to get his case heard in Rwandan courts were thwarted on the basis of legal technicalities.

There were several arrests, disappearances, and at least one killing of Congolese supporters of Nkunda in Rwanda, including Denis Ntare Semadwinga, who was murdered in June, and Sheikh Iddy Abbasi, who disappeared after being abducted in March.

On October 1 the Office of the UN High Commissioner for Human Rights published the report of its mapping exercise on the most serious violations of human rights and international humanitarian law in the DRC between March 1993 and June 2003 (see chapter on the DRC). Among other things, the report documents grave crimes allegedly committed by the Rwandan army in 1996 and 1997. While the Congolese government welcomed the report, the Rwandan government rejected it, initially threatening to pull out its peacekeepers from UN missions if the UN published it.

Key International Actors

Most Western donors remained broadly supportive of the Rwandan government and few expressed public concern about human rights violations. However, in the pre-election period, and in the face of increasingly critical media coverage of Rwanda in their own countries, some donor governments raised mostly private concerns about political and media restrictions with the Rwandan government. These concerns were also mentioned in the final report of the Commonwealth Observer Group on the presidential election. Relations between Rwanda and the UN came under strain following the publication of the UN mapping report on the DRC.

SIERRA LEONE

Throughout 2010 the government of President Ernest Bai Koroma made meaningful progress in addressing endemic corruption and improving access to justice and key economic rights, notably health care and education. Endemic public and private corruption has for decades undermined development, and was one of the major factors underpinning the 11-year armed conflict that ended in 2002.

High levels of unemployment, persistent weaknesses in the performance of the police and judiciary, and increased political tension in advance of the 2012 elections slowed the consolidation of the rule of law. Through the efforts of the United Nations-backed Special Court for Sierra Leone, however, progress continued in achieving accountability for war crimes committed during the armed conflict.

The discovery of a major offshore oil deposit, and the ratification by parliament of major resource exploitation contracts, notably those involving a large iron ore deposit, raised hopes that Sierra Leone would be better able to address chronic unemployment, improve access to basic economic rights, and minimize donor dependency. It also illuminated the continued importance of focusing on deficits in economic governance and anti-corruption efforts.

Corruption

In 2010 the Anti-Corruption Commission (ACC) secured convictions against several high-level public officials, including the minister of health and sanitation, the minister of fisheries and marine resources, the head of the school feeding program in the Ministry of Education, a judge, and the director of procurement at the Ministry of Defense. At year's end a further five cases and some 90 investigations were ongoing. While President Koroma repeatedly admonished government officials to desist from corrupt practices, the May resignation of ACC Commissioner Abdul Tejan-Cole, reportedly over security concerns and government interference, and the ACC's subsequent failure to investigate or indict several ruling party politicians, raised concerns that recent gains would be reversed. In March President Koroma released the country's first Extractive Industries Transparency Initiative report.

Rule of Law

Serious deficiencies in the judicial system persist, including extortion and bribe-taking by officials; insufficient numbers of judges, magistrates, and prosecuting attorneys; unprofessional conduct and absenteeism by court personnel; and inadequate remuneration for judiciary personnel.

Overcrowding and inadequate food, sanitation, and health care in prisons remain serious concerns. The population of the country's largest detention facility—designed for 324 detainees—stands at over 1,300. In 2010 some 65 percent of prisoners in Sierra Leone were held in prolonged pretrial detention.

However, concerted efforts by the UN, the United Kingdom (through its Justice Sector Development Programme), aid agencies, and the government have led to meaningful improvements in access to legal representation. The Pilot National Legal Aid program (PNLA) supports lawyers in providing legal aid to hundreds of people detained within police stations and prisons in Freetown, the capital. By the end of August 2010 the cases of over 1,000 individuals had been processed, of which 506 were discharged. A UN Development Program (UNDP) funded project also helped clear the backlog of cases throughout the country by supporting lawyers from the Bar Association in representing indigent detainees, establishing a few new permanent court houses and temporary special tribunals, and deploying itinerant judges. A donor-funded program that deployed tens of paralegals, backed by lawyers, to some 30 locations throughout Sierra Leone helped bridge the gap between the customary and formal legal systems.

Police and Army Conduct

The police in Sierra Leone continue to engage in unprofessional and at times criminal behavior. There were persistent allegations of crime victims being required to pay for investigations and of police involvement in extortion, solicitation of bribes, and other criminal acts. In late 2009 the Sierra Leonean army stepped in to help the police address a spike in armed robberies.

The UK-led International Military Advisory and Training Team has been working since 1999 to reform the Republic of Sierra Leone Armed Forces (RSLAF). In 2010 some 40 mostly British military officers were deployed to Sierra Leone. Over the last several years the army has been downsized from 17,000 to its goal of 8,500 personnel. The Military Court Martial Board within the RSLAF, established in 2009, encouraged discipline by adjudicating the cases of several soldiers implicated in misconduct, misappropriation, and criminality. A milestone was achieved in early 2010 when the first-ever contingent of RSLAF troops was deployed as peacekeepers, to Sudan.

Sexual and Gender-Based Violence and Treatment of Children

Incidents of sexual and gender-based violence against girls and women remained high; in 2009, the latest year for which figures exist, victims reported 927 cases of rape and other forms of sexual assault and 1,543 of domestic violence. While Family Support Units within police stations led to increased reporting, fear of stigma and weaknesses within the judiciary resulted in very few prosecutions. Child labor within artisanal diamond mining areas continued to be a major cause of concern. However, the completion of construction of remand facilities for juvenile offenders successfully kept children from entering adult prisons, as was previously the practice.

Accountability for Past Abuses

Between 2004 and 2009, eight individuals associated with the three main warring factions were tried and convicted by the Special Court for Sierra Leone for rape, murder, mutilation, enslavement, recruitment of child soldiers, forced marriage, and attacks against UN peacekeepers. All eight were transferred in October 2009 to Rwanda to serve out their sentences.

During 2010 the trial of former Liberian president Charles Taylor—charged with 11 counts of war crimes and crimes against humanity for his role in supporting Sierra Leonean rebel groups during the conflict—made notable progress. The defense, which closed its case in November, brought forward 21 witnesses, including Charles Taylor. Earlier, 94 witnesses testified for the prosecution. Closing arguments are scheduled for February 2011 and a judgment is expected later in the year. Taylor is the first sitting African head of state to be indicted and face trial before an international or hybrid tribunal. Due to security concerns, his trial is taking place in The Hague, Netherlands, instead of in Freetown.

Meanwhile, the Special Court began closing down operations in Freetown. In May the Special Court handed over control of its detention facility to the Sierra Leone prison service. It also reached an agreement with the government on residual functions of the court, which include witness protection, court archives, supervision of sentences, and the trial of the last person indicted, Johnny Paul Koroma, who remains at large. The Special Court—whose largest donors include the United States, the United Kingdom, the Netherlands, and Canada—continues to lack the resources to complete its work. The Special Court relies solely on voluntary contributions from the international community.

Reparations programs for war victims, as recommended by the Truth and Reconciliation Commission, provided financial and medical assistance and skills training to some 20,000 victims with support from the UN Peacebuilding Fund and UN Development Fund for Women.

Economic and Social Rights

In 2010 the government launched a free healthcare plan for pregnant women, breast-feeding mothers, and children under five years old; raised the salaries of health workers; and announced plans to increase the number of midwives trained each year from 30 to 150, representing a significant step toward improving access to basic health care. To improve access to education, the government increased the number of teachers, awarded grants to girls and the disabled attending secondary school and university, and investigated and prosecuted Education Ministry personnel engaged in corrupt practices.

According to the 2009 UN Human Development report, Sierra Leone ranked 180th out of 182 countries for overall development. A 2009 report of the UN Department of Economic and Social Affairs found that Sierra Leone had the world's worst indicators for infant mortality (123 deaths per 1,000 live births) and maternal mortality (the lifetime risk of maternal death is 1 in 8).

National Human Rights Commission and Legislative Developments

The National Human Rights Commission carried out its mandate to investigate and report on human rights abuses and generally operated without government interference. In January a revised Mines and Minerals Act envisioned to improve Sierra Leone's benefits from its vast natural resources was signed into law. In November the Right to Access Information Bill was introduced into parliament. However, the government has yet to act on the report of the Constitutional Review Committee, submitted in 2008, or conduct a promised review of the Criminal Libel Law.

Key International Actors

In 2010 UN Secretary-General Ban Ki-moon and World Bank President Robert Zoellick visited Sierra Leone. The UN and the UK government continued to take the lead in helping to reform and support Sierra Leone's rule of law sectors. The UK remained Sierra Leone's largest donor, providing some £50 million (US$80 million) in the last fiscal year, including support for the health sector, anti-corruption efforts, security sector reform, and access to justice.

In July the World Bank gave $20 million to be used over three years to address high unemployment by supporting skills training and cash-for-work programs. The EU gave €52.5 million ($73.7 million) to support infrastructure, agriculture, and governance.

In September the UN Security Council extended the mandate of the UN Integrated Peacebuilding Office in Sierra Leone (UNIPSIL) for one year and lifted an arms embargo and travel ban on former rebel leaders that had been imposed in 1997. UNIPSIL plays a largely advisory role in strengthening democratic institutions and addressing organized crime, drug trafficking, and youth unemployment.

The UN Peacebuilding Fund has approved more than $35 million since 2007 to support justice, security, youth employment, and good governance in Sierra Leone.

SOMALIA

The Transitional Federal Government (TFG), supported by the African Union Mission in Somalia (AMISOM), lost control of further territory to opposition groups in Somalia in 2010, with bitter fighting imposing a significant toll on civilians, especially during an upsurge of attacks in August and September. Al-Shabaab and Hizbul Islam, the militant Islamist groups that spearhead the opposition, consolidated control over much of south-central Somalia, where the population experienced relative stability but also increasingly harsh and intolerant repression, in the name of Sharia law. A humanitarian crisis exists across the country. Humanitarian agencies have limited access due to ongoing insecurity, and armed opposition groups threatened humanitarian workers, journalists, and civil society activists with attack.

The northern region of Somaliland, a self-declared independent republic, provided a rare positive note in the region when its long-delayed presidential election took place in a largely free and fair atmosphere in June 2010.

Indiscriminate Warfare in Mogadishu

Continual fighting between militant Islamist groups and the TFG raged in Mogadishu, Somalia's capital, throughout 2010, with all parties conducting indiscriminate attacks causing high civilian casualties. Opposition fighters have deployed unlawfully in densely populated civilian neighborhoods and at times used civilians as "shields" to fire mortars at TFG and AMISOM positions. These attacks are conducted so indiscriminately that they frequently destroy civilian homes but rarely strike military targets. Often AMISOM or TFG forces respond in kind, launching indiscriminate mortar strikes on the neighborhoods from which opposition fighters had fired and then fled, leaving only civilians to face the resulting devastation.

The TFG lost further ground to al-Shabaab during the year and at this writing controls just a few square blocks around the presidential palace at Villa Somalia in Mogadishu, with the AU forces defending the capital's port, the airport, and a few other strategic sites.

Clashes and attacks intensified in August and September—during the Islamic holy month of Ramadan—after al-Shabaab claimed responsibility for the July 11 bomb blasts in Kampala, Uganda's captial. At least 76 civilians died in those attacks, which struck crowded public gatherings the day of the football World Cup final. Uganda provides the largest contingent of the 7,100-member African Union Mission in Somalia. AMISOM forces were accused of indiscriminate shelling in retaliation for the Kampala blasts, particularly in Bakara Market. Bakara and other residential areas were repeatedly hit on July 12 and 13, again in late August, and on September 9; dozens of civilians were killed and injured in these attacks.

On August 23 al-Shabaab and Hizbul Islam called for an escalation in the fighting, and al-Shabaab claimed responsibility for an August 24 suicide attack at the Muna Hotel, which killed 32 people, including civilians and several members of parliament. Another suicide attack on Mogadishu's international airport on September 9 killed at least nine people, including civilians.

Much of the remaining population of Mogadishu fled this new round of fighting and is now displaced in makeshift camps on the outskirts of the capital, primarily in the Afgoi corridor, with little access to humanitarian aid and at risk of harassment by local militia groups.

Both the armed opposition groups and the TFG have used children in their ranks.

Abuses in Opposition-Controlled Areas

South-central Somalia was under the control of local administrations linked to armed opposition groups throughout 2010. In many areas al-Shabaab rule brought relative stability and order, which contrasts dramatically with the chaos in Mogadishu. Residents from some of these areas credit al-Shabaab with ending a constant menace of extortion, robbery, and murder from bandits and freelance militias. But even where this holds true, security has come at a steep price, especially for women.

Grinding repression characterizes daily life in communities controlled by al-Shabaab, and many local administrations have sought to implement harsh and intolerant measures in the name of Sharia law. These measures control minute details of personal lives, including the way people dress and work. The punish-

SOMALIA

Harsh War, Harsh Peace

Abuses by al-Shabaab, the Transitional Federal Government, and AMISOM in Somalia

HUMAN RIGHTS WATCH

ments for even minor offenses are often summary, arbitrary, and cruel. A climate of fear prevents most people from speaking out against abuses of power. As one resident of the southern town of El Wak said, "We just stay quiet. If they tell us to follow a certain path, we follow it."

Freedoms women took for granted in traditional Somali culture have been dramatically rolled back. In many areas women have been barred from engaging in any activity that leads them to mix with men, even small-scale commercial enterprises on which many of them depend for a living. Al-Shabaab authorities have arrested, threatened, or whipped countless women for trying to support their families by selling cups of tea.

Al-Shabaab and other opposition forces often threaten to kill people they suspect of harboring sympathies for their opponents or who resist recruitment. These are not empty threats; opposition groups have murdered civilians regularly and with complete impunity.

Elections in Somaliland and Instability in the North

After almost two years of delay, Somaliland finally held its presidential election on June 26, 2010. International observers deemed the polls reasonably free and fair despite an isolated incident in the Sool region, where one person was killed. The incumbent President Dahir Riyale accepted defeat and peacefully ceded power to an opposition candidate, further advancing hopes for stability in the northern region.

The situation remains unstable in the contested regions of Sool, Sanag, and Cayn, which lie between Somaliland, in Somalia's northwest, and the autonomous state of Puntland in the northeast. Thousands of civilians were displaced by clan-based clashes and conflicts over resources in the disputed area in June.

Attacks on Journalists, Human Rights Defenders, and Humanitarian Workers

Somalia remains one of the world's most dangerous places to be a journalist. At least three journalists were killed in 2010, bringing the total killed since 2007 to

22. Two were targeted killings: Sheikh Nur Mohamed Abkey of state-run Radio Mogadishu was killed by three gunmen in May, and Abdullahi Omar Gedi was stabbed by unknown assailants in Galkayo. Barkhat Awale was killed by a stray bullet in Mogadishu on August 24. Both TFG and opposition forces have harassed the dwindling number of journalists still struggling to operate in Somalia. In April al-Shabaab banned all BBC broadcasts in Somalia and confiscated equipment.

Journalists also suffered detentions and harassment in the northern Somali regions of Somaliland and Puntland. In January Puntland authorities released Mohamed Yasin Isak, a local correspondent for Voice of America, after 17 days of detention without charge.

The majority of human rights defenders fled the country in the past years amid increasing threats to civil society and media; the few individuals remaining in south-central Somalia censor themselves.

The delivery of humanitarian assistance to south-central Somalia has been partially blocked by insecurity as well as measures imposed by armed opposition groups specifically targeting humanitarian agencies. At least eight agencies have been expelled from Somalia by al-Shabaab since January. In addition, United States sanctions on support to terrorist groups have restricted the delivery of food aid toward southern and central Somalia. As a result, some agencies had to cancel their operations, and access is reportedly at its lowest point since 2006.

Key International Actors

Western governments, the UN, the AU, and neighboring countries, with the exception of Eritrea, are united in supporting the TFG as the government of Somalia. The July 2010 bombings in Kampala, Uganda, increased regional concern over the threat posed by al-Shabaab and its connections to al-Qaeda. At this writing the principal response has been to increase the number of AMISOM troops to approximately 7,100 and pledge further funds.

Of the US$213 million pledged by a joint UN, European Union, and AU conference held in Brussels in April 2009, little has reached Somalia. The EU, Ethiopia, Uganda, and Kenya trained TFG soldiers and police in neighboring countries throughout 2010. But efforts to bolster the TFG's weak military and police capacity have been plagued by allegations of corruption and the defection of newly trained troops, some with their weapons; many of the trainees complain that they never received their salaries.

Since withdrawing from Mogadishu in early 2009, Ethiopian troops have repeatedly entered into Somalia for security operations near the border. Ethiopia, along with Eritrea, remains a key player in Somalia, with both countries providing various types of support to proxy forces, although Eritrea's support for armed opposition groups has reportedly declined, according to UN experts.

SOUTH AFRICA

South Africa's pro-human rights constitution, stable government, democratic institutions, independent judiciary, and strong economy mean it has great potential to become a global human rights leader. However, government efforts to realize this potential at home have been inconsistent, and recent trends suggest possible constriction of civil and political rights. In addition, inadequate policies and poor implementation of good ones has slowed the realization of social and economic rights for many South Africans.

In the international arena, South Africa's government has refrained in recent years from condemning abuses in China, Sri Lanka, Iran, Burma, Sudan, and the Democratic Republic of Congo, dashing hopes that it would be a reliable partner in promoting human rights. South Africa's foreign policy role will be in the international spotlight again following its assumption of a seat on the United Nations Security Council on January 1, 2011.

Freedom of Expression

Two separate but interrelated developments in 2010 led to widespread criticism and concern that the government is trying to limit freedom of expression. Ahead of its policy conference in September the ruling African National Congress party (ANC) resurrected a 2007 resolution pushing for the establishment of a Media Appeals Tribunal, arguing that media cannot be counted on to regulate themselves, and that "freedom of the press is not an absolute right and must be balanced against individuals' rights to privacy and human dignity." The ANC's proposal seeks to establish a regulatory mechanism accountable to the ANC-dominated Parliament, which would constitute a back-door path to censorship and suppression of dissent.

On August 4 Mzilikazi Wa-Afrika, a prominent journalist with the *Sunday Times* who had exposed corruption by officials, was arrested without a warrant by 20 policemen in six vans. He was then taken to a secret location in Mpumalanga and interrogated at 2 a.m. without a lawyer. The police also searched his home and took notebooks without a search warrant. Wa-Afrika was eventually released on R5,000 (US$725) bail after his newspaper went to the High Court; the charges cited upon his arrest have since been dropped. The incident heightened fears that such politically motivated intimidation of the press could become the norm if the ANC-proposed tribunal is established.

In April 2010 the Department of State Security tabled a draft of the Protection of Information Bill (PIB) for parliamentary consideration. In 2008 Parliament first tabled and rejected the bill—which aims to replace the existing, expansive 1982 apartheid-era law that prevents and penalizes disclosure of state secrets—for being too draconian. Parliament instructed the Department of State Security to revise the bill in line with the constitution. But when it was re-presented in July 2010, offending elements of the bill had been retained and even made harsher.

The PIB currently gives the government sweeping powers to classify information and impose jail terms of up to 25 years for publishing classified information. It sets no limits on which officials or state bodies can classify information, and has no clear criteria for classifying information. The bill also extends the protection of secrecy to commercial entities, exempts intelligence agencies from scrutiny, and imposes serious punitive measures against those who disclose information.

If enacted as currently written, the bill would seriously impede the free flow of information, erode the right of access to information, and violate key constitutional provisions. The Right to Know Campaign, which represents a broad spectrum of civil society groups, has pressured to squash the bill in its current form. Parliament gave the adhoc committee tasked with finalizing the bill until January 28, 2011 to incorporate all inputs and present a final draft.

Refugees and Migrants

On May 11 the Consortium for Refugees and Migrants in South Africa (CoRMSA) reported 10 incidents of xenophobic violence in Siyathemba, Atteridgeville, Mamelodi, Orange Farm, and Sasolburg, where large crowds looted foreign-owned shops.

CoRMSA also reported mounting threats of violence following the football World Cup, held in South Africa in June and July, leading thousands of migrants—mainly Zimbabweans—to flee South Africa or relocate to other communities. Responding to public pressure, the government moved swiftly, establishing a heavy police presence and deploying the military in Alexandria, Katlehong, and other town-ships where xenophobic violence had been predicted. The anticipated violence did not materialize, but migrants in South Africa continue to report scattered inci-dents of xenophobic attacks.

In September South Africa moved to "regularize the presence of Zimbabweans in South Africa" by ending the special dispensation for Zimbabwean nationals that the government introduced in April 2009, and resuming deportations of those without the new special permits. After the January 2011 lifting of the moratorium on deporting Zimbabweans, they have two options to lawfully enter and remain in South Africa: apply for asylum, or apply for a temporary residence permit under the Immigration Rules' work, study and business provisions. Most are unlikely to qualify under either regime. South Africa's Department of Home Affairs already had a backlog of 309,794 unresolved applications at the end of 2009, according to the UN High Commissioner for Refugees.

Socioeconomic Rights

Millions of South Africans suffer from inadequate access to shelter, water, educa-tion, and health care. South Africa is unlikely to meet the UN health-related Millennium Development Goals (MDGs), and is one of only eight countries in the region where the rate of maternal deaths seems to be increasing. The South African government estimates that the maternal mortality ratio was 625 deaths per 100,000 live births in 2007, up from 150 deaths per 100,000 live births in 1998. The under-five mortality rate was 104 deaths per 1000 live births in 2007, up from 59 deaths in 1998, while the infant mortality rate was 53 deaths per 1,000 live births in 2007, compared to 54 in 2001.

South Africa also has one of the world's largest populations affected by HIV/AIDS, with more than 5 million people living with HIV, and more than 1 million needing AIDS treatment. The country's response to the epidemic has significantly improved under Health Minister Aaron Motsoaledi. On April 25 the government launched the HIV Testing and Counseling campaign (HTC), which aims to see 15 million people accepting voluntary HIV testing and counseling by 2011, and 1.5 million receiving antiretroviral treatment by June 2011. However, weaknesses in

South Africa's public health system are already hampering the campaign's success.

Sexual Orientation and Gender Identity

While South Africa has attempted to foster a culture of tolerance by outlawing discrimination based on sexual orientation and by legalizing same-sex unions,
social conservatism means that gays, lesbians, and gender-nonconforming individuals remain vulnerable to violence and discrimination. In a study by the
Human Sciences Research Council (HSRC) in 2008, over 80 percent of respondents across age groups "consistently" expressed the view that sex between two
men or two women "was always wrong," and that gays and lesbians were "un-
African." The cases of Sizakele Sigasa and Salome Masooa, who were tortured,
raped, and brutally murdered on July 7, 2007, in Soweto, as well as subsequent
cases of Eudy Simelane, Zoliswa Nonkonyane, and others has highlighted the vulnerability of black lesbians and gender-nonconforming individuals to violence
and hate crimes. The 07-07-07 Campaign continues to take up cases of violence
against black lesbians and gender-nonconforming individuals, and advocate for
an end to hate crimes. However, the government has yet to develop and implement measures to end these human rights abuses.

International Role

South Africa plays a significant role on the African continent, where it is one of
the largest contributors to peacekeeping missions and a key player on regional
bodies, such as the African Union and the Southern African Development
Community.

South Africa continues to drive mediation efforts in Zimbabwe, which have taken
a bolder approach toward President Robert Mugabe under President Jacob
Zuma's stewardship. Yet South Africa has not publicly pushed Zimbabwe's coalition government on key rights reforms and the need to end ongoing violations. It
failed to condemn the violence that erupted in Zimbabwe during September's
constitution-outreach process, and neglected to speak out against abuses committed in the Marange diamond fields in eastern Zimbabwe, despite ample evidence that the Zimbabwean military is using forced adult and child labor.

At a high-level meeting on Sudan in September, organized by UN Secretary-General Ban Ki-moon, International Relations Minister Maite Nkoane-Mashabane appealed for international support to guarantee a peaceful referendum outcome in January in South Sudan and Abyei. South Africa has also supported the work of the AU Panel on Sudan and contributed to the joint AU-UN operation in Darfur (UNAMID).

In 2010 South Africa lobbied aggressively and successfully to regain a non-permanent seat at the UN Security Council, which will allow it to exert influence on key international issues. Its past performance in multilateral institutions has been disappointing from a human rights perspective. As a member of the Security Council in 2007-2008, South Africa opposed a resolution condemning abuses by the military junta in Burma, while at the UN Human Rights Council in 2007, South Africa attempted to block discussions of rights abuses in Zimbabwe and voted to end monitoring of abuses in Iran and Uzbekistan. South Africa's seat on the UN Security Council beginning in 2011 affords the country an opportunity to translate its constitutional commitment to human rights into critical involvement on international issues where protecting human rights is a central concern.

SUDAN

Sudan's human rights environment deteriorated in 2010 during the April elections and in the months leading up to the historic referendum on southern self-determination, scheduled for early January 2011. The referendum was called for as part of the 2005 Comprehensive Peace Agreement (CPA), which ended Sudan's 22-year civil war.

The April multi-party national elections, also prescribed by the CPA, were marked by serious human rights violations and resulted in the consolidation of power for both the national ruling National Congress Party (NCP) and the Sudan People's Liberation Movement (SPLM), which controls Southern Sudan. Omar al-Bashir – subject of an arrest warrant from the International Criminal Court for crimes committed in Darfur – was re-elected president of the national government, and Salva Kiir as president of Southern Sudan and vice president of the national government.

In the second half of the year domestic and international attention shifted to the referendum, in which southerners will vote to either remain part of a united Sudan or secede. Should southerners secede, a parallel referendum in Abyei, the disputed oil-rich area straddling the north-south divide, will determine whether that area remains part of Sudan or joins Southern Sudan.

The parties made slow progress in resolving key issues around the referendum such as voter eligibility in the Abyei referendum, and post-referendum arrangements concerning citizenship rights, oil- and wealth-sharing, and debt allocations.

Darfur, in western Sudan, saw continued large-scale attacks by government forces on rebel forces and civilians, as well as an increase in armed clashes between ethnic groups, particularly in South and West Darfur. The United Nations and humanitarian agencies increasingly came under attack and were targeted for robberies, kidnappings, and killings by armed elements in Sudan's western region.

In January the parliament amended the Child Act, setting 18 years as the legal age of majority. The previous year Sudan executed Abdulrahman Zakaria Mohammed in El Fasher, North Darfur, for a crime he committed at the age of 17. It remains unclear whether the amendments to the child act will lead to a ban on the juvenile death penalty in accordance with international law.

Rights Abuses in National Elections

Human Rights Watch documented numerous rights violations across Sudan by both northern and southern authorities in connection with the April elections. International and domestic election observers reported widespread technical irregularities such as multiple voting, ballot-stuffing, and other acts of fraud.

In the months leading up to the elections in the north, the ruling NCP arrested opposition party observers and civil society groups, suppressed peaceful assemblies by opposition party members in the north, and restricted free association and speech. During the week of the election, there were fewer cases of such restrictions, but Human Rights Watch documented several cases of harassment, intimidation, and arrests of opposition members and election observers in the north.

In Darfur, continued insecurity presented an obstacle to holding free and fair elections. Large areas of Darfur were inaccessible to election officials and candidates; insecurity due to banditry and ongoing conflict restricted candidates' freedom of movement.

In Southern Sudan, throughout the elections process, security forces engaged in widespread intimidation, arbitrary arrest, detention, and mistreatment of opponents of the SPLM as well as of election observers and voters.

In the weeks following the elections the human rights situation across Sudan deteriorated, with renewed political repression in the north, incidents of election-related violence in the south, particularly where SPLM candidates ran against independent candidates, and ongoing conflict in Darfur. The lack of accountability for abuses during the elections did not bode well for a free and fair referendum process nine months later.

Political Repression in Northern Sudan

The national government failed to enact institutional and legal reforms, which are required by the CPA. The national legal framework continues to allow censorship of the press and restrictions on freedom of assembly and political expression. The new National Security Act, passed in January, retains broad powers of arrest and detention for up to four-and-a-half months, in violation of international treaties to which Sudan is a party. Legal immunities for security forces remain in place.

The post-election crackdown in Khartoum, Sudan's capital in the north, included the May 15 arrest and six week detention of the opposition figure Hassan al-Turabi and the arrest of four journalists from *Rai al Shaab*, the newspaper affiliated with al-Turabi's Popular Congress Party (PCP). One of the journalists was subjected to electric shocks while in the custody of national security agents. In July three of the journalists received prison sentences on charges of "attempting to destabilize the constitutional system."

In addition, authorities resumed pre-print censorship, a practice that al-Bashir publicly declared had ended in September 2009. Officials banned articles that reported on the arrests of al-Turabi and the journalists, and the escalating violence in Darfur. In the weeks that followed authorities continued to censor papers through site visits and telephone calls to editors—what Sudanese journalists call "remote control censorship"—and shut down several newspapers.

National security forces continued to harass human rights activists and target student members of the United Popular Front (UPF), a student group that the government alleges has links to the Darfuri rebel group led by Abdel Wahid al-Nur. Members of the group were subjected to arrest, detention, ill-treatment, and torture.

Insecurity and Human Rights Violations in Southern Sudan

Vote-rigging and intimidation during the elections in the south led to anger and frustration. Grievances over the election results led to armed clashes, particularly in areas where the SPLM faced strong opposition.

SUDAN

Democracy on Hold

Rights Violations in the April 2010 Sudan Elections

HUMAN
RIGHTS
WATCH

In northern Jonglei state, for example, forces loyal to a former deputy chief of staff of the Sudan People's Liberation Army (SPLA) who unsuccessfully ran for state governor as an independent candidate, clashed with the SPLA on multiple occasions after the results were announced. The SPLA's efforts to capture the renegade commander resulted in numerous human rights abuses against the civilian population in northern Jonglei including sexual violence. In Upper Nile state, SPLA soldiers clashed with local militia whom they accused of links to the SPLM-DC, a breakaway political party led by former SPLM leader Lam Akol. The soldiers were responsible for killings and rapes of civilians during these operations.

Patterns of intercommunal violence stemming from cattle-rustling and other localized disputes across Southern Sudan continued to put civilians at risk of physical violence and killings. The Lord's Resistance Army also continued to pose a significant security threat in western parts of the region, with attacks, abductions, and killings reported on a monthly basis.

Neither the Government of Southern Sudan nor the UN Mission in Sudan has adequately been able to protect civilians from these sources of violence. Weaknesses in the justice sector and lack of accountability mechanisms fostered an environment of impunity for violence and human rights violations.

Civil and Political Rights and the Referendum

In the weeks preceding the referendum, Southern Sudanese communities living in Khartoum and other northern states reported heightened anxiety over the status of their citizenship rights following the referendum. NCP officials publicly threatened that southerners may not be able to stay in the north in the event of a secession vote. A higher-than usual number of southerners returned to Southern Sudan toward the end of 2010, with tens of thousands arriving in southern states during voter registration in November. Although SPLM and Government of Southern Sudan officials stated that they would protect the rights of northerners living in the South, some northern traders reported facing intimidation and moved to northern states. As of mid-November, however, the two ruling parties had not formally agreed to post-referendum citizenship arrangements. Both southerners in the north and northerners living in Southern Sudan said that they feared retaliation, even expulsion, if secession were approved.

Journalists and civil society activists across the country reported that they were not free to speak openly about any opposition to the prevailing sentiment regarding the outcome of the referendum. In October security forces arrested a group of southern students speaking out in support of secession at a pro-unity rally in Khartoum, underscoring growing tensions. Although the head of the national security service in early August lifted pre-print censorship in northern states, repressive policies toward the media have caused many Khartoum-based papers to self-censor on sensitive topics, including the referendum outcome.

Deterioration in Darfur

Fighting in Darfur intensified in 2010, with armed clashes between government and rebel forces, among rebel factions, and between armed ethnic Arab groups in South and West Darfur. In Jebel Mara, a stronghold of the Sudan Liberation Army (SLA) faction led by Abdel Wahid al-Nur, fighting among SLA groups over support for the Doha, Qatar peace talks and clashes between government forces and rebels continued throughout the year. Government attacks on Jebel Mara intensified again in September, destroying dozens of villages and causing mass displacements. In Jebel Mun, another rebel stronghold, and elsewhere, clashes between government forces and the Justice and Equality Movement (JEM) intensified early in the year, following the January rapprochement between Chad and Sudan, in which both governments agreed to end support to rebel groups fighting in each other's territory and to jointly patrol their common border.

The UN-African Union Mission in Darfur (UNAMID) was unable to access most of the areas affected by violence, despite its mandate to protect civilians under imminent threat of physical violence. Both government and rebel authorities blocked the peacekeepers and humanitarian agencies at various times. An increase in banditry, abductions, and attacks on UN and humanitarian aid operations undermined the international response.

Meanwhile the peace process at Doha foundered. JEM and the SLA faction led by Abdel Wahid al-Nur and other groups boycotted the process, leaving only one rebel group, the Liberation and Justice Movement (LJM), to negotiate.

In September the Sudanese government released a new strategy on Darfur that focused on the return of displaced persons to their home villages. The plan did not provide clear safeguards for the rights of displaced persons, such as their voluntary return. The government repeated its intention to dismantle the camps, particularly the volatile South Darfur Kalma camp, where political violence between armed groups killed 10 people in August.

Between October 30 and November 3, Sudanese national security officials arrested and detained more than 10 Darfuri activists and journalists in Khartoum, and continue to hold them in unknown locations without access to family or lawyers. The arrests were widely viewed as a means to suppress information and advocacy on Darfur.

Key International Actors

International engagement on Sudan increased and intensified with the elections and referendum, particularly by key CPA stakeholder countries like the United States. The UN continues to deploy two major peacekeeping missions in the country: the UN Mission in Sudan (UNMIS) and UNAMID.

On September 24 the UN convened a high-level meeting on Sudan in which the Sudanese parties to the CPA and 40 heads of state re-affirmed their commitment to a timely, peaceful referendum in January 2011.

With the focus on the referendum, international attention shifted away from Darfur, despite the deteriorating situation there and lack of progress on a peace deal. The Sudanese government made little progress in implementing recommendations of the AU High Level Panel on Darfur; the AU and other influential leaders did not press the government to do so. In general, the key stakeholder countries engaged on Sudan continued to be divided in approach and willingness to use pressure to influence the Sudanese government.

In Geneva, in September, the UN Human Rights Council renewed the mandate of the Independent Expert on Sudan, maintaining a much-needed avenue for human rights reporting, over objections from Sudan and its allies. The two major peacekeeping missions in Sudan, UNMIS and UNAMID, did not publicly report on their human rights concerns except through regular reports to the UN secretary-general.

The ICC continued its investigation of crimes committed in Darfur and issued a second arrest warrant for President al-Bashir in July 2010, adding genocide to charges on war crimes and crimes against humanity. The same month, the AU reiterated a July 2009 call for its member states not to cooperate in the arrest of al-Bashir. In a setback for accountability Kenya and Chad – both states parties to the ICC – allowed al-Bashir to enter their territories in July and August, citing the AU decision.

UGANDA

Freedoms of assembly and expression in Uganda have come under attack in 2010, the pressure intensifying in advance of presidential and parliamentary elections scheduled for February 2011. Journalists critical of the government face intimidation and sometimes criminal charges from state agents and members of the ruling party. Security and quasi-military organizations continue to illegally detain and torture suspects, in some instances leading to death. Impunity for human rights abuses persists. For example, Uganda failed to carry out investigations or prosecutions for the deaths of at least 40 people killed, some by military police, in riots in September 2009.

On July 11, 2010, two bomb blasts in Kampala, the capital, killed 76 people who had gathered to watch the football World Cup final. The Somali armed Islamist group al-Shabaab claimed responsibility and threatened further attacks if Uganda continued to supply troops to the African Union Mission in Somalia (AMISOM). Uganda arrested scores of suspects, charged 36 with terrorism, and eventually committed 17 for trial. The judiciary issued an injunction barring the press from covering the investigations and, on July 28, police broke up an opposition demonstration, stating that public gatherings were banned until the perpetrators of the bombings were arrested.

Some fear of violence around the 2011 elections was furthered by irregularities surrounding the ruling National Resistance Movement primaries in August 2010. Roughly 350 petitions were filed with the party's electoral commission, alleging beatings, intimidation, and bribery. Investigations are ongoing at this writing.

Freedoms of Assembly and Expression

Opposition demonstrations protesting the composition of the electoral commission were met with police brutality. For example, in January 33 women from an opposition coalition were charged with illegal assembly, and in June police severely beat these women as they exited a court appearance causing four to be hospitalized.

Ugandan officials have repeatedly failed to hold state actors involved in election-related violence accountable. That continued in 2010, for example in March at the Rukiga by-election, where police detained six opposition supporters and beat others who attempted to bring food to detainees leaving one person in a coma. Police were not charged with any crime.

In June an ad hoc group known as the *kiboko* (stick) squad assaulted Forum for Democratic Change presidential candidate Kizza Besigye and other opposition leaders at a rally in Kampala. The opposition accused the state of supporting and mobilizing the squad. Police denied the allegations, but failed on several occasions to arrest squad members. In July police in 13 towns arrested at least 80 people during a nationwide demonstration against the electoral commission. In Mbale, eastern Uganda, police used their guns to strike unarmed opposition demonstrators.

The Ugandan government uses media and penal laws to prosecute journalists, restrict who can lawfully work as a journalist, and revoke broadcasting licenses without due process. Journalists face harassment and threats, especially outside the capital. After being forced off air by security agents during the September 2009 riots, CBS Radio was permitted to operate again in October 2010. The government never provided evidence in court of any wrongdoing.

In August the constitutional court ruled, after five years, that the crime of sedition is unconstitutional. The court upheld the constitutionality of the crime of "promoting sectarianism," which prohibits any act promoting "feelings of ill will or hostility" on account of religion, tribe, ethnicity, or regional origin. At least four journalists and some opposition politicians who criticized alleged government favoritism of some ethnicities over others currently face this charge, which has effectively silenced debate.

At this writing, the government is considering draft amendments to the media law, which would further imperil freedom of expression.

Extrajudicial Killings, Torture, and Illegal Detention

As the Ugandan People's Defence Force (UPDF) continued a disarmament exercise in the northeast region of Karamoja, soldiers have killed civilians with impunity.

A Media Minefield

Increased Threats to Freedom of Expression in Uganda

**HUMAN
RIGHTS
WATCH**

"As If We Weren't Human"

Discrimination and Violence Against Women
with Disabilities in Northern Uganda

HUMAN
RIGHTS
WATCH

The Uganda Human Rights Commission stated that soldiers killed civilians, including children and the elderly, in Kotido district, and two Karamoja parliamentarians accused the army of killing between 48 and 55 civilians between April and August. UPDF officials acknowledged that soldiers killed 10 Karamojong, four of them children, during crossfire on April 24 in Kotido, but said that no soldiers would be punished.

The Rapid Response Unit (RRU), formerly known as Operation Wembley and the Violent Crimes Crack Unit, a section of the police created to combat armed crime, continues to detain people without charge, well beyond the constitutionally mandated 48 hours. At least two individuals died this year as a result of torture in RRU custody. Those arrested by the RRU await trial before military courts for long periods of time. The slowness of the military courts has resulted in instances of defendants serving longer periods on remand than would result from the maximum sentence for their charges.

The RRU in September arrested Kenyan human rights activist Al-Amin Kimathi, who had criticized the handover of Kenyan suspects in the July bombings to the Ugandan authorities without due process. Kimathi was detained for six days without charge, denied access to a lawyer, and eventually charged with terrorism in the July bombing. At this writing, he is awaiting trial with 16 other suspects. Human Rights Watch was denied access to all the detainees on this file.

Bills Violating International Human Rights Law

Indicating a troubling authoritarian trend as elections loom, Parliament and the Cabinet drafted and debated a raft of repressive legislation.

The draft Public Order Management Bill would grant the inspector general of police and the minister of internal affairs wide discretionary powers over the management of all public meetings. The draft bill imposes extensive obligations on meeting organizers, which violates rights to freedom of assembly and speech. The bill would also allow state actors to regulate the conduct and content of discussions. The Constitutional Court has already deemed some of these provisions unconstitutional in previous cases.

The draft Press and Journalist Amendment Bill requires print media to be annually registered and licensed by government regulatory bodies. It empowers the Media Council to deny licenses based on its assessment of the newspaper's "values" and revoke them at will.

Homosexual conduct is already criminalized in Uganda, a violation of international standards, but the proposed 2009 Anti-Homosexuality Bill would go further, punishing homosexuality with up to life imprisonment, and "serial" homosexuality with the death penalty. The bill, still pending at this writing, would also punish failure to report acts of homosexuality and prohibit the "promotion" of homosexuality through advocacy on sexual minority rights, threatening work of human rights groups. In early October 2010 a new newspaper, *Rolling Stone*, published photographs, names, and locations of some Ugandan lesbian, gay, bisexual, and transgender rights activists and individuals under a headline that included the phrase "Hang Them." Some have since gone into hiding. The government has taken no action to protect them. The High Court issued a temporary injunction barring further publication of such articles, though *Rolling Stone* went on to allege that sexual minorities supported the July bombings.

The draft HIV/AIDS Prevention and Control Act criminalizes intentional or attempted transmission of HIV, an approach discredited by international principles. Contravening international standards of voluntary counseling and testing the bill also makes testing mandatory for pregnant women, their partners, and other specified groups. The bill allows medical practitioners to disclose HIV status without the patient's consent potentially exposing women and girls to domestic violence.

Lord's Resistance Army

While relative calm continued to prevail in northern Uganda, the Ugandan armed rebel group the Lord's Resistance Army (LRA) continued killings and abductions across Central African Republic, southern Sudan and northern Democratic Republic of Congo (see chapter on the DRC).

Warrants issued by the International Criminal Court for LRA leaders in 2005 remain outstanding. President Museveni reportedly signed a bill domesticating

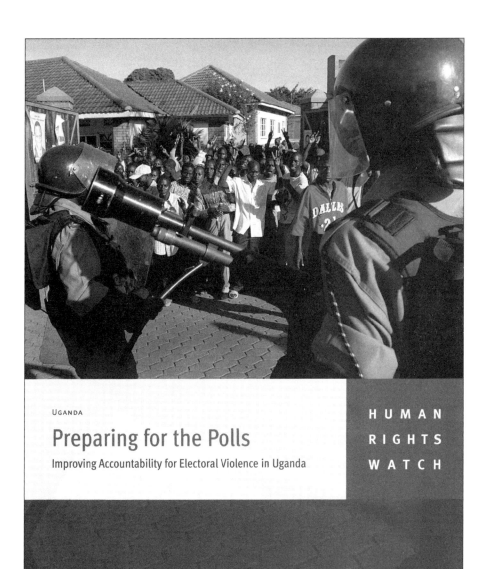

Preparing for the Polls

Improving Accountability for Electoral Violence in Uganda

HUMAN
RIGHTS
WATCH

the Rome Statute in May prior to the ICC Review Conference in Kampala. The newly created War Crimes Division of the Ugandan High Court is expected to begin its first trial in 2011 of LRA fighter Thomas Kwoyelo, charged with willful killing, taking hostages, and extensive destruction of property. Kwoyelo has applied for amnesty.

Refugees and Internally Displaced Persons

After two decades of conflict in Uganda's northern region, internally displaced persons (IDPs) have largely moved out of the camps. For persons with disabilities there are significant hurdles to returning home. Research by Human Rights Watch found that women with disabilities experience stigma and isolation, gender-based violence, and obstacles in accessing health care and justice.

The government, cooperating with Rwandan authorities, forcibly repatriated more than 1,700 Rwandan refugees and asylum seekers from southwestern Uganda in July. Ugandan officials reportedly deceived the residents of Kyaka and Nakivale camps into gathering around trucks by announcing a food distribution and information on asylum appeals. Police and camp commanders then forced the residents onto the trucks at gunpoint. In the ensuing panic 25 people were injured and at least two died.

Key International Actors

Uganda's Joint Budget Support partners—the European Commission, the World Bank, the United Kingdom, Germany, Demark, Belgium, Ireland, Norway, the Netherlands, Austria, and Sweden—reduced their US$360 million contribution to Uganda's budget by 10 percent due to concerns about unaddressed corruption.

A range of international actors, including United States President Barack Obama, actively condemned the Anti-Homosexuality Bill, which appeared to have contributed to retarding the bill's progress in Parliament. Other key human rights issues, particularly accountability for extrajudicial killings and torture by state agents, were not raised with similar zeal.

The US and the UK, among other donors, put significant effort into enhancing the election process in advance of 2011, including training for police in public order management and support to reduce legal and regulatory restrictions on freedom of expression. Some raised concerns about the independence of the electoral commission, but the government made no concessions.

The US continues to provide considerable logistical support and training to the Ugandan army, both in counterterrorism efforts and for the ongoing UPDF-led operations against the LRA. The FBI provided substantial resources to investigate the July 11 bombings, but denied reports that its agents were present during interrogations of suspects.

ZIMBABWE

Two years into Zimbabwe's power-sharing government, President Robert Mugabe and the Zimbabwe African National Union- Patriotic Front (ZANU-PF) have used violence and repression to continue to dominate government institutions and hamper meaningful human rights progress. The former opposition party, the Movement for Democratic Change (MDC), lacks real power to institute its political agenda and end human rights abuses.

The power-sharing government has not investigated widespread abuses, including killings, torture, beatings, and other ill-treatment committed by the army, ZANU-PF supporters, and officials against real and perceived supporters of the MDC.

Political Violence during Constitutional Outreach Program

In 2010 the power-sharing government began a series of community outreach meetings called the Constitutional Outreach Program to elicit popular views on a new constitution. However, the meetings were marked by increasing violence and intimidation, mainly by ZANU-PF supporters and war veterans allied to ZANU-PF. In February police disrupted MDC-organized preparatory constitutional reform meetings, beat participants, and arbitrarily arrested 43 people in Binga, 48 in Masvingo, and 52 in Mt. Darwin. The violence worsened in Harare, the capital, and led to the suspension of 13 meetings in September.

On September 19, ZANU-PF supporters attacked MDC supporters and prevented some from attending an outreach meeting in Mbare, Harare. The meeting ended when violence broke out. ZANU-PF supporters and uniformed police assaulted 11 residents and MDC supporters from Mbare with blunt objects as they left the meeting. One resident, Chrispen Mandizvidza, died from his injuries on September 22.

Human Rights Violations in Marange Diamond Fields

Diamond revenue, particularly from the Marange diamond fields in eastern Zimbabwe, is providing a parallel source of revenue for ZANU-PF and its repres-

ZIMBABWE

Deliberate Chaos

Ongoing Human Rights Abuses
in the Marange Diamond Fields of Zimbabwe

HUMAN
RIGHTS
WATCH

ZIMBABWE

Sleight of Hand

Repression of the Media and the Illusion of Reform in Zimbabwe

HUMAN
RIGHTS
WATCH

sive state apparatus. Companies with connections to ZANU-PF are mining diamonds in Marange, where military control and abuses continue. Corruption is rife, and smuggling of diamonds by soldiers in the fields is prolific. The diamond revenues continue to benefit a few senior people in the government and their associates rather than the people of Zimbabwe. Soldiers continue to perpetrate abuses in Marange, including forced labor, beatings, and harassment, which Zimbabwe's government has failed to investigate or prosecute.

State security agents have harassed local civil society organizations attempting to document smuggling and abuses in the fields. On June 3, police arrested Farai Maguwu, the head of the Centre for Research and Development, after he provided sensitive information on the activities of soldiers in the fields to Abbey Chikane, a monitor appointed by the Kimberley Process Certification Scheme, an international body that oversees the diamond trade (also known as the Kimberley Process). Police also beat, arrested, and detained members of Maguwu's family. Maguwu was charged with "communicating and publishing falsehoods against the State with the intention to cause prejudice to the security or economic interests of the country" under section 31 of the Criminal Law (Codification and Reform) Act.

The Kimberley Process has struggled to address state abuses in the fields. It's mandate narrowly defines "blood diamonds" as those mined by abusive rebel groups, not abusive governments. In November 2010, at their annual meeting in Jerusalem, Israel, Kimberley Process members failed to reach a consensus on whether Zimbabwe should be allowed to resume exports of diamonds from parts of the Marange diamond fields. However, Zimbabwe threatened to go ahead with diamond exports, arguing that it had met the minimum standards required by the Kimberley Process.

Media Freedom and Freedom of Expression

With ZANU-PF still in control, the power-sharing government continues to use an arsenal of repressive legislation and unlawful tactics to restrict the right to freedom of expression, and harass and punish critical journalists. While the government has lifted restrictions on the international media and allowed independent local daily papers to resume operations, it has not reformed media-related laws as promised. It has also not reviewed criminal defamation laws that impose severe penalties, including prison terms, on journalists. The government continues to block free expression through senior officials aligned to ZANU-PF and partisan state security agents.

Journalists and media practitioners routinely face arrest for allegedly violating the state's repressive media laws. On January 17, police arrested Barnabas Madzimure and Fortune Mutandiro, two directors of a distribution company for *The Zimbabwean,* a weekly newspaper published in South Africa and distributed in Zimbabwe. The police questioned them for two hours about the operations of the newspaper and then released them. On February 11, they were charged as accomplices in "publishing falsehoods prejudicial to the state" in violation of the Criminal Law (Codification and Reform) Act.

Journalists and media outlets have also been subjected to threats and harassment from the authorities and security forces, creating major obstacles to reporting on Zimbabwe's political system and continuing abuses by ZANU-PF. On January 16 freelance journalist Stanley Kwenda was forced to flee the country, following death threats from a senior police officer. The death threats were prompted by a story that Kwenda wrote for *The Zimbabwean*. The story reported that a named senior police officer had barred Prime Minister Morgan Tsvangirai from visiting police stations across the country.

In an example of restrictions on freedom of expression, police arrested artist Owen Maseko on March 26 after he displayed an exhibition that portrayed massacres that took place in Matabeleland in the 1980s, allegedly carried out by troops loyal to President Mugabe. Maseko was initially arrested on charges of violating section 33 of the Criminal Law (Codification and Reform) Act for insulting or undermining the authority of the president. The charges were later altered to section 31 of the same act which deals with the publication of false statements prejudicial to the state. Maseko spent four days in police custody before he was released on bail, and is awaiting trial at this writing.

Human Rights Defenders

The working environment for human rights defenders continues to be restrictive. For example, 83 men and women from the group Women of Zimbabwe Arise were arrested in Harare on September 20 as they demonstrated against the lack of professionalism by the Zimbabwean police. The group was detained at the Harare Central Police Station for two days. On September 22 they were charged with criminal nuisance under the Criminal Law (Codification and Reform) Act and released on free bail.

In a raid at the offices of the organization Gays and Lesbians of Zimbabwe (GALZ) on May 21, police arrested staff members Ellen Chadenama and Ignatius Mhambi, charging them with possession of "obscene, indecent or prohibited articles" and confiscating educational material. On May 24 a Zimbabwean magistrate's court added the charge of "undermining authority of or insulting [the] president" because the GALZ office displayed a placard that made a critical reference to President Mugabe. Two days later police searched the house of the acting director of GALZ, confiscating his birth certificate, several GALZ magazines, books, and business cards. Chadenama and Mhambi spent six days in detention before they were released on bail; they pleaded not guilty to the charges. Mhambi and Chadenama reported that they were physically assaulted by the police while in custody. Mhambi said that police hit him with empty glass bottles on his knees. The arrests, which Human Rights Watch considers to be politically motivated, occurred shortly before the opening of the Constitutional Outreach Program, through which GALZ is seeking to remove discriminatory provisions and secure constitutional protections for lesbian, gay, bisexual, and transgender people. The trial is ongoing at this writing although Mthambi has been acquitted of the first charge.

Rule of Law

In a worrying development for respect for the rule of law, heads of state of the Southern African Development Community (SADC), at their annual summit in August, upheld Zimbabwe's objections to the jurisdiction of the SADC Tribunal. Zimbabwe formally withdrew from the tribunal, arguing that the court did not exist by law. In 2008 the tribunal ruled in favor of 79 white commercial farmers who took the government to the tribunal in a bid to block the compulsory acquisition of their farms by the state, and has made a number of other rulings against the state. Zimbabwe's courts have refused to enforce rulings by the tribunal.

Key International Actors

The South African government deepened its engagement with the power-sharing government, but failed to make full use of its leverage to ensure meaningful human rights improvements. Despite visiting the country several times, President Jacob Zuma and his mediation team have failed to engage the power-sharing government on critical issues that include cessation of human rights abuses, institutional reform targeting constitutional and electoral processes, as well as security sector reform.

Instead Zuma and other heads of state from the SADC community have called for the lifting of targeted sanctions against President Mugabe and his inner circle, arguing that these were a major obstacle to the progress of the power-sharing government. In September SADC announced that it had asked for regional leaders to embark on a tour of the United States and European Union calling for the lifting of sanctions. In the absence of meaningful progress, the US and the EU have maintained targeted sanctions on Mugabe and others within his government.

Paramilitaries' Heirs

The New Face of Violence in Colombia

WORLD REPORT

2011

AMERICAS

ARGENTINA

Argentina continues to make significant progress in prosecuting military and police personnel for "disappearances," killings, and torture during the country's "dirty war" in the 1980s, although trials have been subject to delays.

Argentina passed legislation to regulate broadcast and print media in 2010, and is considering bills to promote access to information. The impact of the new media legislation on freedom of expression in Argentina will depend on how it is implemented by a new regulatory body established by the law. A landmark law passed in July legalized same-sex marriage.

Significant ongoing rights concerns include deplorable prison conditions and arbitrary restrictions on women's reproductive rights.

Confronting Past Abuses

Several important human rights cases from Argentina's last military dictatorship (1976-1983) were reopened in 2003 after Congress annulled the 1986 "Full Stop" law, which had forced a halt to the prosecution of all such cases, and the 1987 "Due Obedience" law, which granted automatic immunity in such cases to all members of the military except those in positions of command. Starting in 2005 federal judges struck down pardons issued by then-president Carlos Menem in 1989-90 of former officials convicted or facing trial for human rights violations.

As of October 2010, 748 people were facing charges for these crimes and 81 had been convicted. In December 2009, after long delays, the trial began of 19 officers who worked in the infamous Navy Mechanics School (ESMA) for their alleged responsibility for the torture and enforced disappearance of 87 victims. In April 2010 former military president Gen. Reynaldo Bignone received a 25 year prison sentence for the kidnapping and torture of 56 people at the Campo de Mayo military camp on the outskirts of Buenos Aires.

Delays in judicial proceedings, however, continue to undermine accountability. According to the Center for Legal and Social Studies (CELS), by October 2010, 253 people implicated in crimes committed during the dictatorship had died before being brought to justice. One of the main causes of delay was the failure to allocate sufficient courtrooms in Buenos Aires. There have also been long delays at the appellate level: as of March 2010 the Supreme Court had confirmed final sentences in only two of the cases reactivated after the annulment of the amnesty laws.

The security of witnesses in human rights trials continues to be a serious concern. Jorge Julio López, age 78, a former torture victim who "disappeared" from his home in September 2006,the day before he was due to attend one of the final days of a trial, remains missing.

In September the government filed a criminal complaint charging the owner and president of the newspaper *Clarin*, the director of *La Nacion*, and the former owners of *La Razon* with crimes against humanity. The complaint alleged that the three newspapers had illegally appropriated the newsprint company Papel Prensa in 1976, during the military dictatorship. In 1977 government agents kidnapped and tortured five members of the Graiver family, which owned majority shares in Papel Prensa. The government alleges that representatives of the newspapers, in concert with the military government, used threats to pressure the members of the family into signing over their shares. *Clarin* and *La Nacion* insisted that the acquisition of the shares was legal and denied any link between their purchase and the detention of the Graiver family. They accused the government of attacking the papers because of their criticism of President Cristina Fernández de Kirchner.

Freedom of Expression and Information

A bill to regulate the broadcast media, approved by Congress in October 2009, aims to promote diversity of views by limiting the ability of corporations to own large portions of the radio frequency spectrum. The new law contains vague definitions of what "faults" could lead to sanctions such as the revocation of broadcasting licenses. Responsibility for interpreting and implementing the law is assigned to a new regulatory body. Courts have issued injunctions suspending the application of some of its articles while they review the law.

 In October 2010 commissions of the Chamber of Deputies approved draft legislation presented by President Fernández to regulate the company that produces and distributes paper for newsprint in Argentina. The law would also declare that the supply of newsprint is a matter of public interest, granting oversight powers to an implementing body that reports to the executive.

In 2010 both chambers of Congress debated bills to ensure public access to information held by state bodies. In September the Senate approved a bill presented by an opposition senator to ensure public access to information held by all three branches of government as well as other public institutions such as universities, state-funded enterprises, and the Central Bank. The bill would establish a body to apply the regulations, with members appointed by each branch of government, the ombudsman, the comptroller general, and the National Archive. By October Congress had not yet agreed on a final text.

The absence of transparent criteria for allocating government advertising contracts, at the federal level and in some provinces, creates a risk of political discrimination against media outlets that criticize government officials. In a case against the provincial government of Neuquen, the Supreme Court ruled in September 2007 that, while media companies have no right to government advertising revenue, officials may not apply discriminatory criteria in deciding where to place advertisements. Several bills to regulate the matter remain pending.

Judicial Independence

President Fernández, her husband (former president Néstor Kirchner, who died in October 2010), and high level authorities repeatedly questioned decisions adopted by the judiciary in 2010. For example, in September the Supreme Court ordered the province of Santa Cruz to reinstate a former state attorney general who had been removed from his post in 1995, when former President Kirchner was governor of Santa Cruz, without following the legal procedure for his removal. President Fernández supported the governor, who refused to reinstate the attorney general, and stated that the ruling was unconstitutional.

Transnational Justice

To date no one has been convicted for the 1994 bombing of the Jewish Argentine Mutual Association in Buenos Aires (AMIA), in which 85 people died and over 300 were injured. Criminal investigations and prosecutions have been hindered by judicial corruption and political cover-ups in Argentina, and by the failure of Iran, which is suspected of ordering the attack, to cooperate with the Argentine justice system. An Argentine federal court issued an international warrant for the arrest of former Iranian president Ali Akbar Hashemi-Rafsanjani and six Iranian officials in 2006, but demands for their extradition fell on deaf ears. In a speech at the United Nations in September 2010 President Fernández offered Iranian President Mahmoud Ahmadinejad the possibility of holding the trials in a neutral third country. In a letter to the UN in October Iran rejected the proposal as "unsustainable."

In September 2010 the Argentine Supreme Court approved a request by Chile for the extradition of Galvarino Apablaza, a Chilean citizen facing criminal investigation for his alleged role in the assassination of former Chilean senator Jaime Guzmán, a close civilian advisor of General Pinochet. A former leader of a left-wing armed group, Apablaza was also wanted in Chile for allegedly ordering the kidnapping of the son of a prominent newspaper owner. Both crimes were committed in 1991 after Chile's return to democratic rule. The Supreme Court ruled that the crimes were not political and approved the extradition subject to a ruling by Argentina's National Refugee Commission (CONARE) on Apablaza's long-standing request for political asylum in Argentina. CONARE, an inter-ministerial panel on which only government officials have the right to vote, decided unanimously to grant Apablaza political asylum. The grounds for the decision were not made public.

Conditions in Detention Facilities

Overcrowding, abuses by guards, and inmate violence continue to be serious problems in detention facilities. In a landmark ruling in May 2005 the Supreme Court declared that all prisons in the country must abide by the UN Standard Minimum Rules for the Treatment of Prisoners, highlighting the deplorable conditions in the province of Buenos Aires. According to a report submitted to the Supreme Court in October 2009 by CELS, 4,507 people were being held in police stations in the province which are unsuited for long-term detention. CELS estimated that the provincial prison population was nearly 40 percent above capacity, the figure rising to nearly 65 percent if individuals held in police stations were included. Responding to this report in March 2010 the court again urged the province's Supreme Court to correct the "inhuman conditions" in detention facilities.

Detainee and prisoner access to medicines and medical services continues to be inadequate in many facilities despite HIV prevalence rates far higher than in the general population and conditions conducive to ill health.

Reproductive Rights and Marriage

Women face numerous obstacles to reproductive health products and services such as contraception, voluntary sterilization procedures, and abortion after rape. The most common barriers are long delays in obtaining services, unnecessary referrals to other clinics, demands for spousal permission contrary to law, financial barriers, and, in some cases, arbitrary denials. As a direct result of these barriers, women and girls may face unwanted or unhealthy pregnancies. Unsafe abortions have been a leading cause of maternal mortality for decades. Government oversight of reproductive health care and accountability practices are woefully deficient.

In a major advance for lesbian, gay, bisexual and transgender rights, Argentina in July became the first Latin American country to legalize same-sex marriage.

Key International Actors

In June 2010 the Inter-American Commission on Human Rights expressed "deep concern" about conditions in Argentina's police jails and prisons, and urged the government to end the use of police stations as detention centers.

Argentina continued to positively engage on human rights issues at the UN Human Rights Council and in other international settings. At the Council, Argentina has consistently voted in a principled way to ensure scrutiny of human rights violators. It also has played a key role in opposing a proposed UN resolution on defamation of religion that would undermine freedom of expression standards.

ARGENTINA

Illusions of Care

Lack of Accountability for Reproductive Rights in Argentina

HUMAN
RIGHTS
WATCH

BOLIVIA

Lack of accountability for rights abuses remains a serious problem in Bolivia. The fate of scores who "disappeared" before democracy was re-established in 1982 has still not been clarified, and most perpetrators of disappearances and extrajudicial executions have escaped justice. In 2010 officials of President Evo Morales's government backed the military when it failed to comply with court orders to provide access to information. During the same year the Bolivian Legislative Assembly passed anti-corruption laws that do not fully adhere to the rights to a fair trial and due process.

Due Process and Judicial Independence

Laws enacted in 2010 that are intended to strengthen accountability for past human rights abuses and corruption by government officials include provisions that contravene international standards of due process and fair trial, including the prohibition on the retroactive application of criminal law and the right to be present during trial.

An anti-corruption law establishing new crimes and harsher penalties passed in March 2010. It allows for individuals to be prosecuted for actions and behavior that was not criminalized before the law was adopted, a breach of the international law principle that criminal provisions may not be applied retroactively. The anti-corruption law also makes it possible to try former heads of state in absentia, a provision incompatible with the right to be present during trial in order to exercise a proper defense.

In February 2010, responding to the crisis provoked by the legislature's inability to agree on judicial appointments, President Morales obtained legislative approval to appoint five temporary justices to the Supreme Court, as well as temporary magistrates to the Constitutional Court, in a process that lacked the usual safeguards for selecting judges. The judges are to be replaced by permanent judges to be elected by universal suffrage in December 2010.

Accountability for Past Abuses

Efforts in 2010 by prosecutors to reopen investigation into serious abuses committed under previous governments, particularly the military dictatorships of Hugo Banzer (1971-1978) and Luis García Meza (1980-1981), met with resistance from Bolivian armed forces. Instead of guaranteeing full military cooperation with such investigations, the government backed the armed forces in conflicts with prosecutors and judges.

In February 2010 an investigating judge ordered the army to turn over information that could help clarify "disappearances" that occurred in 1980. The defense minister assured that access would be granted. However, when the public prosecutor, Milton Mendoza, visited army headquarters to request a view of the files, he was turned away on the grounds that the army first needed to put the documents in order. Another prosecutor was allowed into the building a week later, but was allowed only to view the contents of a filing cabinet, and not to remove or photocopy documents. The armed forces eventually provided only a photocopied register of personnel on active service in 1980. In April 2010 the Supreme Court issued a further ruling ordering the declassification of files covering the first year of the García Meza dictatorship. However, at this writing the army continued to defy the order and has provided no information to help clarify the fate of the "disappeared." Mendoza, whom Vice-President Alvaro García Linera publicly criticized for overstepping his mandate, was taken off the case.

In October 2010 the Supreme Court upheld the conviction of 11 former police and military officers for their role in the murder in 1980 of socialist leader Marcelo Quiroga Santa Cruz. It sentenced three of them in absentia to 30 years in prison on charges including terrorism and murder, and the others to shorter prison terms for covering up the crime. Quiroga's remains have still not been found.

In November 2008 Bolivia's government requested the extradition of former president Gonzalo Sánchez de Lozada and two of his ministers to stand trial for killing at least 60 people in anti-government protests in September and October 2003, when the army used lethal force to quell violent demonstrations in the highland city of El Alto. As of November 2010 it has received no response from the United States government.

Sánchez de Lozada resigned and fled to the US after the events, known in Bolivia as "Black October." The three men, as well as other ministers who were given asylum in Peru, have been declared fugitives from justice. In August 2010 the prosecutor filed charges against three senior military officials, including a former commander-in-chief of the armed forces, for destroying military documents, including a log believed to have recorded details of the events and the personnel who participated.

Military Jurisdiction

The determination of Bolivia's military courts to assert jurisdiction over human rights abuses has been a major obstacle to accountability for many years. The military has often refused to allow members of the armed forces to testify before civilian courts, instead insisting on trying the cases in military court, which invariably ends in acquittals. However, in an important precedent in September 2010, the army commander-in-chief—at President Morales's insistence—ordered four officers accused of subjecting a conscript to water torture in September 2009 to appear before a civilian court.

Political Violence and Impunity

Impunity continued to be a problem in 2010. Investigations into deaths and injuries that occurred during violent protests in 2008 and 2009 over Bolivia's new constitution and demands for autonomy by five regional departments were ineffective and subject to long delays.

In June 2010, after long delays due to conflicts over jurisdiction, a court in La Paz began to hear a case against 26 defendants in connection with the killing of at least nine pro-Morales demonstrators in Porvenir, Pando department, in September 2008. The accused included the former prefect of Pando department, Leopoldo Fernández, who was indicted in October 2009 on charges of homicide, terrorism, and conspiracy. He was still in preventive detention in September 2010.

The Attorney General's Office also failed in 2010 to conduct a thorough and impartial investigation into the circumstances in which three Europeans were shot dead in April 2009 when an elite police unit broke into their rooms in a Santa Cruz hotel. The public prosecutor accused the men of being mercenaries engaged in a plot to kill President Morales, and named several government opponents alleged to have hired them. However, the evidence he offered to support the official version that the three men were involved in a firefight when they were killed was widely questioned. The government rejected calls from European governments for an independent investigation.

Media Freedom

Bolivia enjoys vibrant public debate, with a variety of critical and pro-government media outlets. However, in what remains a politically polarized atmosphere, President Morales sometimes aggressively criticizes the press, accusing journalists of distorting facts and seeking to discredit him. In January 2010, he warned journalists that he would establish norms "so that the media don't lie." However, at this writing the government has presented no proposals for legislation on the media.

Under a law against racism and other forms of discrimination, passed in October 2010, media that "authorize or publish racist or discriminatory ideas" can be fined and have their broadcasting licenses suspended. Media outlets protested these provisions, claiming they were so broad that they could be used against media critical of the government.

Human Rights Defenders

In August 2010, police searched and removed computers from the office and home of Jorge Quiroz and Claudia Lecoña, lawyers for the parents of two students killed when police broke up a protest in May in Caranavi, in the department of La Paz. Quiroz, who worked as a volunteer for the La Paz Permanent Assembly of Human Rights, reportedly accused police of using excessive force. Government officials accused Quiroz of a string of offenses, including drug-trafficking, immigration irregularities, acting as an "infiltrator" for the US embassy in the Caranavi protests, and trafficking prostitutes. However, no proof was provided or charges leveled, raising concern that the government aimed to discredit Quiroz because of his accusations against the police.

Sexual Orientation and Gender Identity

The new constitution explicitly bans discrimination based on sexual orientation and gender identity. The anti-racism law under debate in Congress provides a penalty of up to five years imprisonment for anyone who discriminates on the basis of sexual orientation or gender identity, and an even higher penalty of up to seven-and-a-half years if the offender is a public official.

Key International Actors

In October 2010 the Inter-American Court of Human Rights found Bolivia responsible for multiple violations of human rights in relation to the enforced disappearance of Rainer Ibsen Cárdenas, a student, and his father, José Luis Ibsen Peña, during the military dictatorship of Hugo Banzer in the early 1970s.

BRAZIL

Brazil has consolidated its place as one of the most influential democracies in regional and global affairs in recent years, but important human rights challenges remain. Faced with high levels of violent crime, some Brazilian police officers engage in abusive practices instead of pursuing sound policing policies. Detention conditions in the country are often inhumane, and torture remains a serious problem. Forced labor persists in some states despite federal efforts to eradicate it. Indigenous peoples and landless peasants face threats and violence, particularly in rural conflicts over land distribution.

Public Security and Police Conduct

Most of Brazil's metropolitan areas are plagued by widespread violence perpetrated by criminal gangs and abusive police. Violence especially impacts low-income communities. There are more than 40,000 intentional homicides in Brazil every year. In Rio de Janeiro hundreds of low-income communities are occupied and controlled by drug gangs, who routinely engage in violent crime and extortion.

Police abuse, including extrajudicial execution, is a chronic problem. According to official data, police were responsible for 505 killings in the state of Rio de Janeiro alone in the first six months of 2010. This amounts to roughly three police killings per day, or at least one police killing for every six "regular" intentional homicides. The number of killings by police in Sao Paulo, while less than in Rio de Janeiro, is also comparatively high. A 2009 Human Rights Watch report found that police in Sao Paulo state had killed more people over the prior five years than had police in all of South Africa, a country with a higher homicide rate than Sao Paulo.

Police claim these are "resistance" killings that occur in confrontations with criminals. While many police killings undoubtedly result from legitimate use of force by police officers, many others do not, a fact documented by Human Rights Watch and other groups and recognized by Brazilian criminal justice officials. Reform efforts have fallen short because state criminal justice systems rely almost entirely on police investigators to resolve these cases, leaving police largely to police themselves.

In 2010 the attorney general of Sao Paulo took an important step to address the problem of police violence by establishing that all cases involving alleged police abuse be investigated by a special unit of prosecutors.

The state of Rio de Janeiro has installed Pacifying Police Units (UPP) in some *favelas* (shanty towns) since 2008, with the aim of establishing a more effective police presence at the community level. However, the state has not yet taken adequate steps to ensure that police who commit abuses are held accountable.

Some police officers also commit abuses while off duty. In Rio de Janeiro, police-linked militias control dozens of neighborhoods at gunpoint, extorting residents and committing murders and other violent crimes. The government has undertaken significant efforts to dismantle some of these groups, and dozens of alleged militia members have been arrested, but the problem remains critical.

In April 2010, 23 people were executed in the region of Santos, in the state of Sao Paulo. Local residents have attributed the killings to a death squad known as the "Ninjas" which allegedly includes police officers among its members.

In July 2010, four military police officers were convicted of murdering and decapitating a mentally disabled person. They were identified as being members of a death squad known as the "Highlanders", a nickname derived from the group's practice of cutting off the heads and hands of their victims in an effort to cover up their crimes (a practice from the 1986 fictional film *Highlander*).

Detention Conditions, Torture, and Ill-Treatment

Brazil's prisons and jails are plagued by inhumane conditions, violence, and severe overcrowding. Delays within the justice system contribute to the overcrowding: some 44 percent of all inmates in the country are pretrial detainees.

Over the past three years the National Council of Justice, the judiciary's oversight body, ordered the release of more than 25,000 prisoners who were being held arbitrarily.

The use of torture is a chronic problem within the penitentiary system. A report by the multiparty National Parliamentary Commission of Inquiry on the Penitentiary

BRAZIL

Lethal Force

Police Violence and Public Security in Rio de Janeiro and São Paulo

HUMAN
RIGHTS
WATCH

System concluded that the national detention system is plagued by "physical and psychological torture." In one case from Goias, the Commission received evidence that the National Security Force subjected female detainees to kicks and electric shocks, stepped on the abdomen of a pregnant woman, and forced another woman to strip naked. A 2010 report by the Pastoral Prison Commission found that these problems continue.

Gangs continue to dominate the prisons in Brazil. In early 2010 gang rivalry in a prison in Parana state led to a riot involving 1,200 prisoners. Five people were killed, including two burned to death.

HIV and tuberculosis prevalence rates in Brazilian prisons are far higher than rates in the general population; overcrowded conditions facilitate the spread of disease and prisoners' access to medical care remains inadequate.

There were also continued reports of substandard conditions at Rio de Janeiro's juvenile detention centers run by the General Department of Socio-Educational Measures (DEGASE). In 2010, 44 DEGASE agents were charged with participating in a torture session in 2008 that resulted in the death of one juvenile and left another 20 injured.

A 2001 law sought to overhaul the system of mental health institutions, which had been plagued by overcrowding and inhumane conditions, but it has not yet been fully implemented.

Reproductive Health Rights

Raids on family planning clinics and aggressive prosecution of abortion limited women's access to reproductive health services in 2010. In May a bill to prioritize the human rights of a fertilized ovum over those of the pregnant woman carrying it was voted favorably out of the Family and Social Security Commission of the Brazilian House of Representatives. The bill is still pending at this writing.

Forced Labor

Since 1995 the federal government has taken important steps to eradicate forced labor, including creating mobile investigation units to monitor conditions in rural areas and establishing a list of employers found to have used forced labor. More than 36,000 workers have been freed since 1995. However, the Pastoral Land Commission reported that more than 6,000 workers were subject to forced labor in 2009. Criminal accountability for offending employers remains relatively rare.

According to the United Nations special rapporteur on contemporary forms of slavery, forced labor is also present in urban centers in the garment industry. Bolivian workers are recruited by Brazilian sweatshops and trafficked to Sao Paulo, where they have to endure harsh living and working conditions. They are often locked in basements, work up to 18 hours a day, and receive very little pay.

Rural Violence and Land Conflicts

Indigenous and landless peoples face threats and violence, particularly in land disputes in rural areas. According to the Pastoral Land Commission, 25 people were killed and 62 were attacked in rural conflicts throughout the country in 2009. In September 2010 José Valmeristo Soares, a member of the Landless Rural Workers' Movement, was killed by gunmen in Para, the state with the highest numbers of such killings.

Confronting Past Abuses

Brazil has never prosecuted those responsible for atrocities committed during the period of its military dictatorship (1964-1985). A 1979 amnesty law has thus far been interpreted to bar prosecutions of state agents, an interpretation reaffirmed in April 2010 by the Supreme Federal Tribunal.

The federal government in 2010 presented a bill creating a national truth commission to investigate dictatorship-era abuses, but at this writing its approval is still pending in congress.

Human Rights Defenders

Some human rights defenders, particularly those working on issues of police violence and land conflicts, suffer intimidation and violence. In January 2009 Manoel Mattos, a human rights lawyer, was shot and killed in the border area between the states of Paraiba and Pernambuco. The main suspect, a police offi-cer linked to a death squad under investigation by Mattos, has been arrested. In October 2010 in an unprecedented decision, the judiciary ruled in favor of a request by the Attorney General's Office to grant federal prosecutors jurisdiction over the case to ensure an independent investigation and prosecution.

Media Freedom

In July 2009 a court issued an injunction prohibiting the newspaper *O Estado de Sao Paulo* from publishing stories containing information from the "Operacao Faktor" police investigation involving Fernando Sarney, son of Senate President José Sarney. Despite strenuous criticism from national and international press freedom organizations, the ruling was confirmed by the Supreme Federal Tribunal in December 2009. At this writing the restrictions are still in force.

In September 2010 the Supreme Federal Tribunal suspended an electoral law pro-vision that had imposed restrictions on radio and television broadcast of pro-grams that "degrade or ridicule" political candidates.

Key International Actors

In March 2009 the Inter-American Commission on Human Rights filed an applica-tion at the Inter-American Court regarding the "Guerrilha do Araguaia" case, ask-ing the court to hold Brazil responsible for the enforced disappearance of guerrilla members carried out by the Brazilian military in the 1970s, during the military dic-tatorship. It also petitioned the court to instruct the Brazilian government to ensure that the country's amnesty law does not continue to bar the investigation and prosecution of past human rights abuses. In May 2010 the Brazilian defense minister declared that Brazil would not comply with such a ruling. The court's decision is still pending at this writing.

The Inter-American Court of Human Rights issued a ruling against Brazil in September 2009 in the case of *Garibaldi v. Brazil*, declaring that Brazilian author-ities had not acted with due diligence in investigating the death of Sétimo Garibaldi, who was killed in 1998 during an extrajudicial operation aimed at evict-ing families of landless workers in Parana.

Brazil increased its influence at the UN Human Rights Council. In 2009 the government controversially abstained from supporting strong scrutiny of North Korea, Sri Lanka, and the Democratic Republic of the Congo. In 2010 it improved its record, supporting continued UN monitoring of human rights conditions in North Korea and Sudan and convening a session on Haiti. Brazil also proposed in 2010 that the Council develop a more cooperative, less adversarial approach to its work, an idea that could weaken the Council if not accompanied by new mechanisms to ensure human rights accountability.

CHILE

Chilean military courts that fall short of international standards of independence and impartiality continue to investigate and try police accused of human rights abuses. Counterterrorism legislation has been used inappropriately to deal with common crimes committed by indigenous protesters. Legislation enacted in 2010 only partially corrected these problems.

Judges continue to convict former military personnel accused of committing grave human rights violations during the military dictatorship (1973-1990). However, final sentences are often unacceptably lenient given the seriousness of the crimes. Overcrowding and inhumane conditions in many Chilean prisons remains a serious problem.

Military Jurisdiction

Beginning in 2000, Chile has overhauled its criminal justice procedure and reinforced due process guarantees, however, until 2010, military courts continued to exercise jurisdiction over civilians accused of acts of violence against *Carabineros* (uniformed police), which is part of the armed forces. Military courts still hold jurisdiction over crimes committed by *Carabineros* against civilians, such as use of excessive force, torture, and ill-treatment.

In a 2005 ruling in the Palamara case, the Inter-American Court of Human Rights ordered Chile to ensure that military courts no longer exercise jurisdiction over civilians. Subsequent court decisions have held that members of the armed forces accused of humans rights violations should also be tried under civilian jurisdiction.

Legislation approved by Congress in September 2010 finally complied with Chile's obligation to ensure that civilian courts try civilians in all cases. However, it did not transfer to civilian jurisdiction cases of abuse by police officers against civilians, thereby failing to meet Chile's obligations under international law to ensure that law enforcement officials accused of human rights abuses are tried by independent and impartial courts.

Police Abuses

In repeated incidents, carabineros have used excessive force during operations in indigenous Mapuche communities in the Araucanía region. Abuses typically occur when police try to control Mapuche protests and prevent land occupations, or when they enter communities to pursue activists suspected of crimes allegedly committed during land disputes with farmers and logging companies.

Since 2002, police have been responsible for the deaths of at least three Mapuches. As noted, such cases are investigated by military courts that do not meet international standards of independence and impartiality; sentences have either resulted in acquittals or been extremely lenient. In August 2010, for example, Corte Marcial (the military appeals court) placed on probation for three years a police corporal convicted of using excessive force by shooting a Mapuche activist, Matías Catrileo, in the back with a submachine gun. Three military judges on active service have a majority on the panel, which also includes two civilian appellate judges. The same court acquitted a policeman accused of shooting a young Mapuche, Alex Lemun, in 2002. In July 2010 it ordered charges dropped against four policeman accused of beating Carlos Curinao, the son of a Mapuche community leader, while he lay prostrate on the ground.

Counterterrorism Laws

Since 2004 Human Rights Watch has expressed concern about inappropriate use of counterterrorism legislation to deal with common crimes, such as arson, committed by indigenous Mapuche activists. Under Chile's counterterrorism law, crimes against property, such as burning homesteads, woods, or crops; or damaging vehicles or machinery, are considered terrorist crimes if judges believe they are intended to spread fear among the population. Defendants under the law have restricted due process rights and face much higher sentences. As of June 2010 more than 50 Mapuches faced terrorism charges and five had been convicted of terrorist crimes.

In October 2010 the government enacted legislation to modify the counterterrorism law in response to a hunger strike by 32 Mapuche prisoners protesting the law's application to their cases, as well as their prosecution by military courts.

The reforms of the counterterrorism law strengthened some due process guarantees, such as allowing witnesses whose identity can be concealed by prosecutors to be cross-examined by defense attorneys. The government also announced it would drop all accusations of terrorism against Mapuches currently in the courts, and accuse them only under the ordinary criminal law. However, the inclusion in the law of crimes against property was left unchanged, and public prosecutors continued to apply the law to such crimes.

Confronting Past Abuses

Cases of human rights abuses committed during military rule under investigation by the courts rose from 350 in April 2010 to 452 in June 2010 due to relatives' associations filing new cases. President Sebastian Piñera continues to provide government support for the Human Rights Program attached to the Ministry of the Interior, whose lawyers help relatives of victims pursue their cases before the courts.

As of June 2010, 292 former military personnel and civilian collaborators had been convicted on charges of enforced disappearances, extrajudicial executions, and torture (of whom 210 had the verdict confirmed on final appeal). Sixty-four were serving prison sentences; 490 more were facing charges.

In July 2010 Piñera announced he would exclude prisoners convicted of human rights violations from presidential clemency measures that the Catholic Church had requested to mark the 200th anniversary of Chile's founding as a republic.

In July 2010 the Supreme Court's criminal chamber confirmed the conviction of Augusto Pinochet's secret police chief, Manuel Contreras, and eight other agents for the 1974 car bomb assassination of former army commander Carlos Prats and his wife. The court sentenced Contreras and his associate Pedro Espinoza to 20 years in prison for aggravated homicide and criminal association. The court held these were crimes against humanity, and that Chile is bound under the Geneva Conventions to judge and punish those responsible for such crimes, regardless of the self-amnesty law that Pinochet introduced in 1977.

However, in many cases the Supreme Court has routinely used its discretionary powers to reduce sentences against human rights violators in recognition of the time elapsed since the criminal act. Often the sentence finally imposed is low enough to exempt those convicted from going to prison. This practice raises concerns about Chile's fulfillment of its obligation to hold perpetrators of disappearances accountable by imposing appropriate punishment or sanctions; less than one-third of those convicted were actually serving prison time in August 2010.

Prison Conditions

Chile has yet to take effective measures to relieve severe overcrowding in its prisons, and alleviate conditions that a senior justice official has described as "inhumane."

In Chile's most crowded prisons in 2010, at least two prisoners on average occupied facilities intended for one. Prison conditions include overcrowding; poor sanitation, ventilation, and nutrition; and lack of potable water. Yet despite conditions conducive to ill-health and the spread of infectious disease, access to medical care remains inadequate. According to a report that a government-appointed prison review commission issued in March 2010, the problem stems from delays in the construction of new facilities, the introduction of faster criminal procedures, harsher sentencing policies, and failure to implement effective alternatives to prison. Following visits to facilities across the country in July and August, Minister of Justice Felipe Bulnes said that the problem of overcrowding had been "invisible for a long time," and announced measures to improve conditions.

Reproductive Rights

Chile is one of a handful of countries that prohibits abortion in all circumstances, even in cases of rape or incest, or to save the life or health of a pregnant woman. Despite this, an estimated 60,000 to 200,000 clandestine abortions occur annually, corresponding to between 20 and 40 percent of all pregnancies. The lack of precise statistics on the prevalence of abortion speaks to the highly stigmatized and clandestine nature of the practice. Chile also has one of the highest teenage pregnancy rates in the world, with over 15 percent of all births corresponding to adolescent mothers. There was continued controversy in 2010 over the distribution of modern contraceptive methods. For example, the main health authority of Coquimbo region withdrew the authority of midwives to distribute contraception, contravening national norms. Many women, especially in rural or less accessible areas, lose real access when only medical doctors can distribute contraception.

Key International Actors

United Nations experts have repeatedly criticized the use of counterterrorism legislation against Mapuche activists, including the Committee on the Elimination of Racial Discrimination and the special rapporteur on the situation of human rights and fundamental freedoms of indigenous peoples.

In September the Inter-American Commission on Human Rights filed a case with the Inter-American Court on Human Rights accusing Chile of discriminating against Karen Atala, a judge who is an open lesbian, by depriving her of custody of her children because of her sexual orientation. The Supreme Court refused to participate in a panel formed by the Ministry of Foreign Affairs to debate ways of implementing the commission's recommendations, arguing the final court decision was not subject to discussion. The Inter-American Court will decide for the first time whether such discrimination violates the American Convention on Human Rights.

Colombia

Colombia's internal armed conflict continued to result in serious abuses by irregular armed groups in 2010, including guerrillas and successor groups to paramilitaries. Violence has displaced millions of Colombians internally, and displaces hundreds of thousands every year. Armed actors frequently threaten or attack human rights defenders, journalists, community leaders, trade unionists, indigenous and Afro-Colombian leaders, displaced persons' leaders, and paramilitaries' victims seeking land restitution or justice.

In August 2010 President Juan Manuel Santos replaced former President Alvaro Uribe, whose administration was racked by scandals over extrajudicial killings by the army, a highly questioned paramilitary demobilization process, and the national intelligence service's illegal surveillance of human rights defenders, journalists, opposition politicians, and Supreme Court justices. President Santos has promoted legislation to restore land to displaced persons and compensate victims of abuses by state agents, publicly voiced respect for an independent judiciary, and denounced threats against human rights defenders. However, it remains to be seen whether his approach translates into concrete results in light of serious ongoing abuses.

Guerrilla Abuses

The Revolutionary Armed Forces of Colombia (FARC) and the National Liberation Army (ELN) continue to carry out serious abuses against civilians. The FARC especially is often involved in killings, threats, forced displacement, and recruiting child combatants.

The FARC and ELN frequently use antipersonnel landmines. The government reported that 76 civilians were injured between January and August 2010 by antipersonnel landmines and unexploded munitions.

In September 2010 the Colombian military killed top FARC military commander Victor Julio Suárez, alias "Mono Jojoy," responsible for numerous grave abuses during his decades of leadership.

Paramilitaries and their Successors

Since 2003 more than 30,000 individuals have participated in a paramilitary demobilization process, although there is substantial evidence that many were not paramilitaries, and that others never demobilized.

Successor groups to the paramilitaries, often led by mid-level commanders of demobilized paramilitary organizations, exercise territorial control in certain regions and are responsible for widespread atrocities against civilians. The Colombian National Police reported the groups had 3,749 members as of July 2010; however, the Colombian NGO Instituto de Estudios para el Desarrollo y la Paz estimates the groups have 6,000 armed combatants, and have expanded operations to 29 of Colombia's 32 departments. Toleration of these successor groups by members of the public security forces is a main factor in their growth.

Like previous paramilitaries, the groups engage in drug trafficking, actively recruit, and commit widespread abuses, including massacres, killings, rapes, and forced displacement. Successor groups repeatedly target human rights defenders, trade unionists, and victims groups seeking justice and recovery of land. In Medellín homicides have surged since 2008, apparently due to these groups.

Successor groups contribute significantly to forced displacement. State agencies often refuse to register people as displaced if they say paramilitary successor groups forced them to flee, contributing to disparities between government and NGO estimates of Colombia's internally displaced population. While the state agency Social Action registered 154,040 newly displaced in 2009, the respected Colombian NGO CODHES holds that 286,389 persons were displaced that year. Social Action has registered 3.3 million displaced persons between 1997 and July 2010, compared to 3.9 million that CODHES reports between 1997 and 2009.

Colombia's Supreme Court has in recent years made considerable progress investigating Colombian Congress members accused of collaborating with paramilitaries. In the "parapolitics" scandal, more than 150 Congress members – most from President Uribe's coalition – have been investigated, and at least 20 convicted. The Uribe administration repeatedly took actions that could have sabotaged investigations, including issuing public and personal attacks against

Supreme Court justices. President Santos has publicly stated his commitment to respecting the court's independence.

The Supreme Court is currently investigating more than 20 members of Congress amid concerns of high levels of paramilitary infiltration. Investigations by the Attorney General's Office into senior military officers and businesspersons who allegedly collaborated with paramilitaries have been slow.

Implementation of the Justice and Peace Law, which offers dramatically reduced sentences to demobilized paramilitaries who confess their atrocities, has also been slow and uneven. As of November 2010, more than five years after the law was approved, there have only been two convictions and prosecutors have recovered a negligible fraction of the millions of acres of land that paramilitaries seized. The Santos government has promoted legislation to return millions of acres of land to Colombia's displaced population through a procedure separate from the Justice and Peace Law.

Paramilitary leaders' confessions in the justice and peace process suffered a setback when President Uribe extradited most paramilitary leaders to the United States between May 2008 and August 2009 to face drug trafficking crimes. Paramilitary cooperation declined significantly thereafter, and several commanders refused to continue testifying, fearing reprisals against family in Colombia.

Military Abuses and Impunity

In recent years Colombia's Army has been blamed for an alarming number of extrajudicial killings of civilians, including extrajudicial executions known as "false positives," when army members, pressured to show results, kill civilians and report them as combatants killed in action. The alleged executions have occurred throughout Colombia and involve multiple army brigades.

The problem continues, despite a significant drop in false positives since 2009. The government does not keep statistics for such cases, but as of May 2010, the Attorney General's Office was investigating 1,366 cases of alleged extrajudicial killings committed by state agents involving more than 2,300 victims. There have only been convictions in 63 cases.

The military justice system's resistance to transferring cases to ordinary civilian courts impeded prosecution of extrajudicial killings. Military courts transferred 266 cases in 2009 but only seven from January to September 2010.

Violence against Trade Unionists

Colombia still leads the world in killings of trade unionists, with more than 2,800 reported killings since 1986, according to the National Labor School (ENS), Colombia's leading NGO monitoring labor rights. Most are attributed to paramilitaries and their successor groups.

While the number of murders dropped in 2007 to 39, statistics are still alarmingly high: 52 murders in 2008, 47 in 2009, and 36 from January to September 15, 2010, according to the ENS. Threats against unionists—mostly attributed to paramilitaries' successor groups—have increased since 2007.

Impunity in such cases is widespread: only 25 percent of more than 2,800 ENS-documented killings of unionists are being investigated by the Attorney General's Office unit mandated to prosecute such crimes. The office has opened investigations into more than 1,300 cases (including several hundred that do not appear on the ENS list), but has only obtained convictions in 14 percent of these cases. There are also concerns the investigations are piecemeal, and do not consider whether the victim's union activities motivated the crime.

Human Rights Defenders

Human rights defenders are routinely threatened and attacked. According to the NGO Somos Defensores, seven defenders were murdered and 51 threatened in the first half of 2010. A coalition of Colombian and international NGOs reported 30 killings of human rights defenders and social leaders between July and October 15, 2010. Over 40 leaders of victims groups seeking to recover land have been killed since the Justice and Peace process started in 2005. In 2010 several leaders of Afro-Colombian and indigenous communities were reported killed. Impunity for these crimes contributes to their persistence.

President Santos has publicly condemned threats against human rights defenders—an improvement from their stigmatization during President Uribe's administration.

The Early Warning System of the Ombudsman's Office, which monitors Colombia's human rights situation, regularly issues "risk reports" warning of threats to communities and individuals. Other Colombian authorities have sometimes ignored these and failed to act to prevent abuses.

Illegal Surveillance

In February 2009 Colombia's leading news magazine, *Semana*, reported the Colombian intelligence service, DAS, which answers directly to the president's office, had for years engaged in extensive illegal phone tapping, email interception, and surveillance directed at trade unionists, human rights defenders, journalists, opposition politicians, and Supreme Court justices. DAS documents indicate the alleged criminal activities included death threats and smear campaigns to link targets to guerrillas. The Attorney General's Office has begun investigating dozens of former and current DAS officials, including the current director and several of his predecessors.

Former DAS functionaries say that high-level officials in the Uribe administration may have ordered the illegal surveillance. In October 2010 the Inspector General's Office meted out disciplinary sanctions against President Uribe's chief-of-staff and three former DAS directors for their part in the surveillance.

Key International Actors

The United States remains the most influential foreign actor in Colombia. In 2010 it provided approximately US $673 million—mostly military and police aid—though an increasing percentage consists of social and economic assistance. Thirty percent of US military aid is subject to human rights conditions, which the US Department of State has not consistently enforced. In September 2010 the State Department certified, for the second time under President Barack Obama's administration, that Colombia was meeting human rights conditions. However, the State Department's 2010 certification did include a comprehensive memorandum outlining Colombia's significant human rights problems.

The US Congress has delayed ratifying the US-Colombia Free Trade Agreement until there is "concrete evidence of sustained results on the ground" regarding impunity for violence against trade unionists and the role of paramilitaries.

The United Kingdom reportedly reduced military assistance to Colombia in 2009, apparently due to scandals over illegal surveillance and extrajudicial executions. The European Union provides social and economic assistance to Colombia, including some aid to the government's paramilitary demobilization programs.

The Organization of American States' Mission to Support the Peace Process in Colombia, charged with verifying paramilitary demobilizations, issued reports in 2009 and 2010 expressing alarm over the activities of paramilitary successor groups.

The Office of the Prosecutor of the International Criminal Court continued to monitor local investigations into human rights crimes. The Office of the United Nations High Commissioner for Human Rights is active in Colombia, and has arranged to monitor the military's internal control structure. In October 2010 Colombia's Congress approved the International Convention for the Protection of All Persons from Enforced Disappearance. It would go into effect after being signed by President Santos and upheld by the Constitutional Court.

CUBA

Cuba remains the only country in Latin America that represses virtually all forms of political dissent. In 2010 the government continued to enforce political conformity using criminal prosecutions, beatings, harassment, denial of employment, and travel restrictions.

Since inheriting control of the government from his brother Fidel Castro in 2006, Raul Castro has kept Cuba's repressive legal and institutional structures firmly in place. While Cuban law includes broad statements affirming fundamental rights, it also grants officials extraordinary authority to penalize individuals who try to exercise them.

Following the death of a political prisoner on hunger strike in February 2010 and the subsequent hunger strike of a prominent dissident, Cuba's government has released more than 40 political prisoners, forcing most into exile. Many more journalists, human rights defenders, and dissidents remain behind bars, while the government increasingly relies on short-term, arbitrary detentions to punish its critics.

Political Prisoners, Arbitrary Detentions, and "Dangerousness"

Cubans who dare to criticize the government are subject to criminal and "pre-criminal" charges. They are exempt from due process guarantees, such as the right to a defense, and denied meaningful judicial protection because courts are "subordinated" to the executive and legislative branches.

In February 2010 political prisoner Orlando Zapata Tamayo died following an 85-day hunger strike. Zapata—who was jailed during a 2003 crackdown on more than 75 human rights defenders, journalists, and dissidents—initiated his hunger strike to protest the inhumane conditions in which he was being held and to demand medical treatment. Following Zapata's death, dissident Guillermo Fariñas initiated a hunger strike to demand medical attention for political prisoners with serious health problems. In July Fariñas ended his hunger strike after 135 days when the Catholic Church announced it had reached an agreement with the Cuban government to release the 52 political prisoners still behind bars from the

2003 crackdown. By mid-November, 39 of the 52 prisoners had been released on the condition that they accept forced exile to Spain, while 12 prisoners, who refused to leave Cuba, remained in prison. One prisoner had been granted provisional freedom and allowed to stay on the island.

Scores of political prisoners remain in Cuban prisons. In October 2010 the Women in White—a respected human rights group comprised of wives, mothers, and daughters of political prisoners—issued a list of 113 prisoners whom it said were incarcerated for political reasons. According to the Damas, there are likely many more prisoners whose cases they cannot document because Cuba's government does not allow international monitors or national groups to access its prisons.

The government continued to rely on arbitrary detention to harass and intimidate individuals exercising their fundamental rights. The Cuban Commission for Human Rights and National Reconciliation documented 325 arbitrary detentions by security forces in 2007; from January to September of 2010, it registered more than 1,220. The detentions are often used to prevent individuals participating in meetings or events viewed as critical of the government. Security officers often offer no charge to justify the detentions—a clear violation of due process rights—but warn detainees of longer arrests if they continue participating in activities deemed critical of the government. For example, from February 23 to 25, more than 100 people were arbitrarily detained across Cuba or placed under house arrest to prevent them participating in memorial services for Orlando Zapata Tamayo.

Raul Castro's government has increasingly relied on a "dangerousness" (*estado peligroso*) provision of the criminal code that allows the state to imprison individuals before they have committed a crime, on the suspicion that they might commit an offense in the future. Scores of individuals have been sentenced to between one and four years for "dangerous" activities including handing out copies of the Universal Declaration of Human Rights, staging peaceful marches, writing critical news articles, and trying to organize independent unions.

Freedom of Expression

The government maintains a media monopoly on the island, ensuring that freedom of expression is virtually nonexistent. Although a small number of independent journalists manage to write articles for foreign websites or maintain independent blogs, they must publish their work through back channels—writing from home computers, saving information on memory sticks, and uploading articles and posts through illegal internet connections. Others dictate articles to contacts abroad. The risks associated with these activities are considerable. For example, blogger Luis Felipe Rojas of Holguin has repeatedly been arbitrarily detained, interrogated, and threatened by authorities for his work. In May 2010, soldiers and police surrounded his house for six days. He was arrested in September along with five human rights defenders when he traveled to attend a pro-democracy meeting, and again in October.

The government controls all media outlets in Cuba and access to outside information is highly restricted. Only a tiny fraction of Cubans have the chance to read independently published articles and blogs because of the high cost of, and limited access to, the internet: an hour of internet use costs one-third of Cubans' monthly wages and is only available in a few government-run centers.

Human Rights Defenders

Refusing to recognize human rights monitoring as a legitimate activity, the Cuban government denies legal status to local human rights groups. The government also employs harassment, beatings, and imprisonment to punish human rights defenders who attempt to document abuses. For example, in October 2010 two members of the Women in White were detained as they marched in Havana holding a banner that read: "Down with racism and long live human rights." Police transferred them to a police station and beat them, fracturing one woman's nose and the other's wrist, and held them without access to communications for seven hours.

Travel Restrictions and Family Separation

The Cuban government forbids the country's citizens from leaving or returning to Cuba without first obtaining official permission, which is often denied. For example, internationally acclaimed blogger Yoani Sanchez has been denied the right to leave the island to accept awards and participate in conferences eight times in the past three years.

Widespread fear of forced family separation gives the Cuban government a powerful tool for punishing defectors and silencing critics. The government frequently bars citizens engaged in authorized travel from taking their children with them overseas, essentially holding children hostage to guarantee their parents' return.

The government restricts the movement of citizens within Cuba by enforcing a 1997 law known as Decree 217. Designed to limit migration to Havana, the decree requires Cubans to obtain government permission before moving to the country's capital. It is often used to prevent dissidents traveling to Havana to attend meetings, and to harass dissidents from other parts of Cuba who live in the capital. For example, in January 2010 authorities repeatedly threatened to remove human rights defenders Juan Carlos González and Tania Maceda Guerra from Havana. Security officers visited their home, called them "counterrevolutionaries," and warned they would be forcibly returned to their native province under Decree 217 if they did not leave Havana voluntarily.

Prison Conditions

Conditions for prisoners are overcrowded, unhygienic, and unhealthy, leading to extensive malnutrition and illness. Political prisoners who criticize the government, refuse to participate in ideological "reeducation," or engage in hunger strikes and other forms of protest are routinely subjected to extended solitary confinement, beatings, visit restrictions, and denial of medical care. Prisoners have no effective complaint mechanism to seek redress, giving prison authorities total impunity.

Key International Actors

In October 2010 the European Union renewed its "Common Position" on Cuba, adopted in 1996, which conditions full economic cooperation with Cuba on the country's transition to a pluralist democracy and respect for human rights. At the same time the EU dispatched its top foreign police official, Catherine Ashton, to initiate a dialogue with Cuba's government on how to improve relations.

The United States' economic embargo on Cuba, in place for more than half a century, continues to impose indiscriminate hardship on the Cuban people, and has done nothing to improve human rights in Cuba. At the United Nations General Assembly in October, 187 of the 192 member countries voted for a resolution condemning the US embargo; only the United States and Israel voted against it. In April 2009 the US government eliminated all limits on travel and remittances by Cuban Americans to Cuba. Legislation introduced in the US House of Representatives in February 2010 would restore the right travel to Cuba for all Americans and remove obstacles to sales of US agricultural commodities to Cuba. It has not yet been brought to a vote.

As of October 2010 Cuba's government had yet to ratify the core international human rights treaties—the International Covenant on Civil and Political Rights and the International Covenant on Economic, Social and Cultural Rights—which it signed in February 2008. Cuba is currently serving a three-year term on the UN Human Rights Council, having been reelected in May 2009.

ECUADOR

On September 30 President Rafael Correa was held captive inside a hospital for several hours by police who were protesting a law that diminished benefits for law enforcement officers. During the standoff, the government declared a state of emergency and ordered all TV stations to transmit the official channel's programming. A shootout broke out when members of the military rescued President Correa, resulting in at least five deaths. The government stated the events constituted an attempted coup d'etat. At this writing hundreds of police officers are under investigation.

At least a dozen participants in protests and demonstrations were prosecuted or investigated in 2010 on the exaggerated charge of terrorism, due to the overly broad provisions of the criminal code. Police officers responsible for abuses in previous years have not been held accountable.

Criminal defamation laws that restrict freedom of expression remain in force. Some articles of the draft Communications Law could open the door to media censorship. At this writing there is still no date set for the debate on the bill in the National Assembly.

Misuse of Anti-Terror Laws in Dealing with Social Protests

Prosecutors have applied a "terrorism and sabotage" provision of the criminal code in cases involving protest marches that have ended in confrontations with police. Involvement in acts of violence during lawful protests should be an ordinary criminal offense. Yet Ecuador's criminal code includes, under the category of sabotage and terrorism, "crimes against the common security of people or human groups of whatever kind, or against their property," by individuals or associations "whether armed or not." Such crimes carry a possible prison sentence of four to eight years.

In June 2010 Marlon Santi, president of the Confederation of Indigenous Nationalities of Ecuador (CONAIE), Ecuador's largest indigenous organization, and two other indigenous leaders were under criminal investigation for terrorism and sabotage after leading a protest during a meeting of the Bolivarian Alliance for the Americas (ALBA) in the city of Otavalo. Protesters broke through a police barrier to gain entry to the building where Presidents Hugo Chávez, Evo Morales, and Rafael Correa were meeting. In September a judge charged Pepe Acacho, a Shuar indigenous leader, and 10 others, with sabotage and terrorism for their alleged participation in violent protests in September 2009 in the city of Macas in the Ecuadorean Amazon, in which a teacher was killed. According to the Ministry of Justice, Acacho was accused of using a community radio station he directed, Radio La Voz de Arutam, to incite demonstrators to take to the streets with poisoned spears to protest the government's alleged intent to privatize water.

In August a judge ordered the preventive detention of Juan Alcívar, a reporter for La Hora newspaper and El Nuevo Sol radio station, on terrorism charges. Two employees of the La Concordia town council accused Alcívar of throwing a tear gas canister at President Correa during a demonstration, causing the Ecuadorean leader to have to cover his face with a mask. Alcívar, who was an outspoken critic of La Concordia's mayor, argues he merely pushed the canister away. In September the judge lifted the detention order, but the terrorism case against him continued.

Accountability

Impunity for police abuses, including extrajudicial executions, is widespread, and those responsible for murders often attributed by police to a "settling of accounts" between criminal gangs are rarely brought to justice. In a June 2010 statement Philip Alston, the United Nations special rapporteur on extrajudicial executions, described the justice system as "broadly dysfunctional." The same month a truth commission created by the Correa administration published a report documenting 68 extrajudicial executions and 17 "disappearances" between 1984 and 2008, and named 458 alleged perpetrators of abuses. According to the commission, few of those responsible for the abuses had been held accountable due to statutes of limitations, jurisdictional disputes, and procedural delays. In October 2010 a team of prosecutors appointed by the attorney general to investigate cases reported by the commission began re-interviewing suspects and witnesses.

Indigenous Justice

Competing jurisdiction of the ordinary courts and of traditional indigenous authorities, which have equal status under the 2008 constitution, has been a source of controversy. Critics of indigenous justice maintain that it is responsible for a number of recent lynchings, which received wide press coverage. In 2010 two UN rapporteurs—on extrajudicial executions and on indigenous peoples—criticized these allegations as unfounded. Both urged dialogue to resolve possible conflicts between the two spheres of justice. At this writing the government is working on draft legislation to determine the scope of each jurisdiction.

Freedom of Expression

The Ecuadorean criminal code still has provisions criminalizing "desacato," under which anyone who "offends" the president or other government authorities may receive a prison sentence of up to three months (for offending officials), and up to two years (for offending the president).

Journalists also face prison sentences for criminal defamation of public officials. In March 2010 Emilio Palacio, an editorial writer for the Guayaquil newspaper *El Universo*, received a three-year prison sentence for calling the president of a government-run financial institution "a thug" in an August 2009 editorial. The Inter-American Commission on Human Rights has urged member states to abolish "desacato" provisions, and to use only civil sanctions to guarantee protection of public officials' reputations.

From September 2009 until June 2010 a National Assembly committee debated draft legislation to regulate media. The draft Communications Law contains positive elements that would strengthen free expression if enacted. It explicitly prohibits monopolies and oligopolies in media ownership, potentially extending the range and diversity of public debate. It broadens access for those with hearing disabilities by promoting subtitles and sign language.

However, the bill contains several provisions that could undermine freedom of expression. It includes restrictions whose vague language could open the way for prior censorship, which the American Convention on Human Rights explicitly prohibits. Employing the same language included in the constitution, it refers to the right to freedom of expression as "the search, reception, exchange, production and dissemination of truthful, verified, opportune, contextualized and plural information." Such definition is at odds with Principle 7 of the Declaration of Principles of Freedom of Expression, endorsed by the Inter-American Commission on Human Rights that states that the "prior conditioning of expressions… is incompatible with the right to freedom of expression." Moreover, the bill allows an exception to the prohibition of prior censorship "in those cases established… in the law."

In addition, the proposed law includes sanctions that impose unreasonable restrictions on free expression, and could allow undue interference in the work of media outlets. Infractions for which an outlet could be punished include failure "to observe its ethics code," and publishing unsigned or anonymous letters. At this writing the bill had still to be debated on the floor of the legislature.

Human Rights Defenders

President Correa has frequently accused environmental activists and NGOs defending indigenous rights of interfering in politics, promoting violence, and receiving funds from abroad to destabilize the country. In July 2010 Correa threatened NGOs that "meddle in politics" with expulsion from the country. In October he stated that he would review the list of some 50,000 NGOs registered in Ecuador, some of which he said were suspected of tax evasion and prejudicing the state.

In July unidentified assailants kidnapped Germán Antonio Ramírez Herrera, a forensic expert specializing in investigating torture and extrajudicial executions, forced him into a car, and later shot him. Ramírez, an expert consultant for PRIVA, a member organization of the International Rehabilitation Council for Torture Victims, had been investigating prisoners' injuries following a police raid at the prison of Quevedo, where he was a forensic doctor. He was killed on the same day that he presented evidence to the UN's special rapporteur on extrajudicial executions. Ramírez was reported to have received death threats previously.

Key International Actors

Members of the Union of South American Nations organized an emergency meeting in Buenos Aires to support the presidency of Rafael Correa after he was held by police in September. Other governments and international institutions, including the United States and the Organization of American States (OAS) also expressed support for Ecuador's democratic institutions.

After visiting Ecuador in July, the UN's special rapporteur on extrajudicial executions criticized the justice system's failure to hold accountable those responsible for execution-style killings, whether committed by state agents, hired assassins, or illegal armed groups. The OAS rapporteur on persons deprived of liberty, who visited Ecuador in May 2010, stated that he had received reports of continuing police torture. He urged Ecuador to ratify the Optional Protocol to the Convention against Torture.

In May 2010 a court in Ontario, Canada struck out a claim for damages that three Ecuadorean community leaders had filed against two directors of the Copper Mesa Mining Corporation and the Toronto Stock Exchange, where the company is listed. Since 2006, residents of Imbabura province, northern Ecuador, have received repeated death threats because of their opposition to a mining project in the area. On one occasion, Copper Mesa company guards physically attacked them, an incident captured on film. The court argued the plaintiffs had failed to establish the responsibility of the company directors and the stock exchange in causing the alleged harm.

GUATEMALA

Guatemala's weak and corrupt law enforcement institutions have proved incapable of containing the powerful organized crime groups and criminal gangs that contribute to one the highest violent crime rates in the Americas. Illegal armed groups, which appear to have partly evolved from counterinsurgency forces operating during the civil war that ended in 1996, are believed to be responsible for targeted attacks on civil society actors and justice officials. More than a decade after the end of the conflict, impunity remains the norm for human rights violations. The ongoing violence and intimidation threaten to reverse the little progress that has been made toward promoting accountability.

Public Security, Police Conduct, and the Criminal Justice System

Illegal armed groups and criminal gangs contribute significantly to violence and intimidation, which they use to further political objectives and illicit economic interests, including drug trafficking.

Powerful and well-organized youth gangs, including the "Mara Salvatrucha" and "Barrio 18," have also contributed to escalating violence in Guatemala. The gangs use lethal violence against those who defy their control, including gang rivals and former members, individuals who collaborate with police, and those who refuse to pay extortion money. The gangs are believed to be responsible for the widespread killings of bus drivers targeted for extortion. According to the National Police, 57 drivers and 30 drivers' assistants were murdered in the first seven months of 2010.

Police have used repressive measures to curb gang activity, including arbitrary detentions and extrajudicial killings. Investigations by the Human Rights Ombudsman's Office and NGOs have found police involvement in "social cleansing," killings intended to eliminate alleged gang members and criminals. Moreover, abuses committed by police officers routinely go uninvestigated.

Guatemala's justice system has proved largely incapable of curbing violence and containing criminal mafias and gangs. According to official figures, there was 99.75 percent impunity for violent crime as of 2009. Deficient and corrupt police, prosecutorial, and judicial systems, as well as the absence of an adequate witness protection program, all contribute to Guatemala's alarmingly low prosecution rate. In addition, members of the justice system are routinely subject to attacks and intimidation.

Accountability for Past Abuses

Guatemala continues to suffer the effects of the 36-year civil war. A United Nations-sponsored Commission on Historical Clarification (CEH) estimated that as many as 200,000 people were killed during the conflict. The CEH attributed 93 percent of the human rights abuses it documented to state security forces and concluded that the military had carried out "acts of genocide." Very few of those responsible for the grave human rights violations during the civil war have been held accountable. Of the 626 massacres documented by the commission, only three cases have been successfully prosecuted in Guatemalan courts.

Guatemala's first conviction for the crime of enforced disappearance occurred in August 2009, when an ex-paramilitary leader was sentenced to 150 years in prison for his role in "disappearing" individuals between 1982 and 1984. The verdict was made possible by a landmark ruling by the country's Constitutional Court in July 2009, which established that enforced disappearance is a continuing crime not subject to a statute of limitations so long as the victims are still unknown.

The July 2005 discovery of approximately 80 million documents of the disbanded National Police, including files on Guatemalans who were killed or "disappeared" during the conflict, could play a key role in prosecuting past human rights abuses. Documents in the archive led to the March 2009 arrest of two former National Police agents for their alleged participation in the 1984 "disappearance" of student leader and activist Edgar Fernando García.

In September 2008 Congress passed the Law of Access to Public Information, which orders that "in no circumstances can information related to investigations of violations of fundamental human rights or crimes against humanity" be classified as confidential or reserved. In March 2009 President Alvaro Colom created the Military Archive Declassification Commission, tasked with sorting and declassifying military documents from 1954-1996.

Human Rights Defenders and Journalists

Attacks and threats against human rights defenders are common, significantly hampering human rights work throughout the country. Journalists, especially those covering corruption, drug trafficking, and accountability for abuses committed during the civil war, also face threats and attacks. Rolando Santiz, a reporter for the national television station Telecentro 13, was shot to death in Guatemala City on April 1. Antonio de León, a station cameraman, was injured in the attack.

Labor Rights and Child Labor

Freedom of association and the right to organize and bargain collectively are endangered by increasing anti-union violence, including attacks on union offices, and threats, harassment, and killings of trade unionists. The International Trade Union Confederation reports that 16 trade unionists were killed in 2009, the second highest total in the Americas. Seven trade unionists were reportedly killed in the first eight months of 2010.

Workers pressing for their rights in labor cases must rely on labor courts, whose work is stymied by dilatory legal measures, lengthy backlogs, and an inability to enforce rulings. According to a 2009 United States Department of State report, only two of the 216 companies operating in export processing zones (where export-processing factories known as "maquilas" are located) had recognized labor unions, and none had a collective bargaining agreement.

Guatemala has one of the highest rates of child labor in the Americas. The International Labour Organization reported in 2008 that 16.1 percent of children aged five to fourteen are obliged to work, many in unsafe conditions. Some of these children are employed in the construction, mining, and sex industries.

Sexual and Gender-Based Violence

Violence against women is a chronic problem in Guatemala, and most perpetrators are never brought to trial. Despite legislative efforts to address this violence, there has been wide impunity for crimes against women.

According to the UN special rapporteur on extrajudicial, arbitrary, and summary executions, investigations into crimes against women, including transgender women, are often inadequate and obstructed by investigating police operating with a gender bias.

Reproductive Rights

In a positive development, in September 2010 Guatemala's Congress adopted a law guaranteeing pre-natal and maternal health care. The law also mandates the appropriation of public funds for contraceptives to be distributed in the public health care system.

Key International Actors

In September 2007 the UN secretary-general appointed Carlos Castresana, a Spanish former prosecutor and judge, to lead the newly-founded International Commission Against Impunity in Guatemala (CICIG). The commission's unique mandate allows it to work with the Guatemalan Attorney General's Office, the police, and other government agencies to investigate, prosecute, and dismantle the criminal organizations operating in Guatemala. The CICIG can participate in criminal proceedings as a complementary prosecutor, provide technical assistance, and promote legislative reforms. As of September 2010 the commission has undertaken 56 investigations and participated in 11 prosecutions. An investigation by CICIG led to the March 2010 arrest of Baltazar Gómez, Guatemala's national police chief, and Nelly Bonilla, the head of its antinarcotics unit, who were charged with drug trafficking and obstruction of justice, as well as involvement in a gunfight that resulted in the death of five antidrug police officers. CICIG also helped to improve the witness protection program and purge 1,700 officers from the National Civilian Police.

Originally set to expire in 2009, CICIG's mandate was extended by Congress for another two years until the end of 2011. However, on June 7, 2010, Castresana abruptly resigned, citing lack of cooperation from several high ranking government officials, including the then-attorney general. The UN has since appointed Francisco Dall'Anese, who was Costa Rica's attorney general, as CICIG's new head.

In October 2010 Spanish police arrested Carlos Vielmann, Guatemala's former interior minister, in Madrid. Vielmann was allegedly involved in the extrajudicial killing of seven detainees in 2006. CICIG had requested his capture some months earlier.

The UN high commissioner for human rights has maintained an office in Guatemala since 2005 that provides observation and technical assistance on human rights practices in the country.

In June 2010 James Anaya, UN special rapporteur on the situation of human rights and fundamental freedoms of indigenous people, visited Guatemala to investigate alleged human rights violations affecting the country's indigenous people. Anaya concluded that the right to previous consultation, according to which indigenous people are entitled to be consulted before any commercial enterprise occurs in their territory, is not being adequately protected.

In July 2010 the Office of the US Trade Representative announced it would file a case against Guatemala under the Dominican Republic-Central America-United States Free Trade Agreement (CAFTA-DR) alleging that it has failed to meet its obligations on labor rights.

HAITI

A devastating earthquake near Haiti's capital, Port-au-Prince, on January 12, 2010, left an estimated 222,750 people dead, 300,000 injured including 4,000 to 5,000 amputees, and up to 1.6 million homeless and displaced. In total 3 million people were affected by the earthquake. Assessments calculate the material damage at about 120 percent of the country's annual GDP. Twenty-eight of twenty-nine government ministry buildings and approximately 300,000 homes were damaged or destroyed. Estimates from a range of NGOs, media outlets, and the World Bank suggest that Haiti's government lost between 20 and 40 percent of its civil servants.

Ten months after the earthquake approximately 1.3 million people still live in some 1,300 informal settlements or camps, where conditions leave residents vulnerable to flooding, disease, and violence. The government and humanitarian actors prepared for a cholera epidemic, which broke out at the end of October, to spread to the camps by the end of 2010. Many of these camps formed spontaneously on private land, and most internally displaced persons (IDPs) face mounting threats of eviction. The United Nations reports that 29 percent of closed camps have been shut down due to forced evictions or negotiated departures.

The situation after the earthquake has exacerbated Haiti's chronic human rights problems, including violence against women and girls, inhumane prison conditions, and vulnerability of children. Most prisoners who escaped from jail during the earthquake remain at large. Already weak, the diminished capacity of the state since the disaster continues to significantly undermine its ability to safeguard fundamental human rights.

Public Security and the Justice System

Haiti has been plagued by high levels of violent crime for many years. Police ineffectiveness and abuse, along with severe shortages of personnel, equipment, and training, existed prior to the quake and contributed to overall insecurity in Haiti. The earthquake has further weakened the capacity of Haitian National Police (HNP), with 75 officers reported killed, 70 missing, and 253 injured in the quake.

Haiti's justice system, long-troubled by politicization, corruption, shortage of resources, and lack of transparency, also suffered severe losses as a result of the quake. At least 10 members of the judiciary died in the earthquake, and the Ministry of Justice and the Palace of Justice were destroyed, along with many judicial documents. The UN reported that the Supreme Court of Haiti remained non-functioning as of September.

In recent years kidnappings posed a serious security threat. The UN reported the rate of kidnappings increased 33 percent in the first eight months of the year compared to the same period in 2009.

Gender-Based Violence

High rates of sexual violence existed before the earthquake, but the precarious safety situation in the informal camps has left women and girls even more vulnerable to such abuse. It is difficult to get accurate data on sexual violence in the camps. The HNP reported that 534 arrests (24 percent of all arrests) from February-April 2010 involved sexual violence. In other reports the HNP officials indicate that 20 rapes were reported in Port-au-Prince for January-March 2010. This inconsistency in data reflects a lack of coordinated governmental response to sexual violence in the camps. On September 13, 2010, the UN launched a campaign against rape and gender-based violence in Haiti.

Detention Conditions

Haiti's prison system suffered from chronic and severe overcrowding when the earthquake hit. The largest prison in Haiti, the Civil Penitentiary in Port-au-Prince, housed over 5,400 prisoners, all of whom escaped after the quake. Eight months after the quake the UN stabilization mission in Haiti (MINUSTAH) and HNP had re-incarcerated 629 of the escapees. The rest remain at large.

Prior to the earthquake pre-trial detainees constituted almost 80 percent of all prison inmates in Haiti. The UN reports that the loss of judicial files and registries will increase prolonged pre-trial or arbitrary detentions and detentions of people never formally charged. Damage to prison facilities since the earthquake has led to limited cell space and even more dire prison conditions then existed before.

On July 26, 2010, Haiti's government, with UN support, established an independent commission of inquiry into the HNP's violent response to a prison uprising in Les Cayes just days after the earthquake. The GOH called for the commission inquiry after the New York Times published an in-depth report, which claimed that on January 19, 2010, UN and HNP officers circled the prison to prevent a massive outbreak after its 400 detainees began to riot due to worsening conditions after the quake, and that HNP officers stormed the prison. Details of the event are not independently confirmed, but the Times estimated that 12 to 19 inmates died and up to 40 were wounded. The commission had not completed its report at this writing.

Access to Education and Child Labor

Prior to the earthquake only about half of primary school-age children in Haiti attended school. United Nations Children's Fund (UNICEF) estimates that the earthquake damaged or destroyed almost 4,000 schools and that 2.5 million children experienced an interruption in their education. Schools resumed several months after the earthquake; however, many experienced a sharp drop in enrollment.

In 2009 the UN special rapporteur on contemporary forms of slavery estimated there were from 150,000 to 500,000 child domestic workers in Haiti, called "restaveks." Restaveks are children, 80 percent of whom are girls, from low-income households sent to live with other families in the hope that they will be cared for in exchange for them performing light chores. These children are often unpaid, denied education, and physically and sexually abused. The UN and civil society organizations warned that unaccompanied minors and orphans, who increased in number after the earthquake, are vulnerable to this form of forced labor.

Some groups have also raised concerns about improper processing of inter-country adoption in violation of domestic and international standards.

Human Rights Defenders

The human rights community lost three prominent women's rights activists in the quake: Myriam Merlet of Enfofamn, Magalie Marcelin of Kay Fanm, and Anne Marie Coriolan of Solidarite Fanm Ayisen (SOFA).

Human rights defenders in Haiti have often been the targets of threats and attacks. The Institute for Justice and Democracy in Haiti (IJDH) reports that criminal gangs have threatened some women's rights activists living and working on gender-based violence in the IDP camps, forcing them to relocate.

Key International Actors

MINUSTAH, which has been present in Haiti since 2004, has played a prominent role in increasing stability and protecting human rights in the country, but suffered heavy losses in the earthquake; the head of mission and 96 staff were killed, constituting the largest loss of life for the UN in a single incident. The UN has since increased MINUSTAH's capacity and extended its mandate through October 15, 2011. The UN force contains 8,548 troops and 3,063 police.

In April 2010 parliament extended the state of emergency for eighteen months, providing additional powers to the executive and establishing the Interim Haiti Recovery Commission (IHRC). President René Préval then issued a presidential decree to grant necessary powers to the IHRC. Prime Minister Max Belle-rive and former US President Bill Clinton were named as co-chairs, and the board of the IHRC was constructed to include representatives from Haiti and donor countries. IHRC's mandate is to oversee billions of dollars in reconstruction aid and to conduct strategic planning and coordination among multi-lateral and bilateral donors, NGOs, and the private sector. Clinton also remains the UN special envoy for Haiti, with Dr. Paul Farmer serving as deputy special envoy.

Honduras

President Porfirio Lobo took office in January 2010, seven months after a military coup ousted democratically elected President Manuel Zelaya. The Lobo administration created a truth commission to look into the events surrounding Zelaya's ouster. But Honduras is failing to hold accountable those responsible for the widespread human rights violations committed by the de facto government installed after the coup. At this writing no one has been held criminally responsible for these abuses.

Other continuing human rights concerns include lack of judicial independence and violence and threats against journalists, human rights defenders, political activists, and transgender people.

Lack of Accountability for Post-Coup Abuses

Following the military coup, the de facto government suspended key civil liberties, including freedoms of the press and assembly. In the ensuing days the military occupied opposition media outlets, temporarily shutting down their transmissions. Police and military personnel responded to generally peaceful demonstrations with excessive force. This pattern of the disproportionate use of force led to several deaths, scores of injuries, and thousands of arbitrary detentions.

The human rights unit in the Attorney General's Office is investigating approximately 200 cases of alleged abuses committed by security officials since the coup, many of which involve multiple victims. At this writing, it has filed charges in 20 cases. In eight, the defendants were acquitted, leaving many acts committed by security forces after the coup unaccounted for. Most of the others remain pending before the courts, some of them stalled because the defendants are at large.

The human rights unit's progress on these cases has been hindered by its limited resources and by the government's failure to allocate funds to the existing witness protection program. The unit must rely on an investigative police force institutionally tied to the Ministry of Security, an arrangement that could affect the impartiality and thoroughness of the investigations.

Security forces have obstructed investigations of abuses committed after the coup. Under the de facto government, military and police personnel systematically refused to cooperate with investigators. They failed to turn over firearms for ballistics tests, to respond to information requests to identify officers accused of committing abuses, and to grant access to military installations. The situation has improved somewhat under Lobo, but the prior lack of cooperation has had a lasting impact on the investigations.

In October, the Honduran Congress approved an increased budget for the unit only for 2011.

Judicial Independence

Immediately after the 2009 coup the Supreme Court held that the replacement of Zelaya was a legitimate "constitutional succession of power." The court subsequently failed to resolve in a timely manner appeals challenging the constitutionality of measures by the de facto government that undermined basic rights. It waited until the de facto government revoked the measures and ruled that the appeals were then moot.

The Supreme Court has absolute power to appoint and remove judges, and the court has used this power to advance a politically partisan agenda, seriously damaging the reputation of the judiciary. The court can fire judges applying vague definitions of "fault," such as carrying out "activities that are incompatible with the honor of the position or that somehow affect its dignity." There is no provision to appeal the removals before an independent body.

In May 2010 the Court fired four judges who opposed the coup. One judge had presented an appeal in favor of Zelaya, two others were present in anti-coup demonstrations, and another said in an academic conference that there had been a coup. While the court argued it was firing them because judges may not get involved in politics, it applied a clear double-standard, failing to sanction judges who supported the coup.

Attacks on Journalists, Human Rights Defenders, and Political Activists

2010 also saw a series of attacks on and threats against journalists, human rights defenders, and members of the political opposition. For example, in February Julio Benitez, a member of the opposition who had received numerous threatening phone calls warning him to abandon his participation in opposition groups, was shot by men on a motorcycle while on his way home. He died in the hospital shortly afterwards. In March gunmen opened fire on Nahúm Palacios, who directed TV Channel 5 of Aguan, while he was driving his car. He died at the scene. Palacios had covered several politically sensitive issues, including anti-coup demonstrations, corruption, drug trafficking, and agrarian conflicts.

In April Father Ismael Moreno, a Jesuit priest and human rights advocate, received a text message threatening to kill the family of an opposition member who had been raped by police officers. Father Moreno had been helping the woman and her family leave Honduras. In June Eliodoro Cáceres Benitez, a political activist, received three death threats by phone, stating that members of organized crime would kill him and his family. Days later, his son went missing and remains missing at this writing.

On September 15, police and military members attacked the offices of Radio Uno, which had been critical of the coup. They threw tear gas bombs at the radio station's offices and at the people inside, broke windows in the building, damaged equipment, and seriously injured one person.

Violence against Transgender Persons

Bias-motivated attacks on transgender people are common in Honduras. At least 19 transgender persons have been killed in public places in Honduras since 2004; many more have been injured in beatings, stabbings, or shootings.

These attacks are rarely followed by rigorous investigations let alone criminal convictions. In a welcome change, a court in September 2010 sentenced an off-duty police officer to 10-13 years for stabbing a female sex worker 17 times, the first time since 2003 an officer has been convicted for a crime against a transgender person.

Key International Actors

Influential allies and neighbors, as well as multilateral institutions—including the European Union, Latin American governments, the Organization of American States (OAS), and United Nations General Assembly—immediately condemned the coup d'etat that ousted Zelaya. The United States also condemned the coup, but waited several weeks before imposing key sanctions (including freezing the visas of key officials) to pressure the de facto government to restore Zelaya to office. Most governments gradually lifted the measures and sanctions after Lobo took office, but Honduras' membership to the OAS remains suspended.

The Inter-American Commission on Human Rights has played a critical role in Honduras since the coup, producing comprehensive reports documenting abuses, including killings, threats, and attacks on journalists.

The UN has also sought to promote human rights in the country. In August the UN appointed a human rights officer in Honduras. In September the Lobo administration requested the creation of a UN commission to fight impunity in the country, which has yet to be established. In November several countries expressed concern about the human rights situation in Honduras during the UN Human Rights Council's Universal Periodic Review of the country.

MEXICO

Many of Mexico's most significant human rights issues in 2010 stemmed from violent confrontations between state security forces and organized crime, as well as clashes among criminal groups. The Mexican military continues to commit serious abuses in public security operations, yet those responsible are virtually never held accountable. Journalists, human rights defenders, and migrants are increasingly the targets of attacks by criminal groups and members of security forces, yet Mexico has failed to provide these vulnerable groups with protection or adequately investigate the crimes against them.

Efforts to implement comprehensive reform to the criminal justice system, which would address endemic problems such as police torture, continued to progress slowly in 2010, leaving in place a system rife with abuses. Meanwhile, serious restrictions on the exercise of reproductive rights remain and Mexican laws still provide inadequate protections against domestic violence and sexual abuse.

Impunity for Military Abuses

President Felipe Calderón has relied heavily on the military to fight drug-related violence and organized crime. While engaging in law enforcement activities, the armed forces have committed serious human rights violations, including killings, torture, and rapes. Mexico's National Human Rights Commission has issued detailed reports on 65 cases involving army abuses since 2007, and received complaints of more than 1,100 additional human rights violations in the first six months of 2010.

In April 2010 Martín and Bryan Almanza, ages nine and five, were killed, and five other people were wounded, when the car they were riding in came under fire in Tamaulipas. The army claimed it was a shoot-out between soldiers and criminals but a subsequent investigation by the National Human Rights Commission revealed that the military had manipulated the crime scene and that soldiers were responsible for the killings.

Military authorities routinely assert jurisdiction to investigate and prosecute crimes in which members of the military are accused; the vast majority are never successfully prosecuted. The military justice system lacks the independence necessary to carry out reliable investigations and its operations suffer from a general lack of transparency. According to military authorities, since 2007 only one military officer has been sentenced by military courts for human rights violations.

In October President Calderón proposed a reform to the Code of Military Justice that would subject cases of rape, torture, and enforced disappearance to civilian jurisdiction; other serious violations would continue to be investigated and prosecuted within the military justice system. While the transfer of any cases of human rights violations from military to civilian jurisdiction represents a step in the right direction, the proposed reform would guarantee that serious abuses such as extrajudicial killings would still be investigated by the military justice system, leaving a significant gap in accountability for most abuses. It would also grant military authorities discretion in classifying abuses, despite a track record of downgrading the severity of charges against soldiers. At this writing, the reform is being debated by the Congress.

Criminal Justice System

The criminal justice system routinely fails to provide justice to victims of violent crime and human rights violations. The causes of this failure are varied and include corruption, inadequate training and resources, and abusive policing practices without accountability.

Torture remains a widespread problem. One perpetuating factor is the acceptance by some judges of confessions obtained through torture and other mistreatment. Another is the failure to investigate and prosecute most cases of torture.

Over 40 percent of prisoners in Mexico have never been convicted of a crime. Rather, they are held in pretrial detention, often waiting years for trial. The excessive use of pretrial detention contributes to prison overcrowding, which in turn leads to inhumane, unsanitary, and dangerous conditions. In January 2010, 23 prisoners were killed in a riot in an overcrowded prison in Durango.

Prison inmates are subject to abuses by guards, and are routinely denied adequate medical care, particularly among women. Children are often detained in poor conditions in police stations and other institutions.

In June 2008 Mexico passed a constitutional reform that creates the basis for an adversarial criminal justice system with oral trials, and contains measures that are critical for promoting greater respect for fundamental rights, such as including presumption of innocence in the constitution. The government has until 2016 to implement the reform. At present only a handful of states have undertaken substantive changes.

In addition to its positive aspects, the reform also introduced the provision of *arraigo*, which allows prosecutors, with judicial authorization, to detain individuals suspected of participating in organized crime for up to 80 days before they are charged with a crime—a power that is inconsistent with Mexico's due process obligations under international law.

Freedom of Expression

Journalists, particularly those who have reported on drug trafficking or have been critical of security forces and authorities, have faced serious harassment and attacks. From 2007 to October 2010, 35 journalists were killed, and eight more are missing and feared dead. News outlets in Sinaloa, Coahuila, and several other states were attacked with explosives or firearms in 2010. In July, police officers in Veracruz kidnapped, robbed, and beat a journalist who had witnessed an earlier incident in which police attacked a reporter.

In spite of the increasing attacks, authorities have failed to adequately investigate and prosecute perpetrators or to protect journalists who face serious risk, generating a climate of impunity and self-censorship. In July 2010 the Office of the Special Prosecutor for Crimes against the Press was given a broader mandate and greater autonomy, but has since failed to improve on its poor record of prosecuting cases. In October Mexico announced plans to create a protection mechanism for journalists under threat, a positive step, but at this writing the system has not yet been created.

Defamation as a federal criminal offence was abolished in 2007. However, criminal defamation laws that remain in place in many states undermine freedom of expression.

A 2002 federal law on transparency and access to information and a 2007 constitutional reform increased avenues for public scrutiny of the Mexican government.
However, progress in promoting transparency within the federal executive branch
has not been matched in other parts of the government.

Human Rights Defenders

Human rights defenders continue to suffer harassment and attacks, and authorities consistently fail to provide them with adequate protection. For example, two
human rights defenders in Tijuana received menacing phone calls and emails
from November 2009 to May 2010 and were constantly followed by the police and
the military. A masked man told one of the defenders to leave town if she did not
want her family to be harmed, while a car was firebombed outside of the family
home of the other defender. Receiving little protection from authorities, they
eventually fled from Tijuana.

Migrants

Hundreds of thousands of migrants pass through Mexico each year and many are
subjected to grave abuses en route including physical and sexual assault, extortion, and theft. Approximately 18,000 migrants are kidnapped annually, often
with the aim of extorting payments from their relatives in the United States.
Seventy-two kidnapped migrants originating from Central and South America
were executed en masse in August 2010 in Tamaulipas by armed gangs.

Authorities have not taken adequate steps to protect migrants, or to investigate
and prosecute those who abuse them. Authorities rarely inform migrants of their
rights, such as the right to seek asylum, and the authorities themselves are often
the perpetrators of abuses. The National Migration Institute has fired 350 agents
since 2007—roughly 15 percent of its total force—for suspected links with organized crime and crimes such as human trafficking. In September 2010, immigration
agents beat and robbed more than 100 migrants as they disembarked from a
train in Oaxaca.

The federal Population Law requires public officials to demand that foreign citizens show proof of their legal status before offering any service, such as provid-

ing medical care and registering human rights complaints. As a result, migrants who suffer abuses often choose not to report crimes out of fear of deportation. In September 2010 the Senate approved a reform that would require all authorities to attend to individuals who suffer abuses, regardless of their citizenship status. President Calderon signed the reform into law in November.

National Human Rights Commission

Mexico's official human rights institution has provided authoritative information on specific human rights cases and usefully documented some systemic problems. Under the leadership of President Dr. Raul Plascencia, the commission has played a decisive role in investigating landmark cases, such as the March killing of two students at Monterrey Tec, and in advocating for improved protection for human rights defenders and journalists.

Human Rights Reforms to the Constitution

In April 2010 the Senate approved a series of human rights reforms to the Constitution which would affirm the relevance of international law in Mexico, establish the circumstances in which a state of emergency may be declared, and protect against the arbitrary expulsion of foreigners, among other changes. The reform has not yet been approved by the House of Deputies.

Domestic Violence, Reproductive Rights, and Same-Sex Marriage

Mexican laws do not adequately protect women and girls against domestic violence and sexual abuse. Some provisions, including those that make the severity of punishments for some sexual offenses contingent on the "chastity" of the victim, contradict international standards. Ninety percent of women who have suffered human rights violations do not report them to authorities, while those who do report them are generally met with suspicion, apathy, and disrespect. Such underreporting undercuts pressure for necessary legal reforms and leads to impunity for violence against women and girls.

In August 2008 the Supreme Court affirmed the constitutionality of a Mexico City law that legalized abortion in the first 12 weeks of pregnancy. Since that time 16 of Mexico's 32 states have adopted reforms that recognize the right to life from the moment of conception. In May 2010 the Supreme Court ruled that all states must provide emergency contraception and access to abortion for rape victims. However, only five states have reformed their procedural codes accordingly and efforts to inform women and girls of their rights have been very limited.

In August 2010 the Supreme Court recognized the right of same-sex couples in Mexico City to adopt children and to marry, and ruled that all states in Mexico must recognize same-sex marriages that take place in Mexico City.

Key International Actors

The United States to date has allocated $1.5 billion in aid to Mexico through the Merida Initiative, a multi-year aid package agreed upon in 2007 to help Mexico combat organized crime. Fifteen percent of the aid can be disbursed only after the US secretary of state reports to the US Congress that the Mexican government is meeting four human rights requirements: ensuring that civilian prosecutors and judicial authorities investigate and prosecute federal police and military officials who violate basic rights, consulting regularly with Mexican civil society organizations on Merida Initiative implementation, enforcing the prohibition on use of testimony obtained through torture or other ill-treatment, and improving the transparency and accountability of police forces.

The impact of these requirements, however, was undermined when the United States twice allocated the funds despite evidence that Mexico was not meeting the conditions, most recently in September 2010. In a positive step, the State Department announced in September that it would withhold an additional $26 million in Merida aid for 2010 pending Mexico's passage of human rights reforms to the Constitution and issuance of a proposal to reform the military justice system.

In November 2009, the Inter-American Court ruled that Mexico was responsible for the forced disappearance of a Rosendo Radilla-Pacheco in 1974, and had failed to adequately investigate the crime. The binding decision ordered Mexico to modify its Code of Military Justice to ensure that "under no circumstances can military jurisdiction be applied" in cases where the military violates the human rights of civilians. In August 2010, the Inter-American Court found that Valentina Rosendo Cantú and Inés Fernández Ortega, indigenous women from Guerrero, were raped and tortured by members of the army in 2002 and again ordered Mexico to modify its military code.

The OAS and UN special rapporteurs on freedom of expression conducted a joint visit to Mexico in August 2010, concluding that grave and diverse obstacles—including serious acts of violence against journalists and widespread impunity—continue to limit free expression in Mexico. In October, the UN special rapporteur on the independence of judges and lawyers released an initial report following her visit, highlighting the lack of access to justice for the poor and a "system deficient in the investigation of crimes," among other problems.

The UN Human Rights Committee conducted its periodic review of Mexico in March. The committee urged Mexico, among other recommendations, to reestablish a special prosecutor's office dedicated to investigating abuses committed during the country's "dirty war" and eliminating *arraigo* detention from legislation and practice.

PERU

Judicial efforts to hold military and police personnel accountable for abuses committed during Peru's internal armed conflict yielded disappointing results in 2010. Government officials have often criticized the process, rather than supported it, and in 2010 President Alan García signed a decree amounting to a blanket amnesty that would leave most of the crimes unpunished. The measure was eventually withdrawn after national and international protests. Nevertheless, the military's refusal to provide information continues to obstruct judicial investigations, and most perpetrators have evaded justice.

There have been several incidents in which police have overstepped international norms on the use of lethal force in controlling protests and demonstrations. Torture, although not practiced systematically, continues to be a problem.

Confronting Past Abuses

According to Peru's Truth and Reconciliation Commission, almost 70,000 people died or "disappeared" during the country's internal armed conflict. They were victims of atrocities committed by the Shining Path and the Túpac Amaru Revolutionary Movement, and of human rights violations by state agents.

In August 2010 President García signed into law a decree that amounted to a disguised amnesty for perpetrators of human rights violations during the armed conflict. Decree 1097 violates Peru's international human rights obligations by allowing a statute of limitations to be applied to crimes against humanity committed before 2003, the year Peru ratified the United Nations Convention on the Non-Applicability of Statutory Limitations to War Crimes and Crimes against Humanity. Such crimes would include atrocities committed during the first government of Alan García, such as the massacre of 122 prisoners at El Fronton prison in 1986. Decree 1097 also obliged judges to close judicial proceedings against military and police personnel if formal charges were not presented within the 36 month maximum allowed by law. Within days a general and several members of the Colina Group, a death squad responsible for killings and "disappearances" during the government of Alberto Fujimori, asked a judge to close investigations against them. President García initially defended the decree but changed his mind after intense international and domestic criticism. In September Congress approved a government bill to repeal the decree with an overwhelming majority.

In December 2009 a Supreme Court panel unanimously confirmed a 25 year prison sentence for former president Alberto Fujimori for the extrajudicial execution of 15 people in the Barrios Altos district of Lima in November 1991, the enforced disappearance and murder of nine students and a teacher from La Cantuta University in July 1992, and two abductions. Fujimori was the first democratically elected Latin American leader to be convicted for grave human rights violations in his own country.

Given the landmark significance of the Fujimori conviction, prosecutions in other human rights cases from the armed conflict period have had disappointing results, with convictions trailing behind the number of acquittals. In June 2010 the National Human Rights Coordinator, an NGO that monitors accountability, reported that the National Criminal Court, created in 2004 to hear cases involving human rights violations and terrorism, had acquitted 65 military and police agents, convicted only 15, and dismissed 23 cases.

The Peruvian military has consistently failed to provide information to help prosecutors identify officers who participated in atrocities. Mainly as a result of this lack of cooperation, prosecutors and lawyers for relatives of victims have had difficulty assembling evidence that meets the rigorous standards courts demand. For instance, army and Ministry of Defense officials denied the detention of two students, Alcides Ccopa Taype and Francisco Juan Fernández Gálvez, who "disappeared" in Huancayo in October 1990. In June 2010 the National Criminal Court acquitted two army generals responsible for military operations in the zone. The court discounted the testimony of a former detainee, who had seen the students held at the army base, and the evidence of other witnesses who claimed to have seen them in custody.

Several former senior military officials facing charges have used tactics to delay court proceedings and then filed habeas corpus petitions to the Constitutional Court, claiming that their right to a trial within a reasonable time had been violated.

Unjustified Use of Lethal Force

In recent years there have been several violent clashes between protesters and police, with deaths on both sides. In some of these incidents police appear to have used lethal force unjustifiably.

In April 2010, five civilians were killed and 16 were wounded by gunshots when police opened fire to clear a demonstration by 6,000 striking miners who had blocked a major highway in Chala, Caraveli province. A woman, who was not participating in the events, reportedly died of a heart attack. As of September, 61 police officers were facing charges.

Controversy continues to surround the circumstances in which 33 people were killed (23 police and 10 civilians) in June 2009 in violent clashes between police and indigenous protesters in the provinces of Utcubamba and Bagua in the Peruvian Amazon. An investigative commission appointed in July 2009 placed most of the blame on the indigenous protesters, and the interference of "outside actors." However, two commissioners, including an indigenous member, refused to sign the commission's report. They published a minority version, citing evidence that the protesters were unarmed when the police started to shoot at them. In May 2010 Alberto Pizango, an indigenous leader who was accused of instigating the protest, was arrested on charges of sedition and incitement on his return from exile in Nicaragua. No ministers or police commanders were prosecuted for their handling of the protest.

In August 2010 the president issued a decree that would allow the armed forces to confront a "hostile group" in law enforcement situations using military rules of engagement. The definition of "hostile group" is loosely worded to include those armed with spears or knives or heavy objects such as rocks, raising concerns that the decree could be used to justify the use of excessive force against indigenous protesters.

Torture and Ill-Treatment

Torture remains a problem. The Human Rights Ombudsman and human rights NGOs continue to report beatings by police and by members of municipal security patrols. They also report victimization of military recruits by superior officers, such as the case in August 2010 of a soldier doing military service in Iquitos who was allegedly forced by an army major to swallow keys after a dispute. Courts often classify cases of torture according to the seriousness of physical injuries, considering less serious injuries to be cases of "wounding," which carries a lower penalty that does not normally involve incarceration.

Reproductive Rights

Peru's restrictive abortion laws and policies, which generally criminalize abortion and provide only vague guidance on when an abortion may be procured lawfully, contribute to maternal death and disability. In 2005 the UN Human Rights Committee ruled that the Peruvian state's failure to provide an abortion for an adolescent girl carrying an anencephalic pregnancy constituted a violation of several human rights, including the right to freedom from torture, and that the government had an obligation to ensure that a similar situation would not occur in the future. Even so, and despite much pressure from Peruvian civil society groups, the government has yet to adopt clear legal guidelines for the provision of legal abortion.

Media Freedom

Journalists in Peru's provinces are vulnerable to intimidation and threats. Individuals acting in support of, or working for, municipal authorities have assaulted, and even murdered, journalists who publicize abuses by local government officials.

In October 2010 the Ministry of Transport and Communications provisionally restored the broadcasting license of Radio La Voz de Bagua, a local radio station in the Peruvian Amazon, which was revoked in June 2009 after the minister of the interior and members of the president's American Revolutionary People's Alliance accused it of inciting violence during its coverage of the civil unrest in Bagua.

Human Rights Defenders

Former President Fujimori's supporters in Congress, as well as some top government officials, have aggressively sought to discredit NGOs that advocate for human rights accountability. Such NGOs have been falsely accused of sympathy with terrorist groups or of undermining the armed forces.

In recent years NGOs defending indigenous and environmental rights in areas affected by mining operations have been subject to threats and judicial harassment for allegedly organizing or participating in protests. The government abruptly revoked the residency permit of Paul McAuley, a British lay member of a Catholic order who heads an environmental association in Iquitos in the Peruvian Amazon, and who has lived in Peru for 20 years.

Key International Actors

Following a visit to Peru in September 2010, the UN special rapporteur on human rights and terrorism described Decree 1097 on the use of force by the military as "likely to lead to breaches of international law." He also expressed concern that the decree could lead to the use of unjustifiable force against unarmed protestors.

In September 2010 the Inter-American Commission on Human Rights expressed concern that Decree 1097 "could lead to impunity in hundreds of cases of human rights violations."

VENEZUELA

The Venezuelan government's domination of the judiciary and its weakening of democratic checks and balances have contributed to a precarious human rights situation. Without judicial checks on its action, President Hugo Chávez's government has systematically undermined journalistic freedom of expression, workers' freedom of association, and the ability of human rights groups to promote human rights. It has also harassed political opponents.

Police abuses and impunity are a grave problem. Prison conditions are deplorable, and fatality rates high due to inmate violence.

Independence of the Judiciary

In 2004 President Chávez and his supporters in the National Assembly launched a political takeover of the Supreme Court, filling it with government supporters and creating new measures that make it possible to purge justices from the court. Since then the court has largely abdicated its role as a check on executive power, failing to uphold fundamental rights enshrined in Venezuela's constitution in key cases involving government efforts to limit freedom of expression and association.

The government shows scant respect for democratic checks and balances. Individual judges may face reprisals if they rule against government interests. In December 2009, Judge Maria Lourdes Afiuni was detained on the day she authorized the conditional release of Eligio Cedeño, a banker accused of corruption. Afiuni was following a recommendation by the UN working group on arbitrary detentions, given that Cedeño had been in pre-trial detention for almost three years despite, although Venezuelan law prescribes a two-year limit. A day after her arrest, Chávez branded Afiuni a "bandit" who should be sentenced to the maximum 30 years in prison. Accused of corruption, abuse of authority, and "favoring evasion of justice," the judge's right to due process was violated in several respects in criminal proceedings against her. Three UN human rights experts issued a joint press release describing her arrest as "a blow to the independence of judges and lawyers in the country," and called for her release. Still, the

Supreme Court denied her appeals for the protection of her rights. As of October 2010 she was still held in deplorable conditions in a Caracas women's prison.

Media Freedom

Venezuela enjoys vibrant public debate in which anti-government and pro-government media are equally vocal in criticizing and defending the president. However, the government has discriminated against media that air views of political opponents, and has strengthened the state's capacity to limit free speech and created powerful incentives for government critics to self-censor. Laws contributing to a climate of self-censorship include amendments to the criminal code extending the scope of "desacato" laws that criminalize disrespect of high government officials, despite international standards that require such laws be abolished, and a broadcasting statute that allows arbitrary suspension of channels for the vaguely defined offense of "incitement."

In June 2010 journalist Francisco Pérez was sentenced to three years and nine months in prison, stripped of his professional certification, and ordered to pay a fine of almost US$20,000 for defaming Valencia's mayor. Perez had published two articles in *El Carabobeno* newspaper accusing the mayor of nepotism and corruption.

The government has abused its control of broadcasting frequencies to punish radio and television stations with overtly critical programming, while obliging private media to transmit speeches of the president and other officials. Since taking office in February 1999 Chávez has compelled radio and TV stations using public airwaves to transmit more than 2,000 of his speeches live.

In January 2010 the government broadcasting authority CONATEL ordered the country's cable providers to suspend transmitting channels that did not comply with the broadcasting statute—including the requirement to transmit presidential speeches—until they applied for, and received, the status of "international" channels (to which the statute does not apply). The suspension affected seven channels, including RCTV International, the cable channel created after RCTV—a critic of Chávez—was taken off public airwaves in 2007. CONATEL rejected RCTV

International's application for status as a national broadcaster. At this writing the channel was only available online and unable to transmit in Venezuela.

In June 2010 Chávez created by decree a Center for Situational Studies of the Nation (CESNA), which has broad powers to limit public dissemination of "information, facts or circumstance[s]" that it decides should be confidential. The decree's language is so broad it could allow the government to block information disseminated by civil society groups and media entirely at its discretion.

Human Rights Defenders

The Chávez government has aggressively sought to discredit local and international human rights organizations. Officials, including the president, have repeatedly made unsubstantiated allegations that human rights advocates are engaged in efforts to destabilize the country.

Rights advocates have been targeted for prosecutorial harassment. In July 2010, President Chávez stated that prosecutors should "thoroughly investigate" the "millions and millions of dollars" that the US State department gives Venezuelan NGOs. His statements came a day after a pro-Chávez organization presented a formal complaint before prosecutors seeking an investigation into funding received by two leading human rights groups in Venezuela. The judiciary has offered no protection in such cases. The Supreme Court ruled the same month that "obtaining financial resources, either directly or indirectly, from foreign states with the intent of using them against the Republic, [and] the interest of the people [could constitute] treason."

Human rights defenders are often stigmatized in government-controlled media and harassed or intimidated by unidentified individuals aligned with the government. Carlos Correa, director of Public Space, was the subject of an aggressive publicity campaign in 2010, including an animated sequence aired by state television (VTV) depicting him leaving the US embassy in a limousine with a suitcase overflowing with US dollar bills.

Prosecution of Government Critics

Several prominent critics of the Chávez government have been targeted for criminal prosecution. The courts' lack of independence diminished the accused parties' chances of receiving a fair trial.

The Attorney General's Office opened an investigation into Guillermo Zuloaga, president of Globovisión, a television station critical of the Chávez government, for "disseminating false information, offense and insulting the President of the Republic." In a speech at a public meeting Zuloaga had accused the president of having "ordered the shooting" of demonstrators during the April 2002 coup against him. In June, the president voiced outrage in a televised speech that Zuloaga was still free. A week later, police arrived at Zuloaga's house to arrest him and his son for alleged irregularities in their car sales business, an investigation their lawyers said had been stalled for months. In August the Venezuelan Supreme Court authorized a request for Zuloaga and his son's extradition from the United States, where they had fled to escape arrest.

In May a prosecutor charged Oswaldo Álvarez Paz, a former governor of the state of Zulia and a Chávez opponent, with "public incitement [to violate laws] endangering public tranquility" and "publicizing false information" for criticizing the Chávez administration during a television interview in March. Álvarez Paz had said that, "Venezuela has turned into a center of operations that facilitates the business of drug trafficking." He was in pretrial detention for almost two months.

Police Abuses

Violent crime is rampant in Venezuela, where extrajudicial killings by security agents remain a recurring problem. The minister of the interior and justice has estimated that police commit one in every five crimes. According to the Attorney General's Office, law enforcement agents allegedly killed 7,998 people between January 2000 and the first third of 2009. Impunity for all violent crimes, including those committed by police, remains the norm.

In April 2008 the Chávez administration issued a decree establishing a new national police force, and enacting measures to promote non-abusive policing that were proposed by a commission made up of government and NGO representatives. In2010 agents of the new National Bolivarian Police (PNB), trained in human rights and non-abusive methods, participated in a pilot scheme in Catia, a high-crime district of Caracas. At this writing there had been no independent evaluation of the new police force's performance.

Prison Conditions

Venezuelan prisons are among the most violent in Latin America. Weak security, deteriorating infrastructure, overcrowding, insufficient and poorly trained guards, and corruption allow armed gangs to effectively control prisons. Hundreds of violent prison deaths occur every year. In September 2010 16 prisoners were killed and 35 wounded in a riot between rival armed gangs at the Aragua Penitenciary in Tocorón.

Labor Rights

The Chávez government has systematically violated workers' rights, undercutting established labor unions while favoring new, parallel unions that support its agenda.

The government requires the National Electoral Council (CNE), a public authority, to organize and certify all union elections, violating international standards that guarantee workers the right to elect their representatives in full freedom, according to conditions they determine. Established unions whose elections have not been CNE-certified are barred from participating in collective bargaining.

The government has for several years promised to reform the relevant labor and electoral laws to restrict state interference in union elections. Reforms that explicitly state that union elections held without CNE participation are legally valid were still pending before the National Assembly at this writing.

Key International Actors

Venezuela's government has increasingly rejected international monitoring of its human rights record. In its December 2009 report on human rights in Venezuela, the Inter-American Commission on Human Rights stated that by impeding it from visiting the country, Venezuela was "contributing to the weakening of the Inter-American system for the protection of human rights." Chávez described the report as "ineffable" and "ignominious."

INDONESIA

Unkept Promise

Failure to End Military Business Activity in Indonesia

HUMAN
RIGHTS
WATCH

WORLD REPORT

2011

ASIA

AFGHANISTAN

While fighting escalated in 2010, peace talks between the government and the Taliban rose to the top of the political agenda. Civilian casualties reached record levels, with increased insurgent activity across the country. An additional 30,000 United States troops increased international forces to more than 150,000.

Endemic corruption and violence marred parliamentary elections in September 2010.

Negotiations

The Afghan government made greater efforts in 2010 to promote a negotiated settlement with the Taliban and Hezb-e Islami (Gulbuddin). In June a Consultative Peace Jirga brought together around 1,500 Afghan elders, politicians, and civil society representatives in Kabul. The government offered limited reassurances it would seek to protect the rights of Afghan women and religious and ethnic minorities during the peace process. In October a newly appointed High Level Peace Council drew criticism from a wide range of Afghan civil society organizations and human rights defenders because it included numerous former warlords implicated in war crimes.

The Conflict

The armed conflict remains most acute in the south and southeast, with a marked deterioration in security in the north. In the first nine months of 2010 the United Nations documented the deaths of 2,135 civilians, an increase of more than 10 percent compared to the same period in 2009, largely due to increased insurgent attacks that often take the form of drive-by shootings or suicide bombings. US and NATO-caused civilian casualties dropped in the first six months of the year compared to the previous year. However, the third quarter saw an increase in civilian casualties, which matched an increase in the use of air attacks and night raids. US, NATO, and Afghan forces were responsible for more than 350 civilian deaths during the first nine months of 2010.

Insurgent-targeted killings in violation of international humanitarian law increased, particularly in the south. The UN estimates 183 assassinations in the first six months of the year, up 95 percent compared to 2009. Amongst the most senior officials killed was the governor of Kunduz, northern Afghanistan, who was targeted in an October suicide bombing.

In February and March the US military carried out a major operation in Marjah, Helmand, aimed at expelling the Taliban and installing a local government capable of providing basic services. The operation led to significant civilian displacement, and increased insurgent activity in the area, including heavy mining. According to the UN, more than 70 civilians were killed in Marjah between February and April.

In June the US and NATO launched a civil and military campaign in Kandahar. Although there was emphasis on governance reform as a central component of winning popular support, little action was taken to reduce the stranglehold of a few dominant tribal strongmen on the local government and economy, including that of the president's brother, Ahmad Wali Karzai, and Kandahar's former governor, Gul Agha Sherzai. Combat operations increased in September, with civilian casualties and displacement rising due to the increased Taliban and international military presence. The International Committee of the Red Cross reported close to a thousand new patients with weapon-related injuries in August and September 2010, double the previous year.

So-called "night raids" against suspected insurgents intensified, despite a tactical directive in January 2010 encouraging commanders to use daytime raids when possible.

Timely and transparent inquiries or accountability for forces in the event of wrongdoing are often lacking when civilians are hurt or killed in night raids, airstrikes, or escalation of force incidents. A notable exception may be the response to allegations that five US soldiers deliberately killed and mutilated Afghan civilians in early 2010; several soldiers will face a court martial—for which no date has yet been set—on charges of premeditated murder.

At this writing the US has almost doubled the number of detainees it is holding in Afghanistan to more than a thousand. Despite modest procedural improvements, including the right to call witnesses, detainees do not receive adequate due process, including the right to legal counsel or to see evidence against them.

In August unidentified insurgents killed ten aid workers in Badakhshan, including eight foreign nationals and two Afghans. Insurgents abducted British aid worker Linda Norgrove in Kunar province in September; she was killed during a US special operations forces rescue operation in early October.

Attacks on Women and Girls in Taliban-Controlled Areas

Women in de facto Taliban-controlled areas face "night letters"—threatening missives often delivered at night—and death threats by phone. In recent years several high profile women have been assassinated; their killers have not faced justice. While men in Taliban-controlled areas are also threatened and attacked, there is an additional gender-related dimension to the pressures on women connected to the Taliban's interpretation of Sharia law, which is used to justify harsh punishments for women seen to be mixing with men outside their immediate families.

The Taliban and other insurgent groups continued to target schools, particularly for girls over 10-years-old. According to the Ministry of Education, between March and October 2010, 20 schools were attacked using explosives or arson, and insurgent attacks killed 126 students.

Parliamentary Elections 2010

Parliamentary elections took place in September 2010, with insecurity and fraud disenfranchising a large segment of the electorate. More than 30 were killed on polling day.

The Taliban claimed responsibility for killing three candidates during the campaign period: Sayedullah Sayed, killed by a bomb while speaking in a mosque; Ghazni candidate Najibullah Gulisanti, abducted and, after failed demands for prisoner release, killed; and Haji Abdul Manan Noorzai, shot dead while walking to a mosque in Herat. In August five campaign workers supporting Fauwzia Gilani in Herat were abducted and killed. Women campaigners throughout the country told election observers of threats and intimidation.

AFGHANISTAN

The "Ten-Dollar Talib" and Women's Rights

Afghan Women and the Risks of Reintegration and Reconciliation

HUMAN
RIGHTS
WATCH

There were serious attacks on election officials; in September, 28 election staff in Baghlan were kidnapped and two were killed in Balkh. Election monitors were also threatened and abducted during the campaign period.

Candidates and their supporters were responsible for a significant amount of the violence, with little sign at this writing that disqualifications or criminal prosecutions will follow.

Impunity

In January 2010 it emerged that a law had been quietly brought into effect in late 2009 that provides amnesty to perpetrators of war crimes and crimes against humanity, despite earlier pledges by President Hamid Karzai that the National Stability and Reconciliation law would not be promulgated. In 2007 a coalition of powerful warlords in parliament pushed through the amnesty law to prevent prosecution of individuals responsible for large-scale human rights abuses in the preceding decades. It was revived in 2010 to facilitate amnesties for reconciliation and reintegration of the Taliban and Hezb-i Islami (Gulbuddin).

Lack of due process of law remains a major failing of the legal system; Afghans continue to face arbitrary detention, and are frequently denied access to a lawyer and the right to challenge the grounds of their detention before an impartial judge. Corruption and abuse of power often taint court proceedings. Reports persist of torture and ill-treatment of detainees held by the National Directorate of Security, with human rights officials gaining only erratic access to detention facilities where abuses are thought to occur.

Kidnapping for ransom is common, with an estimated 450 Afghans abducted annually according to the Afghanistan NGO Security Office. Insurgent groups also use kidnapping to demand prisoner releases.

Attacks on Human Rights Defenders, NGOs, and Journalists

Threats, violence, and intimidation are regularly used to silence opposition politicians, journalists, and civil society activists, particularly those who speak out about impunity, war crimes, government officials, or powerful local figures.

Women's rights defenders are regularly threatened and intimidated. Government failure to bring perpetrators to justice compounds fear among other women activists.

Journalists in the conflict areas face severe pressures. Insurgent groups use arson, kidnapping, and intimidation to try to stop reporting they see as unsympathetic. The government and local strongmen also intimidate and detain journalists.

Key International Actors

Safeguards against the potential human rights implications of reconciliation and reintegration have been poorly articulated by most key international actors involved, including the US, United Kingdom, and UN. While most have stressed the need to protect women's rights, notably US Secretary of State Hillary Clinton, the constitution is cited as sufficient protection, without explicit guarantees that women's right to work and freedom of movement and education will be protected in a negotiated settlement.

While the main international actors now acknowledge that impunity has fuelled the insurgency, they have not effectively addressed systemic concerns, including the entrenched power of strongmen and former warlords, misuse of presidential powers, police corruption, and judicial weakness. This was exacerbated by continued international support for powerbrokers with past and present records of human rights abuses. The US military has introduced guidelines and a system of oversight for contracting to try to reduce perceptions it is fuelling corruption, though this has not yet led to a break with notorious powerbrokers providing logistical and security services.

The US and NATO continued to operate in Afghanistan without an adequate legal framework, such as a status-of-forces agreement. It is rare for the US and NATO to hold independent and transparent investigations into possible acts of wrongdoing, or to hold individuals to account. This is particularly true of special operations forces, and the opaque irregular Afghan forces working with both special operations forces and the CIA.

Bangladesh

The elected government of Prime Minister Sheikh Hasina Wazed made strong commitments to address serious human rights problems in 2010, but those promises were not realized, as extrajudicial executions and torture continued, as well as impunity for members of the security forces. The government mounted sustained attacks on the right to freedom of expression of the media and political opposition. Labor union activists protesting for higher wages were systematically targeted and, in some cases, arrested and jailed on trumped-up charges.

Abuses by the Rapid Action Battalion and Other Forces

Soon after elections in December 2008, officials in the Awami League-led government promised to institute a zero-tolerance policy and bring the perpetrators of extrajudicial killings to justice. Yet little change has taken place, and in 2010 the home minister and other officials denied any wrongdoing by law enforcement agencies, including the Rapid Action Battalion (RAB), the elite anti-crime, anti-terror force whose officers regularly kill with impunity. The RAB acknowledges that its officers have killed at least 622 people since the force was established in 2004. But in press statements, the RAB has claimed that the victims were shot and killed in "crossfire" after their accomplices opened fire on the force. The home minister has also supported the claim that RAB officers who have killed were acting in self-defense. In a worrying development, the police appear to have increasingly adopted the RAB's extrajudicial methods, and several hundred killings have been attributed to the police force in recent years.

Investigations by human rights organizations regularly find that victims were executed while in RAB custody. The bodies of the dead often bear marks of torture, and many survivors of RAB custody have repeatedly alleged ill-treatment and torture. The chairperson of the National Human Rights Commission recommended in December 2009 that all allegations of RAB killings be investigated by an independent commission of inquiry. At this writing the government has taken no action on this, and not a single member of the RAB has been criminally prosecuted for involvement in torture or killings.

In one abortive attempt at justice, the High Court issued a *suo moto* ruling calling on the government to explain why action should not be taken against the RAB officers responsible for the "crossfire" killing of Lutfar and Khairul Khalashi in November 2009. However, before a ruling could be issued, the relevant judicial bench was reorganized and the case has not since been heard by the court.

Attacks against Civil Society and Media

In July 2010, officials forced the closure of the daily Amar Desh, an opposition-linked newspaper that had reported critically on the government. The editor, Mahmudur Rahman, was arrested under the Anti-Terrorism Act, and he later claimed in court that police officers beat him and that RAB officers blindfolded him, handcuffed him to window bars in a cell, and deprived him of food and water. At this writing the newspaper's closure is under court appeal.

In another assault on free expression, the police in Dhaka, the capital, temporarily shuttered the Drik Picture Library on March 22, shortly before the opening of an exhibit titled "Crossfire" by Shahidul Alam. Police claimed the show, which featured photographs and installations relating to alleged extrajudicial killings by the RAB, would "create anarchy." After a public outcry and a legal challenge by the gallery, the exhibit was finally able to open on March 31.

Harassment and Intimidation of Apparel Industry Workers

In 2010 the government continued to severely restrict the work of trade unionists pressing for an increase in the minimum wage. On June 3 the government's NGO Affairs Bureau suddenly revoked the operating license of the Bangladesh Centre for Workers Solidarity (BCWS), a group with ties to international trade union and labor rights groups and representatives of foreign clothing brands sourcing from Bangladeshi factories.

In July the government raised the monthly minimum wage for garment workers from 1,662 to 3,000 taka (US$24 to $43). Workers contended that the increase was inadequate to meet the rising urban cost of living. On July 30 and 31, as they have often done in the past, angry garment workers took to Bangladesh's streets.

They blocked roads and damaged factories and other property. Government security forces responded with force, injuring scores of protesters.

On July 30 the government accused Kalpona Akhter, Babul Akhter, and Aminul Islam, the directors of the BCWS, of inciting workers to protest, which the directors denied. Babul Akhter later alleged that on the night of August 28, he was beaten in custody. Kalpona and Babul Akhter were released on bail in September and are awaiting trial at this writing. Islam, who had managed to escape police custody after being detained and allegedly physically abused by the police in June, remains in hiding.

Impunity

In 2010, members of the security forces regularly escaped accountability for killings, acts of torture, and illegal detentions. Several legal provisions effectively shield members of the security forces and other public officials from prosecution by requiring government approval for criminal actions to be initiated.

Military and police regularly employ torture and cruel, inhuman, or degrading punishment against detainees, despite constitutional guarantees against torture and Bangladesh's ratification of the United Nations Convention against Torture and Other Cruel, Inhuman or Degrading Treatment or Punishment. The government failed to investigate the causes of numerous deaths in custody, and there was little action to hold accountable those responsible for the deaths of alleged mutineers from the Bangladesh Rifles border force.

In 2009 the parliament passed amendments to the International Crimes (Tribunals) Act of 1973 in order to bring to trial those responsible for human rights crimes in the war of 1971, but the law still falls short of international standards. Five members of Jamaat-e-Islami, a religious right-wing political group alleged to have collaborated with Pakistani forces, were in 2010 charged with war crimes, including genocide, and at this writing are awaiting trial before a special war crimes tribunal established in March to investigate crimes committed during Bangladesh's battle for independence four decades ago.

Women's and Girls' Rights

Discrimination against women remains common in both the public and private spheres, despite the presence of women in several key government positions. Bangladesh maintains a reservation against article 2 of the Convention on the Elimination of All Forms of Discrimination against Women, which requires it to effectively adopt laws and policies to provide equal rights for women and men.

Domestic violence is a daily reality for many women, and there was no progress made in adopting laws on domestic violence and sexual harassment during 2010. The Acid Survivors Foundation reported 86 acid attacks, primarily against women, between January and September. The courts convicted only 15 perpetrators of acid attacks in 2009.

Sexual Orientation and Gender Identity

Section 377 of Bangladesh's criminal code punishes consensual homosexual conduct with penalties up to life imprisonment.

Border Killings

According to Odhikar, a Bangladesh human rights monitoring group, at least 930 Bangladeshi nationals were killed by India's Border Security Force between the year 2000 and September of 2010. A number of Indian nationals have also been killed by Indian forces deployed at the border.

Acute poverty and unemployment prompts millions of Bangladeshi nationals to cross the border into India in search of jobs and commerce. While some of those killed are engaged in smuggling goods and contraband, Indian border forces systematically use lethal force without justification.Bangladeshi authorities have repeatedly complained about killings of Bangladeshis, as have human rights groups in both countries. Bangladeshi Home Minister Sahara Khatun in May 2010 said that she would again ask officials in New Delhi, India's capital, to stop these incidents. Indian authorities declared that their forces have been instructed to exercise restraint, but there was little sign of progress in ending violations during 2010.

Discrimination in Corruption Cases

Prime Minister Sheikh Hasina and her Awami League party reiterated the government's strong commitment to address the problem of corruption in 2010. Yet the government recommended that the courts and the Anti-Corruption Commission withdraw hundreds of corruption cases initiated against Awami League supporters on the grounds that they were "politically motivated" cases filed under previous governments. The government has not recommended similar cases against the political opposition for withdrawal, raising significant concerns about discriminatory treatment and politically motivated prosecutions.

Refugees

Bangladeshi authorities did little to prevent a wave of intensifying violence and discrimination against Rohingya refugees from Burma, and refugees were driven out of communities and into makeshift camps. Newly arriving Rohingya were systematically denied the right to seek asylum in 2010.

Key International Actors

Foreign governments—including the US and members of the European Union—raised concerns about extrajudicial executions, stressed the importance of addressing impunity, and called for respect for human rights, but also continued to view the RAB as an important anti-terrorism force. The US has provided training on investigation methods and human rights to the RAB, but has failed to vigorously enforce the Leahy Law and deny US assistance and training to all RAB units credibly implicated in human rights abuses where justice has not been done.

After the arrests of key labor leaders in the garment industry, the US Congress sent a letter in August to US garment importers urging them to put economic pressure on Bangladesh to secure the release of the prisoners. The US Congress also called for action to withhold Generalized System of Preferences trade benefits for Bangladesh on labor rights grounds.

BURMA

Burma's human rights situation remained dire in 2010, even after the country's first multiparty elections in 20 years. The ruling State Peace and Development Council (SPDC) continued to systematically deny all basic freedoms to citizens and sharply constrained political participation. The rights of freedom of expression, association, assembly, and media remained severely curtailed. The government took no significant steps during the year to release more than 2,100 political prisoners being held, except for the November 13 release of Nobel Peace Prize winner Aung San Suu Kyi.

Calls mounted for an international commission of inquiry into serious violations of international law perpetrated by all parties to Burma's ongoing civil conflict. The Burmese military was responsible for ongoing abuses against civilians in conflict areas, including widespread forced labor, extrajudicial killings, and forced expulsion of the population. Non-state armed ethnic groups have also been implicated in serious abuses such as recruitment of child soldiers, execution of Burmese prisoners of war, and indiscriminate use of anti-personnel landmines around civilian areas.

The November 2010 Elections

In November Burma held long-planned elections. These took place in an atmosphere of intimidation, coercion, and widespread corruption, with laws and regulations strongly favoring military controlled parties.

In March the SPDC formed the Union Electoral Commission (UEC) and released a series of laws governing the conduct of the elections, which included provisions barring any person serving a prison sentence from party membership. This effectively forced the National League for Democracy (NLD) to decide whether to dismiss Aung San Suu Kyi–who was under house arrest–and more than 430 of its jailed members, in order to re-register with the UEC. The NLD ultimately did not re-register, and the UEC declared it illegal.

Other provisions tightly regulated the campaigning of parties and candidates, warned against public disturbances, and expressly outlawed public criticism of the constitution and the military. The government declared illegal a boycott campaign that some NLD members organized, and warned the public that election boycotters could face one year in prison.

In April Prime Minister Lt. Gen. Thein Sein and 27 SPDC and government cabinet ministers resigned their military commissions and formed the Union Solidarity and Development Party (USDP). In August the USDP absorbed all the assets and infrastructure of the Union Solidarity and Development Association (USDA), a mass-based social welfare movement formed by the military in 1993 with more than 26 million nominal members. The military conducted its biggest reshuffle in years, with scores of senior officers resigning in order to run as USDP candidates.

The USDP was the only party that fielded candidates for virtually all 1,168 seats open for contest in the national bicameral assembly and 14 regional assemblies. The remaining seats, out of a total of 1,551, are reserved for serving military officers as stipulated in the 2008 constitution.

By November 37 parties had registered and were contesting the elections. Many were small, ethnic-based parties only contesting a limited number of regional seats. Voting was not conducted in parts of 32 townships in ethnic border areas where the government alleged there was armed conflict and instability. Widespread irregularities, such as advance bulk voting by local officials, were reported in some regional areas.

The USDP won more than 80 percent of the seats in the bicameral national parliament. Results were mixed in the 14 state and regional assemblies, with some ethnic parties gaining half the number of seats, particularly in Arakan and Shan states. Burman-dominated regions had majority USDP candidates elected. Many opposition parties lodged official complaints with the electoral commission citing widespread corruption, particularly by USDP members and officials.

Ethnic Conflict, Displacement, and Refugees

The Burmese military continues to direct attacks on civilians in ethnic areas, particularly in Karen, Karenni, and Shan states of eastern Burma, and parts of western Burma in China and Arakan states. Tensions increased with ethnic armed groups that had agreed to ceasefires with the government, such as the Kachin

Independence Organization (KIO) and the United Wa State Army (UWSA), over the government's plans to transform these militias into Border Guard Force units under direct Burmese army control. By the end of 2010 only five militias had agreed, leaving large groups such as the Kachin, Wa, and Mon facing increased military pressure to transform, partly demobilize, and surrender territory. As a result of increased tensions, parts of 32 townships in Burma– including most of the Wa area on China's border–did not conduct polls in November. There are widespread fears of resumed conflict in 2011 in ethnic areas that have experienced uneasy peace for the past two decades.

Abuses by the Burmese military against civilians in violation of international humanitarian law include the widespread use of anti-personnel landmines, sexual violence against women and girls, extrajudicial killings, forced labor, torture, beatings, targeting of food production and means of civilian livelihood, and confiscation of land and property. All parties to Burma's conflicts continue to actively recruit and use child soldiers, with the *Tatmadaw* (state military) continuing to use them even as the SPDC cooperates with the International Labour Organization (ILO) on demobilizing child soldiers.

Approximately half-a-million people are internally displaced due to conflict in eastern Burma, with more than 140,000 refugees in camps in Thailand. In Bangladesh, there are 28,000 Rohingya refugees in official camps, and another 200,000 live in makeshift settlements or mixed in with the local population around border areas. Millions of Burmese migrant workers, refugees, and asylum seekers live in Thailand, India, Bangladesh, Malaysia, and Singapore.

Humanitarian Assistance

Burma's humanitarian situation did not markedly improve in 2010 despite attempts by international relief agencies and Burmese civil society to expand operating space and programs in the country.

The Tripartite Core Group (TCG), a multilateral mechanism formed by the Association of Southeast Asian Nations (ASEAN), the SPDC, and the United Nations in the aftermath of Cyclone Nargis in May 2008, concluded its operations in July. The UN continued to slowly expand its humanitarian initiative in Northern

BURMA

"I Want to Help My Own People"

State Control and Civil Society in Burma after Cyclone Nargis

HUMAN
RIGHTS
WATCH

Arakan State to assist Rohingya, who have been denied citizenship and suffered abuses by state and paramilitary forces for decades, including restrictions on movement, livelihoods, and freedom of religion. Abuses against Rohingya women, including restrictions on the right to marry and access maternal health, are particularly grave. Humanitarian space throughout Burma constricted markedly ahead of the November elections, with international humanitarian organizations being denied work visas for staff, travel permits, and permission to expand programs in some areas.

Calls for Accountability

In his report to the UN Human Rights Council (HRC) in March, Tomás Ojea Quintana, the special rapporteur for the situation of human rights in Myanmar, outlined a "pattern of gross and systematic violation of human rights which has been in place for many years." He concluded that "UN institutions may consider the possibility to establish a commission of inquiry (CoI) with a specific fact finding mandate to address the question of international crimes." At this writing more than 13 countries publically supported the formation of a CoI, including the United States, the United Kingdom and several other European countries, Australia, and Canada. UN Secretary-General Ban Ki-moon has not publically commented on Quintana's call.

During a general debate at the UN Human Rights Council in Geneva on September 17, Burmese ambassador U Wunna Maung Lwin denied the situation in Burma warranted an inquiry, saying there were "no crimes against humanity in Myanmar... (w)ith regard to the issue of impunity, any member of the military who breached national law was subject to legal punishments...there was no need to conduct investigations in Myanmar since there were no human rights violations there."

Quintana's report to the UN General Assembly in October elaborated on the possible parameters of a CoI, possible areas of investigation, and time frames. In late October US Secretary of State Hillary Clinton said she wanted to "underscore the American commitment to seek accountability for the human rights violations that have occurred in Burma by working to establish an international Commission of Inquiry." China has actively tried to block the proposal. The European Union, which drafted the annual Burma resolution, did not pursue calls for the CoI to be included in the resolution in the UN General Assembly.

Key International Actors

UN Secretary-General Ban expressed "disappointment" and "frustration" with the SPDC's lack of cooperation in responding to the UN's long-standing call for release of political prisoners; a free, fair, and inclusive election; and the start of a genuine process of national reconciliation. Despite requests to the SPDC, Ban's special advisor on Burma, Vijay Nambiar, was not permitted to visit Burma in 2010.

Tomás Ojea Quintana visited Burma in February, but the SPDC denied him access for further visits after his report to the HRC.

China continued to be Burma's most supportive international ally, routinely blocking criticism of Burma's human rights record in multilateral forums. Chinese Premier Wen Jiabao conducted a state visit to Burma on June 2, and Burmese President Than Shwe visited China from September 7-11. Than Shwe paid his second state visit to India in late July, where he signed numerous bilateral investment deals with Prime Minister Manmohan Singh. India failed to voice criticism or concerns over Burma's elections.

US Assistant Secretary of State for East Asian and Pacific Affairs Kurt Campbell visited Burma in May and met senior military leaders and Aung San Suu Kyi as part of the Obama administration's "pragmatic engagement" policy with the SPDC. Campbell expressed his "profound disappointment" at the SPDC's lack of reciprocity, and the US government was consistently critical of the election process. US Senator Jim Webb, who had been conducting private visits to Burma to talk with senior SPDC leaders, postponed a trip in June due to media allegations over Burma's suspected nuclear program and cooperation with North Korea.

Association of Southeast Asian Nations (ASEAN) reduced its previous criticism of Burma in 2010. In a statement, Vietnam, the current chair of the association, stated that ASEAN emphasized the importance of "national reconciliation in Myanmar" and "holding general elections in a free and fair manner with the participation of all interested parties," which it said contributed to the country's stability and development. However, Indonesia and the Philippines criticized the lack of reform in Burma, particularly the elections which Philippines President Benigno Aquino III called a "farce."

Burma's neighbors China, India, and Thailand, continued to invest and trade extensively, especially in the extractive and hydro-electric energy industries. China is building two energy pipelines from western Burma to Yunnan, and a series of massive hydro-electric dams on the Irrawaddy River in upper Burma. Sales of natural gas to Thailand still account for the largest share of the SPDC's foreign exchange earnings, which will increase markedly when the Chinese gas pipeline project is completed in 2013.

Russia and North Korea continued to sell arms to the SPDC, despite US concerns that North Korean sales could breach UN Security Council Resolution 1874, which imposes curbs on weapons proliferation.

CAMBODIA

The Cambodian government increased its repression of freedoms of expression, assembly, and association in 2010, tightening the space for civil society to operate.

Prime Minister Hun Sen's ruling Cambodian People's Party (CPP) used the judiciary, new laws, and threats of arrest or legal action to restrict free speech, jail government critics, disperse workers and farmers peacefully protesting, and silence opposition party members.

Cambodia also regressed in respecting international rights treaties. In December 2009 the government deported 20 Uighur asylum seekers at risk of torture and mistreatment to China, violating Cambodia's obligations under the 1951 Refugee Convention. The controversial refoulement took place on the eve of a visit by senior Chinese officials that finalized a massive aid package to Cambodia.

Freedoms of Expression, Association, and Assembly

Journalists who criticize the government face biased legal action, imprisonment, and violence. At least 10 opposition journalists have been killed in the past 15 years.

Under a new penal code that came into force in November 2009, government critics who peacefully express views about individuals and government institutions risk criminal prosecution for defamation and disinformation. These include the editor of *Khmer Amatak* newspaper who was charged in March with defamation and disinformation for a feature on governmental corruption, and the editor of *Prey Nokor* newspaper, which covers Khmer Krom affairs, who was forced to resign in August. In May authorities banned a public screening in Phnom Penh of a documentary about the 2004 assassination of labor leader Chea Vichea. There was no progress in his murder investigation or that of two other union leaders murdered in 2004.

Pending legislation on nongovernmental organizations and trade unions is expected to further tighten restrictions on freedom of association.

In September tens of thousands of garment workers seeking a higher minimum wage began a legal strike, which union leaders suspended after government officials agreed to negotiate. However, employers suspended or fired more than 200 union leaders and members for their roles in the strike, fueling worker protests.

Authorities continue to forcibly and often violently disperse public protests. A new law allows local officials to ban protests deemed threats to "security, safety, and public order."

Judiciary

The government made no efforts during 2010 to improve the judiciary's impartiality or independence.

Politically motivated court cases continue to target opposition members. In January a provincial court convicted opposition leader Sam Rainsy and two villagers on charges of racial incitement and destroying border demarcation posts. In a closed trial, the court refused to consider defense evidence and sentenced Rainsy to two years in jail in absentia. In September he was sentenced to 10 more years for disinformation and falsifying maps.

The judiciary's lack of independence was further highlighted in August, when the Takeo provincial court convicted four people on unfounded charges of disinformation.

A long-awaited anti-corruption law hastily passed in March, with little time for public comment. The government threatened to expel the UN resident coordinator when UN agencies called for more public debate on the law, which lacks adequate protections for whistle-blowers and fails to ensure independence for legally-created anti-corruption agencies.

Arbitrary Detention and Torture

Police and military police routinely use torture to extract confessions from detainees. Courts fail to address the illegal torture and use coerced confessions to convict the accused. The Cambodian League for the Promotion and Defense of

CAMBODIA

"Skin on the Cable"

The Illegal Arrest, Arbitrary Detention and Torture
of People Who Use Drugs in Cambodia

HUMAN
RIGHTS
WATCH

"*[A staff member] would use the cable to
beat people... On each whip the person's skin
would come off and stick on the cable...*"
—M'NOH, AGE 16

CAMBODIA

Off the Streets

Arbitrary Detention and Other Abuses
against Sex Workers in Cambodia

HUMAN
RIGHTS
WATCH

Human Rights (LICADHO) received reports of 60 cases of torture in the first half of 2010 alone.

More than 2,000 people were arbitrarily detained in 11 government drug detention centers. Mandated to treat and "rehabilitate" drug users, the centers subject detainees to violence (including electric shocks and whippings), forced labor, and military-style drills. Many detainees are children and people with mental illnesses. In December 2009, 21 drug users were illegally detained and forced to test an unregistered Vietnamese herbal formula purported to "cure" drug dependence.

Women and girls, including transgender women, involved in sex work face beatings; rape; sexual harassment; extortion; arbitrary arrest; and detention by police, government-hired security guards, and employees in social affairs centers. A 2008 law on trafficking and sexual exploitation criminalizes trafficking but also makes "solicitation" illegal, exposing sex workers to arbitrary detention and abuse. Police crackdowns on "trafficking" focus on closing brothels and arbitrarily detaining sex workers rather than prosecuting traffickers.

Homeless children, families, beggars, the mentally ill, and other indigent people gathered in police sweeps are also detained and mistreated in government social affairs centers.

Cambodia's prisons continue to be overcrowded and lack sufficient food, water, sanitation, and healthcare. Prey Veng prison experienced a major cholera outbreak in July, while 15 prisoners in Kampong Thom, who tried escaping in early 2010, were shackled to iron bars for over a month.

Land Confiscation and Forced Evictions

Illegal land confiscation and forced evictions continue to escalate. During the first half of 2010, more than 3,500 families – approximately 17,000 people – were newly affected by land grabbing, according to a survey of 13 of Cambodia's 24 provinces by LICADHO.

Land rights activists faced violence and arrest, with more than 60 people imprisoned or awaiting trial for protesting forced evictions and land grabbing.

In Kampong Speu, more than 800 families had their land confiscated due to sugar concessions granted to a CPP senator. Soldiers, military police, and courts facilitated the arrest and charging of farmers protesting seizure of their land.

In January company guards and soldiers from Brigade 31 wounded at least four people when they forcibly evicted 116 families from their land in Kampong Som which is slated for development by a Chinese-owned company. Using military force to conduct evictions is illegal in Cambodia.

Land conflicts affecting indigenous peoples continue unabated. In March the United Nations Committee on the Elimination of Racial Discrimination criticized the government for granting numerous concessions on indigenous peoples' lands without their consent and harassing peaceful protesters. In Kampong Speu, a Singaporean concession holder partnered with PM Hun Sen's sister to oversee the clearing of farmland belonging to indigenous Suy people, threatening the resource base of 350 families.

On April 26, unknown assailants in Battambang shot and killed community activist Pich Sophan, who had led fellow villagers to contest military confiscation of their land, and was a witness to the April 4 shooting of fellow activist Sim Mey. Mey survived but was jailed in May on charges of destruction of property.

Khmer Rouge Tribunal

In July the Extraordinary Chambers in the Courts of Cambodia (ECCC), the UN-backed Khmer Rouge tribunal, sentenced the former chief of Tuol Sleng (S21) prison, Kaing Gech Eav, known as Duch, to 35 years in prison for crimes against humanity and war crimes. He faces just 19 more years because of time served and deducted for his illegal detention before his transfer to the ECCC.

In September the tribunal announced indictments for four other former Khmer Rouge leaders in custody. Charges against them include genocide, crimes against humanity, torture, and murder. Despite the international co-prosecutor's submission of six additional suspects for indictment, Hun Sen continued to publicly oppose further trials beyond the five persons in custody and reiterated this view to the UN Secretary General during a meeting in October.

Refugees and Asylum Seekers

Asylum seekers, especially from Vietnam and China, face forced repatriation in violation of the Refugee Convention. Uighurs were forcibly returned to China three days after Hun Sen signed the refugee sub-decree.

The authorities also refused asylum for Khmer Krom (ethnic Khmers from southern Vietnam) who fled to Cambodia from Vietnam. Despite promises to treat Khmer Krom as Cambodian citizens, authorities failed to grant many Khmer Krom citizenship and residence rights, including 24 who were deported to Cambodia in December 2009 after a failed asylum bid in Thailand. In February 2010 authorities rejected the group's request to receive documents needed to rent housing, get jobs, and access healthcare, education, and other services.

Key International Actors

In June Cambodia's donors pledged US$1.1 billion in development aid for 2010. Years of donor funding for judicial reform have had little effect. Japan, Cambodia's largest donor and the single largest funder of the ECCC, maintained its practice of not publicly confronting the government about its rights violations. China, another major investor and donor, continued to increase aid to Cambodia with no conditions made to improve human rights.

Besides supporting rule of law, health, and human rights projects, the United States continued to aid and train Cambodia's armed forces – including units with records of serious rights violations such as Brigade 31, Battalion 70, and Airborne Brigade 911 – in violation of the Leahy law. Responding to the deportation of Uighur asylum seekers in April, the US cancelled shipment of 200 surplus military trucks to Cambodia. In July US-funded regional peacekeeping exercises took place on land transferred from a military unit involved in illegal land seizures.

In August the European Union convened its first public consultations in Cambodia with civil society ahead of its annual rights dialogue with the government. Rights groups criticized the EU's tax-free policy for imported Cambodian sugar, some of which is grown on plantations that have displaced thousands of rural Cambodians.

In March Cambodia officially accepted all 91 recommendations that UN member states made during the Universal Periodic Review of its rights record by the UN Human Rights Council. Yet when the country representative from the UN High Commissioner for Human Rights criticized the deportation of two Thais in June the government threatened to expel him. According to the Foreign Minister, Hun Sen demanded the expulsion of the representative and closure of the office in a meeting with the UN Secretary General in October. In September a report by the special rapporteur on human rights in Cambodia strongly criticized the lack of judicial independence.

CHINA

Imprisoned dissident Liu Xiaobo's selection as the 2010 Nobel Peace Prize winner in October was a defining moment for China's human rights movement. It also focused global attention on the extent of human rights violations in China, and on its unreformed, authoritarian political system as it emerges as a world power.

The Chinese government tried to censor news about the prize domestically, immediately placing Liu's wife Liu Xia under house arrest and clamping down on rights activists and Liu's supporters. It then attempted to portray the prize as part of a conspiracy by Western countries, insisting that Chinese citizens do not value civil and political freedoms.

That argument was significantly challenged by a public letter that circulated the next week: written by retired Chinese Communist Party (CPC) elders, it called for political reforms to defend the right to free expression and a free press as guaranteed by the constitution. The letter cited the domestic censorship of comments that Premier Wen Jiabao made in New York in October, in which he acknowledged that "the people's wishes for, and needs for, democracy and freedom are irresistible." In an unprecedented move, several newspapers printed Wen's comments the next day, openly challenging censorship orders.

The Nobel Prize and the letter highlighted the growing importance of debate within mainstream society, the party, and the government about the role of "universal values." These ideas were also advocated by Charter 08, the landmark document that called for a gradual overhaul of China's political system. Liu's participation in drafting the charter prompted his December 2008 arrest and his 11-year prison sentence one year later.

Freedom of Expression

The government continued to restrict the rights and freedoms of journalists, bloggers and an estimated 384 million internet users, in violation of domestic legal guarantees of freedom of press and expression. The government requires state media and internet search firms to censor references to issues ranging from the June 1989 Tiananmen massacres to details of the 2010 Nobel Peace Prize.

On January 12, 2010, the US search engine company Google announced it would seek an agreement with China's government to end the firm's self-censorship of Chinese internet users' search results, which it undertook partly because of government requirements. The government refused. On March 22, 2010, Google stopped censoring searches on its http://www.google.cn site and began redirecting them to its uncensored Hong Kong-based site.

On April 22, 2010, the government approved an amendment to the revised draft Law on Guarding State Secrets. The revised law requires internet and telecom firms to "cooperate with public security organs, state security agencies [and] prosecutors" on suspected cases of state secrets transmission.

At least 24 Chinese journalists are jailed on ambiguous charges ranging from "inciting subversion" to "revealing state secrets." They include Gheyret Niyaz, a Uighur journalist and website editor, sentenced to 15 years in June for "endangering state security" related to a foreign media interview he gave after the July 2009 protests in Xinjiang. That same week a Xinjiang court convicted three Uighur bloggers on the same charge. Dilshat Perhat, webmaster of Diyarim; the webmaster of Salkinm who goes by the name Nureli; and Nijat Azat, webmaster of Shabnam, received sentences of five, three, and ten years respectively.

Journalists who overstepped censorship guidelines continued to face official reprisals. Zhang Hong, a deputy editor with the *Economic Observer* newspaper, was fired after co-writing a March 1, 2010, editorial carried in 13 Chinese newspapers advocating the abolition of China's discriminatory *hukou* (household registration) system. *China Economic Times* editor Bao Yuehang was fired in May 2010 in apparent retaliation for a March 17, 2010, story that exposed vaccine quality shortfalls in Shanxi province linked to four children dying and at least 74 others falling ill.

Chinese journalists also continued to face physical violence for reporting on "sensitive" topics. On April 20, 2010, 10 unidentified assailants attacked Beijing News reporter Yang Jie while he photographed the site of a forced eviction. Police at the scene briefly detained the assailants before releasing them, characterizing their actions as a "misunderstanding." On September 8, 2010, security guards beat three reporters from Jilin and Changchun television stations attempting to cover a fire at the City College of Jilin Architecture and Civil Engineering.

Foreign correspondents in China continue to face reporting restrictions despite the government's October 2008 decision to eliminate requirements for official permission to travel the country and interview Chinese citizens. Those restrictions include a prohibition on foreign correspondents visiting Tibet freely.

Legal Reforms

Legal awareness among citizens continues to grow and legal reforms progress slowly, although the government's overt hostility towards genuine judicial independence undercuts legislative improvements. It also defeats efforts to progressively curtail the Chinese Communist Party's authority over all judicial institutions and mechanisms.

Two potentially significant reforms progressed on paper but not in practice. In May the Supreme People's Court, the Supreme People's Procuratorate (the state prosecution), and the ministries of public security, state security, and justice issued two directives regarding excluding evidence obtained through torture. This includes confessions of defendants and testimonies of prosecution witnesses, which underpin most criminal convictions in China.

However, these new regulations were not followed in the case of Fan Qihang, who in a video made public by his lawyer, described daily torture for six months and failed attempts to retract his forced confession during trial. The Supreme People's Court refused to investigate the torture allegations and upheld the original death sentence.

In August the government announced a draft amendment to China's criminal law that would eliminate the death penalty for 13 "economy-related non-violent offences." But in September a senior member of the legislature's Legal Affairs Committee announced the government would not pursue this initiative. China leads the world in executions: five to eight thousand take place every year.

Human Rights Defenders

Most human rights advocates, defenders, and organizations endure varying degrees of surveillance, harassment, or suppression by police and state security agencies. Several leading figures have been jailed in the past three years, and several NGOs shuttered or constrained. Yet the domestic "rights defense movement"—an informal movement connecting lawyers, activists, dissidents, journalists, ordinary citizens, and peasant and workers' advocates—continues to expand as demands grow for the state to respect its own laws.

Despite pervasive state censorship, rights advocates helped generate public and media debate on issues including illegal detention centers for petitioners travelling to the capital to lodge grievances (known as "black jails"), abnormal deaths in custody, widespread torture to extract confessions, use of psychiatric facilities to detain dissenters, socioeconomic discrimination against ethnic minorities in Xinjiang, and endemic abuses linked to forced demolitions and eviction.

Activists nonetheless paid a heavy price for these advances. In addition to routine harassment, they endure aggressive police surveillance, illegal home confinement, interception of communications, warnings and threats, repeated summons for "discussions" with security officers, and short-term detention.

Human rights lawyer Gao Zhisheng has been missing for two years. He reemerged in Beijing in early April 2010 after a year of official obfuscation about his status, telling journalists and supporters that security agents had repeatedly tortured and kept him captive. He disappeared again a few days later. In October police rejected his brother's effort to register him as a missing person.

The blind legal activist Chen Guangcheng was freed from prison in September, only to be confined with his entire family in his home village and denied medical treatment for ailments he developed in prison. Unidentified men working at the behest of local police officials threatened and roughed up journalists and activists who tried visiting him.

On November 10 Zhao Lianhai, the father of a child who developed kidney stones due to the contaminated milk scandal, was sentenced to two-and-a-half years' imprisonment on charges of "causing a serious disturbance" for his role in organizing a victims association to file a class action lawsuit.

Migrant and Labor Rights

The All-China Federation of Trade Unions (ACFTU) remains the sole legal representative of workers in China; independent labor unions are banned. Labor activism—mainly by migrant workers—in several foreign-invested factories in southern Guangdong province in the summer of 2010 challenged that prohibition, resulting in improved pay and benefits for strikers at production facilities for Japan's Honda and Denso Corporation. In August the ACFTU announced reforms aimed at developing a more democratic selection process for union leaders. Yet its insistence that reforms "not deviate from the leadership of the Communist Party" indicates that restrictions on independent union activity will remain.

The government has yet to deliver on longstanding promises to abolish the *hukou* system. Access to public benefits such as education and healthcare are linked to place of birth; China's 230 million migrant workers are denied access to these services when they move elsewhere in the country.

In June 2010 the State Council, China's cabinet, announced a proposal to replace the *hukou* system with a residential permit system, which would extend public welfare benefits to migrants in China's cities. However, the proposal lacks a timetable and financial provisions for the *hukou* system's elimination.

Sexual Orientation and Gender Identity

The government decriminalized homosexuality in 1997 and removed it from the official list of mental disorders in 2001 but does not allow same-sex marriage. In March 2010 former vice-minister of health Wang Longde told state media the government needed to end discrimination against gay men in order to more effectively combat the country's HIV/AIDS epidemic.

Despite such indications of progress, entrenched social and official discrimination against lesbian, gay, bisexual, and transgender people in China limits them from realizing fundamental rights of expression and association. Beijing police forced cancellation of the first Mr. Gay China pageant in January 2010 without explanation. In September 2010 Beijing police detained hundreds of gay men rounded up in a Haidian district park in an apparent effort to harass and intimidate homosexuals. The men were reportedly released only after providing identification and submitting to blood tests.

Women's Rights

Entrenched gender-based discrimination and violence continue to afflict Chinese women. Inequality is particularly serious in rural areas, where gender-based discrimination, unequal access to services and employment, trafficking into forced prostitution, and violence are more common than in cities. In June 2001 the non-governmental Anti-Domestic Violence Network of China Law Society (ADVN) called for revisions to domestic violence provisions of the Marriage Law. The ADVN criticized the current Marriage Law for requiring victims of domestic violence to provide what the organization considers to be impossibly high standards of proof of long-term physical abuse.

Police typically subject suspected female sex workers to public "shaming" parades in violation of their rights of privacy and due process. Public criticism of the practice peaked after a widely publicized June 2010 incident in which police forced two suspected sex workers to walk bound and barefoot through the streets of Dongguan. On July 27, 2010, state media announced an official ban on the practice, although it remains uncertain whether it will be enforced.

Health

The Chinese government moved in 2010 to protect the rights of people with HIV/AIDS. On April 27, 2010, it lifted its 20-year-old entry ban on HIV-positive foreign visitors. And on August 30, 2010, an Anhui provincial court accepted China's first-ever job discrimination lawsuit on the grounds of HIV-positive status. In November the provincial court ruled against the defendant.

However, HIV/AIDS activists and nongovernmental advocacy organizations continued to face government harassment. In May 2010 Wan Yanhai, China's leading HIV/AIDS activist, fled to the United States, citing official harassment of his NGO,

CHINA

"Where Darkness Knows No Limits"

Incarceration, Ill-Treatment, and Forced Labor as Drug Rehabilitation in China

HUMAN
RIGHTS
WATCH

the Aizhixing Institute. On August 16, 2010, police in Henan province detained Tian Xi, a veteran HIV/AIDS rights activist pursuing state compensation for victims of the province's blood contamination scandal, on charges of "intentionally damaging property" after a minor altercation at a hospital. Tian faces up to three years in prison.

Government officials and security forces continue to incarcerate suspected users of illicit drugs without trial or judicial oversight in drug detention centers for up to six years under China's June 2008 Anti-Drug Law. Detainees in drug detention centers suffer widespread human rights abuses, including arbitrary detention, forced labor, physical violence, and denial of medical services, including evidence-based drug dependency treatment and treatment for HIV/AIDS.

China's rapid economic growth has led to widespread industrial pollution. The government is failing to address the public health repercussions resulting from severe environmental degradation. Lead has poisoned tens of thousands of Chinese children, many of whom suffer permanent physical and mental disabilities as a result. Despite Chinese and international law that purport to protect people from polluted and hazardous environments, Human Rights Watch research to be published next year shows that local governments across China have prioritized concealing the problem, turning children away from hospitals, refusing to test them for lead, and withholding or falsifying test results.

Freedom of Religion

Despite a constitutional guarantee of freedom of religion, China's government restricts spiritual expression to officially registered churches, mosques, monasteries, and temples. Religious personnel appointments require government approval. Religious publications and seminary applications are subject to official review. The government subjects employees, membership financial records, and activities of religious institutions to periodic audits. It deems all unregistered religious organizations illegal, including Protestant "house churches," whose members risk fines and criminal prosecution. Certain groups, including the Falun Gong, are seen as "evil cults," and their followers are subject to official harassment and intimidation.

Police and government officials raided a training session on law and theology organized by a Christian house church in Henan's Fangcheng County on March 11, 2010, and temporarily detained three attendees. On May 9, 2010, Guangzhou police broke up an outdoor house church service in a local park and later temporarily detained the church's leader for questioning. On October 10, 2010, Beijing International Airport immigration officials blocked five Protestant house church leaders from boarding planes en route to an international evangelical conference in South Africa.

Tibet

The Tibet Autonomous Region (TAR) and the neighboring Tibetan autonomous areas of Qinghai, Sichuan, Gansu, and Yunnan province, remained tense. The Chinese government gave no indication it would accommodate the aspirations of Tibetan people for greater autonomy, even within the narrow confines of the country's autonomy law on ethnic minorities' areas. There were no mass arrests in 2010 of the kind that followed the spring 2008 protests, but the government maintains a heavy security presence across the Tibetan plateau and continues to sharply curtail outside access to most Tibetan areas.

Tibetans suspected of being critical of political, religious, cultural, or economic state policies are targets for persecution. In June the 15-year sentence given to Karma Sandrup, a prominent art dealer and environmental philanthropist, on unfounded charges of "grave robbing" signaled a departure from the government's previous willingness to embrace economically successful Tibetan elites who abstained from political pursuits. Multiple due process violations marred the trial, including evidence the suspect and witnesses had been tortured.

In July 2010 the government rejected the findings of a comprehensive Human Rights Watch report, which established that China had broken international law in its handling of the 2008 protests. The report, based on eyewitness testimonies, detailed abuses committed by security forces during and after protests, including use of disproportionate force in breaking up protests, firing on unarmed protesters, conducting large-scale arbitrary arrests, brutalizing detainees, and torturing suspects in custody. The government accused Human Rights Watch of "fabricating material aimed at boosting the morale of anti-China forces, misleading the

CHINA

"I Saw It with My Own Eyes"

Abuses by Chinese Security Forces in Tibet, 2008-2010

HUMAN
RIGHTS
WATCH

general public and vilifying the Chinese government," but failed to respond to any of the report's substantive allegations.

Xinjiang

The Urumqi riots of July 2009—the most lethal episode of ethnic unrest in recent Chinese history—continued to cast a shadow over developments in the Xinjiang Uighur Autonomous Region. The government has not accounted for hundreds of persons detained after the riots, nor investigated serious allegations of torture and ill-treatment of detainees that have surfaced in testimonies of refugees and relatives living outside China. The few publicized trials of suspected rioters were marred by restrictions on legal representation, overt politicization of the judiciary, failure to publish public notification of the trials, and failure to hold genuinely open trials as mandated by law.

Pervasive ethnic discrimination against Uighurs and other ethnic minorities persisted, along with sharp curbs on religious and cultural expression and politically-motivated arrests under the guise of counterterrorism and anti-separatism efforts.

In April Beijing installed a new leader for the autonomous region, Zhang Chunxian, to preside over an ambitious economic overhaul. In May the first national Work Conference on Xinjiang unveiled numerous measures that are likely to rapidly transform the region into an economic hub but also risk further marginalizing ethnic minorities and accelerating migration of ethnic Han Chinese into the region.

By the end of 2011, 80 percent of traditional neighborhoods in the ancient Uighur city of Kashgar will have been razed. Many Uighur inhabitants have been forcibly evicted and relocated to make way for a new city likely to be dominated by the Han population.

Key International Actors

China's government became more brazen in thwarting international norms and opinion. In late December 2009 it successfully pressured Cambodia to forcibly return 20 Uighur asylum seekers, despite its record of torturing Uighurs and vocal opposition from the US and others. A few months later, when the US suspended a shipment of trucks to punish Cambodia for violating the 1951 Refugee Convention, China provided a comparable shipment within a few weeks.

The Chinese government also continued to obstruct international efforts to defend human rights by taking steps to derail growing international momentum for a commission of inquiry into war crimes and crimes against humanity in Burma. China's United Nations delegation also opposed the release of a UN report documenting use of Chinese ammunition in Darfur in violation of an arms embargo. The Chinese government has still not issued invitations to the UN high commissioner for human rights or a half-dozen other special rapporteurs who requested visits in the wake of the Tibet and Xinjiang protests.

Although more than a dozen countries continue to pursue human rights dialogues with the Chinese government, few of these opaque discussions produced meaningful outcomes in 2010. While most of these governments offered strong support for the Nobel Committee's choice of Liu Xiaobo as winner of the peace prize, many failed to seize other opportunities, such as conducting high-profile visits to China or meeting senior Chinese officials to raise human rights concerns.

INDIA

India, the world's most populous democracy, has a vibrant media, active civil society, a respected judiciary, and significant human rights problems.

The government's agenda in 2010 was dominated by continuing insurgency and armed conflict in several regions, including Jammu and Kashmir, Maoist-afflicted areas in central India, and Manipur and other parts of the volatile northeast. Impunity for abuses committed by security forces in the context of these conflicts remains a pressing concern.

Authorities made little progress in reforming the police; improving healthcare, education, and food security for millions still struggling for subsistence; ending discrimination against *Dalits* ("untouchables"), tribal groups, and religious minorities; and protecting the rights of women and children.

In many parts of the country, communities protested forcible acquisition of land by state governments for infrastructure and mining projects. These projects frequently go ahead without proper safeguards to protect the rights of those at risk of displacement.

Legislators and officials proposed new laws to prevent torture, ensure food security, and prosecute those responsible for sexual violence, but have yet to repeal laws providing effective immunity from prosecution to government officials, including soldiers and police, responsible for human rights violations.

Accountability for Security Force Abuses

The security forces have at times used excessive force in suppressing violent street protests in Indian-administered Kashmir; the clashes resulting in more than 100 deaths and thousands of injuries to both civilians and security forces. Deaths and injuries to protesters, many of them children, prompted anger and renewed protests, deepening a cycle of tit-for-tat violence. In September the government sought to calm tempers by announcing dialogue, releasing arrested protesters, and providing financial compensation for deaths.

Maoist insurgents (Naxalites), operating in seven states, killed more than 100 police and paramilitary personnel in 2010, prompting a massive government security response. Civilians were often caught up in the fighting.

In Manipur, conflicting separatist demands by rival groups led to repeated unrest, with the security forces continuing to operate under the Armed Forces Special Powers Act (AFSPA). Separatist groups and security forces committed serious abuses against civilians; no members of the security forces were held accountable.

Activists in all of the conflict areas and in major cities demanded repeal of the AFSPA and a larger commitment by officials to holding security forces accountable for abuse, but repeal efforts were stymied by opposition from the army and extreme nationalist political parties.

Bombings and Other Attacks

Prosecutors made some progress in 2010 in pursuing justice for a series of bombings targeting civilians that killed 152 persons in 2008, responsibility for which was claimed by an Islamist militant group called Indian Mujahedin (IM). Police have charged more than 70 alleged IM members or associates from nine states in the 2008 attacks and continue to seek the arrest of more than three dozen fugitives. The IM is also suspected in a February 2010 attack in Pune city that claimed 17 lives and has apparently claimed responsibility for a September attack that injured two foreign tourists in New Delhi.

There were repeated allegations of unlawful detention, torture, and other ill-treatment by police to secure confessions in response to such attacks. In several cases, the police themselves appear to have drafted the confessions. The suspects suffered further abuses while in jail awaiting trial and even in court.

On an encouraging note, the trial of Ajmal Kasab, the sole surviving Pakistani gunman in the November 2008 Mumbai attack that claimed 166 lives, was conducted in a professional manner and was not the summary proceeding that critics had feared.

Police in 2010 reported that extremist Hindu groups may have been responsible for bombing attacks in Ajmer and Hyderabad, prompting the Home Minister to warn against these previously ignored militant groups.

Other Accountability Issues

Impunity for abusive policing remains a pressing concern in India, with continuing allegations in 2010 of police brutality, extrajudicial killings, and torture. While some policemen were prosecuted for human rights abuses, legal hurdles to prosecution remained in place and long-promised police reforms remained in draft form or unimplemented. Alleged perpetrators use political influence, corruption, and intimidation to obstruct investigations, delay proceedings, discourage plaintiffs, and ultimately escape prosecution.

The long backlog and slow progress of cases in India's courts also discourages potential complainants. Victims' family members and human rights lawyers needed several years, for example, to force an investigation into allegations that the Gujarat police summarily executed four persons in 2004. Only after the Supreme Court ordered the Central Bureau of Investigation to investigate the summary execution of an alleged terrorist in 2005 were a state minister and several senior Gujarat police officials arrested.

The government has yet to prosecute those responsible for the mass killings of Sikhs that followed the 1984 assassination of Prime Minister Indira Gandhi by her Sikh bodyguards. Delivery of justice for mass violence against Muslims in Mumbai in 1992-93 and in Gujarat in 2002 has been slow.

In a positive development, a legislator from the ultra-nationalist Bharatiya Janata Party was convicted in June 2010 for his role in violence against Christians in Orissa in 2008 that left at least 40 people dead and thousands displaced when a Hindu mob attacked Christians. In August, 16 others were sentenced to three years in prison for their role in the violence.

Women's Rights

While many serious issues remain, Indian officials took some positive steps on women's rights in 2010. In March long-awaited legislation reserving seats for women in parliament was passed by the upper house and awaits lower house approval. In April authorities introduced nationwide guidelines for maternal death investigations and introduced a separate mechanism to track pregnancies and their outcomes.

"Honor" killings of women and girls continued in 2010, mostly in the northern states of Haryana, Punjab, and Uttar Pradesh. *Khap panchayats* (unofficial village councils) issued edicts condemning couples for marrying outside their caste or religion and censured marriages within a *gotra* (kinship group) as incestuous even though there was no biological connection. To enforce these decrees, family members threatened couples, filed false cases of abduction, and killed spouses to protect the family's "honor." Some local politicians and officials were sympathetic to the councils' edicts, implicitly supporting the violence.

India still lacks comprehensive legislation on sexual violence and child sexual abuse, but authorities in 2010 began to consider reforms to the existing sexual violence law. Among a host of other problems, rape survivors continue to suffer from use of an unscientific and degrading "finger test" in many hospitals to determine whether they are "habituated" to sexual intercourse; the findings of the test can be used in rape cases and other criminal proceedings.

Children's Rights

In Jammu and Kashmir, several children were among those killed or injured during anti-government demonstrations. Children detained for alleged participation in the violent protests were held in jail with adults, in violation of juvenile justice laws.

Although the government issued a directive preventing security forces from occupying and using schools as long-term outposts during anti-Maoist operations in states such as Chhattisgarh, Bihar, and Jharkhand, it failed to effectively implement the measure, resulting in continued disruptions in education. Maoist insurgents continued to bomb government schools and to recruit children into armed combat. The government failed to effectively implement policies that provide for free and compulsory primary education.

Access to Pain Relief

Hundreds of thousands of persons with advanced cancer suffer unnecessarily from severe pain because the Indian government has failed to ensure access to safe, effective, and inexpensive pain drugs. More than half of government-supported regional cancer centers do not offer palliative care or pain management, even though more than 70 percent of their patients need it. Numerous patients told Human Rights Watch that their suffering from cancer and other conditions was so severe that they would rather die than live with the pain. The government also failed to integrate palliative care into HIV treatment programs.

Sexual Orientation and Gender Identity

Building on a 2009 decision of the Delhi High Court, government officials promised to drop section 377—a provision too often abused to treat consensual homosexual conduct between adults as a crime—in proposed amendments to the Penal Code.

India's Foreign Policy

Despite its considerable influence, India continues to miss opportunities to raise concerns about even egregious human rights violations in other countries or to assert leadership on human rights at the United Nations. In several cases, it has actively opposed international efforts to pressure human rights violators.

India played an important role in Afghanistan, providing aid for humanitarian and infrastructure projects. In July the Foreign Minister called on all parties to abjure violence, end links to terrorism, and accept the "democratic and pluralistic values of the Afghan Constitution, including women's rights."

After the conclusion of a Sri Lankan military campaign to defeat the Tamil Tigers in 2009, India provided humanitarian assistance for the rehabilitation of displaced persons and called for political reconciliation. India, however, has continued to be weak on accountability for atrocities committed during the conflict by both Sri Lankan and Tamil Tiger forces.

In July India hosted a state visit by Burma's authoritarian leader, General Than Shwe. India failed to demand greater protection for human rights by the military junta, support an international commission of inquiry into war crimes in Burma, or condemn the deeply flawed processes and rules for Burma's national election held on November 7, 2010.

Relations with Pakistan remained tense, particularly when new evidence showed that Pakistani military intelligence officials may have been involved in supporting the Lashkar-e-Taiba attack in Mumbai in November 2008.

Key International Actors

India's policy in the subcontinent is heavily influenced by its strategic and economic concerns about China's growing influence in countries like Burma, Nepal, Pakistan, and Sri Lanka.

Relations between India and China suffered setbacks in 2010. China disapproves of India's continued support to Tibetan refugees and its hosting of the Tibetan government in exile. However, both China and India agreed to resolve differences through continued dialogue.

India continued to build strong ties with the United States and Europe, built on increasing trade and business opportunities. Both the US and EU insisted they privately pressed India to address a range of domestic rights concerns and to become more of a champion of human rights issues internationally. But there was no evidence such efforts resulted in changes in Indian policy or practice.

INDONESIA

Over the past 12 years Indonesia has made great strides in becoming a stable, democratic country with a strong civil society and independent media. However, serious human rights concerns remain. While senior officials pay lip service to protecting human rights, they seem unwilling to take the steps necessary to ensure compliance by the security forces with international human rights and punishment for those responsible for abuses.

New allegations of security force involvement in torture emerged in 2010. But the military consistently shields its officers from investigations and the government makes little effort to hold them accountable. The government has also done too little to curb discrimination against and attacks on religious, sexual, and ethnic minorities.

In July the US government lifted its ban on military assistance to Kopassus, Indonesia's elite special forces, despite continuing concerns about its human rights record.

Freedom of Expression

While Indonesia today has a vibrant media, authorities continue to invoke harsh laws criminalizing those who raise controversial issues, chilling peaceful expression. Indonesia has imprisoned more than 100 activists from the Moluccas and Papua for "rebellion" for peacefully voicing political views, holding demonstrations, and raising separatist flags.

In August Indonesian police arrested 21 individuals for planning to float pro-independence flags attached to balloons during a visit to the Moluccas by President Susilo Bambang Yudhoyono. Police subjected them to severe beatings that lasted for days including with wooden sticks and bars and forced them to hold painful stress positions. In September Papuan activist Yusuf Sapakoly, convicted of "rebellion" in 2007 for assisting activists who displayed a pro-independence flag, died of kidney failure after prison authorities denied him medical treatment. In July, after 10 months of delay, prison authorities in Papua permitted political prisoner Filep Karma to travel to Jakarta for necessary surgery.

Indonesia's criminal libel, slander, and "insult" laws prohibit deliberately "insulting" a public official and intentionally publicizing statements that harm another person's reputation, often even if those statements are true. In early 2010 Tukijo, a farmer from Yogyakarta, was sentenced to six months' probation and a three-month suspended prison sentence for criminal defamation after he asked a local official to disclose the results of a land assessment.

Military Reform and Impunity

Indonesia still does not credibly investigate most allegations of serious human rights abuse by security forces. Despite parliament's recommendation in September 2009, President Yudhoyono failed in 2010 to authorize an ad hoc court to investigate the 1997-98 enforced disappearances of student activists. Nor was there any progress on a bill before parliament that would give civilian courts jurisdiction to try soldiers accused of committing abuses against civilians. In November a military court in Papua convicted four soldiers for beating unarmed civilians in Papua to sentences of between five and seven months in prison, the incident was captured on film. Other videos of security forces torturing or killing civilians emerged this year but few perpetrators have faced justice.

Ignoring recommendations from a National Human Rights Commission team, police and prosecutors took no steps to reopen the case against former deputy state intelligence chief and one-time Kopassus commander Maj. Gen. Muchdi Purwopranjono, implicated in the 2004 murder of prominent human rights activist Munir Said Thalib.

In January President Yudhoyono appointed Maj. Gen. Sjafrie Sjamsoeddin, implicated in the 1997-98 student disappearances and in serious human rights abuses in East Timor, to the position of deputy defense minister.

Of 18 Kopassus personnel convicted of human rights abuse since 1999, at least 11 continue to serve in the military. On March 22 Defense Minister Purnomo Yusgiantoro publicly pledged to suspend from active duty military officials credibly accused of gross human rights abuses in the future, discharge those convicted of abuse, and cooperate with their prosecution. Six days later soldiers in Depok were accused of severely assaulting four boys who had allegedly stolen a

INDONESIA

Turning Critics into Criminals

The Human Rights Consequences
of Criminal Defamation Law in Indonesia

HUMAN
RIGHTS
WATCH

INDONESIA

Prosecuting Political Aspiration

Indonesia's Political Prisoners

HUMAN
RIGHTS
WATCH

bicycle. Military police said they investigated the soldiers but released no information suggesting that they were prosecuted or disciplined.

The armed forces retain extensive business holdings despite a law requiring the government to shut down these businesses or take them over by October 2009. The government merely ordered a partial restructuring of the entities—cooperatives and foundations—through which the military holds many of its investments. The team overseeing the restructuring failed to meet an August deadline to complete its work, which remains incomplete at this writing.

Freedom of Religion

Senior government officials justify restrictions on religious freedom in the name of public order. In April Indonesia's Constitutional Court upheld a law prohibiting "blasphemy," which criminalizes the practice of beliefs deviating from the central tenets of one of six officially recognized religions, on the grounds that it protects public order.

On several occasions militant Islamist groups mobilized large groups of private citizens and attacked places of worship of minority religious communities. Police frequently failed to arrest the perpetrators of the violence. In July the local authorities tried to seal a mosque where members of the Ahmadiyah religious community worship in Kuningan, West Java. When Ahmadiyah members blocked them, hundreds of anti-Ahmadiyah protesters then attempted to forcibly close the mosque, resulting in minor injuries. Police made no arrests, and in August Indonesia's religious affairs minister called for a ban on Ahmadiyah religious practice, claiming that the violence resulted from the Ahmadiyah's failure to adhere to a 2008 decree requiring them to refrain from spreading their faith.

Several minority congregations alleged that local government officials arbitrarily refused to issue them permits required by law to build a "house of worship." Those who attempted to worship without a permit faced harassment and violence.

In August protesters assaulted a Protestant congregation that had begun holding services in a vacant lot after officials in Bekasi, a Jakarta suburb, denied their permit request and sealed two sites they used for services. Approximately 20 congregants were injured, but police made no arrests. In September assailants attacked two leaders of the congregation, injuring one critically. Police arrested 10 suspects, including the leader of the local chapter of the militant Islamic Defenders Front.

Sexual Orientation and Gender Identity

In a sign of rising social intolerance, threats by the Islamic Defenders Front forced cancellation of a regional meeting of the International Lesbian, Gay Bisexual, Trans and Intersex Association (ILGA) in Surabaya in March and a National Human Rights Commission workshop on transgender issues in April.

Papua/West Papua

In 2010 Indonesia maintained restrictions on access to Papua by foreign human rights monitors and journalists, facilitating a climate of impunity. Indonesia expelled the International Committee of the Red Cross (ICRC) from Papua in 2009; its office there remained closed in 2010.

In May government officials transferred Anthonius Ayorbaba, the warden at Papua's Abepura prison, after the Papua office of the National Commission on Human Rights found him responsible for frequent beatings of prisoners by guards. However, authorities did not investigate Ayorbaba further and took no other steps to address allegations of prisoner abuse at Abepura.

In July Papuan journalist Ardiansyah Matra'is's body was found in a river. Matra'is had reported on plans for a large agri-business development in Papua and illegal logging involving police officers. Police claimed he had committed suicide, but an autopsy revealed he had died before entering the river.

Despite the wide circulation of a video showing police paramilitary (Brimob) officers taunting Yawan Wayeni after they had cut open his stomach, police officials made no effort to investigate or prosecute those responsible for his killing.

In October a 10-minute cell phone video showed Indonesian soldiers brutally torturing two Papuan farmers, Tunaliwor Kiwo and Telangga Gire, as they asked them about weapons. Kiwo screams as a piece of burning wood is repeatedly jabbed at his genitals. The Indonesian government promised to prosecute the soldiers.

Aceh

Aceh's provincial government continued to implement a repressive Sharia-inspired dress code and law on "seclusion"—banning association between unmarried men and women in "isolated" places—primarily through a Sharia police force that harasses, intimidates, and arbitrarily arrests and detains women and men. Local community groups also forcibly enter homes and assault and publicly humiliate couples they suspect to be committing "seclusion." Police make little effort to deter such behavior.

In January 2010, three Sharia police officers raped a young woman they had detained overnight on suspicion of "seclusion." Officials replaced the head of the local Sharia police and two of the perpetrators were tried and sentenced to imprisonment for eight years, but authorities declined to implement broader remedial measures.

In July the West Aceh district government forbade women from wearing tight pants and authorized the local Sharia police to require women wearing pants to immediately change into a government-issued skirt.

In a positive development, Aceh's governor refused to implement an October 2009 draft law that would have added new Sharia offenses that raise human rights concerns, including criminalizing adultery by a married person and imposing penalties including death by stoning.

Migrant Domestic Workers

Migrant domestic workers continue to confront a range of abuses both during the recruitment process in Indonesia and while employed abroad. The government has failed to stop local recruiters from charging prospective migrants exorbitant fees that leave them highly indebted, which contributes to situations of forced labor abroad. Citing concerns about abuse, the government has maintained bans of new migration to Malaysia and Kuwait, and in 2010 imposed and lifted a ban

INDONESIA

Policing Morality

Abuses in the Application of Sharia in Aceh, Indonesia

HUMAN
RIGHTS
WATCH

on migration to Jordan. Negotiations to revise a 2006 memorandum of understanding with Malaysia on domestic workers, initially expected to be concluded in 2009, have repeatedly stalled on establishing a minimum wage and a recruitment fee structure.

Child Domestic Workers

Hundreds of thousands of girls in Indonesia are employed as domestic workers. Many work long hours, with no day off, and are forbidden from leaving the house where they work. In the worst cases, girls are physically, psychologically, and sexually abused by their employers. Presently, Indonesia's labor law excludes all domestic workers from the basic labor rights afforded to formal workers.

The parliament failed to enact a draft Domestic Worker's Law. The committee considering the bill ceased its deliberations in July 2010 following internal disagreements, particularly over a provision that would require domestic workers to be paid the minimum wage.

Migration and Refugees

Indonesia does not offer asylum for refugees and has not ratified the 1951 Refugee Convention. Increasingly, Indonesia has detained asylum seekers, largely as a result of foreign pressure. Indonesia detained nearly 1,300 migrants between January and June 2010, many of whom were attempting to reach Australia. Some organizations have reported mistreatment and substandard care in detention.

Key International Actors

Indonesia continued its leadership role in ASEAN and appointed an independent expert supported by civil society groups as its representative to the ASEAN Intergovernmental Commission on Human Rights (AICHR), which held its first formal session in Jakarta in April. Yet Indonesia failed to press for strengthening the AICHR's weak mandate or for substantial participation by civil society organizations in its work.

The United States broadened bilateral relations with Indonesia by implementing the US-Indonesia Comprehensive Partnership. In July the US lifted an 11-year ban on military aid to Kopassus, despite continuing concerns about impunity and the unit's human rights record. The US requested that Indonesia shift soldiers previously convicted of human rights abuse out of the force but not that they be discharged from the military entirely. In November President Barack Obama visited Jakarta to discuss the US-Indonesia Comprehensive Partnership, signaling closer cooperation between the two nations. He did not raise specific human rights concerns.

The US also continued to provide significant support to Detachment 88, Indonesia's counterterrorism police, but revealed that it cut off aid for the unit in the Moluccas in 2008 as a result of human rights concerns.

In September the US House of Representatives Committee on Foreign Affairs held a hearing to discuss abuses by security forces in Papua and shortcomings in the implementation of special autonomy.

The Australian government continued to cooperate with Kopassus and Detachment 88. In September Australia noted concern about torture allegations in the Moluccas but did not announce a suspension of aid in response.

In June the European Union held the first EU-Indonesia Human Rights Dialogue in Jakarta. The EU reported that it raised areas of concern but did not indicate whether it had called for any specific human rights improvements.

MALAYSIA

Nearly two years after Malaysian Prime Minister Seri Najib Tun Razak assumed office pledging to "uphold civil liberties," there has been only limited progress. Promised amendments to the Internal Security Act (ISA) and other laws permitting preventive detention have not been enacted. Restrictions on freedom of expression continue to be used to limit the right of government critics to express their views. Local police chiefs continue to restrict public assemblies and processions, often on political grounds.

Detention without Charge or Trial

Malaysia's 50-year-old ISA permits indefinite detention without charge or trial of any person deemed by officials to be a threat to national security. Officials in 2010 reiterated their opposition to repeal of the ISA but agreed to consider reforms in five areas, including limiting detention without trial, providing guarantees against mistreatment of detainees, and more precisely defining what behavior triggers application of the ISA. However, in March the home minister declared that the ISA could not be amended without also reviewing six other laws affecting security and permitting preventive detention, including the Emergency (Public Order and Crime Prevention) Ordinance, the Dangerous Drugs (Special Preventative Measures) Act, and the Restricted Residence Act.

The United Nations Working Group on Arbitrary Detention visited Malaysia in June 2010 and reported that it was "seriously concerned" by the laws permitting preventive detention and recommended their repeal or, if amended, their "conformity with article 10 of the Universal Declaration of Human Rights." The working group expressed concerns that Malaysian authorities resort to the Emergency Ordinance even when the alleged crimes, such as stealing, fighting, or involvement in organized crime, fall under the purview of Malaysia's penal code.

Migrant Workers, Refugees, Asylum Seekers, and Trafficking Victims

The Malaysian Immigration Act 1959/1963 fails to differentiate between refugees, asylum seekers, trafficking victims, and undocumented migrants. While other laws and policies provide some protections for some groups, the government does not effectively or consistently screen alleged immigration offenders; resulting in many ostensibly protected individuals end up arrested, detained, and deported.

In October 2010, in an attempt to "prove to the international community Malaysia's commitment to fighting human trafficking," police used the ISA to detain seven Malaysian immigration officers and two foreigners for trafficking offenses. The same month the government implemented amendments to the Anti-Trafficking in Persons Act that conflate trafficking victims with smuggled migrant workers, reduce protections for both groups, and make it less likely that trafficking victims will be able to cooperate in identifying and prosecuting perpetrators. The government continues to hold trafficking victims in closed shelter facilities that resemble detention centers.

Despite announcements to the contrary, some 300,000 migrant domestic workers in Malaysia still lack important protections. Domestic workers are excluded from key protections under Malaysia's Employment Act, including limits on working hours, public holidays, a mandatory day off per week, annual and sick leave, maternity protections, and fair termination of contracts.

In 2009 Indonesia suspended migration of domestic workers to Malaysia until a 2006 Memorandum of Understanding could be revised with stronger protections for workers. Negotiations have stalled repeatedly over the establishment of a minimum wage structure, employees' rights to retain their passports, and division of responsibility for recruitment and placement costs.

Drug Policy

The National Anti-Drugs Agency maintains some 28 *Puspens* (drug detention centers) where detainees are held for a minimum of two years. Although rates of relapse to drug use have been estimated in Malaysia at 70-90 percent, people who are subsequently rearrested for drug use face long jail terms and caning.

Freedom of Assembly and Police Abuse

Police continued in 2010 to restrict the right to peaceful assembly guaranteed in Malaysia's constitution. On several occasions, local police refused to issue permits to activists for public assemblies, marches, and meetings, and used excessive use of force to break up unlicensed events.

On August 1, police dispersed eight candlelight vigils commemorating the 50th anniversary of the ISA, detaining more than 30 people. At some sites, they failed to give proper warning or allow sufficient time for participants to disperse. Lawyers on hand to represent detained individuals were prevented from doing so.

There was no progress on plans announced in August 2009 by Home Minister Hishamuddin Hussein to remove restrictions on public gatherings at certain designated locations.

Freedom of Expression and the Media

As blogs, Twitter, YouTube, and other websites continue to challenge mainstream newspapers, television, and radio for readers and listeners, officials continue to fall short in fulfilling their pledge to preserve an open internet and to realize Prime Minister Najib's vision of a media sector in which journalists are "empowered to report what they see, without fear of consequence."

Officials in 2010 harassed journalists, confiscated published materials for "review," and banned publications outright or suspended them for activities allegedly beyond the scope of their publishing licenses. The 1984 Printing Presses and Publications Act requires that all publications renew their licenses annually.

In September Najib explained the gap between his rhetoric and the government's noticeably more vigorous crackdown on free expression, saying, "I did say that press must be responsible. I did not say that we will waive all the laws in Malaysia... if you go against the law, whether it is defamation or whether it is inciting racial hatred, religious hatred, then you have to be responsible for your action."

In June and July the government temporarily shut down newspapers published by the opposition coalition's three major parties. Printing license renewals came with restrictive conditions, such as requirements that sales be limited to party offices and party members.

Also in June, the Home Ministry banned *1Funny Malaysia*, a book of political cartoons, and two other books by *Malaysiakini* cartoonist Zulkifli Anwar Ulhaque, popularly known as Zunar. In September, hours before the launch of *Cartoon-o-phobia*, a another Zunar book, police raided his office, seized copies of the work, and arrested him on sedition charges for publishing books detrimental to public order. In October Home Minister Hishamuddin denied application for yet another book by Zunar.

That same month the Malaysian Communications and Multimedia Commission investigated *Malaysiakini*, a popular online newspaper often critical of government policy, over its reporting on Prime Minister Najib's opening speech at the general assembly of the ruling coalition, the United Malays National Organization. The Home Ministry has repeatedly refused *Malaysiakini*'s applications to publish a daily print version.

Sexual Orientation and Gender Identity

The government continued to reject efforts to repeal article 377 of the penal code, which criminalizes consensual "carnal intercourse against the order of nature," or to replace the law's section on non-consensual sexual acts with a modern, gender-neutral law on rape. The government ceased banning gay-themed films, but only if certain acts are not depicted and gay characters repent by the movie's end.

Due Process and Trial of Anwar Ibrahim

The trial of Anwar Ibrahim, leader of Malaysia's political opposition, continued on the charge of "sodomy" in a case involving alleged consensual homosexual conduct. The prosecution refused to hand over documents crucial to the defense, including a list of witnesses, witness statements, and clinical notes and specimens from the medical examination of the accuser two days after the alleged incident took place. Malaysia's Criminal Procedure Code, section 51A, includes a provision requiring the prosecution to turn over "any" document it will use as evidence and a written statement of facts favorable to the defense with the exception of any act that "would be contrary to public interest."

Freedom of Religion

Although Islam is Malaysia's official state religion, the constitution affirms that Malaysia is a secular state protective of religious freedom for all. However, Malaysia's dual-track legal system permits Sharia courts, in which non-Muslims have no standing, to rule on religious and moral offenses involving Muslims and on issues involving marriage, inheritance, divorce and custody battles, and burial rites, many of which involve interreligious disagreement. In a widely publicized and potentially far-reaching decision in March, Malaysia's high court awarded custody of three children to a Hindu woman whose husband had, without her knowledge, converted to Islam and had the children converted, but other cases remained mired in the courts.

Key International Actors

United States officials emphasized trade and investment, nuclear non-proliferation, and regional security in discussions in 2010 with their Malaysian counterparts, but did address some concerns relating to human rights, democracy, and rule of law. In a visit in November US Secretary of State Hillary Clinton did not meet with human rights groups or with Anwar Ibrahim.

Malaysia invited the UN Working Group on Arbitrary Detention to visit but then tried to stop civil society representatives from meeting privately with visiting group members.

In May Malaysia was elected to the UN Human Rights Council.

Malaysia continued to play the primary role in thwarting efforts by the intergovernmental Association of Southeast Asian Nations (ASEAN) Committee on Migrant

Workers to negotiate a legally binding ASEAN instrument for the protection and promotion of the rights of migrant workers.

NEPAL

Nepal's political and peace processes remained stalled in 2010, resulting in instability, weak governance, and no progress on accountability for human rights violations. Prime Minister Madav Kumar Nepal of the Unified Marxist-Leninist party
(CPN-UML) resigned on June 30, under pressure from the Maoists who demand a
unity government with themselves at the helm. At this writing the parliament has
failed to form a new government, despite 16 rounds of parliamentary votes. The
Constituent Assembly missed the May 28 deadline to draft a new constitution. In
a last-minute deal, political parties concluded a three-point agreement to extend
the Constituent Assembly by another year.

The government made little progress in 2010 on realizing people's economic,
social, and cultural rights though economic development. Reports of lawlessness
persist in many parts of the country, especially in the southern plains of the Terai
and the eastern hills. Armed groups and ethnically based organizations have
been involved in killings and extortion with impunity.

Accountability for Past Abuses

The government and political parties still fail to show the will to establish
accountability for human rights violations committed during the war. No one from
the security forces or among the Maoists has been held criminally responsible for
abuses committed during the conflict. In many cases, those accused of violations
actively receive protection from the security forces or political parties.

In October the Nepal Army extended the tenure of Colonel Raju Basnet by two
years, though he was at the Maharajgunj army barracks in 2003 and 2004 when
various cases of torture, arbitrary detention, and enforced disappearance took
place. The National Human Rights Commission (NHRC) and the UN Office of the
High Commissioner for Human Rights (OHCHR) have repeatedly requested that
the government start proceedings against Basnet.

In spite of a court order, the army refused to hand over Major Niranjan Basnet,
accused in 2004 of the torture, rape, and murder of 15-year-old Maina Sunwar.
After Basnet was returned at the request of the UN from a peacekeeping mission

in late 2009, the army took him into its custody. In July a military tribunal, established to probe the circumstances of Basnet's return from Chad, concluded he was "innocent."

The Unified Communist Party of Nepal (Maoist) (UCPN-M) leadership has likewise failed to cooperate with criminal investigations into alleged crimes committed by Maoists during and after the conflict.

Although the Comprehensive Peace Agreement does not provide a broad amnesty for serious crimes, the government continues to discuss the withdrawal of cases deemed "political," including cases of murder. In January the Supreme Court upheld the conviction of Maoist Constituent Assembly member Balkrishna Dhungel for the 1998 murder of Ujjwal Kumar Shrestha. However, police have failed to arrest him, and Maoists claim the case is against the Comprehensive Peace Agreement and interim constitution.

In September police and the NHRC exhumed the bodies of four people in Dhanusha district. The four are believed to be among five students that security forces allegedly disappeared and killed in 2003. So far, the police have failed to question officials and claim they are waiting for DNA results to pursue further investigations.

The draft bills to establish a Truth and Reconciliation Commission and a Disappearances Commission have been tabled in parliament but await debate by the Statute Committee. While the bills are a step towards ensuring justice for war victims, several provisions remain that are inconsistent with international law.

Integration of Maoist Combatants

For more than four years, 19,602 Maoist former combatants have been held in UN-monitored cantonment sites. In January 2010 the process began of discharging 4,008 of them, who were disqualified as children (2,973 of them) and as late recruits. A UN monitoring mechanism was formed to scrutinize UCPN-M compliance with its commitment to a 2009 action plan with the government and the UN representatives, including a provision on the non-recruitment of children. A special committee established in mid-2009 to address the integration of Maoist combatants into the security forces was unable to function for several months due to the continuous absence of UCPN-M from meetings.

Dalits

Dalits ("untouchables") suffer from discrimination in economic, social, and cultural spheres. In September 2009 Nepal announced its support for the UN-agreed-upon guidelines on the elimination of caste discrimination. However, Nepal has yet to implement recommendations made in 2004 by the Committee on the Elimination of Racial Discrimination, including adopting relevant statutory law to enable the National Dalit Commission—a state agency—to fulfill its mandate.

Sexual Orientation and Gender Identity

The Nepal government has made significant strides towards ensuring equality for lesbian, gay, bisexual, and transgender people in recent years. The government has promised that the 2011 national census will allow citizens to identify themselves as male, female, or transgender.

Yet progress remains tenuous. According to local NGOs, there are 280 discriminatory legal provisions affecting the LGBT community. In September sexual minorities alleged that the Home Minister refused to issue citizenship cards to transgender people, contravening a Supreme Court directive three years ago. In response, dozens of LGBT individuals staged protests in the capital. Police detained some protesters without charge for several hours.

Women's Rights

While women have constitutional guarantees and a strong representation in the Constituent Assembly, women and girls continue to face widespread discrimination. Violence and exploitation, including trafficking, domestic violence, dowry-related violence, rape, and sexual violence remain serious problems. Sexual violence cases are often settled in private, and even when complaints are filed, police rarely carry out effective investigations.

Female members of the Constituent Assembly have formed a caucus to pressure committees to discuss women's concerns. Some of the members' demands include for women's perspectives to be included on the issues of citizenship and property, and for the government to reserve positions for women in administration and the judiciary, and to provide dedicated public services for sexual and reproductive health.

Many women migrate to the Middle East as workers through recruitment agencies; once they arrive in these countries, they are often vulnerable to abuse and have very few legal protections.

Terai

Tensions persist over the rights of the different ethnic groups, including Madheshi communities near the Indian border in the Terai, who want greater autonomy and proportionate representation in government jobs. Public security remains a major concern in many districts of the Terai. The UN secretary-general, in his periodic report to the UN Security Council expressed concern that the extortion of officials, teachers, and business people by armed groups and ethnic organizations is on the rise despite increased police patrols.

According to human rights groups, the government's special security policy, which aims to address the deteriorating security situation, has led to increased human rights violations. For instance, OHCHR documented 57 cases of deaths as a result of the unlawful use of lethal force by security forces between January 2008 and June 2010. In several Terai districts, armed groups have recruited children as messengers for extortion notes and ransom collection, and for enforcing bandhs (strikes) called by the armed groups.

Tibetan Refugees

The current administration continued to endorse the "One China Policy" and Tibetan refugees faced increased harassment by Nepali authorities in efforts to appease China. Several instances of arrests, criminalization of entry, detention, refoulement, and attempted refoulement of Tibetan refugees were reported in 2010. In June Nepali authorities forcefully deported three Tibetan new arrivals from Humla district. Two of them are believed to be in detention in China. In October police in Kathmandu confiscated ballot boxes during annual elections held by Tibetan refugees to nominate candidates for the government in exile. The Home Minister reportedly issued a statement saying the polling "violated Nepal's foreign policy and existing laws of the host country."

Key International Actors

Nepal is dependent on aid and relies heavily on its traditional donors, such as Japan, the United States, the United Kingdom, India, and the European Union. It has to maintain a balance in its relations with its two powerful neighbors, India and China. In an effort to correct their heavy dependency on India, Nepali political parties—particularly the Maoist-led government—have attempted to strengthen ties with China. In December 2009 China provided military aid of about US$3 million, including training for the Nepal Army.

In December 2009 the US president signed into law the 2010 Consolidated Appropriations Act, which includes a prohibition on assistance to the Nepal army unless, among other things, it fully cooperates with investigations and prosecutions by civilian judicial authorities of violations of internationally recognized human rights.

India played a positive role in bringing about the comprehensive peace agreement between political parties to end the Maoist conflict. But since then, India stands accused of meddling in the selection of a consensus prime minister, adding to the political instability.

The UK continues to provide military assistance to Nepal. In October Nepal's army chief, Gen. Chhatraman Gurung, visited the UK to boost military ties.

The UCPN-M remains on the US list of banned terrorist organizations. In June, the US embassy in Kathmandu denied a visa to Agni Sapkota, a senior Maoist member, for his alleged involvement in the extrajudicial killing of Arjun Bahhadur Lama during the Maoist insurgency.

Nepal continues to be a key troop-contributing country to UN peacekeeping missions.

In June the government renewed OHCHR's mandate for a year but demanded a phased closure of all offices outside Kathmandu, thus weakening human rights monitoring in the field.

The mandate of the UN Mission in Nepal is ending in January 2011. UN Under Secretary-General for Political Affairs B. Lynn Pascoe visited Nepal in October to discuss the peace process with the prime minister.

NORTH KOREA

Despite lip service to human rights in its constitution, conditions in the Democratic People's Republic of Korea (North Korea) remain dire. There is no organized political opposition, free media, functioning civil society, or religious freedom. Arbitrary arrest, detention, lack of due process, and torture and ill-treatment of detainees remain serious and endemic problems. North Korea also practices collective punishment for various anti-state offenses, for which it enslaves hundreds of thousands of citizens in prison camps, including children. The government periodically publicly executes citizens for stealing state property, hoarding food, and other "anti-socialist" crimes.

Vitit Muntarbhorn, then-United Nations special rapporteur on human rights in North Korea, wrote in his final report in February 2010 that the country's human rights situation "can be described as sui generis [in its own category], given the multiple particularities and anomalies that abound." He added that, "simply put, there are many instances of human rights violations which are both harrowing and horrific."

Inter-Korea relations plunged after 46 South Korean sailors died when their warship, the *Cheonan*, sank in March 2010. A South Korea-led team that included investigators from the United States, the United Kingdom, Australia, and Sweden blamed North Korea for the attack. In July the UN Security Council adopted a statement condemning the attack. However, North Korea's strongest ally, China, declined to name North Korea as the party responsible, and shielded it from significant Security Council action.

A campaign for a UN commission of inquiry on North Korea gained momentum in 2010, with a growing number of international and South Korea-based human rights organizations pressing governments to support the initiative.

Monetary Devaluation and Food Shortages

Reports of deaths from starvation surfaced in the months following North Korea's ineptly managed monetary devaluation scheme, which effectively demonetized savings in the old currency in November 2009. North Korea abolished its old bank notes with virtually no advance notice and only allowed North Koreans to exchange up to 100,000 won (approximately US$25 to US$30 according to the then-market exchange rate) of the old currency for the new bills. Authorities also banned the use of foreign currencies and closed markets. It later lifted those bans.

Many people saw their entire private savings wiped out overnight, while prices for food and other basic commodities skyrocketed as merchants stopped selling goods in expectation of further price hikes.

South Korea-based NGOs and media with informants inside North Korea reported on new hunger-related deaths, especially among vulnerable groups. North Korea reportedly executed Pak Nam Ki, the former finance minister who implemented the currency revaluation, accusing him of being a South Korean spy intent on wrecking the economy. Although several international humanitarian agencies continued to deliver food and services, they have continued to have difficulty confirming delivery to the most needy.

Torture and Inhumane Treatment

Testimony from escaped North Koreans indicates that persons arrested on criminal charges often face torture by officials aiming to enforce obedience and to extract bribes and information. Common forms of torture include sleep deprivation, beatings with iron rods or sticks, kicking and slapping, and enforced sitting or standing for hours. Detainees are subject to so-called "pigeon torture," in which they are forced to cross their arms behind their back, are handcuffed, hung in the air tied to a pole, and beaten with a club. Guards also rape female detainees.

Executions

North Korea's Criminal Code stipulates that the death penalty can only be applied to a few crimes, such as "crimes against the state" and "crimes against the people," although at least one scholar believes a December 2007 law extended the penalty to many more. In reality, North Koreans are executed for a wide range of crimes, including vaguely defined non-violent offenses.

Forced Labor Camps

Testimony from escapees has established that persons accused of political offenses are usually sent to a forced labor camp, known as *gwalliso*.

The government practices collective punishment, which results in an offender's parents, spouse, children, and even grandchildren also being sent to a forced labor camp. These camps are notorious for abysmal living conditions and abuse, including severe food shortages, little or no medical care, lack of proper housing and clothes, mistreatment and torture by guards, and executions. Death rates in these camps are very high.

North Korea has never acknowledged these camps exist, but US and South Korean officials estimate some 200,000 people may be imprisoned in these facilities, which include No. 14 in Kaechun, No. 15 in Yodok, No. 16 in Hwasung, No. 22 in Hoeryung, and No. 25 in Chungjin.

Refugees and Asylum Seekers

North Korea criminalizes leaving the country without state permission. Those who leave face grave punishment upon repatriation such as lengthy terms in horrendous detention facilities or forced labor camps with chronic food and medicine shortages, harsh working conditions, and mistreatment and torture by camp guards. Some are even executed, depending on their offense and who they met abroad.

Most North Koreans who leave do so across the country's northern border with China. Hundreds of thousands have fled since the 1990s, and some have settled in China's Yanbian Korean Autonomous Prefecture. Beijing categorically labels North Koreans in China "illegal" economic migrants and routinely repatriates them, despite its obligation to offer protection to refugees under both customary international law and the Refugee Convention of 1951 and its 1967 protocol, to which China is a party.

Many North Korean women in China live with local men in de facto marriages. Even if they have lived there for years, they are not entitled to legal residence and face arrest and repatriation. Some North Korean women and girls are trafficked into marriage or prostitution in China. Many children of such unrecognized marriages are forced to live without a legal identity or access to elementary education in order to avoid their mothers being identified and repatriated.

Government-Controlled Judiciary

North Korea's judiciary is neither transparent nor independent. All personnel involved in the judiciary, including judges, prosecutors, lawyers, court clerks, and jury members are appointed and tightly controlled by the ruling Workers' Party of Korea. In cases designated as political crimes, suspects are not even sent through a nominal judicial process; after interrogation they are either executed or sent to a forced labor camp with their entire families.

Labor Rights

The ruling Korean Workers' Party firmly controls the only authorized trade union organization, the General Federation of Trade Unions of Korea. South Korean companies employ some 44,000 North Korean workers in the Kaesong Industrial Complex (KIC), where the law governing working conditions falls far short of international standards on freedom of association, the right to collective bargaining, and gender discrimination and sexual harassment.

Restrictions on Information, Association, and Movement

The government uses fear—generated mainly by threats of forced labor and public executions—to prevent dissent, and imposes harsh restrictions on freedom of information, association, assembly, and travel.

North Korea operates a vast network of informants to monitor and punish persons for subversive behavior. All media and publications are state-controlled, and unauthorized access to non-state radio or TV broadcasts is severely punished. The government periodically investigates the "political background" of its citizens to assess their loyalty to the ruling party, and forces Pyongyang residents who fail such assessments to leave the capital.

Key International Actors

The UN Human Rights Council reviewed North Korea's human rights record at a Universal Periodic Review session in December 2009. North Korea failed to formally state whether it accepts any of the 167 recommendations that it took under advisement from that session. The same month the UN General Assembly adopted a resolution against North Korea for the fifth straight year, citing member states' serious concerns about continuing reports of "systemic, widespread, and grave violations of civil, political, economic, social, and cultural rights." In April 2010 the council adopted a resolution against North Korea for the third year for abysmal, systematic human rights violations.

In July 2010 the European Parliament adopted a resolution calling for the European Union to sponsor a resolution to establish a UN commission of inquiry to assess past and present human rights violations in North Korea.

The Six-Party talks on denuclearizing the Korean peninsula remain stymied. Citing the attack on the *Cheonan*, the US announced new sanctions targeting Office 39, a secretive Korean Workers' Party organization known to raise foreign currency for the party. North Korea jailed Aijalon Mahli Gomes, a US citizen who crossed the border, on charges of illegal entry and other unspecified crimes. Former US President Jimmy Carter secured Gomes' release in August 2010.

North Korean leader Kim Jong Il visited Chinese leaders in Beijing in May and August 2010 to discuss economic and other cooperation schemes. Observers speculate the trips were tied to building support for a future transfer of power from Kim to his third son, Kim Jong Un.

North Korea's relations with Japan remained frosty, largely due to a dispute over abductees. North Korea admitted in 2002 that its agents had abducted 13 Japanese citizens in the 1970s and 1980s to use them for training North Korean spies. It returned five to Japan, but claimed the other eight had died. Japan insists the number of abductees is higher. No legal means of immigration between the two countries exists; of the nearly 100,000 migrants from Japan to North Korea between 1959 and 1984, only 200 have been able to return to Japan by escaping clandestinely.

PAKISTAN

In July Pakistan experienced a devastating flood that swamped one-fifth of the country, displacing 20 million people and causing billions of dollars in damage. Already reeling from attacks by militant groups and skyrocketing food and fuel prices, the fragile civilian government struggled to cope. Although criticized as chaotic, the flood relief effort was largely free of systematic discrimination against at-risk minorities.

The security situation continued to deteriorate in 2010 with militant groups carrying out suicide bombings and targeted killings across the country. The Taliban and affiliated groups increasingly targeted civilians and public spaces, including marketplaces, hospitals, and religious processions. In Karachi targeted killings of political activists escalated.

Ongoing rights concerns include the breakdown of law enforcement in the face of terror attacks; confrontations between the judiciary, lawyers' groups, and the government; continuing torture and mistreatment of criminal suspects; unresolved enforced disappearances of terrorism suspects and opponents of the former military government; abuses by the military during operations in the tribal areas and Swat; and discriminatory laws and violence against religious minorities.

Militant Attacks, Counterterrorism, and Reprisals

Suicide bombings, armed attacks, and killings by the Taliban, al Qaeda, and their affiliates targeted nearly every sector of Pakistani society, including journalists and religious minorities, resulting in hundreds of deaths. The country's largest cities bore the brunt of these attacks. Two attacks in late May against the Ahmadiyya religious community in Lahore claimed nearly 100 lives. On July 1 a suicide bombing at Data Darbar, shrine of the patron saint of Lahore, killed 40 people.

In the tribal areas and the Swat valley, suicide bombings against and targeted killings of police and civilians deemed to be army informants or peace activists were commonplace. On July 15 at least five people were killed and nearly 50 wounded in a suicide bomb attack near a crowded bus stop in Mingora, the main town of the Swat valley.

Security forces routinely violated basic rights in the course of counterterrorism operations. Suspects were frequently detained without charge or convicted without a fair trial. Credible reports emerged that a few thousand suspected members of al Qaeda, the Taliban, and other armed groups were rounded up in a country-wide crackdown that began in 2009 in Swat and the Federally Administered Tribal Areas, but few were prosecuted before the courts. The army repeatedly refused to allow lawyers, relatives, independent monitors, and humanitarian agency staff access to persons detained in the course of military operations.

Since the military regained control of Swat in September 2009, Taliban-perpetrated abuses such as public floggings and hangings have mostly ended. Despite this, Human Rights Watch continued to receive credible reports of military and police abuses in the district, including summary executions, arbitrary detention, forced evictions, and house demolitions. Human Rights Watch investigated some of these allegations and documented scores of executions. Army chief Gen. Ashfaq Parvez Kayani promised to investigate a video allegedly documenting soldiers executing a group of men and boys in Swat. At this writing, however, no perpetrators have been held accountable for the killings.

Abuses by Pakistani police, including cases of extrajudicial killing, also continued to be reported throughout the country in 2010.

Aerial drone strikes by the United States on suspected members of al Qaeda and the Taliban near Pakistan's border with Afghanistan escalated in 2010. As of October 15, 2010, 87 strikes had been reported, many more than in any other previous year. These strikes were accompanied by persistent claims of large numbers of civilian casualties but lack of access to the conflict areas has prevented independent verification.

In July the federal government presented amendments to anti-terrorism laws to the Senate (upper house of Parliament) that would enable authorities to place suspects under pre-charge detention for 90 days without judicial review or the right to bail. Confessions made before the police or military would be deemed admissible as evidence despite evidence that torture is routine. At this writing the amendments remain before the Senate.

Balochistan

A package of reforms aimed at improving provincial autonomy and providing redress for ethnic Baloch grievances was passed by Parliament in 2010. But civilian authorities struggled to implement the reforms as conditions markedly deteriorated in Balochistan. Armed groups launched several attacks against security forces in the province. Pakistan's military publicly resisted government reconciliation efforts and attempts to locate ethnic Baloch "disappeared" during Gen. Pervez Musharraf's military rule, a key source of continued tension.

As documented by Human Rights Watch, Pakistan forces continued to be implicated in the enforced disappearance of suspected ethnic Baloch militants. Militant groups increased attacks against non-Baloch civilians, teachers, and education facilities. At least nine education personnel were killed between January and October 2010. Many teachers, particularly ethnic Punjabis, Shia Muslims, and other targeted minorities, sought transfers out of fear for their safety.

Legal Reforms and the Judiciary

In April parliament unanimously passed the 18th Amendment to the Constitution, limiting presidential power and giving parliament, the prime minister, the judiciary, and provincial governments greater autonomy. Politicians and civil society groups hailed the amendment as an important step in restoring Pakistan's parliamentary system of democracy. The Supreme Court sparked a confrontation with parliament by voluntarily agreeing to hear legal challenges to parts of the amendment, including those dealing with mechanisms for judicial appointments.

In June Pakistan ratified the International Covenant on Civil and Political Rights and the Convention Against Torture. However, Pakistan made its ratification contingent on a number of broad and vaguely defined reservations, including excluding "anything repugnant" to the Constitution of Pakistan.

PAKISTAN

"Their Future is at Stake"

Attacks on Teachers and Schools in Pakistan's
Balochistan Province

HUMAN
RIGHTS
WATCH

Relations between the judiciary and some of its erstwhile allies in the "Lawyer's Movement," which helped restore Chief Justice Iftikhar Mohammad Chaudhry to office in 2009, deteriorated markedly during the year. In October lawyers attempted to physically attack the chief justice of the Lahore High Court in his chambers. The following day provincial police permitted into the court premises by the Lahore chief justice beat and arrested some 100 lawyers and charged them under Pakistan's Anti-Terrorism Act.

In October Asma Jahangir, a highly regarded human rights activist and former UN rapporteur was elected the first woman president of the Supreme Court Bar Association, the country's most prominent forum for lawyers. Jahangir emphasized the need to create professional distance between lawyers and the judges they helped restore to office in 2009.

Treatment of Minorities and Women

Violence and mistreatment of women and girls, including rape, domestic violence, and forced marriage, remain serious problems. The Domestic Violence (Prevention and Protection) Bill, unanimously passed by the National Assembly in August 2009, lapsed after the Senate failed to pass it within three months as required under Pakistan's constitution.

On November 7, 2010, Aasia Bibi, a Christian from Punjab province, became the first woman in the country's history to be sentenced to death for blasphemy. The sentence was greeted with international and domestic condemnation amid renewed calls by rights groups for repeal of Pakistan's infamous blasphemy laws.

In 2010 Ahmadis continued to be the primary target for prosecutions under various provisions of the blasphemy laws across Pakistan. Islamist armed groups also targeted them for attack. On May 28, militants attacked two Ahmadiyya mosques in Lahore, killing 94 people and injuring well over a hundred. Three days later, unidentified gunmen attacked Lahore's Jinnah Hospital where victims and one of the alleged attackers were under treatment. A Taliban statement "congratulated" Pakistanis for the attacks, calling people from the Ahmadiyya and Shia communities "the enemies of Islam and common people."

Media Freedom

Pakistan's media remained a vocal critic of the government and experienced less interference from the elected government than in previous years. However, the media rarely reported on human rights abuses by the military in counterterrorism operations.

As in previous years, journalists known to be critical of the military continued to be harassed, threatened, and mistreated by military-controlled intelligence agencies. On April 12, shots were fired at the house of journalist Kamran Shafi, a vocal critic of the armed forces and their influence over the state. In September investigative journalist Umar Cheema, who had reported critically on civilian and military authorities in 2010, was abducted, tortured, and then dumped 120 kilometers from his residence in Islamabad. Cheema alleged his abductors were from one of Pakistan's secret intelligence agencies.

Throughout 2010 the Taliban and other armed groups threatened media outlets over their coverage, a practice documented by Human Rights Watch in 2009, and a number of journalists were killed in the tribal areas and Khyber Pakhtunkhwa province. On April 19 reporter Azmat Ali Bangash was killed in a suicide bombing in Orakzai tribal agency while reporting on food delivery at a displaced persons camp. On July 28, grenade attacks on the homes of journalist Zafarullah Buneri and Imran Khan injured at least six women and children. Journalists Mujeebur Rehman Siddique and Mirsi Khan were both shot dead in September.

Bomb blasts in Quetta claimed by Islamist armed groups killed cameraman Malik Arif on April 16 and cameraman Ejaz Raisani and television station driver Mohammad Sarwar during a religious procession on September 3.

British-Pakistani documentary filmmaker Asad Qureshi was finally released on September 9 after being held captive for five months by a group calling itself the "Asian Tigers."

In October the ruling Pakistan Peoples Party announced a boycott of Geo TV, an anti-government television channel, and affiliated newspapers. When the government's former information minister Sherry Rehman appeared on the channel,

President Asif Ali Zardari in retaliation ordered PPP activists to besiege Rehman's Karachi home for several hours, threatening her and her family.

Chief Justice Chaudhry and provincial high courts effectively muzzled criticism of Pakistan's judiciary in the media. Journalists told Human Rights Watch that major television channels were informally advised by judicial authorities that they would be summoned to face contempt of court charges for criticizing or commenting unfavorably on judicial decisions or specific judges. Publications including the English-language newspapers Dawn and the News had to apologize publicly to the court and editors of the former faced contempt proceedings for publishing a story alleging misuse of office by the chief justice of the Sindh High Court.

Key International Actors

The US remained Pakistan's most significant ally and was the largest donor to Pakistan's flood relief effort in 2010. However, as documented by Human Rights Watch throughout 2010, there were several instances where US aid to Pakistan appeared to contravene the Leahy Law. That law requires the US State Department to certify that no military unit receiving US aid is involved in gross human rights abuses, and when such abuses are found, they are to be thoroughly and properly investigated. In October the US sanctioned six units of the Pakistani military operating in the Swat valley under the Leahy Law even as it announced a US$2 billion military aid package for Pakistan to help the country meet unprecedented counterterrorism challenges.

On July 6, British Prime Minister David Cameron announced a judicial inquiry into Britain's role in torture and rendition in Pakistan since September 2001. Several of the cases involve allegations of torture committed against British citizens in Pakistan with British complicity.

In April a three-member United Nations inquiry commission concluded its investigation into the December 2007 assassination of Prime Minister Benazir Bhutto. The commission concluded that not only did Pakistani authorities fail to provide Bhutto the security that could have saved her life, but elements within the powerful military may have played a role in her assassination. The panel was highly critical of the "pervasive role" played by Pakistan's intelligence agency, Inter-Services Intelligence.

PAPUA NEW GUINEA

As construction of a US$15 billion project to tap Papua New Guinea's rich lique-
fied natural gas (LNG) reserves got underway in 2010, Prime Minister Michael
Somare predicted that his troubled country was on the verge of transformation.
But longstanding problems that have consistently hobbled progress in the country were on display throughout the year. Corruption scandals grabbed the headlines, a UN investigation highlighted by now familiar patterns of brutal police
abuse, and violence against women and girls continued to be widespread.

Just as troubling are signs that the government is more committed to avoiding
accountability than improving its capacity to govern responsibly. In 2010 the government moved to curtail the powers of its own widely-praised Ombudsman
Commission, while also trying to enact legislation that would strip citizens of their
right to challenge the legality of controversial extractive industry projects in court.

Extractive Industries

The government has staked the country's future on its extraordinary abundance of
natural resources. Extractive industries are the main engine of the economy, but
the government has a long track record of failing to adequately regulate them. In
2010 there were already worrying signs that the LNG project could generate violent disputes among landowners over compensation payments, this a full four
years before the gas is expected to flow.

In many ways the government has left large multinational extractive companies to
regulate themselves. For instance private security forces at the sprawling Porgera
gold mine—operated by Barrick Gold, a Canadian company—have been implicated in incidents of gang rape and other human rights abuses. Yet the government
provides no meaningful oversight of such private security forces or effective,
accessible channels for victims to report such abuses.

In 2010 a group of citizens filed suit to prevent the Chinese-owned Ramu nickel
mine from building a pipeline that would deposit mine waste into the ocean. The
government responded by introducing amendments to the country's Environment
Act that would strip citizens of their right to challenge government-sanctioned

projects in court. At this writing the amendments have been passed by parliament but not signed into law. Supporters of the Ramu mine also reportedly intimidated and harassed the plaintiffs in the case.

Torture, Rape, and Other Police Abuses

Human Rights Watch has previously documented widespread patterns of abuse by Papua New Guinea's police force, including use of excessive force, torture, and sexual violence, against children as well as adults. These abuses remain rampant and almost all of those responsible continue to enjoy impunity. In the face of widespread violent crime, such tactics have deeply eroded the public trust and cooperation crucial to effective policing.

In May the UN special rapporteur on torture visited the country and documented routine beatings of criminal suspects that often rise to the level of torture, extortion of sex from female detainees, corruption, and other abuses. Police sometimes deliberately disable suspects of serious crimes and escapees by cutting their tendons with bush knives and axes. The UN special rapporteur found that conditions in correctional institutions were "poor" and in police lockups "appalling." Children are regularly detained with adults in police lockups.

In July mobile police squads housed and fed by Barrick Gold at the company's Porgera gold mine allegedly kidnapped and raped three teenage girls. In an unusual and positive move, the police suspended the alleged culprits from duty and opened a criminal investigation into the incident. More than five years after the police beat and sexually assaulted several dozen women and girls (and gang raped at least four in detention) in a raid on the Three-Mile Guest House in Port Moresby in March 2004, the Ombudsman Commission issued a report finding that police had unlawfully arrested and detained the victims, used excessive force, and raped and humiliated them. The Commission also found that senior officials failed to supervise or control the officers under their command.

Violence against Women

Violence against women and girls is epidemic in Papua New Guinea, with studies indicating that more than half of all women in Papua New Guinea have suffered physical assault by a male partner. Sexual violence against women and girls is also commonplace. Support services such as shelters and emergency health care are grossly insufficient and victims face formidable barriers to obtaining redress through the justice system, including lack of information, limited legal aid, and geographic distance. Many village courts rely on customary laws that fail to protect women's rights. The system often leaves perpetrators unpunished, a problem exacerbated by some police officers' own propensity to engage in sexual violence.

Government Corruption and Institutional Decay

The government has regularly become embroiled in corruption scandals over the years and 2010 was no exception. A judicial report that came to light in April detailed how top-level government officials and others siphoned off some $300 million through phony compensation claims. Meanwhile the capacity of key public institutions continues to decay, especially in rural areas where the government often fails to provide basic services like health and education. The government–against widespread civil society protests–supported moves to curtail the powers of its Ombudsman Commission, the very institution tasked with unearthing patterns of government corruption and abuse.

The Rights to Health and Education

Papua New Guinea performs poorly on most indicators of economic and social well-being. Rates of maternal and child mortality are among the highest in the region. The closure of rural aid posts and health centers, declining transportation infrastructure, the failure of allocated funds to reach local governments, and a shortage of drugs, medical equipment, and trained health professionals all limit access to quality healthcare.

The country has the highest prevalence of HIV/AIDS in the Pacific: around 34,100 people are living with the disease (0.92 percent of adults in 2010), with young women most likely to be diagnosed. Gender-based violence and discrimination, as well as poor access to healthcare, fuel the virus's spread. People living with HIV/AIDS often face violence and discrimination. Antiretroviral therapy is inaccessible to most. Despite training, police undermine prevention efforts by targeting female sex workers and men and boys suspected of homosexual conduct for beatings and rape. Police do so in part because they can threaten arrest using laws criminalizing homosexual conduct and certain forms of sex work, and because social stigma against homosexuals and sex work shields the police from public outrage.

Primary education is neither free nor compulsory. Recent estimates of net primary school enrollment rates range from around 45 to 55 percent. Barriers include long distances to schools, a shortage of upper secondary placements, high school fees, and school closures due to insecurity. Girls in particular suffer from sexual abuse by other students and teachers, lack of water and sanitation facilities, and face daily dangerous journeys to and from school.

The Role of Key International Actors

Australia, Papua New Guinea's former colonizer, is the country's most important international partner. Australia provides some $450 million in assistance annually, more than it provides to any other country.

The home governments of most multinational companies working in the country provide few if any enforceable human rights standards to govern overseas corporate behavior. In 2010 Canada's parliament rejected a bill that would have taken modest steps towards establishing such standards for Canadian companies, including companies with operations in Papua New Guinea. The bill encountered fierce resistance from the mining industry.

In 2011 Papua New Guinea's human rights record is due to be examined at the UN Human Rights Council.

The Philippines

Benigno Aquino III, the son of the late president Corazon Aquino, swept to power in the May presidential elections on a platform of fighting corruption and promoting justice for victims of crime. The national and local elections were considered largely free and fair, though marred by violence, including dozens of killings prior to election day. Political violence continued after the elections as more than 20 activists, journalists, party members, and politicians were killed since Aquino took office on June 30.

The Philippines is a multiparty democracy with an elected president and legislature, a thriving civil society sector, and a vibrant media. But several key institutions, including law enforcement agencies and the justice system, remain weak and the military and police commit human rights violations with impunity.

In September Andal Ampatuan Jr. and 18 others went on trial for the November 23, 2009, massacre of 58 people, including more than 30 media workers in Maguindanao on the southern island of Mindanao. Several witnesses to the massacre and their family members were killed in late 2009 and 2010.

Extrajudicial Killings and Enforced Disappearances

Hundreds of leftist politicians and political activists, journalists, and outspoken clergy have been killed or abducted since 2001. So far only 11 people have been convicted of these killings—none in 2010—and no one has been convicted of the abductions. While soldiers, police, and militia members have been implicated in many of these killings, no member of the military active at the time of the killing has been brought to justice.

In December 2009 the Philippines enacted the Crimes Against International Humanitarian Law, Genocide, and Other Crimes Against Humanity Act (Republic Act 9851), which defines and penalizes war crimes, genocide, and crimes against humanity. It provides for senior officers to be held criminally liable for abuses committed by subordinates if they knew or should have known of the abuses and did not take the necessary steps to stop them.

At least five witnesses and family members of witnesses to Ampatuan family abuses, including the Maguindanao massacre have been killed since December 2009. On June 14 an unidentified gunman shot and killed Suwaib Upahm, an Ampatuan militia member who had participated in the massacre and had offered to testify for the government if afforded witness protection. Three months before he was killed, Human Rights Watch had raised concerns with Justice Department officials in Manila about his protection. The department was still considering his request for protection at the time of his killing.

President Aquino has proposed an 80 percent budget increase for the witness protection program, but his administration has not taken steps to make the program independent and accessible and to extend protection from the onset of a police investigation until it is no longer necessary, including after the trial.

Optimism over Supreme Court writs to compel military and other officials to release information on people in their custody and take steps to protect people at risk continued to be dampened by hesitancy to grant inspection orders and difficulty in enforcing them. In two cases, the Supreme Court held that investigations had been inadequate, but simply referred the case to the national Commission on Human Rights for further investigation and monitoring—a role that the commission should already be carrying out. One of these cases involved the 2007 abduction of leftist activist Jonas Burgos who remains missing.

"Private Armies"

In numerous provinces, ruling families continue to use paramilitary forces and local police as their private armies. By recruiting, arming, and paying members of these various militias, often with national government support, local officials ensure their continued rule, eliminate political opponents, and engage in corruption. The Maguindanao massacre, the most egregious atrocity implicating a ruling family in recent years, was allegedly carried out by a private army consisting of government-endorsed paramilitary members, as well as police officers and soldiers.

In 2010 the government created task forces to dismantle private armies in Masbate and Abra provinces, but they continue to operate. In July President

THE PHILIPPINES

"They Own the People"

The Ampatuans, State-Backed Militias, and Killings
in the Southern Philippines

HUMAN
RIGHTS
WATCH

Aquino directed the police and military to take control of paramilitary forces, properly train them, and ensure that all forces are insulated from political entities. Aquino continues to defend the use of these forces, which often provide manpower for private armies and have a history of perpetrating rights abuses.

Torture

The August release of a cell phone video showing a Manila precinct chief pulling on a rope tied around a suspect's genitals and beating him during interrogation focused public attention on police torture. Investigators have filed charges of torture against nine of the police officers involved in the video. The victim, Darius Evangelista, is thought to be dead.

The 2009 Anti-Torture Act criminalizes torture and introduces mechanisms to prevent against torture. For example, it requires the police and military to declare each month the location of all detention facilities to the Commission on Human Rights. The police and military conducting trainings on the law but have yet to declare the location of detention facilities.

Targeted Killings of Petty Criminals and Street Youths

So-called death squads operating in Davao City, General Santos City, Digos City, Tagum City, and Cebu City continued to target alleged petty criminals, drug dealers, gang members, and street children. The number of killings has declined following a Commission on Human Rights investigation.

In January the Ombudsman preventatively suspended 26 police officers for failing to solve the summary killings in Davao City, but this order was reversed by the Court of Appeals in July.

At this writing the Commission on Human Rights has not reported on the outcome of the investigations of the multi-agency task force into summary killings in Davao City, which commenced in April 2009.

Armed Conflict in Mindanao

A ceasefire remained in place between the Philippine government and the Moro Islamic Liberation Front and peace talks are expected. However, at this writing more than 100,000 people remained displaced after the escalation of the conflict in 2008 and 2009.

The army continued to fight Abu Sayyaf, an armed group implicated in numerous attacks and abductions against civilians, particularly in Sulu and Basilan.

Conflict with the New People's Army

Military clashes between government forces and the communist New People's Army (NPA) continued in 2010, especially in Central and Northern Luzon, Southern Tagalog, Bicol, Eastern Visayas, Negros, and on Mindanao. Around 1,100 people in Surigao del Sur, Mindanao, were displaced twice this year for several days each time after government forces moved into their area.

On February 6 the military and police arrested 43 men and women on firearms charges, and accused them of being NPA members. All but five of the detainees say they are health workers and deny links to the armed group. The arresting officers detained them blindfolded and without access to communication for the initial 36 hours, and refused them legal counsel during this time. Rather than investigating these allegations of abuse, the military granted awards to the two officers that led the arrests.

The NPA continued to kill civilians and extort "taxes" from individuals and businesses. For example, on July 13, NPA members killed the former mayor of Giporlos, Mateo Biong, Jr., in Eastern Samar province. The NPA said that it killed Biong after he was sentenced to death by a rebel "people's court."

Reproductive Rights and Access to Condoms

Restricted access to condoms continues to impede HIV/AIDS prevention efforts in the Philippines, where more than 90 percent of HIV transmission occurs through unsafe sexual contact and both rates of transmission and overall HIV prevalence have increased sharply in recent years, particularly among the most at-risk populations. In September President Aquino pledged to enhance access to all forms of family planning, including condoms. At this writing the Philippines continues to prohibit abortion.

Filipino Workers Abroad

Approximately 2 million Filipinos work abroad, including hundreds of thousands of women who serve as domestic workers in other parts of Asia and the Middle East. While the Philippine government has made some effort to support and protect migrant domestic workers, many women continue to experience abuses abroad including unpaid wages, food deprivation, forced confinement in the workplace, and physical and sexual abuse (see Saudi Arabia, United Arab Emirates, Lebanon, Kuwait, and Malaysia chapters).

Key International Actors

The United States remains the most influential ally of the Philippines and, together with Australia and Japan, one of its three largest bilateral donors. The US military has access to Philippine lands and seas under a Visiting Forces Agreement, and the two militaries hold annual joint exercises. The United States Senate appropriated US$32 million for the Philippines in fiscal year 2009-2010 under Foreign Military Financing for procurement of US military equipment, services, and training. Of that sum $2 million is contingent on the Philippine government showing progress in addressing human rights violations, including extrajudicial killings. In September the Millennium Challenge Corporation granted a five-year economic development compact to the Philippines, totaling $434 million.

Implementation continued on the 2009-11 European Union €3.9 million (US$5.3 million) program to address extrajudicial killings and strengthen the criminal justice system by providing training and technical assistance.

Relations with China, particularly Hong Kong, have remained strained since a dismissed police officer took a busload of Hong Kong tourists hostage in Manila. The police response was incompetent and eight tourists were killed, plus the hostage taker, and nine tourists were injured.

SINGAPORE

In January 2010 Prime Minister Lee Hsien Loong said that "updating" the political system to "ensure a more diverse set of voices in Parliament" was a top priority but did not commit to far-reaching changes. Current Singaporean laws and policies on freedom of expression, assembly, and association sharply limit peaceful criticism of the government and have been used repeatedly to stymie the development of opposition political parties and dissenting voices. Of particular concern is the 2009 Public Order Act, which requires a permit for any "cause-related activity," defined as a show of support for or against a position, person, group, or government, even if only one person takes part.

The ruling People's Action Party (PAP) has been in power since 1959, occupies 82 of the 84 parliamentary seats that have full voting rights, controls all mainstream media outlets, and presides over a government with extensive powers to regulate citizen's lives.

Freedoms of Assembly, Expression, and Association

Singapore's constitution guarantees rights to free expression, peaceful assembly, and association, but also permits restrictions in the name of security, the protection of public order, morality, parliamentary privilege, and racial and religious harmony. The restrictions are interpreted broadly.

Censorship extends to broadcast and electronic media, films, videos, music, sound recordings, and computer games. The Newspaper and Printing Presses Act requires yearly registration and permits authorities to limit circulation of foreign papers which "engage in the domestic politics of Singapore."

The Films Act, which since revisions in March 2009 allows some room for political themes and online election advertising, still restricts political speech. Films and video must still be submitted to censors, "partisan... references" on any political matter are still off-limits, and the Ministry of Information, Communication and the Arts may still ban any film deemed to run contrary to public interest. In July 2010 the Media Development Authority ordered a Martyn See video, "Ex-political prisoner speaks out in Singapore," removed from Youtube and from See's blog.

In November 2010 British author and journalist Alan Shadrake was found guilty on charges of "scandalizing the judiciary" and sentenced to six weeks in jail in addition to a fine and court costs. He claimed in his book, *Once a Jolly Hangman: Singapore Justice in the Dock*, that Singapore's mandatory death penalty for murder, treason, and some 20 drug trafficking-related offenses is not being applied as equitably as the government contends. Shadrake's book concludes that the judicial process is subject to political and economic pressures, including from the ruling party, and biased against the "weak," "poor," or "less-educated." During the trial, the prosecution warned media outlets that publicizing Shadrake's allegations could lead to charges against them.

Government authorities continue to closely regulate public meetings, demonstrations, and processions. In May 2010 Vincent Cheng, held under the Internal Security Act in 1987 as the alleged leader of a Marxist conspiracy, agreed for the first time to speak publicly about his treatment in detention at a seminar, Singapore's History: Who Writes the Script, organized by students from the History Society of the National University of Singapore. The National Library Board, the venue's sponsor, however, rescinded the invitation and the event went ahead without Cheng's participation.

A lower court's 2009 acquittal of three leaders and two supporters of the opposition Singapore Democratic Party (SDP) charged with conducting a procession without a permit became in 2010 yet another setback for free assembly when a high court reversed the decision on appeal. Siok Chin Chee, a member of the central committee of the SDP, was sentenced to five short jail terms in 2010 for distributing political flyers without a permit.

The liberalization of regulations governing Singapore's "Speakers' Corner" in Hong Lim Park in 2008 has had little impact. Although processions and demonstrations are permitted and a police permit is no longer required, the park site is ringed with five CCTVs and speakers must register online and show their IDs before they begin. Speaking at the Corner provides no protection from application of sedition and criminal defamation laws.

The Societies Act requires any organization with more than 10 members to register. However, registration may be denied on grounds that an organization's "purposes [are] prejudicial to public peace, welfare or good order" or that registration would be "contrary to the national interest."

Criminal Justice System

Singapore's Internal Security Act and Criminal Law (Temporary Provision Act and Undesirable Publications Act) both permit arrest and detention without warrant or judicial review. The Misuse of Drugs Act permits confinement of suspected drug users in "rehabilitation" centers for up to three years without trial. Second-time offenders face prison terms and may be caned.

Singapore continues to implement its mandatory death sentences for some 20 drug-related offenses, which has been repeatedly criticized by United Nations human rights bodies and experts. In August a court postponed the scheduled execution of Malaysian Yong Vui Kong, 22 years old, accused of transporting 47 grams of heroin into Singapore in 2007, following international attention to the case.

Judicial caning, an inherently cruel punishment, is a mandatory additional punishment for medically fit males between 16 and 50 years old who have been sentenced to prison for a range of crimes including drug trafficking, rape, and immigration offenses. In addition, a sentencing official may at his discretion order caning in cases involving some 30 other violent and non-violent crimes. The maximum number of strokes at any one time is 24.

The US State Department reported that "through November [2009] 4,228 convicted persons were sentenced to caning, and 99.8 percent of caning sentences were carried out." The case of Oliver Fricker, a Swiss national, drew international attention in June 2010 when he was sentenced to five months in jail and three strokes of the cane for breaking into a subway system depot and spray painting one of its cars. On appeal, Fricker's sentence was increased by two months.

Sexual Orientation and Gender Identity

In violation of international standards, Penal Code section 377A criminalizes sexual acts between consenting adult men. In September a defendant brought a constitutional challenge to the law on grounds that it is discriminatory.

On May 15, 2010, the second annual Pink Dot festival, bringing together over 4,000 LGBT individuals and their families and friends, took place at the government-established Speaker's Corner in Hong Lim Park.

Migrant Domestic Workers and Trafficking

Singapore continues to make improvements in working conditions for some 196,000 foreign domestic workers through vigorous prosecution of employers and recruiters who physically abuse workers or fail to pay wages. However, it refuses to include domestic workers under the Employment Act or to regulate recruitment fees, which can run to 40 percent of the total salary a worker will earn during a two-year contract. Instead, it preserves a sponsorship system that ties a domestic worker to a specific employer who, in turn, retains the right to cancel the migrant worker's contract, making her subject to immediate deportation. Unscrupulous employers often use the threat of contract cancellation to intimidate workers to accept unlawful work conditions, restrict their movements, and prevent them from filing complaints.

A government-mandated standard contract for migrant workers does not address issues such as long work hours and poor living conditions. Instead of guaranteeing one day off per month and a set number of rest hours a day, it makes such breaks a matter of negotiation between employer and employee. It also fails to provide protections against denial of annual or medical leave, requires immediate deportation of pregnant workers, and stipulates that no foreign domestic workers may marry a Singaporean.

Human Rights Defenders

To actively defend human rights in Singapore is to risk being repeatedly fined, jailed, bankrupted, and forbidden from travel outside the country without government approval. Although the number of human rights defenders has increased, the community remains small.

Key International Actors

In March 2010 confirmation hearings before the US Senate, US Ambassador-designate Daniel Adelman said he would "use public diplomacy to work for greater press freedom, greater freedom of assembly and ultimately more political space for opposition parties" in Singapore. Following his confirmation, Adelman backtracked, stating that democracy and press freedom "are for Singaporeans to decide for themselves."

Singapore continues to play an important role in the Association of Southeast Asian Nations (ASEAN), driving forward its economic integration agenda and pressing for full implementation of the Association of Southeast Asian Nations (ASEAN) Free Trade Agreement. As an important financial center for Southeast Asia, Singapore continues to face criticism for reportedly hosting bank accounts containing ill-gotten gains of corrupt leaders and their associates, including billions of dollars of Burma's state gas revenues hidden from national accounts.

SRI LANKA

The aftermath of the quarter-century-long civil war, which ended in May 2009 with the government defeat of the separatist Liberation Tigers of Tamil Eelam (LTTE), continued to dominate events in 2010. As pressure mounted for an independent investigation into alleged laws of war violations, the government responded by threatening journalists and civil society activists, effectively curtailing public debate and establishing its own commission of inquiry with a severely limited mandate. When United Nations Secretary-General Ban Ki-moon established his own panel to advise him on accountability issues in Sri Lanka, the government refused to cooperate.

Sri Lanka held presidential and parliamentary elections in January and April respectively. President Mahinda Rajapaksa easily won re-election, and the ruling United People's Freedom Alliance party remained in power with a significant majority in parliament. Two weeks after the presidential election, the main opposition candidate, former army chief Sarath Fonseka, was arrested and in August found guilty before a court martial of engaging in political activity while still in uniform, and was stripped of his rank and pension. In a second court martial in September, he was found guilty of corrupt military supply deals and sentenced to 30 months imprisonment.

In September, at the Rajapaksa administration's urging, parliament passed the 18th amendment to the constitution, which removed restrictions on central government control over important independent bodies, such as the police, judiciary, electoral bodies, and national human rights commission. The amendment consolidated central government power, in particular executive power.

Accountability

Sri Lanka made no progress toward justice for the extensive laws of war violations committed by both sides during the long civil war, including the government's indiscriminate shelling of civilians and the LTTE's use of thousands of civilians as human shields in the final months of the conflict.

Legal Limbo

The Uncertain Fate of Detained LTTE Suspects in Sri Lanka

HUMAN
RIGHTS
WATCH

Senior government officials have repeatedly stated that no civilians were killed by Sri Lankan armed forces during the final months of the fighting, despite over-whelming evidence reported by Human Rights Watch and others that government forces frequently fired artillery into civilian areas, including the government-declared "no fire zone" and hospitals. When in late 2009, former commander Fonseka, then a presidential candidate, stated he was willing to testify about the conduct of the war, the defense secretary threatened to have him executed for treason.

Rajapaksa established the Lessons Learnt and Reconciliation Commission (LLRC) in May 2010. The LLRC's mandate, which focuses on the breakdown of the 2002 ceasefire between the government and the LTTE, does not explicitly require it to investigate alleged war crimes during the conflict, nor has the LLRC shown any apparent interest in investigating such allegations in its hearings to date.

Internally Displaced Persons

After illegally confining more than 280,000 civilians displaced by the war in mili-tary-controlled detention camps—euphemistically called "welfare centers"—the government released most of the detainees in 2010. Many of those who returned to their homes in the north and the east face serious livelihood and security issues. About 50,000 people remained in the camps, primarily families that could not return to their former homes.

Arbitrary Detention, Enforced Disappearances, and Torture

The government continues to detain without trial approximately 7,000 alleged LTTE combatants, in many cases citing vague and overbroad emergency laws. The detainees are denied access by the International Committee of the Red Cross, and little is known of camp conditions or their treatment. They typically have access to family members but not to legal counsel. While the government asserts that it has withdrawn some of its emergency regulations, the Prevention of Terrorism Act enables security forces to circumvent basic due process.

There were reports in 2010 of new enforced disappearances and abductions in the north and the east, some linked to political parties and others to criminal gangs. The government continues to restrict access to parts of the north, making it difficult to confirm these allegations. Witnesses testified before the LLRC that relatives last known to be in government custody at the end of the war were forcibly disappeared and were feared to be dead.

The emergency regulations, many of which are still in place, and the Prevention of Terrorism Act give police broad powers over suspects in custody. Sri Lanka has a long history of custodial abuse by the police forces, at times resulting in death. In a particularly shocking case in January, a video camera caught police officers brutally beating to death an escaped prisoner.

Attacks on Civil Society

Free expression remained under assault in 2010. Independent and opposition media came under increased pressure, particularly in the run-up to elections. Sri Lankan authorities detained and interrogated journalists, blocked access to news websites, and assaulted journalists covering opposition demonstrations.

News outlets associated with opposition parties came under the most vigorous and sustained attacks. The government particularly targeted *Lanka-e-News*, a news website published in English, Tamil, and Sinhalese, often aligned with the opposition party People's Liberation Front (JVP). A contributor to *Lanka-e-News*, Prageeth Ekneligoda, left his office on January 24 and has been missing ever since.

Lanka-e-News was one of six news websites blocked by the state-controlled Sri Lanka Telecom internet provider for several days starting on January 26, the day of the presidential election. Even after the elections commissioner ordered Sri Lanka Telecom to unblock the website, the editor of *Lanka-e-News,* Sandaruwan Senadheera, was subjected to threats and intimidation. Following several abduction attempts, Senadheera went into hiding.

The government also targeted another JVP-owned bi-weekly newspaper, *Irida Lanka.* On January 29, police questioned senior news editor Chandana Sirimalwatte and two editorial assistants about a recently published article. While police released the assistants after several hours, Sirimalwatte was held without charge for 18 days. The police also sealed the newspaper's offices until a court ordered them opened again.

Some 20 journalists, media workers, and civil society actors went into hiding in the days following the January election out of concern for their safety. At least four journalists left the country, adding to the several dozen who have fled in recent years.

Arrests and Harassment of Opposition Members and Supporters

The sudden emergence of Sarath Fonseka as a plausible political challenger to Rajapaksa in November 2009 galvanized the opposition, bringing together such disparate parties as the left-wing Sinhalese-nationalist JVP and the right-leaning United National Front (UNP). Even the Tamil National Alliance (TNA), previously sympathetic to LTTE goals, pledged its support to Fonseka. Although Rajapaksa won the election by a comfortable margin, his administration targeted Fonseka and his supporters in what seems to have been an effort to remove not only Fonseka, but any strong opposition voice, from the public arena.

A few weeks after the January elections the government raided opposition offices and arrested dozens of staff members, including Fonseka. Some were arrested when security forces surrounded the hotel where Fonseka's staff were staying on election night; another 13 staff members were arrested and accused of conspiring to stage a military coup.

Key International Actors

Mounting pressure from the United States, some European governments, and intergovernmental bodies contributed to the Sri Lankan government's decision to establish the LLRC in May. Other influential international actors, including India and Japan, adopted a "wait and see" approach, failing to insist on more serious justice efforts. A US State Department report issued in August acknowledged that the government had not taken effective steps toward accountability and noted the LLRC's shortcomings. In October Human Rights Watch, Amnesty International, and the International Crisis Group declined an invitation to testify before the

LLRC, citing its limited mandate and lack of impartiality. Also in October, United Kingdom Prime Minister David Cameron stated in parliament that there was a need for an independent investigation into the conduct of the war, seemingly retreating from parliament's prior commendation of the LLRC.

In June UN Secretary-General Ban Ki-moon established a three-member panel to advise him on accountability issues in Sri Lanka. The Sri Lankan government publicly castigated the newly created panel and, in early July, Housing Minister Wimal Weerawansa led a protest outside a UN office in Colombo, preventing staff from entering the building. It was only a few days later, after Ban recalled the UN resident coordinator to New York, that President Rajapaksa intervened and the protests stopped.

In June Japan announced that it would donate 100 million yen (US$1.23 million) through the UN High Commissioner for Refugees for humanitarian assistance to internally displaced persons in Sri Lanka. In July the European Union decided to withdraw Sri Lanka's preferential trade relations, known as the Generalised System of Preferences Plus, effective from mid-August, after it identified "significant shortcomings" regarding Sri Lanka's implementation of three UN human rights conventions. The government responded that the decision amounted to foreign interference and that Sri Lanka could manage without the trade benefits.

In September the International Monetary Fund announced that it had approved a US$2.6 billion loan to Sri Lanka following a two-week mission to the country.

THAILAND

Political instability and polarization continued in 2010, and occasionally resulted in violence. There were at least 90 deaths and 2,000 injuries of civilians and security personnel during politically motivated street battles between March and May. Public pledges by the Thai government to prioritize human rights, political reconciliation, and accountability for abuses have largely been unfulfilled.

Political Violence

After a month of largely peaceful rallies, on April 7, anti-government protesters from the United Front for Democracy against Dictatorship (UDD)–backed by former prime minister Thaksin Shinawatra–stormed Parliament, forcing cabinet ministers and parliamentarians to flee the building. In response, Prime Minister Abhisit Vejjajiva declared a state of emergency and created the Center for the Resolution of Emergency Situations (CRES), an ad hoc body made up of civilians and military officers, to handle the crisis and enforce emergency powers.

On April 10 the CRES deployed thousands of soldiers in an attempt to reclaim public space occupied by the red-shirted UDD, sparking violent clashes around Phan Fa Bridge. At nightfall the soldiers were ambushed by the heavily armed "Black Shirt" militants, apparently connected to the UDD and operating in tandem with it. At the same time some UDD security guards and protesters used weapons such as pistols, homemade explosives, petrol bombs, and slingshots to attack the soldiers. The panicked soldiers withdrew, firing live ammunition at the protesters. The government reported that 26 people (including five soldiers) were killed, and at least 860 wounded (including 350 soldiers).

Between April 23 and 29, groups of armed UDD security guards searched King Chulalongkorn Memorial Hospital every night, claiming hospital officials had sheltered soldiers and pro-government groups. The hospital relocated patients and temporarily shut down most services.

Negotiations in early May, based on Prime Minister Abhisit's five-point proposal, ultimately foundered when Maj.-Gen. Khattiya Sawasdipol, who claimed to represent Thaksin's interests, and other hardliners attempted to seize control of the

THAILAND

"Targets of Both Sides"

Violence against Students, Teachers, and Schools
in Thailand's Southern Border Provinces

HUMAN
RIGHTS
WATCH

UDD from more moderate leaders. On May 12 the prime minister warned that the government planned to disperse UDD protesters at Ratchaprasong junction.

As government troops moved to encircle UDD-controlled areas on May 13, an unknown sniper shot Major-General Khattiya, who died four days later. Violence escalated as UDD protesters and the Black Shirts began to openly fight the security forces surrounding their camps. The CRES set out rules of engagement, permitting security forces to use live ammunition as warning shots to deter protesters from moving closer; for self-defense; and when troops had clear visuals of "terrorists," a term the government failed to define. In reality, the military deployed snipers to shoot anyone who breached "no-go" zones between the UDD and army barricades, or who threw projectiles towards soldiers. Sometimes soldiers also shot into crowds of protesters.

On May 19 the government launched a military operation to reclaim areas around Ratchaprasong junction, sparking another round of street battles, in which soldiers used live ammunition, and some UDD protesters and the Black Shirts fought back. Around midday key UDD leaders surrendered and thousands of protesters sought sanctuary in the Wat Pathum Wanaram temple, which had been declared a safe zone by agreement with the government. A Human Rights Watch investigation, based on eyewitness accounts and forensic evidence, found that soldiers later opened fire on persons sheltering in the temple. Many were wounded, and six people, including a volunteer medic, were killed.

After the surrender of UDD leaders, groups of UDD protesters and the Black Shirts launched a coordinated campaign of looting and arson attacks on the Central World shopping complex and other locations across Bangkok for two days, starting on May 19. Previously key UDD leaders had urged their supporters to loot and burn should the government forcibly disperse the UDD protests.

Street battles injured at least nine reporters and photographers and led to the deaths of two foreign journalists. On May 19, UDD protesters burned the headquarters of Bangkok's TV Channel 3 and provincial branches of NBT TV, accusing both stations of bias.

That same day UDD supporters outside Bangkok rioted and burned government buildings in reaction to events in the capital, inflicting damage in Khon Kaen,

Ubon Ratchathani, Udorn Thani, and Mukdahan provinces. The security forces opened fire on the protesters, killing at least three, and wounding dozens more.

Throughout the year bomb attacks in Bangkok and other provinces targeted government and military locations, as well as political groups, companies, and properties associated with anti-UDD elements. For example, on April 22, M79 grenades fired at pro-government groups near Saladaeng junction killed one person and wounded 85.

As a means to reconciliation, Prime Minister Abhisit endorsed an impartial investigation into the violence committed by all sides. However, the UDD said the inquiry was not fully independent or impartial, and in any case, the military was not fully cooperative. Separate inquiries by the National Human Rights Commission and the specifically appointed Independent Fact-Finding Commission for Reconciliation made little progress.

Emergency Decree Detention

On April 7 the government proclaimed the Emergency Decree on Public Administration in Emergency Situation in Bangkok and other provinces.

The decree allows the CRES to hold suspects without charge for up to 30 days in unofficial places of detention, and gives officials effective immunity from prosecution for most acts committed while implementing the decree.

The CRES questioned, arrested, and detained UDD leaders and members who took part in the protests, as well as accused sympathizers. The CRES summoned hundreds of politicians, former officials, businessmen, activists, academics, and radio operators for interrogation; froze individual and corporate bank accounts; and detained some people in military-controlled facilities. The CRES ordered foreign and Thai journalists and volunteer medics to report to the CRES headquarters and substantiate their public statements that they witnessed abuses committed by the security forces.

At this writing the government has failed to provide the exact number and whereabouts of those detained without charge by the CRES.

Repressions of Media Freedom and Freedom of Expression

The CRES used the emergency decree to shut down more than 1,000 websites, a satellite television station, online television channels, publications, and more than 40 community radio stations, most of which are considered to be closely aligned with the UDD.

In addition, the government continued to use the Computer Crimes Act and the charge of *lese majeste* (insulting the monarchy) to enforce online censorship and persecute dissidents, particularly those connected with the UDD, by accusing them of promoting anti-monarchy sentiments and posing threats to national security. Chiranuch Premchiaporn, webmaster of online news portal Prachatai, was arrested on September 24 and charged with violating the act because of reader comments on the site deemed offensive to the monarchy in 2008.

Abusive Anti-Narcotics Policy

The government supported reopening investigations into the 2,819 extrajudicial killings that allegedly accompanied the 2003 "war on drugs." However, little progress was made to bring perpetrators to justice, or end systematic police brutality and abuse of power in drug suppression operations. In June Ratchaburi province police officers shot and killed Manit Toommuang, a suspected drug trafficker, while he was handcuffed and in their custody.

Concerns remained about the detention of drug users in compulsory drug "rehabilitation" centers, mostly run by the military and the Interior Ministry. "Treatment" is based on military-style physical exercise, with little medical assistance for drug withdrawal symptoms.

Violence and Abuses in the Southern Border Provinces

Human Rights Watch expressed concern about the alleged mistreatment of insurgent suspects in custody after Sulaiman Naesa was found dead at the Inkhayuthboriharn army camp in Pattani on May 30. Muslim people and human rights groups also made a growing number of complaints about the unlawful use of force by Thai security personnel, including assassinations of religious teachers and community leaders suspected of involvement in the insurgency. There have been no successful criminal prosecutions in these cases. On September 1, police dropped criminal charges against army-trained militiaman Suthirak Kongsuwan, who had been accused of leading an attack on Muslim worshippers at Al Furqan Mosque in June 2009, killing 10 people and wounding 12 others.

Separatist groups continued to attack and kill civilians, including teachers from government-run schools, and threaten teachers and principals, forcing them to close schools temporarily. Government security forces frequently occupied schools, impairing education by turning schools into armed camps. Insurgents recruited children from private Islamic schools to participate in armed hostilities, serve as spies, and carry out arson. Thai security forces raided private Islamic schools, and detained teachers and students for questioning.

Refugees, Asylum Seekers, and Migrant Workers

Thai authorities violated the international principle against refoulement by returning refugees and asylum seekers to countries where they were likely to face persecution. Despite international outcry, including strong protests by the United Nations High Commissioner for Refugees (UNHCR) and the UN secretary-general, the Thai army on December 28, 2009, forcibly returned 4,689 Lao Hmong, including 158 UNHCR-designated "persons of concern," to Laos. In November Thai authorities sent back to Burma thousands of Burmese fleeing armed conflicts in border areas before UNHCR could assess whether they were returning voluntarily.

In October the Immigration Police arrested 128 Tamils for illegal entry, including many registered with UNHCR, and threatened to send them back to Sri Lanka.

The Thai government failed to fulfill its promise to conduct an independent investigation into allegations in 2008 and 2009 that the Thai navy pushed boats laden with Rohingyas from Burma and Bangladesh back to international waters, which allegedly resulted in hundreds of deaths. A group of 54 Rohingyas have been held at the Immigration Detention Center since January 2009, without access to any mechanism for refugee determination or sufficient medical care. Two of them died in detention in 2009.

Migrant workers from Burma, Cambodia, and Laos continue to be abused with impunity by local police, civil servants, employers, and thugs; with little enforcement of Thai labor laws. A poorly designed and implemented "nationality verification" registration scheme caused hundreds of thousands of migrant workers to lose their legal status, deepening their vulnerability to exploitation. Female migrant workers are also vulnerable to sexual violence and trafficking.

Human Rights Defenders

The government made little progress in official investigations into the cases of 20 human rights defenders killed, including the 2004 "disappearance" and presumed murder of Muslim lawyer Somchai Neelapaijit.

International Actors

The UN, the United States, Australia, and the European Union expressed strong support for political reconciliation and the restoration of human rights and democracy in Thailand, including by urging the government and the UDD to engage in dialogue and refrain from using violence. The UN provided training and technical assistance to the inquiry process, which aims to bring to justice those responsible for politically motivated violence and abuses.

The UDD, through an international law firm hired by Thaksin, submitted a report to the prosecutor of the International Criminal Court in October, calling for an investigation into the alleged crimes against humanity committed by Thai authorities during the dispersal of the UDD protests.

Thailand made a significant number of human rights pledges in its successful campaign to join the UN Human Rights Council, and expectations for progress were further raised when Sihasak Phuangketkeow, Thailand's ambassador to the UN in Geneva, was selected as the president of the Council in June, but little has been implemented at this writing.

THAILAND

From the Tiger to the Crocodile

Abuse of Migrant Workers in Thailand

HUMAN
RIGHTS
WATCH

Vietnam

The Vietnamese government tightened controls on freedom of expression during 2010, harassing, arresting, and jailing dozens of writers, political activists, and other peaceful critics.

Cyber-attacks originating from Vietnam-based servers disabled dissident websites and the government introduced new restrictions on public internet shops while continuing to restrict access to numerous overseas websites.

Public protests over evictions, confiscation of church properties, and police brutality were met at times with excessive use of force by police. Police routinely tortured suspects in custody.

Vietnam, which served as the chair of the Association of Southeast Asian Nations (ASEAN) in 2010, demonstrated little respect for core principles in the Association of Southeast Asian Nations (ASEAN) Charter to "strengthen democracy" and "protect and promote human rights and fundamental freedoms."

Repression of Dissent

2010 saw a steady stream of political trials and arrests as the government stepped up suppression of dissent in advance of the 11th Communist Party congress in January 2011. In December 2009 and January 2010, five activists linked to the banned Democratic Party of Vietnam, including lawyer Le Cong Dinh, were sentenced to prison on subversion charges, followed by the January 29 sentencing of democracy campaigner Pham Thanh Nghien for disseminating anti-government propaganda. On February 5 writer and former political prisoner Tran Khai Thanh Thuy, who was arrested after trying to attend the trials of fellow dissidents in 2009, was sentenced to three-and-a-half years' imprisonment on trumped-up assault charges.

In February police arrested three activists for distributing anti-government leaflets and organizing worker strikes in Tra Vinh province. They were tried and sentenced to long prison sentences in October on charges of "disrupting security." In April the Lam Dong court sentenced four people to prison for alleged links to the Vietnam Populist Party.

In July and August police arrested land rights petitioners Pham Van Thong and Nguyen Thanh Tam in Ben Tre, Tran Thi Thuy in Dong Thap, and Mennonite pastor Duong Kim Khai in Ho Chi Minh City. On August 13 Ho Chi Minh City math professor Pham Minh Hoang was arrested. He had been an active contributor to a website critical of Chinese-operated bauxite mines in the Central Highlands. The five were charged with subversion, with the banned Viet Tan Party claiming all but Pham Van Thong as members.

Authorities harassed, detained, and interrogated online critics during the year. In October police arrested blogger Phan Thanh Hai and Vi Duc Hoi, an editorial board member of *Fatherland Review*, and extended the imprisonment of Nguyen Van Hai (Dieu Cay), a founding member of the Club of Free Journalists. In November police arrested outspoken legal activist Cu Huy Ha Vu on charges of disseminating anti-government propaganda and detained and interrogated former political prisoner Le Thi Cong Nhan about her poems and interviews on the internet.

Ethnic minority activists also faced arrest and imprisonment. In January the Gia Lai provincial court handed down prison sentences to two Montagnards, Rmah Hlach and Siu Koch, on charges of violating the country's unity policy. After conflicts broke out in June between Montagnards and a rubber plantation company in Gia Lai, authorities reinforced the security presence in three districts and arrested Montagnards belonging to independent Protestant house churches, who they accused of using religion to forward a political agenda. In November the Phu Yen provincial court sentenced Ksor Y Du and Kpa Y Ko to prison for "undermining national unity."

In March land rights activist Huynh Ba, a member of the Khmer Krom (ethnic Khmer) minority group, was sentenced to prison in Soc Trang on charges of "abusing democratic rights." In July authorities in Tra Vinh defrocked and arrested Khmer Krom Buddhist abbot Thach Sophon, charging him with illegal confinement. He was sentenced in September to a nine-month suspended sentence.

Freedom of Expression, Information, and Association

The government does not allow independent or privately-owned domestic media to operate and exerts strict controls over the press and internet. Criminal penalties apply to authors, publications, websites, and internet users who disseminate materials that oppose the government, threaten national security, reveal state secrets, or promote "reactionary" ideas. The government blocks access to politically sensitive websites, requires internet cafe owners to monitor and store information about users' online activities, and subjects independent bloggers and online critics to harassment and pressure.

In April the Hanoi People's Committee—the executive arm of the municipal government—issued Decision 15, which requires all internet cafes in Hanoi to install internet monitoring software approved by the authorities and prohibits the use of the internet to "call for unauthorized protests, strikes, and slow-downs." Since September 1 all internet service providers in Hanoi have been required to shut down internet transmissions at all internet retail providers from 11 p.m. to 6 a.m. every day.

The government bans independent trade unions and human rights organizations, as well as opposition political parties. Current labor law makes it almost impossible to declare a legal strike, and while illegal "wild-cat" strikes do occur, workers found to be leading such work stoppages face retaliation from the authorities and their employers. Activists who promote workers' rights and independent unions are frequently harassed, arrested, or jailed.

Freedom of Religion

The government restricts religious practices through legislation, registration requirements, harassment, and surveillance. A special centrally directed police unit (A41) monitors groups the authorities consider religious "extremists."

Religious groups are required to register with the government and operate under government-controlled management boards. The government bans any religious activity deemed to oppose "national interests," harm national unity, cause public disorder, or "sow divisions."

Adherents of some unregistered religious groups and religious activists campaigning for internationally guaranteed rights are harassed, arrested, imprisoned, or placed under house arrest. During Buddhist festivals in May and August Da Nang police blocked access to Giac Minh Buddhist pagoda and interrogated the pagoda's abbot, who is the provincial representative of the banned Unified Buddhist Church of Vietnam (UBCV). In May religious leader Cam Tu Huynh was sentenced to prison on charges of slander for criticizing police crackdowns against followers of the unrecognized branch of the Cao Dai religion.

Those currently in prison for their religious or political beliefs—or a combination of the two—include more than 300 Montagnard Christians, as well as Hoa Hao Buddhists, and members of the Cao Dai religion. Religious leaders under house arrest include UBCV Supreme Patriarch Thich Quang Do, Catholic priests Nguyen Van Ly and Phan Van Loi, and Khmer Krom Buddhist Abbot Thach Sophon.

Members of officially recognized religious groups, including Roman Catholics, also face harassment, especially church leaders and lay people attempting to pro-tect church property. In January police used tear gas and electric batons to dis-perse villagers from Dong Chiem parish near Hanoi who were trying to stop police from taking down a crucifix.

In May police violently dispersed villagers conducting a funeral procession and protest march to a cemetery located on disputed land in Con Dau parish in Da Nang. Police used truncheons and electric shock batons to beat people and arrested more than 60 persons. Most of those arrested were subsequently released, but seven were charged with opposing law enforcement officers and disturbing public order. Afterwards one of the villagers, Nguyen Thanh Nam, was interrogated and beaten by police on several occasions; he died in July from injuries suffered during a beating by civil defense forces.

Criminal Justice System

Police brutality—including torture and fatal beatings—was reported in all regions of the country, at times sparking public protests and even riots. In July demon-strations erupted in Bac Giang provincial town after a man was beaten to death in police custody after being arrested for a minor traffic violation.

Political and religious prisoners, and others whose cases are considered sensi-tive, are routinely tortured during interrogation, held without access to communi-cations prior to trial, and denied family visits and access to lawyers. Vietnamese courts remain under the firm control of the government and the Vietnam Communist party, and lack independence and impartiality. Political and religious dissidents are often tried without the assistance of legal counsel in proceedings that fundamentally fail to meet international fair trial standards.

The use of dark cells, shackling, and transfer of political prisoners to remote prisons far from family continue to be used as punitive measures. In March, for example, journalist Truong Minh Duc was transferred to K4, a more isolated and harshly supervised section of Xuan Loc prison.

Vietnamese law continues to authorize arbitrary "administrative detention" without trial. Under Ordinance 44, peaceful dissidents and others deemed threats to national security or public order can be involuntarily committed to mental institutions, placed under house arrest, or detained in state-run "rehabilitation" or "re-education" centers.

Between 35,000 and 45,000 people are detained in centers for drug dependence "treatment." Detainees are sentenced for up to four years without a lawyer, court hearing, or an opportunity to appeal the decision. Detainees are forced to perform long hours of "therapeutic labor" with punishments for those who do not meet production quotas. Independent reviews of Vietnam's system of compulsory drug treatment have found that some 90 percent of former detainees relapse to drug use.

Defending Human Rights

At considerable personal risk, a number of activists and former prisoners of conscience in Vietnam continued to publicly denounce ongoing rights abuses in 2010. After his release from prison for medical reasons in March, Father Nguyen Van Ly issued a series of public reports detailing torture in prisons. In August Ho Chi Minh City police detained and questioned another former prisoner, Nguyen Bac Truyen, after he publicly advocated on behalf of peaceful dissidents serving long prison terms.

Vietnam exerted pressure on neighboring countries to repress Vietnamese dissidents and human rights defenders living in those countries. Ongoing requests by Vietnam for the Cambodian government to crack down on Khmer Krom activists in Cambodia, for example, played a role in the conviction of four people—including a Khmer Krom monk—by a Cambodian court in August for allegedly distributing leaflets criticizing Cambodia's relations with Vietnam. In September, in response to a request from the Vietnamese Foreign Ministry, Thai authorities pressured the Foreign Correspondents Club of Thailand to cancel a press conference by Vietnamese human rights activists and barred them from entering Thailand.

Key International Actors

Vietnam continued its rocky relationship with China. In 2010 tensions mounted over China's increasingly aggressive claims to oil—and gas—rich offshore islands, signaled in July by Chinese military exercises in the South China Sea.

Vietnam remained the leader of the Cambodia/Laos/Myanmar/Vietnam bloc in ASEAN.

In July and August United Nations independent experts on minority issues and on human rights and extreme poverty visited Vietnam. Despite repeated requests for invitations, the government continued to refuse access to other UN special procedures, including those on freedoms of religion and expression, torture, and violence against women. Although Japan has considerable leverage as Vietnam's largest donor, it did not publicly comment on Vietnam's deteriorating rights record.

The United States continued to develop its trade, defense, and security ties with Vietnam while also pressing Vietnam—one of the largest recipients of US aid in East Asia—to improve its rights record. Steady improvement in US-Vietnam bilateral relations addressed mutual objectives to offset China's military and economic influence in the region. Vietnam continued its delicate balancing act in order to avoid angering China, its single largest trading partner, or the US, its largest export market.

In October, during US Secretary of State Hillary Clinton's second trip to Vietnam in 2010, she expressed concerns about the arrests of activists—including several shortly before she arrived—attacks on religious groups, and internet censorship, and secured a written commitment from the government to sign and implement the UN Convention Against Torture.

"No Questions Asked"

Intelligence Cooperation with Countries that Torture

HUMAN RIGHTS WATCH

WORLD REPORT
2011

EUROPE
AND CENTRAL ASIA

ARMENIA

Armenian authorities have yet to ensure meaningful investigations into excessive police force during March 2008 clashes in Yerevan, the capital, when opposition supporters protested alleged fraud in the previous month's presidential election. Twelve opposition supporters remain imprisoned following the events.

Torture and ill-treatment in police custody remains a serious problem. Amendments to the Law on Television and Radio threaten to limit media pluralism. Authorities continue to restrict freedom of assembly.

Armenia's international partners did not fully use their leverage to influence the human rights situation. The European Union and Armenia launched negotiations on an association agreement to strengthen ties.

Lack of Accountability for Excessive Use of Force

Authorities have yet to ensure a meaningful investigation into, and full accountability for, excessive use of force by security forces during clashes with protestors in March 2008. Ten people were killed, including two security officials and eight protestors. Only four police officers have been convicted of excessive use of force, in December 2009. They were sentenced to three years, but were amnestied immediately, and are only barred from working in law enforcement.

More than 50 civilians were prosecuted in relation to the March 2008 violence, with some sentenced to lengthy prison terms. Although a June 2009 presidential pardon released many of them, local human rights groups maintain that 11 opposition supporters remain imprisoned on politically motivated charges.

On January 19, a court sentenced Nikol Pashinyan, opposition leader and editor-in-chief of the *Haykakan Zhamanak* newspaper, to seven years imprisonment for allegedly organizing "mass disorders" during the March 2008 events. An appeals court upheld the decision but halved his sentence. In November 2010 Pashinyan claimed two masked men attacked and beat him in Kosh prison; the government denied the allegation.

In April 2010, relatives of nine victims killed in the March 2008 violence, the eight protestors and one of the soldiers, appealed unsuccessfully to court for a thorough investigation into the deaths.

In a March 2010 report analyzing the post-March 2008 trials, the Organization for Security and Cooperation in Europe (OSCE) called on authorities to, among other things, comprehensively investigate allegations of ill-treatment and ban in court evidence obtained through ill-treatment.

Torture and Ill-Treatment

Local human rights groups report continued ill-treatment in police custody. For example, on April 13, 2010, police detained 24-year-old Vahan Khalafyan and four others in Charentsavan, north of Yerevan, on suspicion of robbery. Khalafyan died of knife wounds some hours later. Police say he stabbed himself with a knife obtained in the station, and deny allegations of ill-treatment.

On April 23, investigators charged the head of Charentsavan's Criminal Intelligence Department and three others with abuse of authority. The trial is ongoing at this writing. Khalafyan's relatives and human rights groups want additional murder and torture charges. An internal police investigation led to the dismissal of Charentsavan's police chief and three officers. The Helsinki Citizens' Assembly (HCA) Vanadzor Office reported that police ill-treated two other men detained with Khalafyan. Police failed to conclusively investigate these incidents.

On August 27 a court ordered the investigation into the death in custody of Levon Gulyan be reopened. In May 2007, Gulyan was found dead following a police interrogation. Authorities say he jumped from the second-story of a police station trying to escape. Gulyan's relatives deny this, insisting he was tortured.

During a September 2010 visit the United Nations Working Group on Arbitrary Detention interviewed numerous detainees and prisoners who alleged beatings, other ill-treatment in police custody, and refusal by prosecutors and judges to admit evidence of the ill-treatment into court.

In September a YouTube video showed Army Major Sasun Galstyan beating and humiliating two conscripts. An investigation into abuse of power is ongoing.

In June the European Court of Human Rights (ECtHR) found Armenia had twice violated the prohibition against inhuman or degrading treatment in the case of Ashot Harutyunyan. Convicted of fraud and tax evasion in 2004, Harutyunyan died of a heart attack in prison in January 2009. The court determined authorities had denied him necessary medical care for his multiple chronic health problems, including heart disease, an ulcer, and diabetes. The court also found the government's public restraint of Harutyunyan in a metal cage during his appeal hearings amounted to degrading treatment.

On July 26, 14 human rights groups issued a statement citing a 20 percent rise in the national prison population, which is leading to overcrowding, health problems, and conflicts among detainees.

Media Freedom

In early 2010, as part of the transition to mandatory digital broadcasting, parliament convened a working group to revise the Law on Television and Radio that included NGOs and opposition parliamentarians. Parliament adopted the legislation in a June 10 emergency session before thorough discussion of the draft.

The amendments reduced the number of available television stations, and stipulate that existing broadcasters or those with at least three years experience receive preference in future licensing competitions, creating a barrier for new broadcasters.

In March the Gyumri-based television station GALA reported advertisers withdrew business under pressure from local officials. 26 companies pulled their ads in one month alone. Since 2007, GALA has been subject to apparently politically motivated court cases and harassment by state agencies, seemingly in retaliation for the station's regular coverage of opposition party activities.

The independent television station A1+ remained off the air for an eighth year, despite a June 2008 ECTHR judgment that Armenia had violated freedom of expression due to repeatedly arbitrarily denying the station a broadcast license.

Freedom of Assembly

Authorities continue to restrict freedom of assembly by frequently denying requests to hold demonstrations. Opposition parties and some NGOs allege particular difficulties securing indoor events venues.

On May 31, riot police forcibly prevented opposition demonstrators from entering Yerevan's Liberty Square. They detained 15 demonstrators following clashes with riot police, holding them for several hours and denying them access to lawyers.

During the operation police detained Ani Gevorgian, a correspondent for the opposition *Haykakan Zhamanak* newspaper, and two opposition activists, Gevorgyan's brother, Sargis, and Davit Kiramijyan. Amid local media outrage, police did not press charges against Ani Gevorgyan. Authorities charged Kiramijyan with hooliganism and Sargis Gevorgyan with using force against a police officer. Their joint trial is ongoing.

On November 9, police briefly detained four youth opposition activists protesting outside a Yerevan hotel at the start of an EU-organized human rights seminar. The activists claimed police punched and kicked them in the police station.

Human Rights Defenders

Police closed the investigation into the May 2008 attack on Armenian Helsinki Association Chairman Mikael Danielyan, who was wounded when an assailant shot him with a pneumatic gun after an argument. The investigation was allegedly closed due to lack of criminal intent. A court rejected Danielyan's appeal against the decision.

Mariam Sukhudyan, primarily an environmental activist, publicized on national television in November 2008 the case of two girls who alleged sexual harassment at a Yerevan school. Police charged Sukhudyan with falsely reporting a crime. On March 10, 2010, the United States Embassy awarded Sukhudyan its first ever Woman of Courage Award. A day later, the criminal case against her was dropped.

Key International Actors

Armenia's international partners did not make full use of their leverage to press Armenia to fulfill its human rights commitments.

The EU's annual assessment of Armenia—published in May to report on its progress in meeting benchmarks in the European Neighbourhood Policy Action Plan— commended Armenia for certain progress, but urged the government to try harder to ensure that there is a comprehensive investigation into the March 2008 events. On July 19 the EU launched negotiations on an Association Agreement with Armenia to strengthen political and economic ties.

The May 2010 Universal Periodic Review of Armenia at the UN Human Rights Council raised concerns about investigations and prosecutions related to the March 2008 violence; torture and ill-treatment by police; judicial independence; and freedom of assembly and expression. Armenia said it would "examine all recommendations and implement them."

Following his May visit to Armenia, Parliamentary Assembly of the Council of Europe (PACE) President Mevlüt Çavusoglu called on the authorities to adopt a new electoral code; reform police; and ensure judicial independence, freedom of assembly, and media independence and pluralism. In June the PACE rapporteurs on Armenia welcomed the government's "roadmap" of reforms following the March 2008 election violence, but expressed concerns about the new electoral code and amendments to the broadcasting laws. The rapporteurs acknowledged progress on police and judicial reforms.

In March the Council of Europe's Committee for the Prevention of Torture published a report on its ad hoc visit to Armenia in March 2008, finding that practically all people detained on March 1, 2008, alleged physical ill-treatment during arrest, and some alleged ill-treatment during police questioning.

During a July 4-5 visit to Yerevan, US Secretary of State Hillary Clinton met President Serzh Sargsyan, and separately with civil society leaders. Secretary Clinton discussed the US government's concerns that recent changes to the Law on Television and Radio could hinder freedom of expression.

On August 20 Russian President Dmitry Medvedev and President Sargsyan agreed to extend Moscow's lease of a military base in Armenia until 2044, and Russia committed to updating Armenia's military hardware.

In April 2010 Armenia suspended the ratification process for two protocols it signed with Turkey in 2009 to establish bilateral relations. The unresolved conflict between Armenia and Azerbaijan in Nagorno-Karabakh continues to impede normalization of Armenian-Turkish relations. The EU commended Armenia's commitment to pursuing normalization of relations, but expressed concern about loss of momentum.

AZERBAIJAN

Azerbaijan's human rights record remained poor in 2010. The government continued to use criminal defamation and other charges to intimidate and punish journalists expressing dissenting opinions; an outspoken journalist remained in prison on spurious criminal charges, apparently in retaliation for his work. The parliamentary elections of November 7 failed to meet international standards. Other serious problems persisted, including restrictions on freedoms of religion, assembly, and association, and torture and ill-treatment in custody.

The European Court of Human Rights (ECtHR) found Azerbaijan had violated freedom of expression by imprisoning journalist Eynulla Fatullayev and called for his immediate release.

Media Freedom

Government officials initiated 26 criminal defamation cases against journalists and other critics in the first half of 2010; courts delivered 14 sanctions. In addition officials filed 36 civil defamation claims, 30 of which were successful. For example, in February 2010 a Baku court convicted Ayyub Karimov, editor in chief of the *Femida 007* newspaper, of slander and ordered him to pay a fine, in response to a Ministry of Internal Affairs complaint regarding Karimov's articles criticizing the ministry. Also in February Ministry of Education officials filed a criminal complaint against Alovsat Osmanli, a mathematician, for articles in the *Azadlig* newspaper criticizing the ministry for mistakes in mathematics textbooks.

In July a court sentenced Eynulla Fatullayev, chief editor of two newspapers and an outspoken government critic, to an additional two-and-a-half years in prison on spurious drug charges brought by prison authorities. Fatullayev was sentenced to eight-and-a-half years in prison in 2007 on charges of fomenting terrorism and other criminal charges, which were widely believed to be politically motivated. In April the ECtHR found that Azerbaijan "grossly" and "disproportionately" restricted freedom of expression by imprisoning Fatullayev and ordered his immediate release. In October the decision became final after the court's Grand Chamber refused to admit the government's appeal. Fatullayev remains imprisoned at this writing.

Political activists and bloggers Emin Milli and Adnan Hajizade who were victims of an apparently staged attack in July 2009 and subsequently convicted of hooliganism were released in November 2010 after serving over half of their sentences.

Several journalists suffered physical attacks by police and others; the government failed to meaningfully investigate these incidents. In February a police officer attacked Leyla Ilgar, a correspondent for the *Yeni Musavat* newspaper, as she reported at a local market. Police interrogated her and deleted the photographs from her camera. In May police detained Seymur Haziev, a reporter for the *Azadlig* newspaper, at an opposition rally in Baku. Haziyev was questioned without his lawyer, charged with resisting arrest, and sentenced to seven days imprisonment. Haziyev reported that two officers kicked and hit him periodically during the interrogation.

In July unidentified men attacked Elmin Badalov, a reporter for *Yeni Musavat,* and Anar Garayli, the deputy editor of *Milli Yol*, while they took photographs for an investigative story about luxury villas near Baku believed to be built by the transportation minister. In August an unidentified assailant stabbed Rasul Shukursoy, a sports writer for *Komanda* newspaper, in the arm. Shukursoy links the incident to his article criticizing a famous football player.

Police interfered with journalists' efforts to document public protests. In June as police broke up a Baku demonstration by opposition party Musavat, they also shoved journalists and prevented them from filming. In July presidential administration guards detained and erased the recordings of four journalists filming a protest by Sabirabad region residents complaining about the government's response to severe flooding in southern Azerbaijan.

In May Baku airport security forced Norwegian journalist Erling Borgen to place his camera and recorded DVD footage in his checked bags. Upon arrival in Oslo Borgen discovered that all footage from his visit to Azerbaijan for a documentary on Eynulla Fatullayev had disappeared.

In February the parliament approved amendments to several laws that ban media representatives from videotaping, photographing, or audio recording without a subject's prior knowledge or consent, except in "operative-investigative cases" carried out by law enforcement. In June the government placed restrictions on street newspaper vending in central Baku, allegedly for aesthetic reasons, limiting many newspapers' distributions and revenues.

Elections to Milli Mejlis (Parliament)

The ruling Yeni Azerbaijan Party won an overwhelming majority in the November 7 parliamentary elections; only one clear opposition candidate gained a seat in the country's 125-member parliament. Restrictions on political parties and free expression of political views, due to restrictions on the freedoms of assembly and association, marred the pre-election campaign. International observers criticized the elections for failing to meet international standards.

In September the ECtHR found Azerbaijan violated the right of opposition candidate Flora Karimova to free elections when it invalidated 2005 parliamentary election results in the district she had won.

Freedom of Assembly and Association

The government restricted freedom of assembly. Officials did not authorize any demonstrations in central Baku and police quickly dispersed unauthorized protests. On April 26 the Baku police rounded up about 80 people traveling to a rally on free expression and assembly, releasing some immediately on the outskirts of Baku and detaining others for five hours. Police charged 10 with resisting the police and violating public order. Four days later police briefly detained dozens of political activists outside the State Oil Academy, where they had been commemorating the 2009 deadly shooting there.

The government interfered with the work of NGOs. The Ministry of Justice refused to register the Television and Alternative Media Development Center three times. In August police briefly detained several employees of the Kur Civil Society organization as they monitored flood damage in southern Azerbaijan.

In December 2009, several unknown people beat Ilgar Nasibov and Vafadar Eyvazov of the Democracy and NGO Development Resource Center in the Nakhichivan Autonomous Republic, a landlocked region in southwestern

Azerbaijan. The activists believe the attack came in retaliation for their planned anti-corruption seminar.

In September 2010 Elman Abassov and Hekimeldostu Mehdiyev, Nakhichivan-based employees of the Institute for Reporters' Freedom and Safety, a media monitoring organization, reported that security officials regularly interrogate people with whom the activists meet, pressuring them to cease further contact for "their own safety."

Freedom of Religion

All religious communities were forced to re-register with the State Committee for Work with Religious Organizations by January 1, 2010, or face potential liquidation. The 450 communities that successfully re-registered included 433 mosques and two Protestant churches. The state denied registration to Baku's Baptist Church, its Catholic Parish, and its Seventh-day Adventists, Jehovah's Witnesses, and others. Authorities threatened to close several mosques, including the Fatima Zahra Mosque in Baku and a Sunni mosque in the town of Mushfigabad, after refusing to register them.

In March police detained and prosecuted two Jehovah's Witnesses for "distributing religious literature without state permission," fining each US$250. In September an appeals court upheld the decision to sentence Farid Mammedov, a Jehovah's Witness, to nine months in prison for refusing compulsory military service on religious grounds. In October two Muslim men from the northern Azerbaijan region of Zakatala reported being detained by local police, who harassed them for their long beards and forcibly shaved them off. In October police raided a Baptist harvest festival in the northern Azerbaijani town of Qusar, arresting four participants and sentencing them to five days' imprisonment.

Torture and Ill-Treatment

Widespread torture and ill-treatment in custody continue with impunity. In 2010 the Azerbaijan Committee against Torture, an independent prison monitoring group, received over 150 complaints alleging torture and ill-treatment in custody.

Police disciplined several officers, but failed to criminally prosecute any. At least one prisoner reportedly died in custody in 2010 after alleged ill-treatment.

Political Prisoners

The government continued to hold political prisoners. At this writing, NGO activists counted between 23 and 45 political prisoners, including former government officials, businessmen, and opposition politicians arrested prior to the November 2005 parliamentary elections on allegations of attempting to overthrow the government.

Key International Actors

International and regional institutions and bilateral partners voiced concerns about and criticism of Azerbaijan's human rights record, especially regarding media freedoms. In June 2010 Thomas Hammarberg, the Council of Europe commissioner for Human Rights, published a report on his May visit to Azerbaijan, urging the government to remedy a range of abuses, including police misconduct and violations of freedom of expression and association and fair trial norms.

In a June resolution the Parliamentary Assembly of the Council of Europe called on the government to release imprisoned journalists, decriminalize libel, and refrain from new criminal defamation charges against journalists.

During his United Nations General Assembly speech in September, United States President Barack Obama expressed hope that Azerbaijan would implement democratic reforms and increase human rights protections, including the release of the imprisoned bloggers Milli and Hajizade. Secretary of State Hillary Clinton visited Baku in July and raised a number of concerns with the government, including the imprisonment of the bloggers.

The European Union's April 2010 European Neighbourhood Policy Action Plan progress report commended Azerbaijan for improvements in economic and social governance, but expressed concern about the penitentiary system; torture in custody; and freedoms of expression, assembly and religion. In July 2010 Azerbaijan and the EU began negotiations for an Association Agreement to further strengthen economic relations.

Following its December 2009 review of Azerbaijan's torture record, the UN Committee against Torture urged the government to, among other things, ensure that all allegations of torture are subjected to prompt, impartial, and effective investigation.

BELARUS

The situation for civil society and independent media remains dismal, with Belarusian authorities continuing pressure and threats ahead of the December 2010 presidential elections. Journalists and civil society activists face harassment in the form of interrogations, detentions, arrests, and seizure of personal property. NGOs struggle with registration procedures, and media outlets have been threatened with closure.

Elections

In September the Belarusian parliament scheduled presidential elections for December 2010. President Aleksandr Lukashenka will run for a fourth term. First elected in 1994, Lukashenka was re-elected in 2001 and 2006 despite protests of election fraud from activists, international NGOs, and concerned governments, such as those of the United States and most European Union member states. Government crackdowns on civil society and independent media preceded previous presidential elections, and activists reported continued punitive measures in the run up to the December elections.

Some positive amendments, including eliminating the need for candidates to obtain permission for public events, were made to the electoral code in January, and more candidates were allowed to register in the April 2010 local elections. However, electoral code violations and lack of transparency marred the April elections. In the Maladziechna district, four members of the Divisional Electoral Commission ran for the Council of Deputies, in violation of electoral law. Belarus refused long-term election monitoring proposed by the Organization for Security and Co-operation in Europe (OSCE). The only long-term election-monitoring presence was provided by local observers, who were forced to maintain a distance of 3 to 10 meters from ballot counting.

Freedom of Association

Independent civil society groups report government pressure, but many remain active in Belarus. Four activists—Zmicier Dashkevich, Yauhien Afnahiel, Artur

Finkievich, and Uladzimir Lemiesh—from the youth opposition movements Young Front, Young Belarus, and European Belarus, were kidnapped in public in November and December 2009. Assailants in civilian clothes pulled the men into waiting cars, and dumped them outside the city limits. The kidnappers warned three of the men to cease political activities before releasing them.

In May authorities in more than 20 cities raided apartments and confiscated computer equipment from activists for the "Speak the Truth Campaign," founded in February 2010 to encourage public discussion about social problems. Leaders of the movement were detained for three days on suspicion of disseminating false information. The campaign's founder, Uladzimir Niaklayau, has voiced interest in running for president.

In March 2010 the Ministry of Justice refused for the third time to register the Belarusian Assembly of Pro-democratic NGOs, citing procedural violations in its creation, and alleging that the organization's name does not describe its activities. The assembly serves as an unofficial umbrella organization for more than 250 Belarusian NGOs and provides legal guidance and conducts advocacy on their behalf.

Freedom of Assembly

Activists are required to apply for demonstration permits, but the onerous application process restricts the right to hold peaceful assemblies. Civil society activists are frequently arrested, fined, and detained for participating in unsanctioned assemblies. In January 2010, 43 activists and leaders of the unofficial Union of Poles in Belarus (UPB) were detained while en route to an assembly to re-elect Teresa Sobol as chairperson of the Ivenets Polish House, a culture and education center for the Ivenets region. In February authorities arrested 40 UPB activists for an unsanctioned protest over Sobol's closed trial, in which the court ordered her to hand over control of the Polish House building to the officially-sanctioned Union of Poles in Belarus.

Authorities used force to disburse three unsanctioned democratic opposition demonstrations in February, and detained several participants in an unsanctioned Minsk parade supporting lesbian, gay, bisexual, and transgender rights in

May. When authorities do sanction opposition rallies, they grant permission for locations far from public view.

Media Freedom

The government tightened its control on media through stricter internet controls, harassing and detaining independent journalists, and issuing warnings to publications.

In July 2010 a presidential edict restricting the internet came into force. It requires registration of online resources, identification of users at internet cafes and storage of their internet history for a year, and restricts access to "banned" information on the internet.

Independent news sources –the*Charter97* news website, and *Narodnaya Vola* and *Novaya Gazeta* newspapers—were all investigated for criminal defamation against the former head of the Homel Region KGB Department in 2010. Authorities repeatedly interrogated editors and staff, searched their apartments, and confiscated their electronic equipment. In March police forcibly broke into *Charter97*'s editorial office, injuring web-site editor Natalia Radzina. In September 2010 Aleh Biabienin, founder of *Charter97*, was found hanged in his dacha. Bebenin's colleagues and international NGOs have called for a criminal investigation of his e death, which was officially ruled a suicide. In an unprecedented development, the authorities have allowed the OSCE to send two forensic experts to participate in the investigation. Death threats against other *Charter97* journalists have been posted anonymously to the website since Bebenin's death.

In a positive development, the majority of news publications were able to register under a 2009 law requiring them to re-register, and 107 new publications were registered in the first half of 2010. However, authorities denied registration to at least eight independent newspapers, citing insufficient qualifications of the editors or improper premises for the editorial offices. Additionally, the number of official warnings against news outlets increased in 2010. Under the 2009 law, two official warnings constitute sufficient grounds to close a media outlet. Independent newspapers *Narodnaya Vola* and *Nasha Niva* have already received three warnings, and dozens of other papers, including *Komsomolskaya Pravda in Belarus, Va-Bank, Novy Chas,* and *Tovarishch,* have received at least one warning.

Political Prisoners

Two activists arrested on politically-motivated charges in 2009 were sentenced to prison in May 2010.

The court sentenced civil activist Mikalaj Autukhovich to five years and two months in a maximum security prison for illegal possession and transportation of five shotgun shells and a hunting rifle, despite claims that witness testimony was obtained through intimidation. Autukhovich went on a hunger strike in June to protest prison conditions and demand dental treatment, which he has not received as of this writing.

His co-defendant, Uladzimir Asipienka, received a three-year prison sentence for possessing and transporting firearms and explosives. The men's convictions appear connected with their civil society activism. Asipienka had previously been imprisoned for involvement in an entrepreneurs' movement, while Autukhovich attempted to unite veterans in an opposition organization and ran in parliamentary elections as an independent candidate.

Siariej Kavalenka, a Conservative Christian party activist, was sentenced to three years of house arrest for displaying a white-red-white Belarusian flag, a symbol of protest against the Lukashenka administration.

Death Penalty

Belarus remains the only country in Europe that still allows the death penalty. In March 2010 Belarusian authorities executed Andrej Zhuk and Vasilii Yuzepchuk for murder, even though their cases were pending before the United Nations Human Rights Committee. In May, the Hrodna Regional Court sentenced Aleh Hryshkaucou and Andrej Burdyka to death for murder. The executions and sentences occurred after the Belarus National Assembly established a task force to explore a possible death penalty moratorium—a stipulation for full suspension of EU and Parliamentary Assembly of the Council of Europe sanctions. In 2010, the

Ministry of Justice reported that 321 people had been sentenced to death between 1990 and 2009, with the number of sentences declining in the last decade from its peak of 47 in 1998. The ministry did not provide information on the number of actual executions.

Palliative Care

Belarus' low consumption of morphine and other opioid medicines, reported annually to the International Narcotics Control Board, indicates that access to medicine for pain treatment is available to less than 20 percent of its terminal cancer patients.

Key International Actors

Belarus' relations with both Europe and Russia deteriorated in 2010, and foreign governments failed to hold Belarus accountable for its domestic human rights situation.

Belarus came up for Universal Periodic Review by the UN Human Rights Council in May 2010. The resulting report offered recommendations on freedom of speech, association, and assembly, as well as a moratorium on the death penalty, but Belarus rejected any commitment to implement them. Belarus accepted the recommendations to absolutely prohibit torture and introduce a definition in line with the Convention Against Torture in its legislation, but failed to recognize flaws in investigating complaints of torture.

In October 2010 the EU called on Belarus "to fully cooperate" with the presidential election monitoring of the Office for Democratic Institutions and Human Rights (part of OSCE). The EU also extended its existing travel restrictions against high-level officials, but simultaneously suspended restrictions through October 2011.

US President Barack Obama extended existing travel restrictions against high-level Belarusian officials until June 2011 due to concerns about detentions, disappearances, and political repression.

The Parliamentary Assembly of the Council of Europe (PACE) suspended high-level contact with Belarus in April, declaring the lack of international observers at the April elections, state discrimination against the country's Polish minority, and the execution of Zhuk and Yuzepchuk as "concrete steps backwards." PACE also withdrew its earlier recommendation that the Council of Europe restore Belarus's "special guest status," initially suspended in 1997 over human rights concerns.

In June Belarus signed a customs agreement with Russia and Kazakhstan that removes trade barriers between the three countries. Despite their economic cooperation, Belarus distanced itself from Russia in August after Russia cut oil and gas subsidies to the country.

BOSNIA AND HERZEGOVINA

The protracted political crisis in Bosnia and Herzegovina continued to stall necessary reforms in 2010, including constitutional changes initiated after a ruling by
the European Court of Human Rights (ECtHR) that eligibility restrictions for political candidates discriminate against ethnic minorities. Effective local war crimes
prosecutions were again a bright spot, but the intimidation of independent journalists, the slow rate of return of refugees and internally displaced persons
(IDPs), and the arbitrary detention of national security suspects continued to
stain the country's human rights record.

War Crimes Accountability

The pace of war crime trials continued to be good on both central and local (both
cantonal and municipal) levels, despite practical impediments, such as staffing
and funding shortages, and political sensitivities surrounding the topic. On July
11, 2010, the remains of 775 victims of the Srebrenica massacre were buried in
the Potocari area, at a ceremony marking the 15th anniversary of the worst atrocity
in Europe since World War II. Ratko Mladic, an indicted architect of the massacre,
remains at large. Another indicted architect, Radovan Karadzic, faced trial at the
International Criminal Tribunal for the former Yugoslavia (ICTY). Karadzic made his
opening statement in March and the prosecution began presenting its case in
April.

In June the ICTY convicted Vujadin Popovic and Ljubisa Beara, two high-ranking
Bosnian Serb army officials, of genocide, murder, extermination, and persecution
for their roles in the massacre at Srebrenica, sentencing them to life imprisonment. A third defendant, Drago Nikolic, was convicted of aiding and abetting
genocide, murder, extermination, and persecution, and sentenced to 35 years in
prison. Four others were also convicted of a range of crimes committed during
and following the fall of Srebrenica and Zepa.

The War Crimes Chamber in Sarajevo continued to prioritize the most serious
cases of war crimes and crimes against humanity, and reached final verdicts in
eight cases between November 2009 and September 2010, bringing its total

number of completed cases to 46. Sixteen new cases began during this period, with 53 ongoing trials as of September 2010.

Local courts in the Federation of Bosnia and Herzegovina commenced five war crimes cases and issued verdicts in three cases between November 2009 and September 2010. During the same period Republika Srpska local courts began six cases and completed eight, and Brcko District began two new cases. According to the national war crimes strategy, the most sensitive and serious cases are to be tried centrally, while less controversial and complex ones are to be handled at municipal and canton levels.

Return of Refugees and Internally Displaced Persons

The return of refugees and IDPs to their areas of origin remained slow, and the Office of the United Nations High Commissioner for Refugees (UNHCR) registered the return of only 181 refugees and 177 IDPs during the first six months of 2010. As of June 2010 there were more than 113,465 registered IDPs (including some 7,000 in collective centers): 48,659 in the Federation, 64,560 in Republika Srpska and 246 in Brcko. There are no reliable estimates of the number of refugees outside Bosnia.

Lack of economic opportunity, inadequate housing, and people's reluctance to return to areas where most residents are of a different ethnicity remain the key impediments to return. As of September 2010 Bosnia hosted 129 Kosovo Roma under temporary protection status.

In June the House of Peoples (the upper house of parliament) amended the national returns strategy to reflect the current challenges to returns of the remaining displaced, designating 2014 as the year by which displaced people should be given housing or financially compensated. The strategy also reiterates the need to provide more livelihood opportunities and maintain security for returnees.

National Security and Human Rights

Seven North African and Middle Eastern men were subject to indefinite detention without charge on national security grounds during 2010. At least five of the men had been previously stripped of their acquired Bosnian nationality. In February, Omar Frendi, an Algerian detainee, accepted voluntary departure to Algeria. A second Algerian, Noureddine Gaci, was detained in June; an Egyptian, Muhamed Elfarhati Othman, was detained in October; and in August, in the case of Imad Husin–a Syrian who remains in detention–the ECtHR indicated that it might intervene if Husin was not charged or released by years' end, despite the court's earlier intervention in 2008.

In June a bomb exploded at a police station in the town of Bugojno, killing one police officer and injuring six others. One of seven men subsequently arrested confessed to planting explosives and at this writing is in detention awaiting trial with two others whom were arrested later.

Ethnic and Religious Discrimination in the Political System

October general elections were organized in direct contravention of a binding December 2009 ruling by the Grand Chamber of the ECtHR in the case of *Sejdic and Finci v Bosnia Herzegovina*. The court ruled that the inability of the applicants–a Jew and a Roma– to stand for the presidency or the House of Peoples in Bosnia and Herzegovina amounted to illegal discrimination, and called on Bosnia to make constitutional and electoral reforms to remove discriminatory provisions and allow candidates who are not Serb, Bosniak, or Croat.

Media Freedom

Threats and harassment of independent journalists continued throughout 2010. In February a policeman verbally and physically assaulted Osman Drina, a reporter for Independent Television IC (Nezavisna Televizja IC), while he was reporting on a sporting event. The Ministry of Interior opened an investigation into this incident, which is still ongoing at this writing.

In March a car belonging to Rade Tesic, a journalist for the Euroblic daily newspaper, was burned while parked near Tesic's house in Doboj. No one was injured in the attack. The editorial staff of Euroblic also received several anonymous, threatening phone calls in March regarding Tesic's articles about the activities of local criminal networks.

Bakir Hadziomerovic, the editor in chief of the popular "60 Minutes" TV program, which exposes links between politicians and organized crime, received repeated anonymous death threats against him and his family in writing and by telephone. Police opened an investigation and inspected the program's premises, but at this writing has made no arrests in the case.

Human Rights Defenders

No attacks on human rights defenders were recorded in 2010. The community of lesbian, gay, bisexual, and transgender rights defenders, including Association Q, the main LGBT organization, maintain a low profile and remain weak and vulnerable to intimidation and harassment.

International Actors

The combined Office of the High Representative/European Union Special Representative, backed by the United States and the Peace Implementation Council continue to focus on assisting the country to overcome the protracted political stalemate and forge closer integration with the EU.

An April high-level meeting between US Deputy Secretary of State James Steinberg, Spanish Foreign Minister Miguel Angel Moratinos (whose country then held the EU rotating presidency), and key Bosnia and Herzegovina politicians in Butmir failed to produce significant results, with Bosnian leaders unwilling to support any transfer of power from the governments of the Federation and Republika Srpska to the central government ahead of the October elections. The success of ethnic nationalist parties in the elections underscored the obstacles to such reform.

During a March visit to Bosnia Jean-Charles Gardetto, the Council of Europe Parliamentary Assembly (PACE) rapporteur, identified witness protection as a key challenge to accountability for war crimes in Bosnia and Herzegovina. This concern was echoed in a report by the OSCE Mission to Bosnia and Herzegovina, released in May, which called on the Bosnian authorities to do more to protect witnesses in war crime trials from harassment and violence. PACE also adopted resolutions on the functioning of democratic institutions in Bosnia in January and

April, highlighting the urgent need for constitutional reform, and sent a pre-election assessment mission to the country in September.

In February Bosnia and Herzegovina was subject to Universal Periodic Review by the UN Human Rights Council. Recommendations included the need to implement constitutional reforms, address the continued lack of sustainable financial and social support for the internally displaced, respond adequately to threats and attacks against independent journalists, and remove the death penalty from the constitution of Republika Srpska.

The European Commission's annual progress report, released in November, criticized Bosnia and Herzegovina for failing to implement constitutional reforms, the slow pace of reforms of the justice and penitentiary systems, and political interference and pressure on independent media. The EU commended ongoing efforts to process remaining war crimes cases and cooperation with the ICTY and highlighted improvement in the government's efforts to facilitate the return of remaining IDPs and refugees.

CROATIA

The election in January of a new president pledging to promote human rights, and the opening of a crucial chapter on European Union membership talks in June, put human rights on the agenda in Croatia. But the gap between commitments and progress remained. There was little movement towards deinstitutionalizing persons with intellectual or mental disabilities, and questions about access over-shadowed a long-awaited program to benefit Serb former tenancy rights holders. In absentia trials and concerns over fairness undercut domestic war crimes prosecutions, and the EU called into question Croatia's commitment to freedom of expression and information.

Rights of Persons with Disabilities

More than 9,000 persons with intellectual or mental disabilities remained in institutions as of September, with numbers rising. A master plan for deinstitutionalization and extensive social welfare reforms, both expected in 2010, have yet to be published at this writing. There were also few advances in creating community-based housing and support programs, such as personal assistants and other help with daily activities that would allow people to leave institutions.

There was no progress in reforming the legal capacity system, which routinely results in persons with intellectual or mental disabilities being denied the ability to make decisions and exercise rights, contributing to their institutionalization.

In September the State Attorney's Office in Rijeka brought criminal charges against the former director of Lopaca Psychiatric Hospital for 2008 abuses against Ana Dragicevic, who was forcibly institutionalized because of her sexual orientation, and four other unnamed patients.

The Croatian government and parliament again failed to amend the official Croatian translation of article 19 of the Convention on the Rights of Persons with Disabilities, which erroneously allows confinement in a residential institution to be categorized as a "community living option."

Return and Reintegration of Serbs

In September Croatian authorities issued a decision to permit former tenancy rights holders to buy apartments at discounts of up to 70 percent. The decision could remove a long-standing obstacle to Serbs returning to urban areas, although the United Nations High Commisioner for Refugees (UNHCR) noted that application deadlines and evidential requirements could impede access. The program has yet to commence at this writing.

In the first six months of 2010, 203 refugees—all ethnic Serbs—returned to Croatia. UNHCR estimates that 10,000-15,000 of the approximately 70,000 registered Croatian Serb refugees might consider returning to Croatia if problems with housing and pensions are addressed. As of June there were 2,246 internally displaced persons in Croatia, of whom approximately 1,600 were Serbs.

There were ongoing delays in government-sponsored social housing programs for returnees. As of June, 7,456 of the 13,187 families who applied had been allocated housing, of which 4,623 were Serbs. Around 3,300 families were still waiting for eligibility decisions.

The slow process of recognizing wartime work by Serbs in formerly rebel-held areas for pension eligibility continued. As of May, 18,848 of approximately 22,000 requests had been processed, although only 56 percent were resolved positively, in part because of disputes about admissible evidence. In some regions, positive outcomes were as low as 30 percent, compromising the financial security of returnees.

War Crimes Accountability

The trial of Croatian generals Ante Gotovina, Ivan Cermak, and Mladen Markac at the International Criminal Tribunal for the Former Yugoslavia (ICTY) for war crimes and crimes against humanity against Serbs concluded in September, with a decision expected at the end of 2010. At the request of Croatian Prime Minister Jadranka Kosor, the Croatian government created a task force in October 2009 to search for documents related to the case that the ICTY prosecutor alleged were in the government's possession. The trial concluded without these documents.

In March 2010 the Croatian Supreme Court confirmed the acquittal of General Rahim Ademi, and reduced the sentence of General Mirko Norac for war crimes against Serb civilians from seven to six years, relying on his service in the Croatian Armed Forces as mitigation. It remained the only case transferred from the ICTY to Croatia.

Croatian investigations into war crimes committed by members of the Croatian Armed Forces increased in 2010. In the first nine months of the year, Croatian authorities issued new war crimes indictments against 25 individuals, 11 of whom were Serbs. But Serbs remained the majority of defendants in domestic war crimes prosecutions. Ten trials, involving 13 Serb and 5 other defendants were completed in the same period, 16 of whom were convicted. Another 17 trials involving 29 Serbs and 14 Croats were still ongoing. In absentia war crimes trials remained a problem, with 23 Serbs and 7 others not present to defend themselves.

In September the Court of Bosnia and Herzegovina enforced a Croatian war crimes conviction and eight-year sentence against former Croatian MP Branimir Glavas, following a request from the Croatian Justice Ministry. Glavas, a Bosnian citizen, fled to Bosnia in May 2009 on the same day he was convicted in the Zagreb district court. Bosnian police arrested him after the court ruling which, barring a successful appeal, will see Glavas serve his sentence in Bosnia.

Asylum and Migration

Croatia passed amendments to its asylum legislation in July 2010, requiring quicker judicial review of detention decisions of asylum seekers and increased support to those granted asylum or subsidiary protection, in an effort to move closer to European and international standards. But there were continuing problems with its practices, including delays in processing claims and a lack of access to a state-funded lawyer at first instance and for those seeking to challenge their detention. The refugee recognition rate remained below 10 percent in the second half of 2009 and the first half of 2010.

Croatia lacked a strategy to respond effectively to the increasing numbers of unaccompanied migrant children (160 in 2009, with very few in previous years).

Key problems included an overstretched guardianship system, the absence of a tracking system (with some children disappearing), and lack of access to a state-funded lawyer for children who do not claim asylum.

Media Freedom

Journalists faced government pressure because of their reporting. Sergej Trajkovic and Tomislav Kukec, two journalists from the newspaper *Jutarnji List*, faced government attempts to block publication of reports about commercial abuses within the meat industry, including lack of government oversight in regulating the industry.

In April police in Zagreb interrogated and searched the home of Marko Rakar, a prominent blogger, after he published a leaked list of registered war veterans. The government had resisted efforts to release the list, which civil society activists believe contains people fraudulently receiving pensions as war veterans.

The trial of six suspects in the double murder in 2008 of prominent journalist Ivo Pukanic and his marketing director Niko Franjic ended in November, with the conviction of all six for first degree murder. Sentences ranged from 15 to 40 years.

Human Rights Defenders

Human rights defenders in Croatia remained free to operate but reported difficulties accessing information from Croatia's national and local authorities.

In May, for the third successive year, Croatia's parliament examined but then failed to adopt the People's Ombudsman's annual human rights report. Parliament offered no explanation for its decision.

Key International Actors

The EU remained the most influential international actor in Croatia. The opening of the justice and fundamental rights chapter in June offered encouragement to Croatia, although the challenges of closing the chapter were highlighted in the European Commission progress report released in November, which identified domestic war crimes accountability, freedom of expression, deinstitutionalization of persons with disabilities, and treatment of the Serb and Roma minorities as ongoing areas of concern.

The UN Human Rights Council conducted its first universal periodic review of Croatia in November, calling on Croatia to address concerns about the fairness of domestic war crimes trials and improve its treatment of persons with disabilities and the Serb and Roma minorities.

During a visit to Croatia in April, the Council of Europe commissioner for human rights Thomas Hammarberg identified the importance of addressing housing and other obstacles to return of IDPs and refugees; the need to improve fairness in war crimes proceedings; and the need to tackle access to housing, employment, education, and statelessness of Roma.

After her July visit to Croatia the UN special rapporteur on the right to housing identified the need for available and transparent post-war housing programs for Serb returnees as a key challenge.

EUROPEAN UNION

The EU gained new architecture to protect human rights, with the Charter of Fundamental Rights entering into force in January, a greater role for the European Parliament, and the creation of an EU commissioner for fundamental rights. New commissioner Viviane Reding promised a "zero tolerance" policy for EU states violating the charter.

Infringement proceedings against Greece over its asylum system indicated the European Commission's willingness to hold member states to account for rights violations. The commission publicly faulted France over expulsion of Roma, emphasizing procedural safeguards when limiting free movement of EU citizens, rather than non-discrimination obligations.

The scale of the challenge to ensure full respect of human rights in the EU was underscored by evidence of growing intolerance—manifest in electoral success by far-right parties, including in ruling coalitions, and policies targeting Roma, Muslims, and migrants—and ongoing concerns over abusive counterterrorism policies, inadequate access to asylum, and uneven protection against discrimination.

Common EU Asylum and Migration Policy

Efforts to reform and harmonize asylum procedures across the EU remained stalled. Studies by the United Nations High Commissioner for Refugees (UNHCR) in March and the European Commission in September found significant differences and shortcomings in the way asylum claims are handled across the EU.

Around three-quarters of all irregular migrants entered the EU through Greece in 2009, with early estimates for 2010 suggesting a rising trend. Arrivals by sea dropped significantly in 2010, with the EU border agency, Frontex, reporting a 75 percent decrease in maritime arrivals in the first half of the year. Only 150 people reached Italy and Malta in the first quarter of the year, down from 5,200 in the same period in 2009. Sea arrivals in Spain were also down sharply.

If ui go back my husband and my family kill me. No one to collect me on airport and you know in Pakistan women are not secure in Pakistan. If i go back there is no one who protect me from the world of animals If there in this world a little bit humanity or it can say human rights please protect me from them. If no then allowed me to kill my self as a right of human who have nothing in This world not a

UK Border Agency
Twinwoods Road
Clapham
Bedfordshire
MK41 6HL
Tel: 01234 424000   Fax: 01234 424095

UNITED KINGDOM

Fast-Tracked Unfairness
Detention and Denial of Women Asylum Seekers in the UK

HUMAN
RIGHTS
WATCH

Under paragraph 9-10A of schedule 2 to the Immigration Act 1971 & section 10(1) of the Asylum Act 1999

To

REMOVAL
DIRECTIONS   A   Directions have now been given for your removal from the United Kingdom by (flight) PK786 to Islamabad, Pakistan at 20.25 hrs on 05 October 2009

This is NOT an appealable decision.

The Dublin II Regulation, which requires asylum claims to be made in the first country of entry into the EU, exacerbated the burden placed on Greece's already broken asylum system (discussed below). But European Commission-led efforts to initiate modest reform encountered strong opposition from some member states.

As of mid-2010 the European Court of Human Rights (ECtHR) had issued orders to states to suspend more than 750 "Dublin" returns to Greece, with thousands more pending or blocked at national level. In September the United Kingdom government halted all such returns to Greece. As of early November the Netherlands, Belgium, Finland, Sweden, Iceland, and Norway (the latter two not EU countries) had done the same.

In September the ECtHR heard a challenge to the policy brought by an Afghan returned by Belgium to Greece, where he claims he was subjected to ill-treatment and risked being returned to Afghanistan without proper examination of his asylum claim. A ruling is pending at this writing.

The European Commission's May action plan on unaccompanied migrant children called for a common European approach to ensure durable solutions in children's best interests.

The UK and other EU countries (as well as Norway) pursued plans to build reception centers in Kabul, Afghanistan, in order to repatriate unaccompanied children, despite concerns over security and lack of safeguards.

Dozens of rejected asylum seekers were returned to Iraq in at least three joint flights between April and September, despite objections by UNHCR. Frontex coordinated at least one of these charter flights. The UK and the Netherlands organized their own flights, in addition to participating in joint returns. In November the Netherlands announced a halt to such deportations after the ECtHR intervened. The UK said it would suspend removals if ordered to do so by the ECtHR.

New guidelines for Frontex operations at sea, adopted in April, included a ban on return to persecution and the obligation to consider the needs of vulnerable groups, including asylum seekers, children, and trafficking victims.

Malta withdrew from Frontex missions in March over the guidelines, which require those rescued in international waters to be taken to the mission's host country rather than the closest port. But in July, Malta participated in a controversial joint rescue operation with Libya, which led to some Somali migrants being returned to Libya, while others were brought to Malta.

The European Parliament approved an EU readmission agreement with Pakistan in September, despite serious concerns about respect for human rights clauses. There were also concerns that the agreement would facilitate the repatriation of Afghans, including children, who transited through Pakistan.

The European Commission signed a cooperation agreement with Libya in October, including €50 million (approximately US$67 million) for border management and refugee protection, despite the forced closure of UNHCR's office in Tripoli in June.

Discrimination and Intolerance

The Roma, Europe's largest minority, continued to face discrimination, exclusion, and extreme poverty across the region. In April the European Commission adopted a communication on Roma for the first time, ahead of the second EU Summit on Roma held later that month in Spain, calling for more effective policies to address multiple sources of marginalization of Roma. EU countries, notably Germany, continued to repatriate Roma to Kosovo despite UNHCR guidelines, while France targeted Roma for repatriation to Eastern Europe.

Despite concerns about interfering with the right to freedom of religion and personal autonomy, efforts to restrict face-covering veils in Europe gained political momentum in 2010. France's parliament approved legislation in September banning the wearing of such veils in all public places and making it a crime to coerce women to cover themselves. The Constitutional Council ruled in early October that the law was compatible with France's constitution.

The lower house of the Belgian parliament approved similar legislation in May. At this writing, it has yet to be examined by the Senate. A ban was included in the coalition agreement in the Netherlands in September, with proposals also on the table in Spain, Italy, and Denmark.

In May Germany's interior minister ruled against a similar ban, but a December 2009 Federal Labor Court ruling, which upheld a ban on a teacher in North-Rhine-Westphalia wearing a headscarf in the classroom, underscored the continued presence of state-level restrictions on headscarves for teachers and civil servants.

Germany and other EU states blocked efforts to upgrade EU anti-discrimination laws to prohibit discrimination on grounds of religion, age, disability, and sexual orientation. National obstacles to ending discrimination against lesbian, gay, bisexual, and transgender people also remained, including in the Netherlands, where transgender persons could only officially change gender if they undergo irreversible sex reassignment surgery, and Italy, which still lacked explicit protection against discrimination on the grounds of sexual orientation.

Counterterrorism Measures and Human Rights

UN special rapporteurs on torture and on human rights while countering terrorism concluded in a joint February report that Germany (one case, 2002) and the UK (several cases, from 2002 onward) had been complicit in secret detentions of terrorism suspects. In June the Council of Europe commissioner for human rights criticized the lack of progress towards full accountability for complicity in United States abuses in Poland, Romania, and Sweden. A criminal investigation was launched in January in Lithuania after a parliamentary committee concluded in December 2009 that the CIA had established two secret detention facilities in that country in 2005 and 2006.

Resettlement of Guantanamo Bay detainees in Europe continued. Between January and September, 10 detainees were resettled in EU countries, three each in Spain and Slovakia, two in Germany, one in Bulgaria, and one in Latvia. Italy and Spain both pledged to take two more.

As part of the action plan to counter radicalization and recruitment to terrorism, the Council of the EU agreed in April to systematically collect and share information on radicalization, raising right to privacy concerns.

In September the EU General Court annulled a November 2008 European Commission terrorism finance regulation freezing the assets of Saudi national

Yassin Abdullah Kadi, the second EU Court ruling against his asset freeze, in both cases for lack of procedural fairness.

Human Rights Concerns in Select EU Member States

France

In July the government launched a highly-publicized campaign to expel Roma from France following riots sparked by the fatal shooting of a member of the community of French *gens du voyage* ("travelers") that month by a gendarme (now under criminal investigation). By the end of August, 128 informal settlements had been dismantled–including those occupied by French *gens du voyage*–and almost 1,000 Roma sent back to Romania and Bulgaria. An August 5 directive from the interior minister, leaked in early September and subsequently annulled, ordered prefects to take "systematic action to dismantle illegal camps, priority given to those of Roma" linked to the expulsions, showing discriminatory intent.

In September France agreed to improve procedural safeguards after the European Commission threatened infringement proceedings over its failure to properly implement EU law on freedom of movement. The changes have yet to be introduced at this writing.

Following its August review of France, the UN Committee on the Elimination of Racial Discrimination expressed concern over what appeared to be collective expulsion, as well as the difficulties Roma and French *gens du voyage* face exercising their rights and accessing education and decent housing. The committee also expressed broader concern about discriminatory political discourse in France and increased racist and xenophobic violence.

In October the National Assembly approved a government draft immigration law weakening the rights of asylum seekers and migrants, despite criticism from UN Committee against Torture in May and ECtHR in 2009 about inadequate safeguards for fast-tracked asylum claims. The Senate is to debate the law in early 2011.

The bill also contained last-minute government amendments designed to widen the grounds for expelling EU citizens to include "abusing" France's welfare system, exploitation of begging, and "abusive" occupation of land. The amendments' timing and focus and statements made by government ministers strongly suggested the measures were aimed at Roma.

In late December 2009, French authorities expelled a Tunisian man to Senegal on national security grounds, despite an order from the ECtHR to suspend his removal. Earlier that month the court ruled that France would violate its obligations under the European Convention if it deported an Algerian man who served six years in France on terrorism charges. France complied.

In July the Constitutional Council declared the inadequate safeguards in ordinary criminal cases, including denial of the presence of a lawyer during interrogations, unconstitutional. In October the government introduced draft legislation to reform police custody. Legislation remains pending at this writing. The ECtHR subsequently ruled in October that the current rules violated fair trial standards. Also in October the Court of Cassation, the highest criminal court, ruled that weaker safeguards in terrorism, organized crime, and drug trafficking cases violate the right to an effective defense. At this writing the current draft law does not address these issues.

Germany

In a February report the UN special rapporteur on racism underscored persistent racism, xenophobia, and discrimination when it comes to housing, employment and education, living conditions, and movement restrictions for asylum seekers.

The Grand Chamber of the ECtHR ruled in June that Germany had violated the ban on ill-treatment when it only fined a deputy police chief (later promoted) and his subordinate for threatening a kidnapper with torture in 2002, concluding that the punishment lacked the necessary deterrent effect.

In a judgment that became final in May, the ECtHR ruled that a German law allowing convicted prisoners deemed dangerous to be detained indefinitely after they have served their sentences violated the right to liberty and prohibition on arbitrary detention.

In July Germany lifted its restrictions on the application of the UN Convention on the Rights of the Child, covering a variety of issues, including asylum-seeking children. German rights groups continue to call on the government to bring the treatment of unaccompanied migrant children in line with the convention, including ending accommodation with adults and detention pending deportation of those aged between 16 and 18.

Greece

In September UNHCR described the situation facing migrants and asylum seekers in Greece as a "humanitarian crisis." There were no concrete improvements despite the government's repeated commitments to overhaul its broken asylum system, restore appeal rights, ensure humane treatment for migrants, and police accountability for ill-treatment.

A presidential decree containing modest reforms, including addressing a backlog of more than 46,000 cases, remained stalled, in part because of the country's budget crisis. Only 11 of 30,000 applicants (0.04 percent) were granted asylum at first instance in 2009. Wider reforms have been pushed back to 2011 or later.

The European Commission continued infringement proceedings against Greece for its breach of EU asylum rules, sending the government a second letter of formal notice on June 24. In response to a request from Greece, Frontex deployed 175 border guards to the Greece-Turkey border in November.

Migrants and asylum seekers continued to be detained in substandard conditions. There is little or no assistance for unaccompanied migrant children and other vulnerable groups, many of whom live in destitution or on the streets, at risk of exploitation and trafficking. Following a visit in October, the UN special rapporteur on torture called conditions in many immigration detention facilities inhuman and degrading.

Violence by armed opposition groups, as well as strikes and demonstrations, marked a year of increasing economic crisis and austerity measures in Greece. There were several deadly bomb attacks against public buildings, killing a bystander in March and the assistant to the minister of citizen protection in June. Other attacks caused structural damage. In November police in Greece and elsewhere intercepted over a dozen letter bombs addressed to foreign embassies in Athens, the Greek parliament, heads of state, and institutions in Europe.

A policeman was sentenced in October to life in prison for intentionally shooting a 15-year-old boy in Athens during a demonstration in December 2008, sparking nationwide riots. Another officer was sentenced to 10 years in prison for complicity.

In May the Council of Europe European Committee of Social Rights made public conclusions from December 2009 condemning Greece for widespread discrimination against Roma in access to housing. The same committee had condemned Greece in 2004.

Italy

Racist and xenophobic violence and hostile political discourse remained a pressing problem. In January, 11 African seasonal migrant workers were seriously injured in drive-by shootings and mob attacks over a three day period in Rosarno, Calabria. At least 10 other migrants, 10 law enforcement officers, and 14 local residents required medical treatment. Over 1,000 migrants left the town following the violence, most of them evacuated by law enforcement personnel. Numerous countries expressed concern about racism and xenophobia in Italy during its Universal Periodic Review at February's UN Human Rights Council (HRC).

Roma and Sinti continued to suffer high levels of discrimination, poverty, and deplorable living conditions in both authorized and unauthorized camps. Eastern European Roma, primarily from Romania and living in informal settlements, faced forced evictions and financial inducements to return to their countries of origin. In October the Council of Europe European Committee of Social Rights published conclusions from June condemning Italy for discrimination against Roma in housing and access to justice, economic, and social assistance.

Italy continued to deport terrorism suspects to Tunisia, including Mohamed Mannai in May, despite the risk of ill-treatment, persistent interventions from the ECtHR, and condemnation by the Council of Europe. A June resolution from its Committee of Ministers reiterated Italy's obligation to comply with European Court decisions.

428

The European Committee for the Prevention of Torture said in an April report that Italy violated the prohibition on refoulement when it intercepted boat migrants attempting to reach Italy and returned them to Libya without screening for people needing international protection. Two Italian officials faced prosecution in a Sicily court for their role in the return of 75 people to Libya on an Italian Financial Police boat in August 2009.

Italy failed to offer asylum to approximately a dozen Eritreans it had pushed back to Libya in 2009, where alongside hundreds of other Eritreans they suffered ill-treatment, abusive detention, and threat of deportation to Eritrea.

In May a Genova appeals court convicted 25 out of 29 police officers for violence against demonstrators at the 2001 G8 summit, overturning acquittals by a lower court. The Interior Ministry said it would not suspend the officers. Appeals against the May decision are pending at this writing.

The Netherlands

General elections in June left the anti-immigrant Freedom Party in third place with 24 parliamentary seats. In late September, after months of negotiations, the Liberal Party and Christian Democrats announced a center-right coalition government resting on Freedom Party support.

In October Freedom Party leader Geert Wilders appeared in court for inciting discrimination and hatred against Muslims, non-Western immigrants, and specifically Moroccans, as well as for group defamation of adherents to Islam. Later that month new judges were appointed following a challenge by Wilders over alleged bias; the case remains pending at this writing.

New rules in July extended the 48 hour accelerated asylum procedure to eight days while making it the default procedure, despite domestic and international criticism that eight days are insufficient for a proper assessment, particularly in complex cases and those involving vulnerable groups. In February the UN Committee on the Elimination of Discrimination against Women criticized Dutch accelerated procedures as unsuitable for women victims of violence and unaccompanied children, and urged the government to recognize formally domestic violence and gender-based persecution as grounds for asylum.

The ECtHR ruled in July that the expulsion to Libya of a Libyan man, acquitted of terrorism charges by a Dutch court in 2003, would violate the ban on returns to risk of torture.

In September, under a new policy announced in July, the government deported a Somali who had been refused asylum to Mogadishu, despite UNHCR guidelines advising against all returns to south-central Somalia.

Poland

Official flight records obtained by two national human rights groups in February confirmed that at least six CIA rendition flights landed in Poland in 2003. A criminal investigation launched in 2008 into complicity in a CIA secret prison continued, with reports suggesting the prosecutor was considering war crime charges against former president Aleksander Kwasniewski and other former senior officials. In September the prosecutor in charge of the case said his investigation would include the alleged detention and torture of a Saudi man while in CIA custody in Poland.

Discrimination based on race, gender, and sexual identity remained serious problems. In June the Council of Europe's European Commission against Racism and Intolerance (ECRI) expressed concern over Poland's failure to adequately address discrimination against Roma and non-citizens in education, housing, employment, and health. The European Commission referred Poland to the EU Court of Justice in May for failing to implement the EU directive on race equality. At this writing a government-sponsored anti-discrimination bill is pending final approval in parliament and is expected to come into force in January 2011. A coalition of 40 rights groups criticized the bill as failing to protect against discrimination on the basis of sexual orientation, disability, age, or religion in a variety of spheres, or against gender discrimination in education.

Warsaw hosted a landmark gay rights rally in July. The first EuroPride parade in a former Eastern Bloc country was peaceful, despite strong opposition. In December 2009 the UN Committee on Economic, Social and Cultural Rights had expressed concerns about discrimination against lesbian, gay, bisexual, and transgender persons in Poland. The ECtHR ruled in March that Poland discriminated unlawfully against same-sex couples by denying them the same protection in relation to housing and succession rights afforded to unmarried heterosexual couples.

In a May report the UN special rapporteur on the right to health criticized Poland over the lack of access to legal abortions, contraception, and prenatal testing.

Spain

The violent Basque separatist group ETA announced a unilateral ceasefire in early September after a year of relative inactivity and significant arrests under continuing France-Spain cooperation. A French gendarme was killed in March near Paris in a shoot-out with suspected ETA members. In January the Spanish Supreme Court ruled that 2006 negotiations between elected Basque officials and Batasuna, the Basque nationalist party declared illegal in 2003 for alleged ties to ETA, did not constitute a crime. Three ETA members were convicted for the December 2006 bombing of a Madrid airport. They will serve a maximum of 40 years in jail each, despite the symbolic 1,000 year sentences.

Spain rejected recommendations from peer governments during its Universal Periodic Review at the HRC in May. The rejected recommendations included the improvement of safeguards for terrorism detainees held without access to communication and the implementation of the 2008 justice reform in terrorism cases recommendations made by the UN special rapporteur on human rights while countering terrorism. The Spanish government similarly rejected recommendations to create an independent police complaints mechanism.

Parliament approved in June an overhaul of Spain's criminal code effective December 2010, increasing sentences for over 30 crimes, creating a new system of post-sentence "supervised liberty" for terrorism and sex offenses, and creating a new crime of disseminating information to "provoke, foment or foster" the commission of a terrorism offense.

Judge Baltasar Garzón, known internationally for his efforts to bring former Chilean dictator Augusto Pinochet to justice, was suspended in May and faced trial for investigating alleged cases of illegal detention and forced disappearances of more than 100,000 people during Spain's civil war and under the subsequent

SPAIN

Eternal Emergency
No End to Unaccompanied Migrant Children's
Institutionalization in Canary Islands Emergency Centers

HUMAN
RIGHTS
WATCH

Franco regime, despite a 1977 amnesty law. The UN Working Group on Enforced or Involuntary Disappearances expressed concern in May over Garzón's suspension and criticized Spain's amnesty law.

Around 200 unaccompanied migrant children, mainly from sub-Saharan Africa and Morocco, remain in "emergency" centers set up in 2006 in the Canary Islands despite repeated pledges by the local government to close them. Around half live in La Esperanza, a substandard, large, isolated former detention facility. The UN Committee on the Rights of the Child expressed concern in September over inadequate reception conditions and neglect of children in the Canaries. It recommended that Spain establish child-friendly centers and introduce effective complaints mechanisms for children in care to report ill-treatment.

A new law came into force in July removing restrictions on abortion to make it legal on request up to the fourteenth week of pregnancy. It also increased access to, and information about, reproductive rights and family planning. Prior to the reform, abortion was lawful only on the grounds of serious health risks for the woman, fetal malformations, or in rape cases.

United Kingdom

General elections in May resulted in a coalition between the Conservative and Liberal Democrat parties, Britain's first coalition government since 1945.

In July the new government announced a judge-led inquiry into allegations of complicity of UK intelligence agencies in torture, and for the first time published guidance for intelligence officers on interrogating detainees abroad. The inquiry, whose detailed terms of reference have yet to be published at this writing, is not expected to begin until all ongoing criminal investigations into alleged complicity by British agents in overseas torture were resolved. In November the UK's top prosecutor announced there was insufficient evidence to prosecute a Security Service (MI5) officer over the abuse of Binyam Mohamed. The same month the government announced it would pay former Guantanamo Bay detainees compensation to settle civil suits and avoid disclosure of classified documents, without UK authorities admitting culpability.

Concerns remained that current guidelines on overseas interrogations give too much latitude to intelligence officers, appear to create ministerial discretion to permit use of abusive techniques, and foresee assurances as a means of mitigating the risk of torture or ill-treatment, despite their inherent unreliability.

The Equality and Human Rights Commission warned the government in September that it would seek judicial review by the courts if the guidance was not amended. Lawyers representing civilians detained and allegedly tortured by British forces in Iraq also threatened action because the guidelines do not unequivocally prohibit hooding, an issue central to the public inquiry into the 2003 death of Iraqi hotel receptionist Baha Mousa while in British military custody in Basra. The inquiry's hearings ended in October and a final report is pending at this writing.

Heavily redacted documents were published in July and September following a High Court order in a civil case brought against the UK government by six former Guantanamo Bay detainees. The documents provided evidence that the government was aware as early as January 2002 of allegations that UK citizens and residents were being tortured in US custody but failed to object to transferring UK nationals to Guantanamo Bay. The documents also included 2002 guidance to UK intelligence officers that if they observed the "mistreatment" of prisoners in foreign custody "the law does not require you to intervene to prevent this."

In July the Home Office launched a review of much-criticized counterterrorism measures, including control orders, extended pre-charge detention, stop and search without suspicion, and deportation with assurances. At this writing the government has yet to present its reform proposals to parliament. The government suspended the terrorism stop and search power in July, following the ECtHR's confirmation that the powers violated privacy rights, was too broad, and lacked safeguards.

Despite the Home Office review, the coalition government agreement endorsed the use of diplomatic assurances to deport terrorism suspects.

In May the Special Immigration Appeals Commission (SIAC) blocked the deportation on the basis of diplomatic assurances to Pakistan of two Pakistani terrorism suspects. In July the US government began extradition proceedings against one of

TERRORISM ACT 2000: STOP AND SEARCH EXPLAINED

Police have two stop and search powers under the Terrorism Act 2000.

Under Section 44 officers may search any person or vehicle for items related to terrorism. **They do not need reasonable grounds** to suspect that items will be found.

Section 43 gives officers the power to search any person for items related to terrorism **where they have reasonable grounds** to suspect such items will be found.

Reasonable suspicion an individual is involved in terrorist activity may arise from their behaviour and/or current intelligence.

If you are stopped and searched you have certain rights:

- The officer searching you will use stop and search powers fairly a'

U.K.

Without Suspicion

Stop and Search under the Terrorism Act 2000

H U M A N

R I G H T S

W A T C H

435

the suspects. The case is ongoing at this writing. SIAC ruled in September that an Ethiopian terrorism suspect could be safely deported to Ethiopia despite the risk of torture, the first case involving a 2008 agreement between the two countries. An appeal is pending at this writing.

In June the UK High Court confirmed a moratorium on transfers of terrorism suspects to the National Directorate of Security (NDS) facility in Kabul following allegations of torture. In March the ECtHR ruled that the UK violated the rights of two Iraqis by transferring them from UK military custody in Basra to Iraqi authorities in December 2008. The court rejected the UK government's appeal in October.

The prime minister publicly apologized in June for the "unjustified and unjustifiable" 1972 killing of 14 unarmed protestors in Northern Ireland by British soldiers, following the long-awaited report from the Bloody Sunday Inquiry published the same month. The 12 year inquiry concluded the soldiers did not face any threat and gave no warnings before firing.

The death in October of an Angolan man as he was being deported by private security guards working for the Home Office prompted an inquiry by the Parliamentary Home Affairs Committee into restraint techniques used during such removals. A criminal investigation into the death was ongoing at time of writing.

Children continued to be detained in immigration centers despite the government's pledge in May to stop the practice. Women, including survivors of sexual violence in Pakistan, Sierra Leone and Uganda, continued to be placed in the "detained fast-track" asylum procedure unsuited to considering such complex claims.

The Supreme Court ruled in July that two gay asylum seekers from Iran and Cameroon could not be denied protection on the grounds that they could conceal their sexuality in their countries of origin. The Home Office announced new rules to prevent removals to countries where individuals face persecution based on their sexual orientation or gender identification.

Georgia

Georgia's human rights record remained uneven in 2010. The government evicted hundreds of internally displaced persons (IDPs) from state-owned collective centers in Tbilisi, the capital, often leaving them homeless or without adequate compensation. State actors hindered activists' right to assembly and attacked and harassed journalists and opposition newspapers. Municipal elections on May 30 largely met international standards, but observers also identified significant shortcomings.

More than two years after the August 2008 Georgian-Russian conflict over South Ossetia, the government has not effectively investigated international human rights and humanitarian law violations. Russia strengthened its military presence in and effective control over Georgia's breakaway regions. The European Union started negotiations with Georgia to deepen economic and political ties.

Forced Evictions of Internally Displaced People

Since June the authorities have evicted hundreds of IDPs from state-owned temporary collective centers in Tbilisi, supposedly to provide them with durable housing solutions. The authorities failed to respect international standards regarding evictions: they did not engage in genuine consultation with IDPs, did not provide reasonable advance notice of eviction, and failed to provide adequate alternatives. Some IDPs received no alternative housing; others were sent to homes in remote regions, some of which had damaged roofs or lacked electricity or gas. Georgia has some 246,000 IDPs as a legacy of conflicts in the 1990s and in 2008. Over 40 percent live in 1,658 state or private collective centers, 515 of which are in Tbilisi.

In June officials gave IDPs verbal warnings five days prior to eviction. August 2 amendments to Ministry of Interior Decree No. 747 abolished the five-day warning requirement. Thereafter some IDPs received only a few hours' warning prior to eviction. The evictions violated Georgia's Law on the Internally Displaced, which prohibits the removal of IDPs without written consent and the placement in homes inferior to their current residences.

The Ministry of Refugees and Accommodation says it offered those evicted in August either financial compensation or housing in rural areas. Many IDPs refused to relocate to rural areas citing lack of employment opportunities. They received no financial compensation and became homeless after eviction.

Freedom of Assembly and Police Violence

The authorities interfered with peaceful assembly and failed to meaningfully investigate past excessive use of force by law enforcement. On August 14, police arrested Georgian activists and writers Irakli Kakabadze, Shota Gagarin, and Aleksi Chigvinadze as they peacefully protested on George W. Bush Street in Tbilisi. Police charged the three with disobeying police orders and released them the next day after a court fined each of them GEL400 (US$220). At the closed hearing, the judge heard only police evidence and refused to watch video showing the men cooperating with police at the moment of arrest. Kakabadze alleged that police verbally and physically abused him in the police car. An Ombudsman's representative visited Kakabadze in detention and confirmed injuries on his shoulder and arm.

On November 23, 2009, police arrested Dachi Tsagauri, Jaba Jishkariani, and Irakli Kordzaia– activists from a pro-opposition youth group–as they protested government policies near the parliament. At the time of arrest police told the activists that they had violated the law on rallies, which bans holding rallies in a 20-meter radius from the Parliament building. However, the arrest protocol indicated that the protestors stood 30 meters away from the building. The Tbilisi City Court found the men in violation of rules for holding a rally and for resisting police and fined each GEL500 (US$280). The court did not consider video footage from journalists present at the rally showing that the activists had not obstructed movement of pedestrians and had obeyed police orders at the moment of arrest.

On August 19, 2010, police detained two opposition activists allegedly for resisting police orders also outside parliament, where IDPs and others peacefully protested the spate of evictions. The protestors had informed the city municipality about the rally in advance and did not block the road. The Tbilisi City Court fined the activists GEL400 (US$220) each for resisting police orders.

The government has refused to launch a comprehensive investigation into events of November 7, 2007, when police used excessive force against largely peaceful demonstrations in Tbilisi, resulting in at least 500 injured. The authorities have also failed to conduct an effective investigation into a June 15, 2009 police attack against 50 opposition supporters outside the police headquarters, when at least 17 demonstrators were injured. The government has also failed to conduct a thorough investigation into the March 2006 operation to quell a riot in Tbilisi Prison No. 5, which left seven prisoners dead and dozens injured.

Municipal Elections

National municipal elections took place on May 30, 2010 to elect 63 local councils, including the mayor of Tbilisi, who was directly elected for the first time. The ruling National Movement party won an overwhelming majority in all municipalities. International observers concluded that the polls marked progress towards international standards, but significant shortcomings remained, including legal deficiencies, unlimited campaigning and the use of administrative resources by some public officials, and isolated cases of election-day fraud.

Lack of Accountability for Laws of War Violations

Over two years since the Georgian-Russian conflict over South Ossetia, Georgian authorities have yet to ensure a comprehensive investigation into and accountability for international human rights and humanitarian law violations by their forces.

During the war the Georgian military used indiscriminate force, including firing multiple rocket launchers, an indiscriminate weapon that should not be used in civilian areas. The military also used cluster munitions against the Russian military, including in civilian-populated Georgian territories adjacent to the administrative border with South Ossetia.

The Office of the Prosecutor at the International Criminal Court—to which Georgia is a party—continued with its preliminary examination of the situation and sent delegations to Russia in March and to Georgia in June 2010 to obtain additional information on domestic proceedings.

Some 20,000 ethnic Georgians from South Ossetia remain displaced.

Media Freedom

The media environment remains mixed, with diverse print media, but nationwide television broadcasting limited to the state-owned Public Broadcaster and pro-government Rustavi 2 and Imedi stations. Transparency of media ownership remains a concern.

Several journalists alleged pressure and attacks. On June 25, police assaulted Gori-based Trialeti television journalist Lado Bichashvili and cameraman Imeda Gogoladze as they filmed the removal of a Stalin statue from the city center. About eight policemen beat the journalists and confiscated their camera, which they later returned with materials deleted.

In July Vakhtang Komakhidze, a long-time Georgian investigative journalist, received asylum in Switzerland, citing threats by the authorities. The threats allegedly intensified after Komakhidze started work on an investigative film regarding the August 2008 war in South Ossetia.

In February the opposition newspaper Guria News, published in Western Georgia, alleged that local authorities threatened and intimidated the private distributors who distribute the newspaper. On February 8, police briefly detained Guria News correspondent Irakli Dolidze as he photographed a police official, confiscating his photo camera and cell phone temporarily.

On November 25, 2009, the Ministry of Interior's Special Operations Department called in Tedo Jorbenadze, head of the investigations unit at the independent Batumi-based weekly newspaper *Batumelebi*, and threatened to publish photos of near-naked men, Jorbenadze allegedly among them, if he refused to cooperate with intelligence services.

Criminal Justice System

Prison overcrowding remains a problem, leading to poor conditions. Courts' low number of acquittals is a key factor in overcrowding. In September the Council of Europe's Committee for the Prevention of Torture and Inhuman or Degrading

Treatment or Punishment published a report on its February visit to Georgia, noting a number of positive developments, but expressing concern regarding little or no progress on overcrowding in Georgian prisons and lack of meaningful activities for prisoners.

In February Georgia restored the minimum age of criminal responsibility to 14, after reducing it to 12 in 2008, making it consistent with the country's international commitments. In 2009 the state trained 430 investigators in juvenile interrogation techniques and made the presence of a lawyer and a legal guardian mandatory during interrogation.

Key International Actors

The United States and the EU deepened their engagement and economic ties with Georgia. Meanwhile, Russia continued to occupy Georgia's breakaway regions of South Ossetia and Abkhazia and strengthened its military presence in the region by establishing a military base and placing an advanced surface-to-air missile system in Abkhazia.

In July US Secretary of State Hillary Clinton visited Georgia and met with women leaders from civil society and government. She also met President Mikheil Saakashvili to emphasize the US commitment to Georgia's territorial integrity and pledging support for democracy and economy. Working groups met in Tbilisi and Washington in 2010 to discuss the implementation of the U.S.-Georgia Charter on Strategic Partnership, signed in January 2009, envisaging increased cooperation, including on strengthening human rights.

The April 2010 European Neighbourhood Policy (ENP) Action Plan progress report commended Georgia for improvements in judicial reform and fighting corruption, but raised concerns on several issues including: prison overcrowding, minority rights, and media transparency. In July 2010 Georgia and the EU began negotiations for an Association Agreement, which enhances the ENP, aiming at strengthened economic and political relations.

A report on Georgia by the Council of Europe's European Commission against Racism and Intolerance issued in June expressed concern about discrimination against ethnic and religious minorities and the absence of mechanisms for addressing abuses.

In September Council of Europe Commissioner for Human Rights Thomas Hammarberg published a report on disappearances during and after the August 2008 armed conflict, calling for impartial investigations by both sides. In October Hammarberg published another report on human rights issues following the conflict, including the right to return, rights of displaced persons to care and support, and protection and release of detainees.

In August the United Nations High Commissioner for Refugees expressed concern about forced evictions of IDPs in Tbilisi.

KAZAKHSTAN

During its 2010 chairmanship of the Organization for Security and Co-operation in Europe (OSCE), Kazakhstan's human rights record was marred by continued disappointments. Restrictive amendments to media and Internet laws remained, and a number of websites and weblogs were blocked on a regular basis. The government punished activists for breaking restrictive rules on freedom of assembly. Several activists were put on trial in 2010 and Kazakhstan's leading human rights defender, Evgeniy Zhovtis, remains in prison.

Freedoms of Expression and Information

Government loyalists dominate broadcast media outlets; independent journalists who criticize government policies and practices face threats and harassment; there are prohibitive penalties for civil defamation; and criminal penalties for libel remain in force. Combined, these conditions chill the environment for freedom of expression. In the first half of 2010 five journalists were physically attacked and another five accused of criminal libel, according to the media watch dog Adil Soz.

One of the attacked journalists is Igor Larra, of the independent daily *Svoboda Slova*. On March 22, 2010, three unidentified men assaulted him in Aktobe, breaking his nose and jaw and inflicting multiple contusions to his head. In the weeks prior to the attack Larra had been covering a 19-day strike by oil workers employed by OzenMunaiGaz. The workers had demanded that the company's director resign and that management take back cuts in wages. The biggest shareholder at OzenMunaiGaz is the state-owned company KazMunaiGaz. According to *Adil Soz,* Larra did not file a complaint because he did not trust the authorities to conduct a proper investigation.

In July 2010 a court upheld an April 21 ruling ordering the independent weekly *Uralskaya Nedelya* to pay 20 million tenge (US$136,000) in "moral damages" to Tengizneftestroi, an oil company. The weekly had published an article in August 2009 criticizing the company for being so sure of winning a tender that it had hired workers and bought equipment before the tender was even published. The company confirmed these facts during the trial hearing, raising doubt about the grounds for the ruling.

The authorities denied parole to imprisoned journalist Ramazan Yesergepov, editor of the newspaper *Alma-Ata Info,* after he had completed one-third of his sentence. Yesergepov was sentenced to three years in prison in 2009 for disclosing state secrets, because his newspaper had published information from a letter from the Committee for National Security in which the agency appeared to be attempting to sway a criminal investiation against a local businessman. Yesergepov's trial was not open to the public, and he was denied access to a lawyer of his choice.

On March 1, 2010 the head of the government's Agency for Information and Networks stated that a computer emergency response team had been established and had started to develop "a blacklist of destructive websites." The same official mentioned that religious and political websites in particular would be considered for the list. Currently blocked are more than a dozen websites, including the popular Russian-language blogging platform Livejournal and the website of the independent weekly *Respublika*.

Freedom of Assembly

On March 26, 2010, a court sentenced Vladimir Kozlov, a leading activist with the opposition party Alga!, to 10 days of administrative arrest on charges of holding an unsanctioned protest. The charges were brought because Kozlov had distributed leaflets criticizing the trial and sentencing of Mukhtar Dzhakishev, the former director the state-owned nuclear company KazAtomProm, whose imprisonment many believe is politically motivated. Kozlov had distributed the leaflets along a pedestrian zone in Almaty; other individuals distributing commercial leaflets at the same time where not arrested.

On May 2, 2010, Yermek Narymbaev, leader of the Arman (Dream) social movement, was sentenced to 15 days' administrative arrest for allegedly holding a peaceful unsanctioned mass gathering of 500 people on May 1. During his arrest, he was additionally charged with resisting the police and offending the judge at his trial on May 2. On June 23, a court sentenced him to four years' imprisonment.

In June 2010, courts fined at least five individuals—three journalists and two human rights activists—for organizing and participating in unsanctioned meetings and disobeying the authorities. In each case, the individual had staged a one-person picket on Almaty's main square protesting the highly controversial law, adopted that month, giving President Nursultan Nazarbaev lifetime immunity from prosecution.

Detention of Activists

In July 2010 a court in Aktobe sentenced Aidos Sadykov, a longtime opposition political activist who had assisted oil workers in creating an independent union, to two years' imprisonment for "hooliganism accompanied by resistance to the police," in what appears to be a politically motivated set-up. On May 27, Sadykov was arrested for attacking an unknown man, despite evidence that he was himself attacked and did not retaliate against the attacker. When Sadykov was already handcuffed he resisted police attempts to put the cell phone of the attacker in his pocket. During his court hearing the judge twice declined to show a video that a journalist had recorded shortly after the arrest, which could have proved Sadykov's innocence.

September 3, 2010 marked the one-year anniversary of the imprisonment of Kazakhstan's most prominent human rights defender, Evgeniy Zhovtis. On September 3, 2009, Zhovtis, founding director of the Kazakhstan International Bureau for Human Rights and the Rule of Law, was found guilty of vehicular manslaughter, following an unfair trial marred by serious procedural flaws that denied him the right to present a defense. Zhovtis was sentenced to four years in a settlement colony, a penal establishment which allows for more freedoms than an ordinary prison. The facilty's director had the discretion to allow Zhovtis to live and work outside the establishment but chose not to do so.

On April 26, 2010, the Supreme Court of Kazakhstan declined to review Zhovtis' verdict.

Risk of Refoulement

Since the entry into force in January 2010 of the Law on Refugees, the Kazakh government renewed pressure on refugees and asylum seekers from Uzbekistan who are devout Muslims and fear religious persecution in Uzbekistan. More than 70 asylum seekers and refugees signed a letter to Human Rights Watch stating that when they applied for asylum, migration officials tried to convince them that they have nothing to fear in Uzbekistan.

In June Kazakh authorities rounded up more than 40 Uzbek nationals in Almaty, almost all of whom were registered asylum seekers. Some were released, and at this writing some 31 remain in detention in Kazakhstan, pursuant to extradition requests from the Uzbek government. While the charges on which the Uzbek authorities are seeking extradition have not been made public, they are reportedly related to religious extremism. There is significant, credible evidence that persons prosecuted in Uzbekistan on religious extremism charges face a grave risk of torture or other forms of ill-treatment in detention. Despite these risks, Kazakhstan extradited to Uzbekistan four men; two of them are ethnic Uzbeks but citizens of Tajikistan and Kyrgyzstan.

Labor Abuses and Child Labor in Agriculture

Farmers employing migrant workers from Kyrgyzstan on farms supplying tobacco to Philip Morris Kazakhstan (PMK), a subsidiary of Philip Morris International (PMI) did not provide workers with written contracts or pay them for periods of eight to nine months of employment. They confiscated some workers' passports and subjected some to forced labor. Child labor remains a serious problem in tobacco and cotton farming, which employs children as young as 10. Experts agree that tobacco and cotton farming are two of the worst forms of child labor worldwide owing to the difficulty of the work and the risks associated with exposure to pesticides and tobacco leaves. Beginning in 2010 PMI and PMK have revised their contracts with tobacco farmers to ensure that migrant workers receive regular wages and other protections. PMI and PMK have also committed to implement a mechanism for complaints; to expand training for workers, farmers, and PMK employees regarding labor rights and hazards of child labor; and

KAZAKHSTAN

"Hellish Work"

Exploitation of Migrant Tobacco Workers in Kazakhstan

HUMAN
RIGHTS
WATCH

to develop summer camps and work with the government to facilitate access to schools for migrant workers' children to prevent child labor.

Key International Actors

Key international actors, notably members of the OSCE, uncritically pledged their support for and cooperation with Kazakhstan during its OSCE chairmanship in 2010. They generally failed to use the chairmanship and Kazakhstan's bid to hold a summit at the end of 2010 as a lever to push for outstanding reforms.

During a United Nations Security Council discussion on February 5, the United Kingdom stressed that the role of the OSCE chairmanship "brings with it important responsibilities to promote and embody the principles of human rights ... on which the OSCE is founded." During a meeting with President Nursultan Nazarbaev on April 11, 2010, United States President Barack Obama said the US would continue to support democratic reforms in Kazakhstan, but fell short of expressing concern about Kazakhstan's human rights performance.

On February 12, during Kazakhstan's Universal Periodic Review at the UN Human Rights Council, UN member states raised many concerns about media freedoms. They recommended that Kazakhstan adopt a moratorium on criminal libel, establish a cap on defamation awards in civil suits, stop any attempt to filter internet content or block access to websites, and refrain from adding further unwarranted restrictions to Kazakhstan's media law. Kazakhstan committed to implement most of these recommendations, but denied that its laws criminalize defamation by journalists and rejected allegations of abusive regulation of Internet content.

During a visit to Kazakhstan in April, UN Secretary-General Ban Ki-moon urged the government to implement the UPR recommendations, noting that "a robust and engaged civil society—with full guarantees of free speech and media, and tolerance for ethnic and religious diversity—is a powerful force for modernization."

Following its May 2010 review of Kazakhstan, the UN Committee on Economic, Social and Cultural Rights noted "with concern the low level of awareness of human rights in general, and of the Covenant in particular" and expressed deep concern about "the precarious situation of migrant workers."

KYRGYZSTAN

In 2010 Kyrgyzstan experienced its worst violence and upheaval since independence in 1991, with disastrous results for human rights.

Unrest surrounding President Kurmanbek Bakiyev's ouster in early April led to 85 deaths, hundreds of injured, and contining violence. Between June 10 to 14 ethnic violence shook southern Kyrgyzstan, killing hundreds, injuring thousands, destroying more than 2,600 homes, and resulting in the temporary mass exodus to Uzbekistan of nearly 100,000 ethnic Uzbeks from the country's southern provinces. For several days Kyrgyz authorities failed to contain or stop the killings and large-scale destruction, and did not appear to take every possible measure to protect all citizens.

The country remained extremely volatile after the June violence, especially in the south, where lack of security and accountability has allowed vigilantism and rule of force to prevail over the rule of law. As trials related to the violence began, angry mobs—mostly comprised of relatives of ethnic Kyrgyz killed in June violence—attacked defendants and their relatives, human rights defenders, journalists, and lawyers.

A constitutional referendum on June 27, 2010—just two weeks after the mayhem— transformed Kyrgyzstan to the first parliamentary republic in Central Asia. Parliamentary elections on October 10 were largely peaceful despite the tense atmosphere. With five parties passing the five percent threshold, international observers praised the elections as "pluralistic."

April Turmoil

On April 7, 2010, demonstrators ousted President Bakiyev from office, throwing the country into political turmoil. In precedeing weeks, the political opposition had held a series of demonstrations to air various grievances, including concern regarding President Bakiyev's growing authoritarianism, persecution and imprisonment of influential opposition political leaders, alleged government nepotism and mismanagement, increased energy tariffs, growing corruption, and government closure of several media outlets.

Authorities detained several opposition leaders on the eve of nationwide opposition gatherings planned for early April. Political violence erupted in response to the first detention and was eventually quelled on April 6 in Talas, a city in northwestern Kyrgyzstan. Violence erupted again on April 7 in Bishkek, when security forces tried to disperse a peaceful protest against the detention of more opposition leaders. Thousands of people eventually gathered in front of the White House, the main government building in Bishkek, in a standoff with security forces. Some demonstrators were armed with weapons they had seized from police. As the situation escalated security forces fired on the demonstrators with live ammunition.

Clashes ended in the early morning hours of April 8 when opposition supporters took control of the White House, forcing Bakiyev to abandon his office. He fled the country on April 15, and a 14-member interim government of opposition leaders took charge.

The authorities' investigation into April's events has focused on members of the ousted government. It is unclear to what extent, if any, the authorities have investigated crimes committed by demonstrators, including illegal seizure and use of weapons.

Mayhem in Southern Kyrgyzstan in June

The political power struggle that followed Bakiyev's ouster acquired an ethnic dimension in southern Kyrgyzstan when the area's large Uzbek minority sided with the interim government and helped prevent Bakiyev staging a comeback. The growing role of the ethnic Uzbek community in the political arena led to escalating tensions and violent clashes between ethnic Uzbeks and Kyrgyz in May 2010.

On the evening of June 10, violence erupted in Osh when a large crowd of ethnic Uzbeks gathered in the city center in response to several fights between small groups of ethnic Kyrgyz and Uzbek men earlier that day; the fighting escalated, with crowds clashing throughout the night.

Outraged by the violence and concerned about their bretheren in Osh, crowds of ethnic Kyrgyz from neighboring villages descended on the city and joined local

"Where Is the Justice?"

Interethnic Violence in Southern Kyrgyzstan and its Aftermath

HUMAN
RIGHTS
WATCH

residents in clashing with ethnic Uzbeks, looting and torching Uzbek shops and neighborhoods, and even killing Uzbeks.

Widespread use of heavy military vehicles in the attacks on Uzbek neighborhoods indicated that, in at least some cases, government forces facilitated the attacks by knowingly or unwittingly giving cover to violent mobs. It remains unclear whether government forces actively participated in these attacks, and if so, to what extent.

On June 13, 2010, violence spread to neighboring Jalal-Abad province, causing more deaths, injuries, and destruction.

According to official statistics, more than 400 people died during the violence and around 2,600 homes were destroyed, most of them owned by ethnic Uzbeks.

Aftermath of the Violence

The government's investigation into the violence has included serious violations of Kyrgyz and international law. Arbitrary arrests and extortion were widespread, and there is credible evidence in numerous cases that detainees were ill-treated and tortured. One man died from injuries he sustained in custody.

The authorities systematically denied defendants due process rights, such as the right to representation by a lawyer of their choice and the right to consult with a lawyer in private, which made it impossible for clients to complain confidentially about ill-treatment, extortion, and other violations. Lawyers also said the authorities have routinely refused to order medical examinations of detainees in cases of suspected ill-treatment.

In the vast majority of cases authorities claimed that they had been unable to verify allegations of torture and ill-treatment, and refused to launch criminal investigations. At this writing no official has been charged or prosecuted for the use of torture and ill-treatment.

In August the government acknowledged that most individuals detained in connection with the violence were ethnic Uzbeks, raising concern that the investigation into the violence was biased. As the post-violence crackdown by police on the ethnic Uzbek community intensified in late June and July, ethnic Uzbeks wanting to flee to Uzbekistan could not do so due to the closed land border.

At numerous trials related to the June violence, aggrieved relatives of ethnic Kyrgyz victims attacked ethnic Uzbek defendants, defendants' relatives, lawyers, and journalists, before, during, and after trial hearings. Police did little to stop or prevent these attacks.

For example, on September 15, 2010, a court in southern Kyrgyzstan sentenced Azimjon Askarov, an ethnic Uzbek human rights defender and head of the NGO Air, to life in prison for his alleged role in an incident in which an ethnic Kyrgyz policeman was killed during the June violence. During the trial the victim's relatives and supporters threatened and struck Askarov's lawyer, shouted threats and insults at the defense team, and beat relatives of the defendant. Police were present but did not act. The court heard numerous witnesses for the prosecution, but defense lawyers felt they could not endanger witnesses by calling them to the stand. On two occasions prior to the trial angry groups, allegedly including the policeman's relatives, threatened and physically attacked Askarov's lawyer. Local authorities did not respond.

Similar attacks continued at trials through October.

Threats to Human Rights Defenders

Several of Kyrgyzstan's most prominent human rights leaders received threats in connection with their investigation into the June violence and its aftermath.

In late June Tolekan Ismailova of Citizens Against Corruption, a human rights NGO, fled the country for several months with her family after the Osh prosecutor's office falsely accused her and Aziza Abdirasulova of Kylym Shamy, another human rights NGO, of distributing inaccurate information about a police operation that followed the violence. A few days later Ismailova's neighbors in Bishkek reported that strangers had come to the neighborhood to inquire about her family and where she lived. Abdirasulova received numerous threats. For example in August, angry residents of Bazar-Kurgan threatened to kill one of Abdirasulova's children if their mother monitored Askarov's trial.

In October two unknown men threatened the program coordinator of Spravedlivost (Justice), based in the southern city of Jalal-Abad, for providing free legal assistance to defendants in cases related to the June violence.

Elections

Parliamentary elections on October 10 and the election campaign that preceded them were conducted in a peaceful and rather pluralistic manner—an important step towards future free and fair elections. The Office for Democratic Institutions and Human Rights of the Organization for Security and Cooperation in Europe (OSCE) noted a number of shortcomings though, especially regarding election legislation and the accuracy of voter lists.

Key International Actors

A unified international community expressed concern about the April 2010 disturbances, quickly condemned the June violence, and called for the restoration of law and order. It also called for objective investigations into the events. However, key governments and international organizations such as Russia, the Collective Security Treaty Organization (CSTO), and the UN Security Council were much more hesitant to take necessary measures to protect the civilian population. Despite calls from the Kyrgyz authorities during the June violence, no international body proved ready to deploy stabilization forces.

Six weeks after violence erupted in June OSCE participating states reached an agreement, at the Kyrgyz government's request, to deploy a small unarmed international police force to the region in a monitoring and advisory role. The Kyrgyz government also requested the OSCE Parliamentary Assembly's special envoy for Central Asia establish an independent international commission of inquiry into the June 2010 violence. Due to disagreement within the Kyrgyz government about both initiatives, their deployment was postponed until after the October 10 election. At this writing the international commission has commenced its work, while the government continues to hold up the deployment of the police advisory group.

During his visit to Kyrgyzstan on April 3, 2010—just before the overthrow of the Bakiyev government—United Nations Secretary General Ban Ki-moon said he was "troubled" by the crackdown on independent media in Kyrgyzstan and urged authorities to respect all human rights, including free speech and freedom of the media.

On May 3, 2010, during Kyrgyzstan's Universal Periodic Review (UPR) at the UN Human Rights Council, UN member states issued a number of important recommendations, including ensuring an early return to constitutional order; rule of law and respect for human rights; ending all forms of intimidation, harassment, aggression, arbitrary arrest and detention, and torture against all persons, especially human rights defenders, peaceful demonstrators, and journalists; ensuring judicial independence; ensuring the rights of minorities; and inviting the special rapporteur on torture to visit in 2010. Kyrgyzstan accepted these and other recommendations. On June 18, 2010, the Council adopted a resolution condemning ethnic violence in Kyrgyzstan and called on the high commissioner to keep it appraised of the situation.

RUSSIA

In 2010 Russia demonstrated increased openness to international cooperation on human rights, but the overall human rights climate in the country remained deeply negative. President Dmitry Medvedev's rhetorical commitments to human rights and the rule of law have not been backed by concrete steps to support civil society. The year 2010 saw new attacks on human rights defenders, and the perpetrators of brazen murders in the previous year remained unpunished.

Civil Society

Despite the Kremlin's repeated statements about the importance of normal working conditions for NGOs, human rights defenders remain vulnerable to harassment and attacks, and those working to end impunity in the North Caucasus are especially at risk.

In September Oleg Orlov, chairman of the Memorial Human Rights Center, stood trial for criminal slander, a charge that carries up to three years in prison. The charge stems from Orlov's statement that Ramzan Kadyrov, the leader of Chechnya, was politically responsible for the July 2009 murder of Natalia Estemirova, a leading Memorial researcher in Chechnya. No one has yet been held accountable for Estemirova's murder. It is unclear if the investigation has examined possible official involvement or complicity in the crime.

Memorial resumed its activities in Chechnya in late 2009, following a six-month suspension after Estemirova's murder and threats against other staff. Under the leadership of the Nizhny Novgorod Committee Against Torture, 12 Russian human rights organizations established mobile groups that worked by rotation in Chechnya throughout 2010. The groups assist Memorial in investigating human rights violations in the republic and provide legal aid to victims.

In a May 2010 meeting with NGOs working on the North Caucasus, President Medvedev urged local authorities to cooperate with civil society organizations. However, Kadyrov and other high-level Chechen officials continued to make threatening statements about rights groups. In a televised interview in July,

Kadyrov described human rights defenders and Memorial activists as "enemies of the state, enemies of the people, enemies of the law." The Kremlin failed to react.

Rights activists in the republic of Dagestan, particularly the Mothers of Dagestan for Human Rights, continue to receive threats. In June 2010, human rights lawyer Sapiyat Magomedova was severely beaten by police in the city of Khasavyurt. The alleged perpetrators, although identified, have not been held to account.

Human rights defenders working in other regions also faced harassment and attacks. In February 2010 Vadim Karastelev, a human rights advocate in the port city of Novorossiisk, served seven days of administrative detention for organizing an unsanctioned demonstration in support of Aleksei Dymovsky, a former police officer whose YouTube video exposé of police corruption received nationwide attention. The day after Karastelev's release, unknown assailants brutally beat him, causing serious injuries.

Responding to public outcry about police violence and lawlessness, the government pledged to undertake major reforms. However, the draft law on police proposed in 2010 falls short of what is necessary to best prevent human rights violations by law enforcement officials and ensure civilian oversight over policing.

In May 2010 a court in the Sverdlovsk region sentenced Alexei Sokolov, a prisoners' rights advocate from Ekaterinburg, to five years in prison on spurious criminal charges after an unfair trial. The charges appear to be in retaliation for his work exposing police and prison abuse.

Throughout 2010, police continued to disperse, sometimes violently, the public rallies held in large cities on the thirty-first day of each month in support of Article 31 of the constitution, which guarantees freedom of assembly. The year 2010 opened with the detention of Ludmilia Alexeeva, Russia's leading human rights defender, then aged 82, at a Moscow rally on New Year's Eve. Prominent activist Lev Ponomarev twice faced administrative detention in 2010 for participating in rallies.

Yet there was also a breakthrough in autumn 2010, when the authorities allowed an October 31 rally that drew at least 1,000 peaceful protesters to Triumfalnaya Square in central Moscow. This development stands as a great victory for Russia's civil society movement and its international supporters. Incidentally, the authorities consented to this rally just as the European Court of Human Rights (ECtHR) issued a stinging rebuke to Moscow in the *Alexeev v Russia* ruling, saying that the Russian authorities repeatedly denied activists the right to hold gay pride marches, in violation of the right to freedom of assembly.

In June a Moscow court found the co-organizers of the Forbidden Art-2006 exhibition, Yuri Samodurov and Andrei Erofeev, guilty of inciting religious hostility. The court maintained that the artworks on display contained images offensive to Christians, and fined Samodurov and Erofeev 200,000 (US$6,452) and 150,000 ($4,839) rubles respectively.

NGOs and the media remain vulnerable to vague anti-extremist legislation, which the authorities use to silence critics. In July 2010, new provisions to the law on the Federal Security Service (FSB) were adopted allowing the FSB to issue warnings to individuals, organizations, and media outlets. The warnings require individuals or organizations to stop activities the FSB considers actually or potentially extremist. In September 2010, the Moscow prosecutor's office launched an unprecedented wave of intrusive inquiries into foreign-funded NGOs.

The North Caucasus

The Islamist insurgency in the North Caucasus republics remained active in 2010. In countering it, law enforcement and security agencies continued to commit grave violations of fundamental human rights, such as torture, enforced disappearances, and extrajudicial killings.

The use of unlawful counterinsurgency methods coupled with rampant impunity for abuses, antagonizes the people of Chechnya, Ingushetia, and Dagestan, and widens the gap between the public and the government. On March 29, for the first time since 2004, a major attack was perpetrated in Russia's capital. Two suicide bombers from Dagestan exploded themselves in the Moscow metro during morning rush hour, killing 40 and wounding dozens.

Despite the fact that their monitoring capacity is severely hampered by security concerns, human rights groups continued to document abductions and extrajudicial killings in 2010.

The Chechen government has brazenly adopted a policy of collective punishment. In 2010, high-level Chechen officials, including the president, stated publicly that insurgents' families should expect punishment unless their relatives surrender. Stopping short of directly instructing law enforcement agencies to destroy the house of insurgents' families and apply other collective punishments, such statements encourage lawless actions by police and security personnel.

Violations of women's rights in Chechnya intensified in 2010. Women not wearing headscarves are harassed on the street. Local authorities unambiguously condoned the pelting of unveiled women on the streets with paintball guns, which resulted in the hospitalization of at least one woman in June. In a July television interview, Kadyrov said that the women deserved such treatment for failing to dress appropriately. The Chechen authorities have banned those refusing to wear headscarves from working in the public sector or attending schools and universities.

In the republic of Ingushetia, despite President Yunus-Bek Yevkurov's stated commitment to uphold the rule of law and improve the working climate for human rights NGOs, law enforcement and security agencies continue to perpetrate abductions, torture, and killings. According to Memorial, 12 civilians were abducted, three forcibly disappeared, and 11 were extrajudicially executed between January and September 2010.

The year 2010 saw new insurgent attacks in Dagestan and new abductions of residents by law enforcement and security officials. The appointment of Magomedsalam Magomedov as the republic's new president in early 2010 has had no noticeable impact on the human rights and security situation in Dagestan.

Salafi Muslims are especially vulnerable to persecution in Dagestan because the authorities suspect them of ties to the insurgency. In May seven Salafi men were arbitrarily detained and severely beaten by Kazbekovsky district police officials; one victim died of his injuries. Police torture is endemic beyond unlawful counterinsurgency practices. In July, police detained a 14-year-old boy in the village of Khotoba on suspicion of theft, and severely beat him, causing serious injuries and the loss of hearing in one ear.

Cooperation with the European Court of Human Rights

In January 2010 – after years of delay – Russia ratified Protocol 14 to the European Convention for Human Rights, becoming the last Council of Europe (CoE) member state to do so. Protocol 14 streamlines the case review process at the ECtHR and strengthens the enforcement mechanisms of the CoE's Committee of Ministers.

To date the EctHR has issued more than 150 judgments holding Russia responsible for grave human rights violations in Chechnya. Russia continues to pay the required monetary compensation to victims but fails to meaningfully implement the core of the judgments, in particular conducting effective investigations and holding perpetrators accountable. The Russian authorities have also failed to take sufficient measures to prevent the recurrence of similar abuses and new complaints are lodged with the ECtHR every year. The failure to fully implement the court's judgments denies justice to the victims and fuels the climate of impunity in Chechnya.

Lack of Accountability for Laws of War Violations

Over two years since the Russian conflict with Georgia over South Ossetia, Russian authorities have yet to ensure a comprehensive investigation into and accountability for international human rights and humanitarian law violations by their forces.

Russian forces used cluster bombs in areas populated by civilians in Georgia, leading to civilian deaths and injuries. Russia also launched indiscriminate rocket attacks on civilian areas, causing casualties. Russian forces in Georgia failed to protect civilians in areas under their effective control whilst also preventing Georgian forces from policing these areas.

Health Issues and HIV/AIDS

In 2010 the Russian government continued to violate the rights of hundreds of thousands of drug users who are denied access to effective drug treatment and HIV prevention. The government's 2009 decision to shift funding away from HIV prevention services resulted in the closure of 42 health centers in August 2010. A number of other sites operate under an extended grant from the Global Fund to Fight AIDS, Tuberculosis and Malaria, but these programs also face closure. The government's opposition to drug treatment using methadone or buprenorphine puts injection drug users at grave risk of HIV infection. Unnecessarily restrictive narcotics laws unduly limit the accessibility of morphine for patients with pain due to cancer, HIV/AIDS, and other illnesses, condemning many to severe suffering.

Migrant Worker Rights

Russia has between 4 and 9 million migrant workers, over 80 percent of whom come from the region of the former Soviet Union. Forty percent of migrant workers labor in construction, where they face abuses that include confiscation of passports, denial of contracts, non-payment or delayed payment of wages, and unsafe working conditions. Migrant workers have few effective options for redress. Legislative changes adopted in May tie foreign workers more closely to their employers and may discourage a worker from leaving an abusive employer. Other legislative changes introduced a system for simplifying legal employment of workers employed by private persons as nannies, contractors, and in other non-commercial jobs.

To complete the large-scale construction projects necessary for Russia to host the 2014 Winter Olympic Games in Sochi, employers are hiring large numbers of migrant workers from other parts of Russia and from other countries. Some workers have reported employers' failure to provide contracts, non-payment or severe delays in payment of wages, and substandard employer-provided housing.

Expropriation of Property and Evictions in Advance of the 2014 Olympic Games

To make way for venues for the 2014 Winter Olympics, hundreds of families living in the Adler region of Sochi will lose their property through state expropriations. Some will also lose their livelihoods, such as small hotels and farms. Although the regional government has in most cases promised compensation, serious concerns remain about the compensation amounts and procedures, and the means of challenging official actions.

International Actors

In 2010 Russia showed some improved cooperation on human rights, but Russia's international partners did not do enough to encourage human rights reform.

In February, after two years of stalled negotiations, Russia allowed a delegation from the United Kingdom's parliament to conduct a fact-finding visit to Chechnya.

In March Dick Marty, the rapporteur on human rights in the North Caucasus for the Parliamentary Assembly of the Council of Europe (PACE), made a long-awaited visit to Chechnya, Ingushetia, and Dagestan. Marty's critical report on the lack of legal remedies for victims of human rights violations was unanimously adopted at the June session of PACE, marking the first time the Russia delegation voted in favor of a critical report on the North Caucasus.

The European Union held two rounds of human rights consultations with Russia. While the consultations provide an important forum for working-level discussions on human rights, the lack of follow-up mechanisms, isolation from high-level political meetings, and the absence of high-level Russian participation undermine their effectiveness. The EU continued negotiations on its Partnership and Cooperation Agreement with Russia, which expired in 2007.

The United States and Russia initiated a civil society working group for government representatives and civil society experts to discuss thematic issues in both countries. The working group convened in Washington, DC in January to focus on corruption and children's rights. It met in May in the Russian city of Vladimir to discuss prison reform and migration. The meetings, while providing a good platform for discussion, have not had any practical outcome to date.

The Office of the Prosecutor at the International Criminal Court continued its preliminary examination of the 2008 armed conflict between Russia and Georgia over South Ossetia and sent delegations to Russia in March 2010 and to Georgia in June to obtain additional information on domestic remedies and proceedings.

SERBIA

In March the Serbian parliament adopted a resolution condemning the Srebrenica massacre in Bosnia and apologizing to its victims and their relatives. However the resolution and the parliament's continuing domestic efforts to tackle war crimes were overshadowed by the government's ongoing failure to arrest Ratko Mladic, the Bosnian Serbs' wartime military leader. The European Union nevertheless took steps to strengthen ties with Serbia by unfreezing a trade agreement, relaxing its visa regime, and asking the European Commission to begin assessing Serbia's application for EU membership. These steps were prompted in part by a shift in the Serbian government's stance on Kosovo. Acts of intimidation of independent journalists persisted, along with discrimination against the Roma minority.

War Crimes Accountability

At this writing Serbia has failed to arrest Ratko Mladic and Goran Hadzic, the two remaining fugitives wanted by the International Criminal Tribunal for the former Yugoslavia (ICTY). In a June briefing to the United Nations Security Council, ICTY prosecutor Serge Brammertz noted Serbia's cooperation with requests for assistance, but indicated that efforts to arrest the fugitives "have thus far produced few tangible results." In September Brammertz reiterated his dissatisfaction with Serbia's efforts to secure the arrests of fugitives and called on the EU to press Serbia for cooperation. On a more positive note, Serbian authorities recovered Mladic's wartime notebooks during a search operation in February and provided them to the ICTY, which will likely introduce them as evidence in several trials.

The trial of Zdravko Tolimir, the last suspect in custody of the ICTY to face prosecution, began in February. Tolimir faces charges of genocide, war crimes, and crimes against humanity related to 1995 events in Srebrenica and Zepa.

The Serbian War Crimes Chamber convicted a total of five suspects in three war crimes trials in 2010 the Malic case, the Banski Kovacevac case, and the Medak case, and acquitted a sixth. The Appellate Court of Belgrade reached final decisions in two cases, the Ovcara case and the Podujevo case. There were eight first instance trials ongoing at the chamber during 2010, and a further 10 cases subject to ongoing appeal.

In September the Serbian War Crimes Prosecutor indicted nine men in connection with killings of ethnic Albanians in the village of Cuska (Qyshk in Albanian) in May 1999, during the war in Kosovo. In total, 26 men are currently being investigated for murder and theft in Cuska.

In May the prosecutor indicted six Serbs for war crimes against Croat civilians in Licki Osik, Croatia, in October 1991.

In August the prosecutor indicted Veljko Maric, a former member of the Croatian Armed Forces, for the wartime killing of Serb civilians in the Croatian village of Rastovac. Maric was arrested in April at the Serbian border with Bulgaria. He is the first ethnic Croat to face war crime charges in a Serbian court.

Treatment of Minorities

Throughout the month of June Roma residents of an informal settlement in the village of Jabuka, north of Belgrade, were harassed by local Serbs after a Roma teenager killed a 17-year-old Serb boy and protests escalated into stone-throwing and threats to destroy Roma homes. At this writing, the Roma neighborhood remains under 24-hour police protection. The Serbian local and central level authorities condemned the violence.

In May the Serbian authorities and the European Investment Bank reached an agreement committing the City of Belgrade to provide sustainable housing by the end of 2010 for Roma evicted from an informal settlement under the Gazela Bridge in August 2009. The evicted residents are currently living in metal containers in various municipalities outside Belgrade. In October Belgrade's development agency, with the help of police, demolished a separate Roma informal settlement and evicted its 36 residents without offering them any alternative accommodation, despite interventions from NGOs, Roma political representatives, and the Ministry for Human and Minority Rights.

In February an ethnic Albanian police officer in the Albanian-majority Presevo Valley was injured when a bomb planted under his police vehicle exploded, fracturing his legs and ribs and hurting his wife and two other female passers-by. At this writing no group has claimed responsibility and no one has been charged for the attack.

Integration of Refugees and Internally Displaced Persons

As of September 2010 there were 82,699 refugees registered in Serbia, according to the UN High Commissioner for Refugees (UNHCR), and around 225,000 internally displaced persons (IDPs), mainly from Kosovo, according to the Serbian authorities. Refugees and IDPs continued to face problems throughout 2010 obtaining personal documentation and accessing sustainable housing and social services. According to UNHCR, 3,500 remain in collective centers. Roma IDPs from Kosovo face particularly difficult economic and social conditions.

Deportations to Serbia from Western Europe continued in the absence of assistance programs, with 637 persons (around half of them Roma) deported in the first 9 months of 2010, according to the Serbian Comissariat for IDPs and Refugees.

Media Freedom

In July Teofil Panic, a political commentator for the Serbian weekly *Vreme,* was beaten by two men with metal bars on a packed bus in Belgrade. The reason for the attack remains unclear. Panic suffered a concussion and injuries to his entire body. The perpetrators fled the scene and currently remain at large, despite a criminal investigation.

In February Serbian minister for infrastructure Milutin Mrkonjic assaulted Milan Ladjevic, a journalist at the daily *Kurir,* slapping him across the face and using obscene language after Ladjevic pursued him for an interview. Mrkonjic subsequently apologized publicly for his behavior.

In December 2009 reporter Brankica Stankovic and her staff from the B92 TV channel received repeated death threats after airing a program about football hooligans. In August the Higher Court of Appeal jailed one suspect over the threats and ordered the first instance court to look again at charges against five other suspects, reversing an April ruling by the lower court dismissing charges against all six.

In June the Serbian Parliament adopted a new Electronic Communication Law, which permits the creation of a national database of personal email and internet communication and allows police to view its contents. Serbian and international media organizations argued that the law is unconstitutional and could jeopardize the confidentiality of journalists' sources.

Human Rights Defenders

A June event organized by the Queeria lesbian, gay, bisexual, and transgender organization to collect 10,000 signatures in support of a Belgrade Pride Parade in 2010 was dispersed after a bomb threat, which proved to be false. The 2009 pride event was cancelled over security concerns.

The interior minister and the human rights minister publicly stated their support for the Pride Parade, which took place in October. A few hundred LGBT demonstrators and their supporters marched through the streets of Belgrade, heavily guarded by police and security forces. Violent counterdemonstrators shouting homophobic language attacked police and wounded many officers, but failed to disrupt the parade. The counterdemonstrators also attacked the Democratic Party headquarters and destroyed many shops and vehicles.

In March the Serbian Ministry of Labor and Social Policy denied the NGO Mental Disability Rights International–Serbia access to monitor social care institutions for persons with disabilities, on the grounds that the institutions were too busy implementing reforms. The group had previously had informal access. The ministry promised access at a later unspecified time once reforms were implemented, but at this writing, despite further requests, at this writing the group has yet to gain access.

Key International Actors

In December 2009 the Council of the EU decided to unfreeze implementation of the Interim Trade Agreement with Serbia and to lift visa requirements for all

Serbian citizens. The Serbian government submitted its formal application for EU membership the same month. In October the Council asked the European Commission to begin considering Serbia's application, despite Belgrade's failure to hand over Mladic. In November the European Commission published its annual progress report on Serbia, highlighting the continued liberty of Mladic and Hadzic. The report noted the lack of progress on prison reforms and widespread employment discrimination against women, while marking improvements to media freedom and progress on domestic war crimes trials.

In July the International Court of Justice issued an advisory opinion in a case brought by Serbia and stated that Kosovo's 2008 declaration of independence did not violate international law. Serbia's initial response was a draft UN General Assembly resolution condemning Kosovo's declaration of independence, but after significant diplomatic pressure by the EU and the United States, Serbia agreed to a joint UN General Assembly resolution with the EU calling for negotiations between Sebia and Kosovo that would allow them to normalize their relations. The General Assembly unanimously adopted the resolution in September.

Kosovo

Kosovo's justice system remained weak in 2010, despite efforts to try perpetrators of war crimes and postwar abuses against minorities. Deportations of Kosovars from Western Europe continued, with a disproportionate impact on Kosovo's most vulnerable minorities: Roma, Askhali and Egyptians, the latter, a Romani Albanian-speaking group with mythical origins in ancient Egypt. The finding of the International Court of Justice that Kosovo's declaration of independence "did not violate general international law, Security Council resolution 1244 or [Kosovo's] Constitutional Framework," had little discernible impact on human rights in Kosovo.

Protection of Minorities

Minorities in Kosovo, including Serbs, Roma, and Albanian-speaking Ashkali and Egyptians, remained at risk of discrimination, marginalization, and harassment. According to the Kosovo Police Service, 40 inter-ethnic incidents (including four murders) were reported during the first eight months of 2010: 31 in the divided city of Mitrovica, which remains a flashpoint for violence; as well as five in Pristina, one in Gnjilane, one in Prizren, and one in Pec.

In April ethnic Albanians pelted stones at the tents of Serbian returnees to the village of Zac, in Istok municipality, and also staged protests against the returnees following rumors that there were war criminals among them. UNHCR denied these allegations, and Kosovar and international authorities robustly condemned the violence. But in August, in the same village, a bulldozer was used to demolish three houses of Kosovo Serb returnees. The police arrested two Kosovo Albanian teenagers in the incident, and Kosovo Prime Minister Hashim Thaci condemned the destruction.

In July as Serbs in northern Mitrovica protested the opening of a Pristina government office, an explosion killed one demonstrator and injured 11. Nobody was arrested in the immediate aftermath of that attack. Just three days later Petar Miletic, a Serb member of the Kosovo Assembly, was shot and injured as he left his home in northern Mitrovica. At this writing the perpetrators remains at large. In September an ethnic Albanian man was shot dead in an ethnically mixed area of northern Mitrovica.

The government made limited progress implementing its Roma, Ashkali, and Egyptian integration strategy. Roma, Ashkali, and Egyptians continue to face persistent discrimination, particularly in employment and access to public services, and have the highest unemployment, school dropout, and mortality rates in Kosovo.

In June, 5,000 people demonstrated in the municipality of Pristina following the Municipal Assembly's adoption and implementation of a headscarf ban on both students and teachers in all public schools.

Return of Refugees and Internally Displaced Persons

Voluntary returns to Kosovo increased, though the overall numbers remain small. During the first six months of 2010, UNHCR Kosovo registered a total of 1,036 voluntary minority returns: 417 Serb, 99 Roma, 257 Ashkali/Egyptian, 32 Bosniak, 152 Gorani, and 79 Albanian (to Serbian majority areas, mainly Mitrovica).

Kosovo

Rights Displaced

Forced Returns of Roma, Ashkali and Egyptians from
Western Europe to Kosovo

HUMAN
RIGHTS
WATCH

Meanwhile, deportations of Kosovars from Western Europe continued with little assistance for returnees once they are in Kosovo. According to UNHCR, 1,694 Kosovars were deported from Western Europe during the first nine months of 2010, including 347 people sent to areas where they were in a minority: 193 Roma, 55 Ashkali, 2 Egyptians, 7 Bosniaks, 25 Gorani, 5 Turks, 29 Albanians, and 1 Serb. Deportations have a particularly adverse effect on Roma, Ashkali and Egyptians.

The Kosovo authorities signed a bilateral readmission agreement with the government of Germany in late April 2010. It awarded Kosovo a better visa facilitation regime in exchange for accepting deportations of all persons originating from Kosovo. Around 16,000 people are expected to be returned under it, many of them Roma, Ashkali, and Egyptian. Similar agreements were signed with Albania, Belgium, France, and Switzerland in late 2009 and 2010.

In October a lead-contaminated Roma, Ashkali, and Egyptian camp in Cesmin Lug was closed and demolished after a decade. Most of its inhabitants are being rehoused in reconstructed homes in the original Roma neighborhood (Mahalla) in South Mitrovica, together with some residents from a second lead-contaminated camp at Osterode, which remains open at this writing. A group of Cesmin Lug residents unwilling to return to the Mahalla have been moved to Osterode and are pending their resettlement elsewhere at this writing. Funding comes from a €5 million European Commission project announced in December 2009, including medical treatment, education, community safety, and income generation, and a complementary project funded by the US Agency for International Development.

Impunity, Accountability, and Access to Justice

In July the ICTY Appeals Chamber partially quashed the acquittals of Ramush Haradinaj, a former commander of the Kosovo Liberation Army (KLA) and former Kosovo prime minister; Idriz Balaj, a former member of the KLA in command of a special unit known as the Black Eagles; and Lahi Brahimaj, who served as a deputy commander of the KLA in the Dukagjin area of Kosovo. The appeals court ordered a partial retrial of the case, accepting the prosecution's contention that the trial court had failed to take adequate measures to secure the testimony of two crucial witnesses. In September the ICTY denied Haradinaj's motion for provisional release, citing the integrity of the trial.

In May the EU Rule of Law and Police Mission in Kosovo (EULEX) announced that its investigation into the so-called "Yellow House" case, involving the alleged transfers by the KLA in 1999 of around 400 Serbian and other captives to detention facilities in Albania, had failed to produce evidence to substantiate allegations of organ-trading. At this writing the status of the investigation into the other allegations remains unclear. Investigations into the case by Dick Marty, the rapporteur of the Council of Europe Parliamentary Assembly, and the Serbian war crimes prosecutor continued, but no new facts were made public.

EULEX investigations into separate allegations of abuses in KLA-run camps in Albania resulted in three arrests. In May EULEX police in Pristina arrested Sabit Geci for the alleged torture of civilians in a KLA-run camp in the town of Kukes, northern Albania, in 1999. The same month, EULEX police arrested Zhemsit Krasniqi in Prizren in connection with crimes against civilians of various ethnicities in KLA bases in Albania in 1999. The third arrest took place in June in the municipality of Djakovica. The suspect's name has not been made public.

In the year prior to September 2010, EULEX completed five war crime cases, with eight more ongoing and 27 in pretrial stages. EULEX completed eight cases related to the March 2004 riots during the same period.

The long-running trial of Albin Kurti, a leader of the Vetevendosje movement for self-determination, concluded in June. A mixed judicial panel including EULEX and Kosovo judges convicted Kurti of a minor charge and sentenced him to time served, releasing him immediately. There were credible allegations that the KPS used excessive force during Kurti's arrest earlier in June, prompting an investigation by the Ombudsperson Institution, which remains pending at this writing.

While EULEX took steps to improve collaboration with Kosovo police, judges, and prosecutors, the justice system continued to be hampered by longstanding problems including a lack of skill in judicial policing, the assisting of prosecutors in investigations, and the failure of court staff to systematically use electronic case management software. Witness protection and security remained serious concerns, with few Western states consenting to host witnesses (no new states agreed to do so during 2010), an inconsistent use of protective measures by the courts, and the continued lack of a comprehensive witness protection law.

According to the International Committee of the Red Cross, 1,837 persons remain missing from the 1999 conflict, the majority Kosovo Albanians.

In May EULEX and the Serbian authorities jointly announced the discovery of a suspected mass grave in southern Serbia believed to contain the remains of as many as 250 Kosovo Albanians who went missing during the war. In September the Kosovo authorities began excavating in a coal mine in the Vucitrn municipality, where the bodies of 20 Kosovo Serbs killed during the 1999 war are believed to have been buried. At this writing no human remains have been found at either site.

Media Freedom

In February Vehbi Kajtazi, a journalist for the daily newspaper *Koha Ditore*, was allegedly threatened by Sabit Geci, a former KLA member, in response to Kajtazi's article criticizing an amnesty for a group of prisoners, including Geci's son, Alban. Kajtazi was discouraged by KPS when he tried to file a complaint against Geci.

In July an explosive device was thrown into the courtyard of the home of Caslav Milisavljevic, editor-in-chief of Radio Kosovska Mitrovica. The device exploded, damaging three vehicles. Nobody was injured. KPS opened an investigation into the incident but no perpetrators have been arrested at this writing.

Human Rights Defenders

In late November 2009 the Council of the EU agreed on the EULEX Human Rights Review Panel (HRRP). The panel reviews complaints of human rights abuse by EULEX from individuals. In May 2010 three members of HRRP (and one alternate) were appointed by the acting EULEX head of mission. The first regular session of HRRP took place in June. At this writing, HRRP had received 16 cases and deemed 12 admissible, including 7 relating to the functioning of the justice system.

The filling of a vacancy in the three-member UN Human Rights Advisory Panel, which hears similar complaints against UN Mission in Kosovo (UNMIK), allowed it to resume functioning. But its effectiveness remained hampered following restrictions introduced by the UN in October 2009.

There were continued instances of the Kosovo authorities ignoring the interventions of the Kosovo Ombudsperson Institution, or responding late.

Key International Actors

In May 2010 peacekeepers from NATO-led Kosovo Force intervened in Mitrovica to assist KPS and EULEX police to quash the week-long civil unrest sparked by Serbian local elections in North Mitrovica.

An April report to the UN Security Council from Secretary-General Ban Ki-moon warned that deportations to Kosovo undermine the country's stability. Thomas Hammarberg, the Council of Europe's human rights commissioner, made similar statements and repeatedly called for a moratorium on deportations.

In June the Parliamentary Assembly of the Council of Europe released a critical report emphasizing the need for Kosovar authorities to cooperate with war crime investigations, combat discrimination and abuse against minorities, create conditions for the safe return of IDPs and refugees, ensure media freedom, promote women's rights, and take urgent steps to close lead-contaminated Roma camps in North Mitrovica.

In November the European Commission's annual progress report highlighted the ongoing weakness of Kosovo's justice system, inadequate attention to war crimes; continued threats to independent journalists; slow progress on missing persons; and widespread discrimination and marginalization of Roma, Ashkali and Egyptians.

TAJIKISTAN

Despite a few small positive steps, Tajik authorities continue to violate rights affecting areas ranging from elections and media freedoms to religious liberty and women's rights.

In February 2010 Tajikistan held parliamentary elections that were marked by fraud, resulting in the ruling party's victory by an overwhelming margin and the further strengthening of President Emomali Rahmon's nearly 20-year rule. The authorities continued to suppress the press, especially in the run-up to the election. The government began enforcing a repressive law that tightens state control over religious activity. Domestic violence against women remains rampant in Tajik society. The judiciary is neither independent nor effective.

In September 2010, Islamist militants attacked a convoy of government troops in the Rasht Valley, killing between 25 and 40 soldiers, and scattered clashes continued through October. The troops had been sent to track down militants who had escaped from a Dushanbe prison in August and were believed to have fled into the valley. The violence marks the first major clash in a decade between government and insurgent forces, giving rise to concerns about creeping instability in Tajikistan, especially in light of the war in neighboring Afghanistan.

Justice System

A report published in March 2010 by the Bureau on Human Rights and Rule of Law, a Tajik nongovernmental organization, revealed a judicial system with little advance notification of hearings, patchy explanations of process and rights, erratic access to interpreters, and efforts by judges to exclude observers.

The politicization of the Tajik justice system was underscored by the treatment of Nematillo Botakozuev, a Kyrgyz human rights activist who had sought asylum in Tajikistan. Botakozuev disappeared in late February 2010; his relatives only learned one month later that he was in the custody of the Tajik police for allegedly lacking identification. He was held without access to communications or a lawyer. When a source known to Human Rights Watch finally saw him in mid-March, Botakozuev appeared to have been tortured. In May Tajikistan extradited

Botakozuev to Kyrgyzstan, where he was held for two weeks, released, and warned by state security to refrain from human rights work.

Fair Elections

The Organization for Security and Cooperation in Europe (OSCE) monitored the February 28, 2010, parliamentary election and found it "failed to meet key... international standards for democratic elections."

District electoral commissions were often staffed by local officials and members of the ruling People's Democratic Party of Tajikistan (PDPT). Registration fees were onerously high. Free television time was allocated late in the campaign.

In its final report on the election, the OSCE noted credible accounts of violations of campaign rules by the authorities: "instances [in which] police prevented activists of the Islamic Revival Party of Tajikistan from campaigning and in some cases detained them for a short time" and "credible allegations of pressure on government employees and voters to vote for or facilitate the victory of PDPT candidates." On election day OSCE and other observers found widespread proxy voting, instances of attempts to influence voters, multiple voting, ballot-box stuffing, and premarked ballots, among other infractions. Furthermore, the OSCE found that vote-counting procedures "were not properly followed in half of the polling stations observed."

Media Freedoms

The press in Tajikistan faced a clampdown in early 2010 in connection first with the parliamentary elections, and later with the clashes in the Rasht Valley. In February Reporters Without Borders issued a statement noting "an all-out drive to intimidate news media and get [independent media outlets] to [self-]censor their coverage of state authorities."

While one independent researcher found the government did not formally shut down any media outlets and even permitted the registration of new ones, debilitating defamation awards resulting from civil suits brought by government officials are threatening the livelihood of independent outlets and seem aimed at muffling the media.

In late January a Tajik court fined the newspaper *Paykon* 300,000 somonis (US$69,000) in a libel suit regarding a report on corruption. The case was brought by Tajikstandart, the state agency that monitors the quality of imported goods. At around the same time two Supreme Court judges and one city court filed libel suits against three independent newsweeklies that ran stories about a press conference regarding alleged corruption within the Tajik judiciary. The Agriculture Ministry brought a libel suit against the *Millat* newspaper, in which it is seeking 1 million somonis ($229,000) in damages.

On October 29, 2010, United States and European ambassadors issued a joint statement raising concern about the "deteriorating climate for independent media in Tajikistan." The statement noted, among other things, that "three news-papers, Farazh, Paikon, and Nigoh, have been effectively shut down by being unable to print their papers, reportedly on orders by government officials," that senior government officials had made public statements "attacking independent media outlets," and that a deputy minister had ordered the blocking of five major news websites. The websites – Tojnews.tj, Avesta.tj, Tjknews.com, Centrasia.ru, and Ferghana.ru – were blocked in the wake of the violence in the Rasht Valley.

Freedom of Religion

Hewing to a new religion law adopted in 2009, the state continued its repression of faith groups. Tajikistan has long curtailed freedom of religion and, under the pretext of battling terrorism, has banned several peaceful Muslim organizations. Certain Christian denominations, such as Jehovah's Witnesses, continue to be banned in Tajikistan. At this writing the law bans all religious activity by unregis-tered religious groups. The government now determines where mosques can be built and how many, and where Muslim sermons can be given, and it has censor-ship authority over religious literature (including material from abroad) and con-trol over children's religious education; faith groups in Tajikistan must register with the state and get government permission to contact foreign religious groups.

Underscoring the importance of state control over religious activity, the new law removed oversight of religious groups from the Ministry of Culture and placed it with the Committee for Religious Affairs, which reports directly to the president. The state has relied on investigations, arrests, and convictions to squelch certain kinds of Muslim religious activity. In January a Dushanbe criminal court convicted Imam Sirojiddin Abdurahmonov (known as Mullo Sirojiddin), a leader of the banned Salafi Muslim religious movement, and six other followers. An Islamic Revival Party leader told Forum 18, an independent religious news service, that Sirojiddin received a seven-year prison term, and his six co-defendants received prison terms of up to six years for "arousing national, racial, local or religious hostility." In April 2009, about 92 followers of the banned Jamaat Tabligh Islamic group were arrested. In March 2010, according to Forum 18, a group of 56 of them were convicted by the Supreme Court and were sentenced on charges of "organisation of banned extremist religious organizations." 23 defendants were given prison terms of between three and six years, and the other 33 defendants were fined between 25,000 somonis(US$5,340) and 50,000 somonis ($10,680), astronomical sums for the average Tajik. In May the remaining 36 Jamaat Tabligh defendants were convicted and received comparable prison and financial penalties. Rights groups in Tajikistan maintain that Jamaat Tabligh is peaceful and the ban on it was never published.

In May 2010, criminal investigations by the state secret police against 17 Jehovah's Witnesses in Khujand were reopened. The group was arrested, interrogated, and threatened in September 2009, but the cases had been suspended after the group complained to the prosecutor general.

Women's Rights

The government took a few small steps forward to protect women from domestic violence, but overall the rights of women remain precarious. A November 2009 Amnesty International report estimated that one-third to one-half of Tajik women "may at some time experience physical, psychological or sexual violence at the hands of husbands or other family members." The report said that given women's severely restricted access to law enforcement and the general practice within the police to blame the victim and preserve the family, perpetrators can harm women with near impunity.

Still, in August 2010 five special police stations with staff trained by the OSCE to deal specifically with domestic violence were opened in Dushanbe, the capital, and other cities. The stations are the only ones of their kind in Central Asia, according to the OSCE, which urged the Tajik government to pass a law on domestic violence that has been pending since 2007. In August officials at a governmental research center said that preliminary results of their research show an increase in polygamy, although the practice is technically illegal, and that at least 10 percent of Tajik men have more than one wife.

In June 2010 President Rahmon signed a law that would raise the age of marriage for girls from 17 to 18 and would also require children to attend school for a minimum of 11 years, starting at age 7.

Key International Actors

The European Union upgraded relations with Tajikistan in early 2010 by concluding a Partnership and Cooperation Agreement. The EU describes the agreement as "enhanc[ing] bilateral relations and heighten[ing] the EU profile in Tajikistan." Its stated aim is also to "promote bilateral trade and investments." Meanwhile, the EU's record in speaking out about abuses remained poor. Human rights concerns appeared to be largely relegated to once-yearly human rights dialogues, held at a relatively low level, with an obscure content and outcome.

In a January report on Tajikistan, the UN Committee on the Rights of the Child (CRC) commended the country on passing several important laws over the years to protect children. But the report went on to document that, in reality, children lack safeguards against abuse and neglect in almost every sphere of their lives. The UN CRC recommended that Tajikistan do more to protect children from institutionalization, violence, and child labor. It urged the state to take more serious action against polygamy, and to do more in general to protect women, girls, and children with disabilities.

TURKEY

Turkey's human rights record remained mixed in 2010. Arbitrary detentions, prosecutions, and convictions under terrorism laws and for speech crimes persisted, while the ruling Justice and Development Party (AKP) partially amended the constitution.

In September voters approved by referendum significant amendments to the 1982 constitution, including lifting immunity from prosecution for military and public officials for crimes committed during and after the September 12, 1980 coup, a reduced role for military courts, changes to judicial appointments, the right of individual petition to the constitutional court, and the creation of a new ombudsperson institution. The amendments open the way for further reform. The need for complete revision of the 1982 constitution to further human rights has been a recurring political discussion since the 2007 general election.

The government made little concrete progress towards realizing its 2009 plan to improve the human rights of Kurds in Turkey. The Constitutional Court in December 2009 closed down the pro-Kurdish Democratic Society Party (DTP) for alleged separatist activities, and hundreds of officials from the DTP and its successor, the Peace and Democracy Party (BDP), faced trial for membership of the Union of Kurdistan Communities, a body connected with the armed Kurdistan Workers' Party (PKK).

There is increasing agreement across the political spectrum on the need for a rights-based and non-military approach to ending the conflict with the PKK. Armed clashes between the Turkish military and the PKK continued. Disagreement erupted over whether the September attack on a minibus in Hakkari province, which killed nine civilians, was staged by the PKK, or by elements of the security forces. The PKK was suspected of the August and September killings of two imams in Hakkari and Sırnak.

In July workplaces and property belonging to Kurds in negol, Bursa province, and in Dörtyol, Hatay province, were attacked. Following police investigations into the incidents–resembling similar ethnically-motivated attacks in recent years–four people were tried for the Dortyol attacks and 21 are imprisoned pending trial for the Inegol attacks at this writing.

Freedom of Expression, Assembly, and Association

Despite a climate of increasingly open debate, individuals continued to be prosecuted and convicted for non-violent speeches, writings, and participating in demonstrations. The practice of holding suspects charged with non-violent crimes in prolonged pre-trial detention continued.

Journalists and editors remained targets for prosecution. Legitimate news reporting on trials was deemed "attempting to influence a judicial process," reporting on criminal investigations was judged as "violating the secrecy of a criminal investigation," and news reports on the PKK was deemed "terrorist propaganda."

Some editors and journalists faced scores of ongoing legal proceedings in 2010. The case of Vedat Kursun stands out among those convicted in 2010. The editor of Kurdish daily *Azadiya Welat*, Kursun received a 166-year prison sentence in May for 103 counts of "terrorist propaganda" and "membership" in the PKK. At this writing he remained in prison pending an appeal.

Long-term restrictions on access to websites, including YouTube, continued. Leftist and pro-Kurdish political newspapers and journals were subject to arbitrary closure. In 2010 the European Court of Human Rights (ECtHR) condemned Turkey twice for using its Anti-Terror Law to ban publication of entire periodicals, saying the move was censorship that violated free expression. The court found Turkey had violated free expression in at least 10 other rulings in 2010.

Courts continued to use terrorism laws to prosecute hundreds of demonstrators deemed to be PKK supporters as if they were the group's armed militants. Most spent prolonged periods in pre-trial detention, and those convicted received long prison sentences. A legal amendment by parliament in July will mean that convictions of children under the laws will be quashed. The laws remain otherwise unchanged.

Hundreds of officials and activist members of the pro-Kurdish party DTP and its successor BDP (which has 20 parliamentary members) were prosecuted during the year, including for links to the Union of Kurdistan Communities (KCK/TM), a body associated with the PKK's leadership.

In October seven mayors, several lawyers, and a human rights defender (see below) were among 151 officials and activists tried in Diyarbakir for alleged separatism and KCK membership. At this writing the mayors have spent 10 months––and the 53 other defendants have spent 18 months–in pre-trial detention, while around 1,000 DTP/BDP officials and members suspected of KCK affiliation were in pre-trial detention nationwide, raising concerns about the right to political participation.

Human Rights Defenders

The ECtHR ruled in September that Turkey had failed to protect the life of Hrant Dink, a Turkish-Armenian journalist and human rights defender, or to conduct an effective investigation into his January 2007 murder. The three-year murder trial of the alleged killer and 19 others continued in Turkey. The ECtHR also found that Dink's conviction for "insulting Turkishness" violated his right to free expression.

Muharrem Erbey, vice-president of the Human Rights Association (HRA) and chair of its Diyarbakir branch, was arrested in December 2009 for alleged KCK/TM membership and held in detention until his trial in October. He remains in detention at this writing. Vetha Aydin, chair of HRA's Siirt branch, was arrested in March for alleged KCK membership. She remained in pre-trial detention at this writing.

Torture, Ill-Treatment, and Use of Lethal Force by Security Forces

Police ill-treatment remained a problem, particularly during street stops, demonstrations, and arrests. Torture and ill-treatment in detention was less common, but at this writing there are at least four cases of deaths in custody in disputed circumstances in 2010.

In May police beat five transgender members of Ankara-based NGO Pembe Hayat (Pink Life Lesbian, Gay, Bisexual, Transgender and Transsexual Solidarity Association) in the street in front of witnesses before detaining them. Following a familiar pattern, the five were promptly charged with resisting police before the prosecutor had concluded an investigation into their ill-treatment, which remains ongoing at this writing. They were acquitted at their October trial. Use of firearms by police and the gendarmerie remained a matter of concern, particularly against unarmed suspects. There was no progress on tightening rules governing use of force. Gendarmes shot dead at least nine suspected smugglers in the border regions of Van, Sırnak, and Urfa during the year.

Impunity

Several of the constitutional changes made in September have implications for ending impunity. Restricting the jurisdiction of military courts is an important step towards ensuring that trials of military personnel for human rights abuses take place in civilian courts. The repeal of a provision in the constitution granting immunity from prosecution to military and public officials for crimes committed during and after the 1980 military coup is significant, although jurists debate whether existing statutes of limitations for torture and murder will impede prosecution.

In a landmark ruling on June 19 prison guards, gendarmes, police officers, and a doctor were convicted in connection with the October 2008 beating to death of Engin Çeber, and the torture of three other political activists arrested with him in Istanbul. Nine guards, including a senior prison official, and police officers received sentences ranging from two-and-a-half years to life imprisonment.

The verdict in the Çeber case remains an exception and impunity remains a formidable problem in Turkey. In general, prosecutors failed to conduct effective, timely, and independent investigations of allegations against the police and gendarmerie, and prosecutions against state officials remained protracted. Two police officers who severely beat lawyer Muammer Öz in Istanbul in July 2007 were given suspended sentences in January 2010, effectively escaping sanction.

Three trials of alleged anti-government coup plotters (the "Ergenekon" gang, comprising senior retired military, police, mafia, journalists, and academics) continued. In related prosecutions, 69 naval officers faced trial for plotting a 2008 campaign of violent attacks aimed at destabilizing the government, and 196 retired and serving military personnel were due to stand trial starting in December 2010 for a 2003 coup plot. Willingness to pursue these cases offers potential for wider efforts to end impunity.

The most significant attempt at bringing to justice state perpetrators of extrajudicial killings and "disappearances" continued with the ongoing trial in Diyarbakır of a now-retired colonel, village guards, and informers for the murder of 20 individuals between 1993 and 1995 in Cizre, Sırnak province.

Key International Actors

Despite concerns about Turkey "turning east," European Union membership and maintaining good relations with the United States and other traditional allies remain stated priorities for the government.

The US failed in 2010 to build on the momentum of President Barack Obama's 2009 visit, focusing on Turkey's foreign policy in the Middle East and Armenia rather than its domestic human rights record.

The EU praised the constitutional reforms, and remains an influential actor in Turkey. But the stalemate over Cyprus stalled Turkey's accession negotiations in many areas, and leading member states such as France and Germany continued to oppose Turkey's membership bid. The European Commission's November progress report on Turkey concluded that reforms made that year were "of limited scope," called for the wholesale revision of the constitution, and raised concerns about freedom of expression, long pre-trial detention, gender equality, and use of anti-terror laws.

In its July review of Turkey, the UN Committee on the Elimination of Discrimination against Women (CEDAW) recommended that Turkey "continue to accord priority attention to the adoption of comprehensive measures to address violence against women."

Following its Universal Periodic Review by the UN Human Rights Council in May, Turkey argued that it was already implementing many of the recommendations made, but notably refused those that would bring its definition of minorities in line with international law, or to wave its reservations to international law that upholds minority rights.

TURKMENISTAN

In 2010 the Turkmenistan government continued a return to the repressive methods of a previous era. President Gurbanguly Berdymukhamedov has ruled Turkmenistan for nearly four years, since the 2006 death of dictator Saparmurad Niazov. During his first two years in office, Berdymukhamedov began to reverse some of Niazov's most ruinous social policies. But then his course appeared to reverse. The government increasingly repressed NGOs and Turkmen activists, and prevented citizens from leaving the country; indeed freedom of movement sharply declined in 2009 and 2010. Instead of continuing needed reforms in education in 2010, the government introduced burdensome requirements for students seeking to travel abroad for university, and allowed "Ruhnama" (The Book of the Soul), Niazov's propaganda book, to remain a subject in university entrance exams. Instead of expanding access to the internet and other media, the government blocked websites and banned the import of some printed materials. Prisons remained closed to the outside for observation. Turkmenistan continued to expand relations with foreign governments and international organizations, but with no meaningful outcomes for human rights.

Civil Society

The repressive atmosphere makes it extremely difficult for independent NGOs to operate. Almost no organizations have applied for registration in recent years.

On September 30, 2010, Berdymukhamedov instructed the Ministry of National Security to lead an "uncompromising fight against those who slander our democratic... secular state." His speech came the day after a satellite channel broadcast an interview with exiled Turkmen activist Farid Tukhbatullin, chair of the Vienna-based Turkmen Initiative for Human Rights (TIHR). In subsequent days hackers disabled the website of the TIHR, and there were credible threats that the Turkmen security services planned to physically harm Tukhbatullin.

In June 2010, the authorities in Turkmenistan began questioning the former classmates and teachers of Tukhbatullin's sons. At least three were threatened with treason charges if they maintained ties with the family.

In December 2009 Medecins Sans Frontieres (MSF) decided to close its Turkmenistan office after the Turkmen authorities repeatedly rejected project proposals, making it impossible for the organization to carry out its work in the country. MSF was the last remaining international humanitarian organization operating in Turkmenistan.

Within Turkmenistan, the Organization for Security and Co-operation in Europe (OSCE) and the United Nations can carry out seminars and offer technical assistance, but little more.

In 2010, for the third year in a row, the Turkmen delegation tried to bar exiled Turkmen activists from registering for the OSCE human dimension review conference and walked out when the activists were admitted to the conference.

Media Freedoms

There continues to be a complete absence of media freedoms. Almost all print and electronic media are controlled by the state. Reporters from foreign media outlets often cannot access the country and, in recent years, local stringers for foreign outlets have been beaten, harassed, and otherwise intimidated.

Many websites are blocked, internet cafes require visitors to present their passports, and the government monitors electronic communications.

It is extremely difficult to obtain foreign newspapers and magazines with any political content. Border guards are known to confiscate foreign printed materials. In August 2010 Berdymukhamedov stated that there were enough publications issued in Turkmenistan to "satisfy domestic demand," so "there is no need to import any," indicating that access to foreign publications would remain limited.

Freedom of Movement

Turkmen authorities arbitrarily interfere with people's right to travel abroad through an informal and arbitrary system of travel bans, commonly imposed on activists and relatives of exiled dissidents.

On July 16, 2010, Turkmen border officials stopped Umida Jumbaeva, an activist, from leaving the country for Kazakhstan. Jumbaeva had helped environmental activist Andrei Zatoka in 2009, when he was arrested on false charges, given an unfair trial, and expelled from Turkmenistan. On June 28, Turkmen authorities barred civic activists Annamamed and Elena Miatiev from traveling abroad for medical treatment. Following an international outcry the couple was allowed to depart on July 10.

For years Radio Liberty stringer Gurbansoltan Achilova and her family endured various forms of harassment by the authorities and were barred from foreign travel. Her son Mukhammetmyrat, who had repeatedly been denied permission to travel abroad, committed suicide on June 12, 2010. One month later the family received a letter from the Turkmen migration services granting him permission to travel.

In 2009, the authorities prevented hundreds of students bound for foreign private universities from leaving the country, and introduced new, burdensome requirements for studying abroad. By August 2010, many of the students were able to depart, except those pursuing their studies at the American University of Central Asia in Kyrgyzstan (AUCA). Throughout 2010 the Ministry of Education, the border services, and the migration service failed explain why students could not leave for study at AUCA; to written requests for information, students received a standard reply of "request declined." By September 2010 the government banned people from leaving the country if they had valid Kyrgyz visas in their passports.

In July 2010 the Turkmen government barred Turkmen citizens who also held Russian passports from traveling to Russia unless they had Russian visas. Turkmenistan abrogated its dual citizenship treaty with Russia in 2003, but had allowed holders of Russian passports to use them for travel to Russia unitl July 2010.

Political Prisoners and the Penitentiary System

As in previous years, in 2010 it was difficult to determine the number of political prisoners because of the wall of secrecy that surrounds their detention. Well-known political prisoners include Annakurban Amanklychev and Sapardurdy

Khajiev, who worked with human rights organizations, and political dissident Gulgeldy Annaniazov.

A report published jointly in February 2010 by two independent human rights groups in exile highlighted serious problems in Turkmenistan's prison system, including overcrowding, degrading treatment of inmates, corruption, and lack of public oversight. In an unprecedented move, Berdymukhamedov responded to the report by acknowledging problems and promising reform. But amendments subsequently made to the criminal code did not address the report's main concerns. No international agency—governmental or non-governmental—has access to monitor Turkmen detention facilities.

Interference with Family Life

Turkmenistan has an unwritten policy against registering marriages of foreign nationals, which, combined with the difficulty of obtaining Turkmen visas, separates families. In April 2010, the authorities expelled to Uzbekistan approximately 30 female Uzbek nationals married to Turkmen men, along with their young children, who were born and raised in Turkmenistan.

In October 2009 a group of 500 ethnic Turkmen from Iran issued a statement against the separation of families of mixed Turkmen-Iranian families. The Iranian nationals said that Turkmen authorities refused to issue long-term visas to non-Turkmen family members.

Freedom of Religion

The government's undeclared campaign against terrorism has involved a crackdown on Muslims branded "Wahhabi," a term the Turkmen government uses to defame followers of a more austere form of Islam and imply their association with terrorism. For example, in June a mullah in Dashagouz province received a three-year prison sentence after security services searched his home and found a fake grenade, which inexplicably vanished from the case materials. Police officers compelled all of the mullah's followers to shave their beards.

In April 2010 an Islamic cleric, Shiri Geldimuradov, was arrested with three of his sons, and all four were convicted on weapons possession charges. Geldimuradov's other four sons are also in prison on unknown charges. In June Geldimuradov died in prison.

The authorities raid sites of worship of unregistered religious groups. Forum 18, an independent, international religious freedom group, reported a raid on a Baptist congregation in Dashagouz in December 2009. Officials confiscated religious books, and congregants were questioned and pressured to sign statements promising to desist from worshipping with the congregation in the future. In June 2010 the authorities again pressured several members of that church to sign similar statements.

On October 21, 2010, a court sentenced Ilmurad Nurliev, head of the Light to the World Pentecostal Church, to four years in prison on what appear to be bogus swindling charges. The prosecution argued that Nurliev had swindled four people who visited a shelter run by the church, even though one of the alleged victims was in prison for much of the time the swindling allegedly took place, and two did not testify in court. The trial judge refused to allow all but three church members to testify for the defense, and the court failed to provide the defense with the written verdict in time to appeal. Light to the World worship services were raided in 2008, and Nuraliev and congregants have endured harassment by government agencies in recent years.

On June 20 the security services detained a group of 47 Protestants who had gathered in Geoktepe for two days of prayer and Bible study. The group was held overnight in a police station, questioned, and released.

The Turkmen government continues to imprison Jehovah's Witnesses for refusing compulsory military service on grounds of religious conscience, and at this writing holds at least eight in custody.

Key International Actors

Seeking to leverage Turkmenistan's energy wealth and strategic importance, several key international actors continued to mute criticism of the government's human rights record. The European Union in particular stood out for its failure to use the prospect of enhanced relations to advance concrete human rights improvements, pressing forward with a Partnership and Cooperation Agreement (PCA), frozen since 1998 over human rights concerns, without requiring any human rights reforms in exchange. At this writing, the PCA was pending approval by the European Parliament. An initial draft opinion green-lighting the agreement stirred significant controversy.

The PCA also requires ratification by two national EU member state parliaments—France and the United Kingdom—before it can enter into force. In a welcome move, the French parliament's Foreign Affairs Committee in April 2010 adopted a resolution requesting the government to refrain from submitting the agreement for ratification until it had secured certain human rights improvements, including the release of political prisoners Amanklychev and Khajiev.

During his early April visit to Turkmenistan, UN Secretary-General Ban Ki-moon was uncharacteristically outspoken about human rights concerns, highlighting in particular the need to allow access to the country for UN special rapporteurs and address prison conditions.

In a new country strategy for Turkmenistan, adopted in April, the European Bank for Reconstruction and Development (EBRD) revised its policy of no public sector investment by reserving the right to increase its engagement with Turkmenistan. In a welcome move, the EBRD set specific human rights benchmarks for the government to fulfill, and made clear the bank's level of engagement would depend on Turkmenistan's progress in meeting them.

Ukraine

The February 2010 presidential election ended the political turmoil that has characterized Ukraine in recent years. Viktor Yanukovich won the election over incumbent Viktor Yushschenko in a contest that international observers declared generally in accordance with international standards. Upon taking office President Yanukovich initiated far-reaching reforms, drawing criticism for pushing through changes without respecting democratic procedures or engaging the opposition.

Ukraine's relationship with Russia improved significantly in 2010. Russian President Dmitry Medvedev, who had clashed frequently with Yushschenko, voiced hope that the "black page" in relations between Russia and Ukraine following the Orange Revolution of 2005 would be turned. Yanukovich, widely-seen as pro-Russian, visited Moscow in March and agreed to extend the lease on Russia's Black Sea fleet in the Crimea for another 25 years. Medvedev reciprocated by discounting gas prices to Ukraine.

The human rights situation in Ukraine remains marred by racial profiling; attacks against foreigners with non-Slavic appearances; government-imposed restrictions on freedoms of media; and migration issues including access to asylum, detention conditions, and protection of vulnerable groups.

Migration and Asylum

The European Union-Ukraine readmission agreement that provides for the return of third-country nationals who enter the EU from Ukraine came into force in January 2010, but implementing protocols has not yet gone into effect at this writing.

A stalemate between the executive and legislature in 2009 led to a year-long breakdown in the Ukrainian asylum system until the authority of the State National Committee on Nationalities and Religions to grant asylum was restored in August 2010. Asylum seekers with pending cases, or those in the process of appealing refugee status rejections, remain vulnerable to arbitrary detention, police harassment, and extortion.

UKRAINE

Buffeted in the Borderland

The Treatment of Migrants and Asylum Seekers in Ukraine

HUMAN
RIGHTS
WATCH

Applying for asylum is riddled with obstacles, including lack of access to lawyers in detention, and failure by detaining authorities to transmit asylum applications to regional migration services. Ukraine's asylum system continues to lack complementary forms of protection. There are only two known cases of refugee status granted to Somalis and only one known case of an unaccompanied child receiving refugee status. Unaccompanied children lack protection, access to state accommodation, and are often detained. Failure to appoint legal representatives in some regions leads to unaccompanied children being barred from entering asylum procedures and forces them to remain undocumented.

A Human Rights Watch fact-finding mission in June 2010 revealed many migrants and asylum seekers apprehended in the border region between Ukraine, Slovakia, and Hungary—or returned from these neighboring EU countries—suffer ill-treatment. In some cases, this includes torture with electric shocks, while in the custody of Ukraine's State Border Guard Service and during interrogations about smugglers' networks.

Judicial Reform

President Yanukovich pledged to undertake judicial reform in compliance with European standards and in close consultation with relevant Council of Europe bodies, particularly the European Commission for Democracy through Law (Venice Commission). However, judicial reform, a central element of Ukraine's commitment to the Council of Europe, is being conducted hastily and without apparent consideration of the commission's opinions and recommendations. Authorities submitted the controversial draft law "On the Judicial System and the Status of Judges" for Venice Commission review in March 2010. The Venice Commission and the Directorate General of Human Rights and Legal Affairs of the Council of Europe recommended substantial changes to the draft law, some of which require constitutional reform. In July 2010 the government signed the bill into law without implementing the Council of Europe's recommendations. The law significantly reduces the power of the Supreme Court and increases the authority of the High Council of Justice, a body criticized for lacking independence. In July 2010 Yanukovich appointed Valery Khoroshkovsky—head of the Security Service of Ukraine (SBU), media owner, and the president's close ally—to the High Council of Justice.

Hate Crimes and Discrimination

Racial profiling, non-violent harassment by police, and hate crimes against persons of non-Slavic appearance and ethnic and religious minorities continue to be a serious concern. The authorities' commitment to combating hate crimes weakened significantly in 2010. The Ministry of Interior Human Rights Monitoring Department, created in 2008 with a mandate to counter racism and xenophobia, was dissolved in June 2010. In August 2010 the same ministry disbanded its hate crimes investigations unit. The government does not gather or publish data on hate crimes. Ukrainian law provides for sentencing enhancements for violent crimes where racial, national, ethnic, or religious hatred is an aggravating circumstance, but this provision is generally not applied by judges due to lack of judicial training on hate crimes.

Crimean Tatars continue to face discrimination and problems with integrating into society, including lack of education in their native language.

Civil Society

Despite Yanukovich's vows to protect freedom and media pluralism, numerous newspapers and independent journalists reported increased pressure by law enforcement agencies and some television stations alleged censorship. 2010 also saw increased pressure and attacks on human rights activists.

In August 2010 Vasyl Klymentyev, editor-in-chief of the Kharkiv-based *Noviy Stil* newspaper known for its critical coverage of the authorities, went missing. Klementyev investigated several high-profile corruption cases involving local officials. Before disappearing, Klymentyev received threats and bribes not to release certain materials, increasing concerns that his disappearance is tied to his work. A national investigation into his disappearance has produced no results at this writing. The case echoes that of Georgy Gongadze, an online journalist who had reported on high-level corruption and was killed in 2000. On September 16, 2010, 10 years after his decapitated body was found, the Prosecutor General's office issued a statement identifying the late interior minister, Yuri Kravchenko, as the mastermind behind Gongadze's murder.

In May 2010 Ukrainian disability-rights activist Andrey Fedosov, who was documenting poor living conditions at several governmental psychiatric institutions in the Crimea region, was hospitalized after an attack by unknown assailants. He had previously received anonymous threats not to publicize his findings. In October Fedosov was informed by the Ministry of Internal Affairs that an inspection was underway into his organization's economic affairs.

On October 15, police searched the office of the Vinnytsya Human Rights Group under the pretext of investigating pornography distribution by the group's coordinator, prominent human rights activist Dmytro Groisman. Police, who did not have a warrant, seized the office's computers and confidential materials related to current refugee cases and two pending cases at the European Court of Human Rights. At this writing, no one has been charged in connection with the alleged investigation and the group's materials and equipment has not been returned.

Health Issues and HIV/AIDS Therapy

Ukraine continued to expand provision of antiretroviral therapy for people living with HIV/AIDS. As of January 2010, 15,871 people were receiving medication. It also expanded the number of people with opioid drug dependence receiving mediation-assisted treatment (MAT) with methadone and buprenorphine, from none in 2004 to about 5,550 in 2010.

However, an increasing number of attacks by law enforcement agencies on drug treatment clinics called into question the new government's commitment to the HIV response.

Police have raided drug treatment clinics; interrogated, fingerprinted, and photographed patients; confiscated medical records and medications; and detained medical personnel in cities nationwide. Many raids appear to have been conducted without probable cause and in violation of Ukraine's rules for police operations. The raids resulted in disrupted treatment, and two doctors face drug trafficking charges punishable by up to 10 years in prison.

Accessibility to palliative care continued to be limited, resulting in tens of thousands of patients suffering unnecessarily. Human Rights Watch research found that Ukraine's narcotics regulations severely limit the availability and accessibility of morphine, essential for treating severe pain, and that most healthcare workers are not properly trained in internationally accepted pain treatment best practices.

Key International Actors

In 2010 the EU and Ukraine continued to seek a closer relationship on economic, trade, and energy issues. President of the European Commission José Manuel Durão Barroso and Yanukovich met in Brussels in September to discuss establishing a visa-free regime between Ukraine and the EU, the vital role of media, and an independent judiciary for Ukrainian democratic development.

After a June 2010 fact-finding mission to Ukraine, the Monitoring Committee of the Council of Europe Parliamentary Assembly (PACE) commented on the increased allegations of state pressure on freedom of assembly and media. In his September visit PACE President Mevlüt Çavusoglu raised issues of media freedom, minority rights, integration of Crimean Tartars, and the integration of Ukraine in the EU. He called on Ukrainian authorities to seek the opinion of the Venice Commission before adopting new legislation to ensure compliance with international standards.

During the second session of the United States-Ukraine Strategic Partnership Commission in July 2010, the sides agreed to establish working groups on nuclear power cooperation, political dialogue and the rule of law. US Secretary of State Hillary Clinton met civil society and independent media leaders to discuss safeguarding media independence and strengthening civil society in Ukraine.

The UN Committee on Elimination of Discrimination against Women reviewed Ukraine during its January 2010 session and concluded that gender inequality and women's rights violations in Ukraine continue. The committee criticized the Ukrainian government for not sufficiently addressing the roots of trafficking in women and girls in the country, and the lack of resources allocated to combating the problem.

Uzbekistan

Uzbekistan's human rights record remains abysmal, with no substantive improvement in 2010. Authorities continue to crackdown on civil society activists, opposition members, and independent journalists, and to persecute religious believers who worship outside strict state controls. Freedom of expression remains severely limited. Government-initiated forced child labor during the cotton harvest continues.

The judiciary lacks independence, and the parliament is too weak to curtail the reach of executive power. In 2010 authorities continued to ignore calls for an independent investigation into the 2005 Andijan massacre, when authorities shot and killed hundreds of mostly unarmed protestors. Authorities also harassed families of Andijan refugees and in April imprisoned a woman who returned to Uzbekistan four-and-a-half years after fleeing.

While Uzbekistan received praise for cooperating with international actors after the June 2010 ethnic violence in Southern Kyrgyzstan caused nearly 100,000 ethnic Uzbek refugees to flee to Uzbekistan, genuine engagement on human rights remained absent.

Human Rights Defenders and Independent Journalists

Uzbek authorities regularly threaten, imprison, and torture human rights defenders and other peaceful civil society activists. In 2010 the government further restricted freedom of speech and increased use of spurious civil suits and criminal charges to silence perceived government critics.

The Uzbek government has at least 14 human rights defenders in prison, and has brought criminal charges against another, because of their legitimate human rights work. Other activists, such as dissident poet Yusuf Jumaev, remain jailed on politically-motivated charges.

In January 2010 Gaibullo Jalilov, a Karshi-based member of the Human Rights Society of Uzbekistan, was sentenced to nine years in prison on charges of anti-constitutional activity and disseminating religious extremist materials. In August new charges were brought against him, and he was sentenced to two years, one month, and five days in prison after a seriously flawed trial.

Members of the Human Rights Alliance were regularly persecuted and subjected to arbitrary detention and de facto house arrest for their activism in 2010. On February 23 two men brutally assaulted Alliance member Dmitrii Tikhonov, leaving him unconscious after choking and hitting him over the head with a metal object.

On September 16 Alliance member Anatolii Volkov was convicted on fraud charges after an investigation and trial marred by due process violations. He was ultimately amnestied. Another Alliance member, Tatyana Dovlatova, faces trumped-up charges of hooliganism.

On February 10 photographer and videographer Umida Ahmedova was convicted of defamation and insulting the Uzbek people for publishing a book of photographs in 2007 and producing a documentary film in 2008 that reflect everyday life and traditions in Uzbekistan, with a focus on gender inequality. Ahmedova was amnestied in the courtroom.

In October Vladimir Berezovskii, a veteran journalist and editor of the Vesti.uz website, was convicted of similar charges based on conclusions issued by the State Press and Information Agency stating that articles on the website were defamatory and "could incite inter-ethnic and inter-state hostility and create panic among the population."

On October 15 Voice of America correspondent Abdumalik Boboev was convicted of defamation, insult, and preparation or dissemination of materials that threaten public security. A substantial fine was imposed.

The Andijan Massacre

The government continues to refuse to investigate the 2005 massacre of hundreds of citizens in Andijan or to prosecute those responsible. Authorities continue to persecute anyone they suspect of having participated in or witnessed the atrocities. On April 30 Diloram Abdukodirova, an Andijan refugee who returned to Uzbekistan in January 2010, was sentenced to 10 years and two months in prison for illegal border crossing and anti-constitutional activity despite assurances to her family she would not be harmed if she returned. Abdukodirova appeared at one court hearing with facial bruising, indicating possible ill-treatment in custody.

The Uzbek government also continues to intimidate and harass families of Andijan survivors who have sought refuge abroad. Police subject them to constant surveillance, call them for questioning, and threaten them with criminal charges or home confiscation. School officials publicly humiliate refugees' children.

Criminal Justice, Torture, and Ill-Treatment

Torture remains rampant in Uzbekistan. Detainees' rights are violated at each stage of investigations and trials, despite habeas corpus amendments that went into effect in 2008. The Uzbek government has failed to meaningfully implement recommendations to combat torture that the United Nations special rapporteur made in 2003.

Suspects are not permitted access to lawyers, a critical safeguard against torture in pre-trial detention. Police use torture and other illegal means to coerce statements and confessions from detainees. Authorities routinely refuse to investigate defendants' allegations of abuse.

In June Yusuf Jumaev, serving a five-year prison sentence since 2008, was put in a cell with men who regularly beat him. During a harsh beating on June 12 he was kicked in the chest and head, causing his ear to bleed. Prison authorities ignored Jumaev's repeated requests to transfer cells.

On July 20, 37-year-old Shavkat Alimhodjaev, imprisoned for religious offenses, died in custody. The official cause of death was anemia, but Alimhodjaev had no known history of the disease. According to family, Alimhodjaev's face bore possible marks of ill-treatment, including a swollen eye. Authorities returned his body to his family's home at night. They insisted he be buried before sunrise and remained present until the burial. Authorities have not begun investigating the death.

Freedom of Religion

Although Uzbekistan's constitution ensures freedom of religion, Uzbek authorities continued their unrelenting, multi-year campaign of arbitrary detention, arrest, and torture of Muslims who practice their faith outside state controls or belong to unregistered religious organizations. Over 100 were arrested or convicted in 2010 on charges related to religious extremism.

Continuing a trend that began in 2008, followers of the late Turkish Muslim theologian Said Nursi were harassed and prosecuted for religious extremism, leading to prison sentences or fines. Dozens of Nursi followers were arrested or imprisoned in 2010 in Bukhara, Ferghana, and Tashkent: at least 29 were convicted between May and August alone.

Christians and members of other minority religions holding peaceful religious activities also faced short-term prison sentences and fines for administrative offenses such as violating the law on religious organizations and illegal religious teaching. According to Forum 18, at least five members of Christian minority groups are serving long prison sentences, including Tohar Haydarov, a Baptist who received a 10-year sentence in March 2010 for drug-related charges that his supporters say were fabricated in retaliation for his religious activity.

Authorities continue to extend sentences of religious prisoners for alleged violations of prison regulations or on new criminal charges. Such extensions occur without due process and can add years to a prisoner's sentence.

Child Labor

Forced child labor in cotton fields remains a serious concern. The government took no meaningful steps to implement the two International Labour Organization (ILO) conventions on child labor, which Uzbekistan ratified in March 2008.

The government continues to force hundreds of thousands of schoolchildren, some of them as young as ten, to help with the cotton harvest for two months a year. They live in filthy conditions, contract illnesses, miss school, and work daily from early morning until evening for little or no money. Hunger, exhaustion, and heat stroke are common.

Human Rights Watch is aware of several instances when local authorities harassed and threatened activists who tried to document forced child labor.

Key International Actors

The Uzbek government's cooperation with international institutions remains poor. It continues to deny access to all eight UN special procedures that have requested invitations, including those on torture and human rights defenders, and blocks the ILO from sending independent observers to monitor Uzbekistan's compliance with the prohibition of forced child labor in the cotton industry.

A March 2010 review by the UN Human Rights Committee resulted in a highly critical assessment and calls for the government to guarantee journalists and human rights defenders in Uzbekistan "the right to freedom of expression in the conduct of their activities," and to address lack of accountability for the Andijan massacre and persisting torture and ill-treatment of detainees.

During a visit to Tashkent in April, UN Secretary-General Ban Ki-moon urged the Uzbek government to "deliver" on its international human rights commitments.

The European Union's position on human rights in Uzbekistan remained disappointingly weak, with virtually no public expressions of concern about Uzbekistan's deteriorating record. The annual human rights dialogue between the EU and Uzbekistan, held in May, again yielded no known results and appeared to have no bearing on the broader relationship. In October the EU Foreign Affairs Council reviewed Uzbekistan's progress in meeting human rights criteria the EU has set for it, noting "lack of substantial progress" on areas the council had outlined the previous year when remaining sanctions imposed after the Andijan massacre were lifted. The council reiterated calls for the Uzbek government to take steps to improve its record, including releasing all jailed human rights defenders, allowing NGOs to operate freely, and cooperating with UN special rapporteurs. However, it again stopped short of articulating any policy consequences for continued non-compliance.

The United States maintains a congressionally-mandated visa ban against Uzbek officials linked to serious human rights abuses. However, its relationship with Uzbekistan is increasingly dominated by the US Department of Defense (DOD), which uses routes through Uzbekistan as part of the Northern Distribution Network to supply forces in Afghanistan. US military contracts with Uzbeks as part of this supply chain are potentially as lucrative for persons close to the Uzbek government as direct US aid would be. Despite the US State Department's re-designation in January 2009 of Uzbekistan as a "Country of Particular Concern" for systematic violations of religious freedom, the US government retained a waiver on the sanctions outlined in the designation. The DOD's prominence in the relationship with the Uzbek government raises concerns over mixed messages about human rights issues among different US agencies.

YEMEN

In the Name of Unity

The Yemeni Government's Brutal Response
to Southern Movement Protests

HUMAN
RIGHTS
WATCH

WORLD REPORT

2011

MIDDLE EAST
AND NORTH AFRICA

ALGERIA

Algeria continued to experience widespread human rights violations in 2010. A state of emergency—imposed in 1992 and renewed indefinitely by decree in 1993—created a backdrop for widespread restrictions on freedom of expression, association, and assembly. Authorities justify the measure as necessary to combat terrorism.

Members of the security forces and armed groups continued to enjoy broad impunity for atrocities committed during the violent internal conflict of the 1990s. The state offered compensation to families of persons forcibly disappeared in the 1990s, but failed to provide answers about their fate. Militant groups continued their deadly attacks, mostly targeting security forces, albeit on a lesser scale than in previous years.

Freedom of Expression and Assembly

The state controls broadcast media, which provides live telecasts of parliamentary sessions but airs almost no critical coverage of government policies. Privately-owned newspapers enjoy freer scope, but repressive press laws and dependence on revenues from public sector advertising limit their freedom to criticize the government and the military.

Prosecutors constantly prosecute journalists and independent publications for defaming or insulting public officials. Courts of first instance sometimes sentence them to prison and heavy fines, which appeals courts often overturn or suspend.

Rabah Lemouchi, correspondent for the national Arabic daily *Ennahar* in Tebessa, is among the journalists who have been jailed in recent years. While most have remained provisionally free pending trial, Lemouchi was incarcerated from his arrest until finishing his sentence six months later. A court of first instance convicted him on July 14, 2009, of defamation and insulting state institutions, mainly due to a personal letter he had addressed in 2006 to President Abdel Aziz Bouteflika. Details of the case indicate that his prosecution and imprisonment were politically motivated.

In the first half of 2010 at least two journalists received prison terms for defamation but remained free pending appeal. On May 13 a court in the city of Mostaganem sentenced Belkacem Belhamideche, director of the French-language *Reflexion* and one of the daily's reporters, to six months in prison for coverage of a letter that a businessman wrote accusing a town mayor of soliciting a bribe from him. A court in the town of Ain Boucif, in the governorate of Medea, sentenced Saleh Souadi of *el-Khabar*, Algeria's leading independent Arabic-language daily, to six months in jail for defaming a local hospital director, even though his articles appeared before the director assumed his post and did not name him.

A 2000 decree banning demonstrations in Algiers remained in effect in 2010. Despite the ban, SOS Disparu(e)s– an organization comprised of relatives of persons forcibly disappeared–has held small vigils in front of the Algiers headquarters of the state human rights commission for most Wednesdays since 1998, in spite of occasional police harassment. In August police dispersed the gathering and briefly arrested the protesters, who were demanding the state provide information regarding the fate of persons whom state security forces abducted in the 1990s and were never seen again.

Authorities require organizations to obtain authorization from the local governor before holding indoor public meetings, and frequently ban meetings organized by human rights organizations or rights organizations working on behalf of Algeria's Kabyle population. Authorities refused to allow the Algerian League for the Defense of Human Rights (LADDH) to hold its national congress on March 25-26 at a public venue in an Algiers suburb. The governorate of Algiers announced the refusal on the eve of the congress, even though the LADDH had formally requested permission a month earlier. The LADDH moved its congress to the Maison des syndicats in Bachdjarrah, a privately owned venue; two months later, the authorities closed that hall, one of the few in the capital where controversial civil society organizations had been able to meet.

On July 23, police in the city of Tizi-Ouzou broke up a human rights seminar organized by the World Amazigh Congress in collaboration with two local Amazigh (Berber) organizations. Police entered the meeting hall, confiscated materials, questioned attendees, and expelled two French participants from the country. Authorities did not explain their action.

Authorities frequently deny journalists and human rights workers entry visas. On October 2, 2010, the Algerian embassy in Washington refused visas for Human Rights Watch to conduct general research, explaining they could visit only the Polisario-run refugee camps near Tindouf. The authorities told Amnesty International the same thing in 2010. Authorities expelled two journalists with the Moroccan weekly *Assahrae al-Ousbouiya* on September 22.

Freedom of Religion

Algeria's constitution defines the state religion as Islam and requires the president to be a Muslim. Algerian laws criminalize non-Muslims proselytizing to Muslims but not the reverse, and forbid non-Muslims from gathering to worship except in state-approved locations. In practice, authorities rarely authorize Algerian Protestant groups to use buildings for worship, subjecting worshippers to possible prosecution. A court in al-Arba Nath Irathen, Tizi-Ouzou province, tried Mahmoud Yahou and three other Christians for "practicing religious rites without authorization." The trial is continuing at this writing. An appeals court in Jijel on June 22 convicted another Christian, Abdelhamid Bouamama, from Grarem in Mila province, of trying to convert Muslims and sentenced him to one year in prison, suspended.

Impunity for Past Abuses

Over 100,000 Algerians died during the political strife of the 1990s. Thousands more were "disappeared" by security forces or abducted by armed groups fighting the government and never found. The 2006 Law on Peace and National Reconciliation provides a legal framework for the continued impunity enjoyed by perpetrators of atrocities during this era. The law provides amnesty to security force members for actions they took in the name of combating terrorism and to armed group members not implicated in the most heinous acts.

The law promises compensation for families of "disappeared" persons, but simultaneously makes it a crime to denigrate state institutions or security forces for the manner in which they conducted themselves during the political strife. Organizations representing the families of the "disappeared" have criticized the state's failure to provide a detailed account of the fate of their missing relatives.

In one case dating to the civil strife of the 1990s, Malik Mejnoun and Abdelkader Chenoui have been in pre-trial detention since 1999 in connection with the assassination one year earlier of Kabyle singer-activist Lounes Matoub. Both men claim they are innocent and say they were tortured while in detention without access to communications. Eleven years later they have yet to be brought to trial.

Algeria amended its penal code in 2004 to make torture an explicit crime. The International Committee of the Red Cross regularly visits ordinary prisons in Algeria, but not places of detention run by the powerful Department for Information and Security (DRS), an intelligence agency within the military.

Algerian courts pronounced death sentences during 2010, some of them against defendants in terrorism cases and most in absentia. Algeria has observed a de facto moratorium on executions since 1993.

Terrorism and Counterterrorism

Militant attacks were down dramatically compared to the mid-1990s, but al Qaeda in the Islamic Maghreb (AQIM) continued to launch fatal attacks, directed mostly—but not exclusively—at military and police targets. On June 25, gunmen—whom Algerian media linked to terrorists—fired on a wedding party in the eastern *wilaya* (province) of Tebessa, killing the bridegroom, a young soldier, and four guests.

In July the United States for the first time sent home an Algerian who had been held at Guantanamo and opposed his repatriation, fearing persecution. The US government said Algeria had given "diplomatic assurances" that Abdul Aziz Naji would be treated humanely. Shortly after arriving, Naji, like other Algerian returnees from Guantanamo before him, appeared before an investigative judge to answer accusations of membership in a terrorist group abroad and was released pending trial, which is continuing at this writing. On November 4 an Algiers court acquitted an earlier Guantanamo returnee, Sofiane Hadarbache, of similar charges. Eight Algerian detainees remain in Guantanamo at this writing, of whom at least five reportedly oppose their return.

Key International Actors

Algeria in 2010 did not extend invitations to five special procedures of the United Nations Human Rights Council that had requested them, including the Working Group on Enforced and Involuntary Disappearances and the special rapporteurs on torture and on human rights while countering terrorism. Algeria announced invitations to visit during 2011 to seven other special rapporteurs, including those on violence against women and on the right to freedom of opinion and expression.

Algeria and the European Union have an association agreement in effect since 2005. In June they signed an agreement that provides Algeria €172 million (approximately US$234 million) in aid during 2011-2013. In 2009 the two sides agreed to create a subcommittee of the Association Council on "Political Dialogue, Security and Human Rights."

According to the US government, Algeria "is a major partner in combating extremism and terrorist networks such as Al Qa'ida and is our second-largest trading partner in the Arab world." The US provides almost no financial aid to Algeria, but is the leading customer of its exports, primarily gas and oil. Other than the annual Country Reports on Human Rights Practices, the US said almost nothing publicly on Algeria's human rights record. In a visit to Algeria in October, Department of State Special Advisor Judith E. Heumann praised the government for ratifying the UN Convention of the Rights of Persons with Disabilities in December 2009.

BAHRAIN

Human rights conditions in Bahrain deteriorated sharply in the latter half of 2010. Starting in mid-August authorities detained an estimated 250 persons, including nonviolent critics of the government, and shut down websites and publications of legal opposition political societies.

Authorities detained 25 of the most prominent opposition activists and accused many of them of "spreading false information" and "meeting with outside organizations." Some rights activists were among those held and allegedly tortured. Authorities prevented detainees from meeting with their lawyers prior to the first session of their trial, and allowed only extremely brief meetings with some family members.

This crackdown came after months of street protests, which often involved burning tires and throwing stones and Molotov cocktails. Among the first people arrested were activists who had just participated in a public meeting in London where they criticized Bahrain's human rights record.

The main exception to these dismal human rights developments involved improved protections for migrant workers.

Torture and Ill-Treatment

Almost all of the 25 prominent activists–whose trial began on October 28–told the court, some in considerable detail, that they had been subjected to torture. Lawyers able to attend the public prosecutor's pretrial interrogations of clients said that in some cases they observed marks and wounds that appeared consistent with the allegations.

A Human Rights Watch report released in February 2010 concluded that in the 2007-2009 period, the authorities regularly resorted to torture and ill-treatment when interrogating security suspects. Officials denied these findings, but apparently conducted no criminal investigations and ordered no disciplinary measures against alleged perpetrators.

On March 28 an appellate court convicted 19 men of the murder of a security officer, overturning their acquittal by a lower court in October 2009. The lower court judge determined that there was no evidence linking them to the crimes other than confessions that appeared to have been coerced.

Counterterrorism Measures

The government charged at least 23 of those detained in August and September under Law 58/2006, Protecting Society from Terrorist Acts, which allows for extended periods of detention without charge or judicial review. The United Nations special rapporteur on human rights and counterterrorism has criticized the law's broad definitions of terrorism.

Freedom of Expression

In September the Information Affairs Authority blocked websites and blogs associated with the opposition. On state-run Bahrain TV on September 20 Abdullah Yateem, the general director of press and publications at the authority, said that websites and bloggers had committed 12 crimes, and he specifically mentioned: offending the person of King Hamad bin Isa Al Khalifa, incitement to overthrow the government, publishing information about bomb-making, and slander and defamation. Yateem also banned publication of the newsletters of several opposition political societies, which are political groups the government allows, unlike other opposition groups that have no legal status.

On September 4 Ali Abdelemam, whose popular Bahrain online blog carried information about human rights developments, responded to a summons to appear at the headquarters of the National Security Agency, a body that operates outside the criminal justice system and reports directly to King Hamad. Authorities refused his request to contact a lawyer, even at his formal interrogation. At the opening session of the October 28 trial of 25 prominent activists, Abdulemam said he was subjected to torture and degrading treatment.

Municipal officials ordered one Waad Party candidate in the National Assembly election scheduled for October 23 to remove billboards with the slogan "Enough to Corruption," saying it was "a breach of the law" but not indicating which law. A court ruled on October 4 that the banners did not violate the law, but the government appealed.

The Ministry of Information suspended the satellite station Al Jazeera on May 18, the day after the channel broadcast a feature about poverty in Bahrain. On July 2, police summoned for questioning two volunteers with the Bahrain Women's Association who had spoken with Al Jazeera about challenges they face being married to non-Bahrainis.

On August 16, 2010, *Al-Wasat*, Bahrain's one independent newspaper, reported that the minister of information suspended its online audio reports. The suspension came after several of the reports featured persons alleging mistreatment of inmates in Jaw prison.

Freedom of Association

In April the minister of social development denied the request of the Bahrain Human Rights Society to hold a monitoring workshop for human rights defenders in the Gulf region, saying it would violate the association law, which prohibits organizations from involvement in political activities. The ministry subsequently allowed the workshop to take place in late May.

In August the ministry wrote to the Migrant Workers' Protection Society saying that the society's shelter was not legally registered and would have to close. This followed an incident in which a migrant domestic worker fled to the shelter from the home of a high ministry official, claiming she had been abused. The society responded by providing a copy of the government's 2005 authorization of the shelter, noting that in previous years the ministry had donated funds to support the shelter.

The government continues to deny legal status to the Bahrain Center for Human Rights (BCHR), which it ordered dissolved in 2004 after the group's then-president criticized the prime minister for corruption and human rights violations.

On April 5 Bahrain's Lower Criminal Court fined Mohammad al-Maskati, president of the Bahrain Youth Human Rights Society (BYHRS), BD500 (US\$ 1,325) for operating an unregistered NGO. The BYHRS attempted in 2005 to register with the

Ministry of Social Development, as required by law, but received no response to its application.

Human Rights Defenders

Those detained in the wave of arrests in August and September and allegedly tortured included Abd al-Ghani al-Khanjar, spokesperson for the National Committee for the Victims of Torture, and Muhammad Saeed al-Sahlawi, a BCHR board member.

On September 1 the pro-government daily *Al Watan* featured a front-page article alleging that BCHR president Nabeel Rajab and former president Abd al-Hadi al-Khawaja were linked to a "terrorist network" responsible for arson attacks and plotting sabotage. A similar article appeared on the official Bahrain News Agency website on September 4, but was removed the following day.

On September 6 Salman Kamaleddin resigned as the head of the newly established official National Institution for Human Rights to protest the institution's failure to criticize the recent arrests.

On September 8–after the Bahrain Human Rights Society (BHRS) criticized the widespread arrests and alleged torture of detainees–the Ministry of Social Development dismissed Abdullah al-Dirazi, the group's secretary general, dissolved the group's board of directors, and appointed a ministry official as "interim director." The minister accused the organization of "only serving one segment of society," communicating with illegal organizations, and conducting "secret training" of regional rights defenders, referring to the May workshops that the ministry expressly approved and that were well publicized at the time. The BHRS had been the main Bahraini organization permitted to monitor parliamentary elections scheduled for October 23; the government refused to allow international observers.

Migrant Worker Rights

Over 460,000 migrant workers, primarily from South Asia, work in Bahrain. Many experience prolonged periods of withheld wages, passport confiscation, unsafe housing, excessive work hours and physical abuse. Government redress mechanisms remained largely ineffective.

In August 2009 Bahrain adopted Decision 79/2009 allowing workers to change jobs more freely. The reform does not apply to domestic workers and many workers remain unaware that they have the right to change employment freely.

A draft labor law circulated in May 2010 extends some rights to domestic workers, including annual vacation and end-of-term pay, but still excludes them from provisions mandating maximum work hours and days off. The law also creates a new "case management" mechanism to ensure the adjudication of labor complaints within two months, potentially making litigation a more viable option for migrant workers seeking redress for abuses.

Women's Rights

Bahrain's first written personal status law (Law 19/2009), adopted in 2009, applies only to Sunnis. Shia religious leaders demand a constitutional guarantee that, should a separate personal status law be passed for Shias, parliament will not be able to amend any provision of the law. Women's groups favor a unified law for all citizens in part because Sharia court judges—generally conservative religious scholars with limited formal legal training—decide marriage, divorce, custody, and inheritance cases according to their own individual readings of Islamic jurisprudence, which consistently favor men. It remains unclear to what extent codification has alleviated these problems for Sunni women.

Key International Actors

Bahrain hosts the headquarters of the United States Navy's Fifth Fleet and provides logistical support for military operations in Iraq and Afghanistan, and the US provides military aid to Bahrain. The US initially did not publicly criticize the government's crackdown on civil society or other serious abuses; on October 31 Secretary of State Hillary Clinton issued a statement congratulating Bahrain for its recent parliamentary election, but also expressing concern about "efforts in the lead-up to the elections to restrict freedom of expression and association targeted at civil society."

British officials expressed little concern publicly about the sharp deterioration of human rights conditions. One of the activists arrested in August, Jaffar al-Hasabi, is a dual national, and it reportedly took a phone call from British Foreign Secretary William Hague to Bahrain's crown prince before a British consular visit to al-Hasabi was permitted, about a month after his arrest. Bahrain publicly called on the United Kingdom to investigate and prosecute or extradite two of those indicted in the alleged terrorism case whom reside in London. The UK responded that it would investigate if Bahrain provided evidence of criminal activity. At this writing, Bahrain has provided no such evidence.

EGYPT

Egypt continued to suppress political dissent in 2010, dispersing demonstrations; harassing rights activists; and detaining journalists, bloggers, and Muslim Brotherhood members. Security officers used lethal force against migrants attempting to cross into Israel and arbitrarily detained recognized refugees.

Despite promising since 2005 to end the state of emergency, the government renewed Law No. 162 of 1958 in May, but promised to restrict its use. Afterward authorities released at least 450 individuals detained under the emergency law, including Bedouin rights defender Mus'ad Abul Fagr and blogger Hany Nazeer. The government continues to refuse to disclose the number of persons detained under the emergency law, but Egyptian human rights organizations estimate the number at around 5,000.

The June 1 elections for the Shura Council, the upper house of parliament, were marred by reports of fraud and voter intimidation. The High Elections Committee failed to issue 2,600 of the 4,000 civil society permits requested by the National Council for Human Rights. People's Assembly elections took place on November 28 with ineffective judicial supervision.

Freedom of Expression

Security officers targeted bloggers and journalists who criticized government policies and exposed human rights violations, and activists supporting Mohamed El Baradei's Campaign for Change. In March State Security Investigations (SSI) arrested Tarek Khedr, who had been gathering signatures for the Baradei petition, and detained him incommunicado at an unknown location for three months. In April SSI officers arrested publisher Ahmed Mehni for publishing a book, "El Baradei and the Dream of the Green Revolution."

In February military intelligence officers arrested Ahmad Mustafa, a blogger and activist in the April 6 Youth Group, after he blogged about corruption in the Military Academy. The prosecutor charged Mustafa with "spreading false information" and transferred the case to a military tribunal, where a judge released him after 10 days on the condition that he apologize.

In the run-up to the parliamentary elections, the government on October 13 brought all live broadcasts by private companies under control of state television, and on November 1 issued directives requiring prior permission for every live broadcast.

Freedom of Assembly and Association

In April security officials cracked down on a peaceful protest–organized by the April 6 Youth Group–calling for an end to the state of emergency; more than 100 were arrested and 33 were brought before a prosecutor, who charged them with demonstrating "to overthrow the regime" and released them. In June a number of peaceful demonstrations expressed outrage at the police killing of Khaled Said in Alexandria. Security officials beat and dispersed protestors, arresting at least 101 in one day.

In February SSI arrested 16 senior Muslim Brotherhood members, including deputy leader Mahmud Ezzat and prominent member Essam El Erian. A state security prosecutor charged them with leading a Brotherhood faction that promotes violence against the government. The prosecutor dropped all charges and released them two months later. After the changes to the emergency law came into effect, the Ministry of Interior released almost all Muslim Brotherhood members detained under the law. As of November 18, Egyptian security officers had arrested 487 members of the Muslim Brotherhood in connection with campaigning for the members of the group who are running as independents in the parliamentary elections, and held 288 of them in preventive detention on charges of "membership in an illegal organization."

Arbitrary Detention and Torture

Officials of SSI appear to have "disappeared" more political detainees in 2010. Security officers "disappeared" those accused of membership in Islamic groups for up to three months and also "disappeared" young political activists for several days. SSI arrested Amr Salah on September 9 and detained him incommunicado at an unknown location before releasing him 30 hours later. In a rare case of a long-term disappearance, the whereabouts and well-being of Mohamed Tork, a 23-year-old student, have been unknown since his arrest in July 2009. Family complaints to the prosecutions and the Interior Ministry have received no response.

Police and security forces regularly engaged in torture in police stations, detention centers, and at points of arrest. In March SSI arrested Muslim Brotherhood member Nasr al-Sayed Hassan Nasr, detained him incommunicado for three months, and tortured him for 45 days during interrogation. They released him without charge in June. Also in June two policemen beat 28-year-old Khaled Said to death on an Alexandria street, causing public outrage. Following widespread protests, a public prosecutor referred the two policemen to court on charges of excessive use of force, but failed to indict their superior officer; at this writing two sessions of the trial have taken place.

Fair Trial and Special Courts

The year 2010 saw increases in the number of trials of civilians before military courts and in reliance on special courts that do not meet fair trial standards. At this writing the ongoing trial of 25 defendants accused of membership in a terrorist organization, the so-called Zeitoun trial, has already been marred by the incommunicado detention of the defendants, their lack of access to counsel, and allegations of torture that prosecutors did not properly investigate. In August prosecutors referred former torture victim Imad al-Kabir to trial before a state security court on charges of possession of an illegal weapon after a neighborhood brawl.

Labor Rights

Egypt witnessed waves of worker protests and unauthorized strikes throughout 2010, and security officers dispersed several of these using excessive force. In August a military court tried eight civilian workers on charges of deliberately stopping production, going on strike, and "disclosing military secrets." The case followed an amendment to the Military Justice Code, after workers from the Helwan Military Factory participated in a protest against factory conditions following another worker's death. The court acquitted three of the workers but gave two others suspended prison sentences and fines, and recommended disciplinary measures against a further three.

Freedom of Religion

Although Egypt's constitution provides for equal rights without regard to religion, there is widespread discrimination against Egyptian Christians, as well as official intolerance of heterodox Muslim sects. In January gunmen shot dead six Coptic Christians as they left a Christmas Mass in Nag' Hammadi, forcing the government to acknowledge increasing sectarian violence. Prosecutors charged three men with premeditated murder in this incident, and transferred the case to a State Security Court. Authorities responded to a subsequent incident of sectarian violence in March in Marsa Matrouh in a more typical fashion, merely urging the parties to drop complaints and not pursuing criminal investigations or holding perpetrators accountable.

In March SSI arrested at least nine members of the Ahmadi faith and detained them for 80 days on charges of "showing contempt for the Islamic faith." Security officials continued to detain eight adherents of the Shia faith under successive emergency law detention orders, despite government promises to release all those detained under the law for reasons other than terrorism and drugs, and despite successive court orders for their release.

Refugees and Migrants

The treatment of refugees and migrants in Egypt deteriorated further. At this writing Egyptian border guards have shot dead at least 27 migrants attempting to cross the Sinai border into Israel since the start of 2010. A government official said that security forces had "only" killed 4 percent of those attempting to cross in 2009. Egypt denied the United Nations High Commissioner for Refugees (UNHCR) access to detained migrants, preventing them from making asylum claims. Egypt also continues to detain UNHCR-recognized refugees and charge refugees and migrants alike with illegal entry, bringing their cases before military courts that do not meet international fair trial standards.

In January SSI officials arrested at least 25 Sudanese refugees and asylum seekers and detained many incommunicado for up to three months. Among them was Faisal Mohamed Haroun, a recognized refugee from Darfur, who disappeared when SSI arrested him on January 7 and did not reappear until April 6, when officials brought him before a state security prosecutor. A prosecutor dropped the charges against Haroun and closed the investigation, but he and at least 14 other refugees and asylum seekers remain in detention. Egypt has made four attempts, one successfully, to deport refugees who have been recognized by UNHCR.

Women's and Girls' Rights

In February the State Council, Egypt's highest administrative court, voted to ban women from serving as judges on the council. The decision was overturned by Egypt's Constitutional Court, but women are still not represented on the State Council and are extremely underrepresented in the Egyptian judiciary.

In June a decision by Egypt's Supreme Administrative Court allowing Christian divorcees to remarry prompted an outcry from the Orthodox Coptic Church, which refused to recognize the decision. In July the Supreme Constitutional Court over-ruled the administrative court's decision, and the Coptic Church approved a draft personal status law for non-Muslims that only allows for divorce under certain conditions, such as adultery, and denies Christian divorcees the right to remarry.

In August officials arrested an Egyptian doctor for illegally performing female genital mutilation on a 13-year-old girl who later died from complications arising from the procedure. The Egyptian government criminalized performing female genital circumcision in 2008.

Egypt still lacks a legal environment to protect girls and women from violence, encourage them to report attacks, and deter perpetrators from committing abuses against them.

Key International Actors

At Egypt's Universal Periodic Review before the UN Human Rights Council in February, the government accepted 140 out of 165 recommendations, but rejected key ones related to abolishing the death penalty, eliminating the crime of "habit-ual debauchery," and permitting NGOs to receive funding without prior authoriza-tion. The United States condemned the renewal of the emergency law and pressed for the release of detainees. US Senators Russ Feingold and John McCain introduced a Senate resolution with broad support calling for ending the state of emergency and abuses by security officers, and establishing free elections in Egypt. Egyptian government lobbyists strenuously opposed the resolution. European Union Heads of Mission issued a statement in July calling for an impartial investigation into the police killing of Khaled Said.

IRAN

Iran's human rights crisis deepened as the government sought to consolidate its power following 2009's disputed presidential election. Public demonstrations waned after security forces used live ammunition to suppress protesters in late 2009, resulting in the death of at least seven protesters. Authorities announced that security forces had arrested more than 6,000 individuals after June 2009. Hundreds—including lawyers, rights defenders, journalists, civil society activists, and opposition leaders—remain in detention without charge. Since the election crackdown last year, well over a thousand people have fled Iran to seek asylum in neighboring countries. Interrogators used torture to extract confessions, on which the judiciary relied on to sentence people to long prison terms and even death. Restrictions on freedom of expression and association, as well as religious and gender-based discrimination, continued unabated.

Torture and Ill-Treatment

Authorities systematically used torture to coerce confessions. Student activist Abdullah Momeni wrote to Supreme Leader Ayatollah Seyed Ali Khamenei in September describing the torture he suffered at the hands of jailers. At this writing no high-level official has been prosecuted for the torture, ill-treatment, and deaths of three detainees held at Kahrizak detention center after June 2009.

On August 2, 2010, 17 political prisoners issued a statement demanding the rights guaranteed to prisoners by law, including an end to their solitary confinement and access to medical facilities. They also complained of severely overcrowded conditions. Reports by international human rights groups indicate that prison authorities are systematically denying needed medical care to political prisoners at Tehran's Evin Prison and other facilities.

Freedom of Expression

Dozens of journalists and bloggers are currently behind bars or free on short-term furloughs. On September 28 blogger Hossein Derakhshan received a nineteen-and-a-half year prison sentence for espionage, "propaganda against the regime," and "insulting sanctities." The judiciary sentenced numerous other journalists, including Isa Saharkhiz and Hengameh Shahidi who were sentenced to three and six years respectively, for crimes such as "insulting" government officials. On June 8 a revolutionary court sentenced Jila Baniyaghoub to a year in prison and barred her from working as a journalist for 30 years.

The Ministry of Islamic Culture and Guidance continued shutting down newspapers and in August directed the press not to publish items about opposition leaders Mir Hossein Moussavi, Mehdi Karroubi, and Mohammad Khatami, the former president.

State universities prevented some politically active students from registering for graduate programs despite undergraduate test scores that should have guaranteed them access. The government initiated an aggressive campaign to "Islamicize" universities, in part by forcibly retiring professors in the social sciences.

The government relied on plainclothes security forces and the *Basij*, a state-sponsored paramilitary force, to target Shia clerics critical of the government, such as Grand Ayatollah Yusef Sanei, Mehdi Karroubi, and Ayatollah Seyed Ali Mohammad Dastgheib. Ayatollah Kazemini Boroujerdi—whose understanding of Islam calls for the separation of religion and government—entered his fourth year in prison following a Special Court for the Clergy conviction on unknown charges. After years under house arrest and government monitoring, Grand Ayatollah Hossein-Ali Montazeri died in December 2009. Security forces arrested scores of mourners who attended his funeral.

The government systematically blocks websites that carry political news and analysis, slows down internet speeds, jams foreign satellite broadcasts, and employs the Revolutionary Guards to target dissident websites.

Freedom of Assembly and Association

Authorities continued a blanket policy of denying permits for opposition demonstrations. Security forces prevented the Mourning Mothers, whose sons and daughters were killed by security forces during the 2009 unrest, from gathering at Laleh Park in Tehran. Authorities also prevented women's rights activists from

IRAN

The Islamic Republic at 31

Post-election Abuses Show Serious Human Rights Crisis

HUMAN
RIGHTS
WATCH

publicly petitioning against existing laws or legislation that discriminate against women.

The government increased restrictions on civil society organizations. On September 27 the general prosecutor and judiciary spokesman announced a court order dissolving two pro-reform political parties, the Islamic Iran Participation Front and the Mojahedin of the Islamic Revolution.

Repression of student groups was particularly harsh. Security forces detained scores of members belonging to the Office for Consolidating Unity, including Ali Qolizadeh, Alireza Kiani, Mohammad Heydarzadeh, and Mohsen Barzegar, who were arrested in early November 2010. The Office for Consolidating Unity is a national independent student association that authorities declared illegal in January 2009. In 2010, revolutionary courts convicted Bahareh Hedayat, Majid Tavakoli, and Milad Asadi, members of Tahkim's alumni group, to prison terms ranging from six to eight-and-a-half years on charges that include insulting government authorities.

Death Penalty

In 2009, the last year for which figures are available, authorities executed 388 prisoners, more than any other nation except China. Iranian human rights defenders believe that many more executions, especially of individuals convicted of drug trafficking, are taking place in Iran's prisons today.

Crimes punishable by death include murder, rape, drug trafficking, armed robbery, espionage, sodomy, and adultery. Under intense international pressure, officials suspended the stoning-to-death sentence of Sakineh Mohammadi Ashtiani who was convicted of adultery in 2006. However, they alleged that Ashtiani helped murder her husband. She remains on death row at this writing.

Iran leads the world in the execution of juvenile offenders. Iranian law allows death sentences for persons who have reached puberty, defined as nine years old for girls and fifteen for boys. According to a human rights lawyer who defended many juvenile offenders on death row, authorities executed a juvenile offender named Mohammad on July 10, 2010. There are currently more than a hundred juvenile offenders on death row, including Ebrahim Hamidi, whom a local court sentenced to death for the alleged rape of another boy in 2010. Hamidi was 16 at the time of the alleged crime.

Authorities have executed at least nine political dissidents since November 2009, all of them convicted of *moharebeh* ("enmity against God") for their alleged ties to armed groups. On January 28 the government hanged Mohammad-Reza Ali-Zamani and Arash Rahmanipour. Although both were arrested prior to the June 2009 presidential election, they were tried as part of the August 2009 mass trials, where they reportedly confessed to planning a deadly 2008 bombing in Shiraz, southwest Iran.

Authorities executed Farzad Kamangar, Ali Heidarian, Farhad Vakili, Shirin Alam Holi, and Mehdi Eslamian by hanging on the morning of May 9 in Evin prison without informing their lawyers or families. Another 16 Kurds presently face execution for their alleged support of armed groups.

Human Rights Defenders

Efforts to intimidate human rights lawyers and prevent them from effectively representing political detainees continued. In September authorities arrested Nasrin Sotoudeh, who represented numerous political prisoners. In November Sotoudeh went on a "dry" hunger strike, refusing to eat or drink anything to protest being held in solitary confinement since her arrest. Mohammad Mostafaei was forced to flee Iran after authorities repeatedly summoned him for questioning and detained his wife, father-in-law, and brother-in-law. Mostafaei represented high-profile defendants such as Sakineh Mohammadi Ashtiani, the woman sentenced to death by stoning, and numerous juvenile detainees on death row. In October 2010, a revolutionary court sentenced Mohammad Seifzadeh, a colleague of Nobel-prize winner Shirin Ebadi and co-founder of the banned Center for Defenders of Human Rights, to nine years imprisonment and banned him from practicing law for 10 years.

Security forces routinely harassed and arrested human rights activists, often without charge. Others were swept up in raids and face charges of attempting to overthrow the government via "cyber-warfare." On September 21 a revolutionary court sentenced Emad Baghi to six years in prison for an interview he conducted with dissident cleric Grand Ayatollah Montazeri several years earlier. Another revolutionary court sentenced Shiva Nazar Ahari and Koohyar Goodarzi, both members of the Committee of Human Rights Reporters, to six years and one year respectively after months of "temporary detention" for alleged national security offenses.

Treatment of Minorities

The government denies adherents of the Baha'i faith—Iran's largest non-Muslim religious minority—freedom of religion. In August the judiciary convicted seven leaders of the national Baha'i organization to 20 years each in prison; their sentences were later reduced to 10 years each. The government accused them of espionage without providing evidence and denied their lawyers' requests to conduct a prompt and fair trial.

Iranian laws continue to discriminate against religious minorities, including Sunni Muslims, in employment and education. Sunni Muslims, about 10 percent of the population, cannot construct mosques in major cities. In 2010, security forces detained several members of Iran's largest Sufi sect, the Nematollahi Gonabadi order, and attacked their houses of worship. They similarly targeted converts to Christianity for questioning and arrest.

The government restricts cultural and political activities among the country's Azeri, Kurdish, and Arab minorities, including the organizations that focus on social issues.

Sexual minorities also face a precarious situation. Law enforcement and judiciary officials discriminate, both in law and in practice, against Iran's vulnerable lesbian, gay, bisexual, and transgender communities. Iran's penal code criminalizes consensual same-sex acts, some of which are punishable by death. During the past few years, a steady stream of LGBT Iranians has sought refugee status in Turkey and are awaiting resettlement in third countries.

Key International Actors

Iran's nuclear program continued to be the center of attention for much of 2010, overshadowing serious concerns regarding the deepening human rights crisis in the country. In June 2010 the United Nations Security Council passed a new round of sanctions against Iran for its failure to comply with previous resolutions on transparency regarding its nuclear program.

During Iran's Universal Periodic Review before the UN Human Rights Council (HRC) in March, Iran rejected 45 recommendations of member states, including allowing the special rapporteur on torture to visit the country; prosecuting security officials involved in torturing, raping, or killing; implementing policies to end gender based violence; and halting the execution of political prisoners.

In October 2010 the UN secretary-general's office released its report on the situation of human rights in Iran, pursuant to UN General Assembly resolution 64/176. The report noted "further negative developments in the human rights situation" in Iran, including "excessive use of force, arbitrary arrests, and detentions, unfair trials, and possible torture and ill-treatment of opposition activists" following the June 2009 election.

In April Iran withdrew its bid to gain a seat on the HRC after strong international opposition. However, it did gain a seat on the Commission on the Status of Women. During the June session of the HRC, 56 states joined a statement expressing concern over "the lack of progress in the protection of human rights in Iran, particularly since the events surrounding the elections in Iran last June." In December 2009 the UN General Assembly passed a resolution criticizing Iran's human rights record.

On September 29, 2010, the Obama administration announced "human rights sanctions" against eight high-level Iranian officials, including individuals from the ministries of intelligence and interior, the police, the *Basij*, the Revolutionary Guards, and the judiciary, who were responsible for systematic and serious human rights violations.

IRAQ

Human rights conditions in Iraq remain extremely poor, especially for journalists, detainees, displaced persons, religious and ethnic minorities, women and girls, and persons with disabilities. The United States officially ended its seven-year combat operations in August 2010, reducing the number of troops to about 49,700.

On March 7, 2010, millions of Iraqis from every part of the country braved mortar shells and rockets to vote in the national legislative election. In a blow to the election's credibility, the Supreme National Commission for Accountability and Justice disqualified more than 500 candidates because of alleged Ba'ath Party links, including several prominent politicians who were expected to do well. Incumbent Prime Minister Nuri al-Maliki, whose State of Law Coalition won 89 of the 325 seats, remained in office pending the formation of a new government, while Ayad Allawi's al-Iraqiya list won 91. The Iraqi National Alliance, a Shia coalition formed by the Islamic Supreme Council of Iraq and the followers of Muqtada al-Sadr, won 70 seats and the Kurdish parties obtained 57. Overall, the election results reflected sectarian divisions.

In November 2010 Iraq's political parties agreed to form a new coalition government eight months after parliamentary elections. The deadlock had created a political vacuum that allowed armed groups to reassert themselves in some areas.

Attacks on Civilians and Displacement

Repeated attacks by armed groups targeted civilians, exploiting the political stalemate and Sunni Arab discontent. Violence killed and injured hundreds of civilians each month, in one of the worst periods, more than 500 people died in August alone. Assailants targeted government buildings and officials, checkpoints, embassies, hotels, factories, markets, and mosques, as well as people gathered for religious pilgrimages, weddings, and funerals, mainly in Shia areas. Violent attacks have caused civilians to flee, creating internally displaced persons and refugees across borders.

Some refugees who had fled to Syria, Jordan, and Lebanon faced economic pressure and difficulties maintaining legal status abroad and returned home to Iraq. The Iraqi government has no adequate plan for the return of Iraqis who have been displaced internally or those who have fled to neighboring countries. Thousands of displaced persons within Iraq reside in squatter settlements without access to basic necessities such as clean water, electricity, and sanitation. Many are widows with few employment prospects. Their desperate situation has contributed to an increase in sex trafficking and forced prostitution.

The ongoing attacks, along with an abundance of abandoned landmines and cluster munitions, have created a disproportionately high number of persons with physical and mental disabilities, many of whom have not received support for rehabilitation and re-integration into the community.

Detention Conditions and Torture

Reports continued of widespread torture and other abuse of detainees in the custody of the defense and interior ministries and police. Government-run detention facilities struggled to accommodate almost 30,000 detainees, and serious delays in judicial review exacerbated overcrowding; some detainees have spent years in custody without charge or trial. The situation worsened in 2010 as the US military transferred most of its remaining prison sites and detainees to Iraqi custody. On July 15, US forces handed over their last prison, Camp Cropper, which housed about 1,700 detainees. US forces retained control over about 200 prisoners, including some former members of Saddam Hussein's government.

In April Human Rights Watch interviewed 42 detainees who had been tortured over a period of months by security forces at a secret prison in the old Muthanna airport in western Baghdad. The facility held about 430 detainees who had no access to their families or lawyers. The prisoners said security forces personnel kicked, whipped, and beat them, asphyxiated them, gave them electric shocks, burned them with cigarettes, and pulled out their fingernails and teeth. They said that interrogators sodomized some detainees with sticks and pistol barrels. Some young men said they were forced to perform oral sex on interrogators and guards, and that interrogators forced detainees to sexually molest one another. As of November government officials had not prosecuted any officials responsible.

Gender-Based Violence

Violence against women and girls continued to be a serious problem across Iraq. Women's rights activists said they remain at risk of attack from extremists who have also targeted female politicians, civil servants, and journalists. "Honor" crimes and domestic abuse remain a threat to women and girls, who also remain vulnerable to trafficking for sexual exploitation and forced prostitution due to insecurity, displacement, financial hardship, social disintegration, and the dissolution of rule of law and state authority.

Female genital mutilation is practiced mainly in Kurdish areas of northern Iraq. In November the Ministry of Health completed a statistical study on the prevalence of FGM and the data suggests that 41 percent of Kurdish girls and women have undergone this procedure. On July 6, 2010, the High Committee for Issuing Fatwas at the Kurdistan Islamic Scholars Union — the highest Muslim authority in Iraqi Kurdistan to issue religious pronouncements and rulings — issued a religious edict that said Islam does not prescribe the practice, but stopped short of calling for an outright ban. At this writing the women's rights committee of the Kurdistan parliament had finalized a draft law on family violence, including provisions on FGM, and the Ministry of Health announced plans to disseminate information on the practice's negative health consequences. But the government has not yet banned FGM or created a comprehensive plan to eradicate it.

Freedom of Expression

In 2010 Iraq remained one of the most dangerous countries in the world to work as a journalist. Extremists and unknown assailants continue to kill media workers and bomb their bureaus. On July 26, a suicide car bomber detonated his vehicle in front of the Al Arabiya satellite television station, killing six and destroying the Baghdad bureau. The Islamic State of Iraq, an armed umbrella group associated with al Qaeda in Mesopotamia, later claimed responsibility for this attack on the "corrupt" channel. In September unknown assailants assassinated two television presenters and injured another in separate incidents in Baghdad and Mosul. On March 12, gunmen opened fire in Baghdad on the car of Mu'aid al-Lami, head of the Iraqi Journalists' Syndicate, killing his driver.

IRAQ

"They Took Me
and Told Me Nothing"

Female Genital Mutilation in Iraqi Kurdistan

**H U M A N
R I G H T S
W A T C H**

Journalists in Iraq also contended with emboldened Iraqi and Kurdish security forces and their respective *image-conscious* central and regional governments. On May 4, assailants abducted, tortured, and killed Sardasht Osman, a 23-year-old freelance journalist and student in Arbil. Friends, family, and other journalists believed Osman died because he wrote critical articles about the Kurdistan region's two governing parties, their leaders, and the ingrained patronage system. Security forces attached to government institutions and political parties harassed, intimidated, threatened, arrested, and physically assaulted journalists. Senior politicians sued publications and journalists for unflattering articles.

Iraq's Communications and Media Commission enforced new restrictions ahead of the March 7 parliamentary elections, ostensibly to silence broadcasters who encouraged sectarian violence, but the regulations encroached unduly on media freedoms. At this writing two pieces of legislation, the Access to Information Law and the Journalists' Protection Law, remain stalled in the Iraqi parliament.

Freedom of Assembly

After thousands of Iraqis took to the streets in June to protest the government's inability to provide sufficient electricity and other basic services, the authorities cracked down on demonstrations. On June 25 the Interior Ministry issued onerous regulations about public protests, and the Prime Minister's Office apparently issued a secret order the following day instructing the interior minister to refuse permits for demonstrations about power shortages. In the months that followed the government refused to authorize numerous requests for public demonstrations, with no explanation. Authorities arrested and intimidated organizers and protesters, and policing actions led to deaths and injuries. The clampdown created a climate of fear among demonstrators.

Violence against Minorities

Armed groups continued to persecute ethnic and religious minorities with impunity. In the three weeks leading up to the March 7 national elections, assailants killed 10 Christians in the city of Mosul in attacks that appeared politically motivated. The violence prompted 4,300 Christians to flee to the Nineveh Plains, a disputed area in northern Iraq that is culturally, ethnically, and religiously diverse. Iraqi and Kurdish government officials condemned the attacks and the government of Iraq established an investigative committee, but as of October no perpetrators had been identified or arrested.

On October 31, gunmen identifying themselves as members of the Islamic State of Iraq attacked a church in Baghdad, taking more than a hundred hostages. Two priests and 44 worshippers were killed when Iraqi forces stormed the building.

Minorities remained in a precarious position as the Arab-dominated central government and the Kurdistan regional government struggled over control of disputed territories running across northern Iraq from the Iranian to the Syrian borders. Leaders of minority communities complained that Kurdish security forces engaged in arbitrary detentions, intimidation, and in some cases low-level violence, against those who challenged Kurdish control of the disputed territories. In other parts of Iraq, minorities have not received sufficient government protection from targeted violence, threats, and intimidation. Perpetrators are rarely identified, investigated, or punished.

Key International Actors

An agreement between the US and Iraq in 2008 calls for a complete US withdrawal—including non-combat military forces—from Iraq by the end of 2011. As of September 2010 the United States had about 49,700 troops in the country, down from 160,000 to 170,000 at the height of the 2007 "surge."

In October Wikileaks released thousands of documents, mostly authored by low-ranking US officers in the field between 2004 and 2009, revealing many previously unreported instances in which US soldiers killed civilians, and the torture of detainees by their Iraqi captors.

The UN Human Rights Council reviewed Iraq under its Universal Periodic Review mechanism in February 2010. The government accepted most of the recommendations but rejected abolishing the death penalty.

In August the UN Security Council voted to extend the mandate of the UN Assistance Mission for Iraq (UNAMI) for another year. The UNAMI Human Rights Office monitors human rights violations as part of a plan aimed at developing Iraqi mechanisms for addressing past and current abuses.

Israel/ Occupied Palestinian Territories

The human rights crisis in the Occupied Palestinian Territories (OPT) continued in 2010, despite marginal improvements. After Israeli commandos enforcing the naval blockade of Gaza killed nine civilians on a flotilla attempting to run the blockade, Israel announced it would ease the severe import restrictions on the territory. Still, Israel continued to block exports, having a devastating impact on the Gaza economy.

Palestinian armed groups in Gaza launched far fewer rocket attacks than in 2009 but continued to target Israeli population centers, killing one civilian, while Hamas claimed responsibility for the killing of four Jewish settlers in the West Bank. Hamas authorities carried out judicial executions for the first time in 2010—in some cases after unfair military trials—and allegedly tortured scores of detainees.

In the West Bank, including East Jerusalem, Israel imposed severe restrictions on Palestinian freedom of movement, demolished scores of homes under discriminatory practices, continued unlawful settlement construction, and arbitrarily detained children and adults. The Palestinian Authority's (PA) security services arbitrarily detained hundreds of people and allegations of torture by the PA's security services increased.

Gaza Strip

Israel

Israel Defense Forces (IDF) attacks in Gaza, including against smuggling tunnels and in response to rocket attacks, killed 21 Palestinian civilians as of October 1, the United Nations reported. The majority of reported cases involved IDF killings of Palestinian civilians in the "no-go" zone along Gaza's northern and eastern borders, often as they were collecting construction material or farming.

On May 31, Israeli naval commandos intercepted a flotilla attempting to break the Gaza blockade, killing nine civilians. A UN Human Rights Council (HRC) committee of inquiry criticized Israeli forces for unlawful killings, abuse of detainees, and other violations; an Israeli inquiry is still ongoing at this writing.

Another HRC committee reported in September that Israel's investigations into dozens of cases of violations during "Operation Cast Lead," including alleged intentional and reckless killings of civilians and wanton destruction of civilian property in 2008-2009, were incomplete, as the authorities failed to investigate some cases of alleged wrongdoing and to examine the responsibility of "high-level decision-makers." The committee found a conflict of interest in the role of the Military Advocate General (MAG), who approved plans for the offensive but was also responsible for prosecuting alleged violations by Israeli soldiers.

As part of the MAG's investigations, the IDF's military justice system convicted three soldiers for crimes during the conflict: one was sentenced to jail for stealing a credit card, while two others were demoted and given suspended sentences for using a boy as a human shield. A fourth soldier was indicted for manslaughter for shooting a civilian waving a white flag. In January Israel paid US$10.5 million for its damage to UN facilities during the conflict.

Blockade

Israel's blockade of the Gaza Strip, imposed since Hamas's takeover of Gaza in June 2007, continued to have severe humanitarian and economic consequences for the civilian population.

International pressure as a result of the May 31 flotilla killings led Israel to ease import restrictions. However, as of September imports amounted to only one-third of pre-blockade levels, the UN reported. Israel approved in principle imports of construction materials for designated UN projects worth $15 million, and work began on upgrading two waste water treatment plants, but as of October materials needed for new schools and health clinics had not yet entered Gaza. The UN Relief and Works Agency for Palestine Refugees (UNRWA) reported that Israeli restrictions had prevented it from building new schools, and that in 2010 it had to refer 40,000 students to Hamas-run schools due to lack of classroom space in its own schools.

Israel continued to impose near-total export restrictions. As of August more than 65 percent of Gaza's factories remained closed, and the rest were working at 20 to 60 percent of their capacity, according to the Palestinian Trade Center. The number of Gaza residents registered with UNRWA living in "abject poverty" tripled since 2007 to 300,000, while unemployment in Gaza increased to 44 percent in the second quarter of 2010.

Israeli officials stated that the blockade, an unlawful form of collective punishment against residents of an occupied territory, would remain in place until Hamas releases soldier Gilad Shalit who was captured in 2006. Israel is Gaza's major source of electricity (Egypt supplies some as well) and sole source of fuel, which Israel does not permit from other sources. In addition, Gaza's sole power plant operated at low capacity due to the PA's failure to pay Israel for industrial fuel shipments. Gaza residents suffered daily blackouts lasting 8 to 12 hours.

Israeli forces regularly shot at Gaza residents up to 1.5 kilometers from the armistice line, creating a "no-go" zone that comprises 30 percent of Gaza's agricultural land. The Israeli navy regularly shot at Palestinian fishing boats that sailed more than two nautical miles from the coast, prohibiting access to some 85 percent of Gaza's maritime area.

Egypt shares responsibility for the blockade by restricting the movement of goods and people at the Rafah crossing it controls on Gaza's southern border. Egypt eased movement restrictions in June for Palestinians needing medical care or with foreign passports and visas, but not others, and continued to restrict imports and exports of goods.

Hamas's rocket attacks from Gaza greatly diminished since 2009. As of October Palestinian armed groups in Gaza had fired 75 largely locally made rockets at population centers in Israel during 2010. In March Ansar al-Sunna, a previously unknown armed group in Gaza, claimed responsibility for a rocket attack that killed a Thai migrant worker in Israel. Israeli police reported that at least four mortars containing white phosphorus were fired from Gaza.

Hamas released two reports claiming that rocket attacks into Israel during "Operation Cast Lead" targeted military objectives, and that civilian casualties were unintended. These claims were belied by repeated attacks toward population centers by rockets that cannot be targeted with any precision and by statements from Palestinian armed groups and leaders indicating an intent to harm civilians as reprisals for Israeli attacks. Rocket, mortar, or other attacks on civilians are never justified under the laws of war, even as reprisals. In September the UN found that Hamas had failed to conduct credible investigations into unlawful rocket attacks or the killings or mistreatment of alleged collaborators or political rivals.

The Hamas Interior Ministry carried out, for the first time, five judicial death sentences, all by firing squad. Three of the men executed had been sentenced to death by military courts for collaboration with Israel, after detentions and trials that violated due process. Hamas civil and military courts also sentenced a further six men to death.

The internal security service of the Interior Ministry and Hamas police in Gaza allegedly tortured 132 people as of August 31, according to complaints received by the Independent Commission for Human Rights (ICHR), a Palestinian rights body.

Hamas continued to detain incommunicado Israeli soldier Gilad Shalit, captured in June 2006, subjecting him to cruel and inhuman treatment by refusing to allow him to communicate with his family or receive visits by the International Committee of the Red Cross.

Hamas police continued to harass, detain, and in some cases torture people suspected of "morality" offenses, including homosexuality and extra-marital sex, and to arbitrarily close or restrict businesses that allowed unmarried and unrelated men and women to "mix." The Interior Ministry closed six NGOs in Rafah in June, and closed a French NGO that provided medical care in August.

West Bank

Palestinian Authority

Complaints of torture committed by West Bank PA security services increased in 2010, with the Independent Commission for Human Rights receiving 106 complaints as of September.

PA courts have not found any security officers responsible for torture or arbitrary detention. In the one case brought to trial, concerning the death of Haitham Amr, 33, after his arrest by the General Intelligence Service (GIS) in 2009, a PA military court ordered the GIS to pay compensation to the family but acquitted all five officers charged with Amr's death due to "lack of evidence" of torture, despite an autopsy confirming the cause of death was "directly due to torture."

The PA's security services arbitrarily prevented or violently dispersed numerous nonviolent protests and press conferences during the year, and assaulted and arbitrarily detained journalists covering the incidents.

Israel

Israeli forces in the West Bank killed at least seven Palestinian civilians as of October. According to B'Tselem, those killed, including two young men collecting scrap metal and two children participating in a demonstration inside their village, posed no danger to Israeli military forces or civilians.

Israeli settlers destroyed or damaged mosques, olive trees, cars, and other Palestinian property, and physically assaulted Palestinians. In October the UN reported 204 attacks by settlers resulting in Palestinian injuries or property damage, almost double the previous year's number. Israeli authorities arrested numerous settlers but convicted few.

Home Demolitions and Evacuations

As of October Israeli authorities had demolished 285 Palestinian homes and other buildings in the West Bank (including East Jerusalem), displacing 340 people, on the grounds that the structures were built without permits; in practice

ISRAEL/OCCUPIED PALESTINIAN TERRITORIES

"I Lost Everything"

Israel's Unlawful Destruction of Property
during Operation Cast Lead

HUMAN
RIGHTS
WATCH

such permits are almost impossible for Palestinians to obtain, whereas a separate planning process available only to settlers grants new construction permits much more readily. Israeli authorities repeatedly demolished the community of al-Farsiye in the northern Jordan Valley, displacing approximately 113 people for living in a "closed military zone." Some of the displaced families had been living there since at least the 1960s.

Settlers also continued to take over Palestinian homes in East Jerusalem, including based on laws that recognize Jewish ownership claims there from before 1948 but that bar Palestinian ownership claims from that period in West Jerusalem.

From November 26, 2009, to September 26, 2010, Israeli authorities "froze" new residential construction in settlements, not including East Jerusalem or roughly 2,000 homes that had already broken ground, or public buildings and infrastructure.

Freedom of Movement

Israel maintained onerous restrictions on the movement of Palestinians in the West Bank, especially in "Area C" which is under exclusive Israeli control. It removed some closure obstacles, but more than 500 remained.

Israel continued construction of the wall or separation barrier. Some 85 percent of the barrier's route falls within the West Bank, placing many settlements on the "Israeli" side of the barrier. The barrier's confiscation of private land separated many farmers and pastoralists from their lands.

Arbitrary Detention and Detention of Children as Adults

Israeli military justice authorities arbitrarily detained Palestinians who advocated non-violent protest against Israeli settlements and the route of the separation barrier. In October a military court sentenced Abdallah Abu Rahme, from the village of Bil'in, to one year in prison on charges of inciting violence and organizing illegal demonstrations, largely on the basis of coerced statements by children. In January the Israeli military released anti-wall activist Muhammad Othman, after detaining him for 113 days without charge.

While Israeli courts define Israelis under 18 years of age as children in accordance with international standards, Israeli military courts continue to treat Palestinians over the age of 16 as "adults," and sentence them as adults according to their age at sentencing even if they were children at the time of the offense. Israel detained at least 286 children under 18, including 20 under the age of 15, as of September. Human rights groups reported dozens of cases in which Israeli authorities detained and questioned Palestinian children without a family member present or access to a lawyer, as required by law, and allegedly mistreated them in custody to coerce them to sign confessions in Hebrew, which they did not understand.

As of September Israel held 189 Palestinians in administrative detention without charge.

Israel

Bedouin citizens of Israel suffered discriminatory home demolitions. From July to October police and the Israel Land Administration destroyed the Bedouin village of Al-Araqib six times, displacing 300 people. At the time residents were contesting in court the state's claims that they had never owned lands in the area. Some 90,000 Bedouin live in "unrecognized" villages with no basic services and at risk of demolitions.

Israel also refused to recognize the legal status of thousands of homes owned by Palestinian citizens of Israel, including the 600-person village of Dahmash in central Israel, which without legal status lacks any basic services. While residents legally own the land on which their homes sit, Israel refuses to rezone the land from its current agricultural status to residential, rendering their homes illegal.

There are an estimated 200,000 migrant workers in Israel, many of whom work in abusive conditions; employers' withholding of wages and underpayment is also reportedly common. The majority of workers are indebted to recruiting agencies and beholden to a single employer for their livelihood, and are unable to transfer their employment without their employer's consent. The government has deported migrant workers and their children born in Israel, pursuant to policies that restrict migrant workers from forming families.

Key International Actors

Israel is the largest overall recipient of foreign aid from the United States since World War II, receiving US$2.775 billion in military aid in 2010. The Obama administration pushed for a resumption of direct peace negotiations between Israel and the PA in September, and offered Israel additional aid to renew a partial "freeze" on settlement construction. The US continued to train and equip Palestinian security forces, providing $350 million for security and program assistance and an additional $150 million to the PA in direct budgetary support, while the EU gave the PA €230 million ($315 million) as of October.

Both the HRC and the UN General Assembly passed follow-up resolutions calling for Israel and Hamas to investigate serious laws-of-war violations. The PA, apparently due to external pressure related to negotiations with Israel, conspicuously failed to refer a Human Rights Council expert report on accountability measures after the Gaza war to higher-level UN bodies for consideration.

JORDAN

King Abdullah dissolved parliament on November 24, 2009, halfway through its four-year term, setting political rights back in 2010. The government ruled by decree through most of 2010, pending new elections scheduled for November 9.

In a missed opportunity for refom, the government on May 18, 2010, issued a new election law that maintained higher parliamentary representation for sparsely populated rural areas– where mainly tribes loyal to the government live–at the expense of urban population centers, where most Jordanians of Palestinian origin live.

A new law decreed on June 16 increased the powers of the Ministry of Justice and diminished judicial independence, over 100 judges said in a protest.

For the first time, a Jordanian court accepted a civil case by an alleged victim of torture demanding compensation, but at this writing has not yet ruled on it. Jordan retains the death penalty but since 2006 has observed a moratorium on its use.

Jordan's General Intelligence Department (GID) continued to influence decisions in most aspects of Jordanian public life, including academic freedom, government appointments, and the issuing of residency permits to non-Jordanians and "good conduct" certificates required for Jordanians seeking work abroad. The GID harassed citizens, including one former senior government advisor, over their criticism of government policies by summoning them for interrogation and threatening them with unspecified harm.

On April 25 the GID re-arrested Jordanian citizen Samir al-Barq, and detained him until summarily deporting him to the Israeli-occupied West Bank on July 11, where Israeli intelligence forces immediately arrested him. On July 18 al-Barq was charged by an Israeli military court with membership in and training with an enemy organization and planning terrorist attacks. The GID had previously detained al-Barq for over two years between 2006 and 2008 without charge.

Deprivation of Nationality

In violation of Jordanian and international law, Jordan continued to arbitrarily withdraw Jordanian nationality from Jordanians of Palestinian origin, rendering them stateless and without rights to education, health care, property, or residency in Jordan. Children of men stripped of their nationality automatically lost theirs too, even if they were adults. The Interior Ministry said it withdrew the nationality of 2,700 Jordanians between 2004 and 2008, but did not discuss numbers for 2009 or 2010.

Torture, Arbitrary Detention, and Administrative Detention

Torture, routine and widespread in recent years, continues, in particular at police stations, where complaints about ill-treatment increased in 2009 and again in 2010, according to the National Center for Human Rights (NCHR).

Perpetrators of torture enjoy near-total impunity, because the police run the system for accountability in places of detention. The process for redress begins with a deficient complaint mechanism, continues with lackluster investigations and prosecutions, and ends in Police Court, where two of three judges on the panel are police officers appointed by the police (in 2010 a change in law added one judge from the regular courts, where judges are more independent). Police Court tends to impose lenient sentences, if any.

Under the Crime Prevention Law, provincial governors can detain people administratively. The law requires governors to have evidence of criminal conduct, but in practice, this is not always the case. Administrative detention is frequently used to circumvent the obligation to present persons suspected of crimes, usually theft or disorderly conduct, to the prosecutor within 24 hours. It is also used to overrule judges who have released suspects on bail. In January 2010, the NCHR reported 16,000 administrative detentions in 2009, up from 14,000 in 2008, and adding up to around one in five prison inmates over the year.

JORDAN

Stateless Again

Palestinian-Origin Jordanians Deprived of their Nationality

HUMAN
RIGHTS
WATCH

Freedom of Expression and Assembly

Criticism of the king, defamation of government officials and institutions, and comments deemed to offend Islam or diminish the prestige of the state or harm international relations carry heavy penalties under the penal code. A June 1 revision of the penal code increased the penalties for some speech offenses. The August 29 Law on Information System Crimes extends these provisions to online expression. Article 5 of the 2007 Press and Publications Law requires publications to adhere to "Islamic values."

On July 28 the military prosecutor at the state security court detained university student Hatim al-Shuli and charged him with insulting King Abdullah and "causing national strife," on the basis of a poem al-Shuli denied writing. On September 8 al-Shuli was released and the charges dropped. In July, the state security court sent Imad al-'Ash to prison for two years for insulting the king in electronic messages sent to a jihadist website.

Under the Public Gatherings Law of 2008, the governor may deny permission—without providing a justification—to hold any meeting on public affairs, including demonstrations. On July 25, police briefly arrested Amina Tariq under the Public Gatherings Law for conducting an unlicensed peaceful street protest to promote vegetarianism by covering herself in lettuce. Article 164 of the penal code also prohibits unlawful gatherings of seven or more persons with the intention to commit a crime or to disturb public order. The State Security Court on July 27 used that provision to sentence Muhammad al-Sunaid, head of the Committee of Day Laborers at Government Offices, to three months in prison for peacefully demonstrating against the dismissal of day laborers at the Agriculture Ministry and heckling the minister at a May 10 event in Madaba.

On December 16, 2010, the grace period ends for civic organizations of any type to comply with a restrictive 2009 Law on Charitable Societies requiring groups registered as nonprofit companies under the less restrictive Companies Law to incorporate as charities under the new law, which grants the government discretionary power to reject applications for new NGOs and to deny their requests for foreign funding, and wide powers to close existing NGOs.

Women's and Girls' Rights

A new draft personal status law introduced in April abolishes a 2001 law providing women with the right to divorce their husbands without having to show fault (khul). It also continues to allow the marriage of girls as young as 15, if a committee of Islamic judges approves. In the two years prior to July 2010, 14,000 Jordanian girls under 18 were married, Agence France-Presse reported.

On May 3, 2010, the government decreed amendments to the penal code to ensure that perpetrators of so-called "honor" crimes receive the full penalty of the law for killing female relatives suspected of illicit relationships. The new article 345 *bis* excludes consideration of mitigating circumstances for committing crimes in a "state of fury" (art. 98) if the victim is under 15 or female. According to Rana Husseini of *The Jordan Times*, there were 12 recorded "honor" killings in Jordan from January to November of 2010.

Changes to the penal code also stiffened penalties for rape from 10 to 15 years in prison and, in a new provision, stipulated 20 years of hard labor if the victim was between 15 and 18 years old. New penalties for physical assaults that result in the death of minors or women were set at a minimum of 12 years in prison.

Labor Rights

Unionized Jordanians may only strike with government permission; non-Jordanians, although allowed to join unions since 2008, are not allowed to strike.

New regulations on migrant domestic workers, issued in August 2009 following the inclusion of domestic workers in the Labor Law in July 2008, restricted essential rights, such as freedom of movement. A Ministry of Labor committee charged with solving labor disputes failed to secure unpaid salaries of domestic workers, or adequately protect workers from working long hours and from remaining trapped in abusive households.

Investigators pursued 34 cases under Jordan's Anti-Human Trafficking Law of March 2009 not all of which were prosecuted. The courts had not yet adjudicated the five cases filed by the Amman prosecutor as of July.

Key International Actors

The United States concluded a five-year agreement, starting in 2010, to provide Jordan with US$360 million in economic assistance annually, and $300 million in foreign military financing. This represents an increase over previous annual requests by the US administration for aid to Jordan, but in the past those were often supplemented with ad hoc aid, which raised actual US aid to over $1 billion in 2008 (compared with the European Union's €265 million, or $369 million for 2007 to 2010).

The EU in November 2009 affirmed its commitment to upgrade relations with Jordan and in May 2010 signed a €223 million ($310million) aid package over three years from 2011 to 2013. One of four priority areas is to address democracy, human rights, media, and justice. This 12 percent increase in EU aid comes despite a lack of progress, and a number of reverses during 2010, in these areas.

KUWAIT

Kuwait's human rights record drew increased international scrutiny in 2010, as proposed reforms for stateless persons, women's rights, and domestic workers remained stalled. Freedom of expression deteriorated as the government continued criminal prosecutions for libel and slander, and charged at least one individual with state security crimes for expressing nonviolent political opinions.

Discrimination against women continues in nationality, residency, and family laws, and in their economic rights, though women gained the right to vote and run for office in 2005.

Kuwait continues to exclude the stateless Bidun people from full citizenship, despite their longstanding roots in Kuwaiti territory. The Bidun also face discrimination accessing education, health care, and employment, as well as violations of their right to marry and establish a family because they are not allowed to register births, marriages, or deaths.

Kuwait significantly advanced workers' rights in 2010 through a new private sector labor law. Minister of Labor Mohammad al-'Afasi announced in September 2010 the government would abolish the sponsorship system in February 2011 and supervise migrant labor recruitment through a government authority. However the new law continued to exclude domestic workers, who make up approximately one-third of the private sector workforce and face recurring abuses. Labor ministry officials informed Human Rights Watch that plans for sponsorship reform also exclude domestic workers.

In May 2010, at the United Nations Human Rights Council in Geneva, Kuwait promised to sign the Convention on the Rights of Persons with Disabilities and to establish an independent human rights institution based on the Paris Principles. At this writing the government has not made definite progress towards either measure.

Women's and Girls' Rights

Kuwait's nationality law denies Kuwaiti women married to non-Kuwaiti men the right to pass their nationality on to their children and spouses, a right enjoyed by Kuwaiti men married to foreign spouses. The law also discriminates against women in residency rights, allowing the spouses of Kuwaiti men but not of Kuwaiti women to be in Kuwait without employment and to qualify for citizenship after 10 years of marriage.

In 2005 Kuwaiti women won the right to vote and to run in elections, and in May 2009 voters elected four women to parliament. In April 2010 an administrative court rejected a female Kuwaiti law graduate's application to become a public prosecutor based on her gender. The advertisement for the position was open to male candidates only. The presiding judge found that article two of Kuwait's constitution, which cites Islam as the state religion and Islamic Sharia as "a main source of legislation," prevented women from holding prosecutorial positions. Kuwaiti women are also denied the right to become judges.

No government data exists on the prevalence of violence against women in Kuwait, although local media regularly report incidents of violence.

Bidun

Kuwait hosts up to 120,000 stateless persons, known as the Bidun. The state classifies these long-term residents as "illegal residents," maintaining that most do not hold legitimate claims to Kuwaiti nationality and hide "true" nationalities from Iraq, Saudi Arabia, or Iran.

Due to their statelessness, the Bidun cannot freely leave and return to Kuwait; the government issues them temporary passports at its discretion, mostly valid for only one journey. Furthermore the Bidun face restrictions in their access to public and private sector employment, as well as to healthcare. Bidun children may not enroll in free government schools. The Bidun also cannot register births, marriages, or deaths, obstructing their rights to family life.

Lawmakers in December 2009 failed to reach the quorum required to discuss a 2007 draft law that would grant the Bidun civil rights and permanent residency, but not nationality. In January 2010 the assembly tasked the Supreme Council for Higher Planning with reporting on the Bidun situation. Bidun from Kuwait continued to seek and receive asylum abroad in countries including the United Kingdom and New Zealand, based upon their treatment by Kuwaiti government authorities.

Freedom of Expression and Media

Freedom of expression markedly deteriorated in 2010. The government continued criminally prosecuting individuals based on nonviolent political speech, denied academics permission to enter the country for conferences and speeches, and cracked down on public gatherings. In April state security forces summarily deported over 30 Egyptian legal residents of Kuwait after some of them gathered to support Egyptian reform advocate Mohammed El Baradei.

In May prominent writer and lawyer Mohammad al-Jassim was detained for over 40 days and charged with "instigating to overthrow the regime, ...slight to the personage of the emir [the ruler of Kuwait],... [and] instigating to dismantle the foundations of Kuwaiti society" over his blog posts criticizing the prime minister. A judge released al-Jassim in June and adjourned the case until October.

Sexual Orientation and Gender Identity

Kuwait continues to criminalize consensual homosexual conduct, in contravention of international best practices. Article 193 of Kuwait's penal code punishes consensual sexual intercourse between men over the age of 21, with up to seven years imprisonment (10 years, if under 21 years old). Article 198 of the penal code criminalized "imitating the appearance of a member of the opposite sex," imposing arbitrary restrictions upon individuals' rights to privacy and free expression. The police continued to arrest and detain transgendered women on the basis of the law, many of whom have previously reported abuse while in detention.

Migrant Worker Rights

More than two million foreign nationals reside in Kuwait, constituting an estimated 80 percent of the country's workforce. Many experience exploitative labor conditions, including private employers who illegally confiscate their passports or do not pay their wages. Migrant workers often pay exorbitant recruitment fees to labor agents in their home countries and must then work off their debt in Kuwait.

For the first time since 1954 the government passed a new private sector labor law in February, which provides workers with more protections on wages, working hours, and safety. However, it does not establish monitoring mechanisms and continues to exclude the country's 660,000 domestic workers who come chiefly from Indonesia, Sri Lanka, and the Philippines and work and live inside employers' homes in Kuwait. No law provides them with a weekly rest day, limits their working hours, or sets a minimum wage. Many domestic workers complain of confinement in the house; long work hours without rest; months or years of unpaid wages; and verbal, physical, and sexual abuse.

A major barrier to redressing labor abuses is the *kafala* (sponsorship) system, which ties a migrant worker's legal residence in Kuwait to his or her employer, who serves as a "sponsor." Migrant workers who have worked for their sponsor less than three years can only transfer with their sponsor's consent (migrant domestic workers always require consent). If a worker leaves their sponsoring employer, including when fleeing abuse, the employer can register the worker as "absconding", a criminal offense that most often leads to detention and deportation. In September the government announced plans to abolish the sponsorship system in February 2011, but provided no details about the system that would replace it, or whether it would include migrant domestic workers.

Key International Actors

The United States, in the 2010 State Department Trafficking in Persons report, classified Kuwait as Tier 3—among the most problematic countries—for the fourth year in a row. However, the US chose not to impose sanctions for Kuwait's failure to combat human trafficking. President Barack Obama determined that sanctions would affect US$2.4 billion in projected foreign military sales to Kuwait and would restrict a US$4 million grant to the Middle East Partnership Initiative, considered a key tool for promoting democracy and respect for human rights in the country.

In April 2010 UN High Commissioner for Human Rights Navanethem Pillay visited Kuwait and spotlighted the sponsorship system and statelessness as pressing human rights concerns.

KUWAIT

Walls at Every Turn

Abuse of Migrant Domestic Workers through
Kuwait's Sponsorship System

HUMAN
RIGHTS
WATCH

LEBANON

Lebanese officials showed increased willingness to discuss human rights concerns in 2010, but failed to implement many of the reforms needed to improve the country's record.

The authorities rejected a proposed law that would grant women the right to pass nationality to their husbands and children, and despite promises to the contrary, made no efforts to shed light on the fate of people who disappeared during the 1975-1990 civil war. In August parliament enacted a long-awaited amendment to ease Palestinian refugees' access to the labor market, but the reform fell short of expectations.

Tension increased in the second half of the year over the United Nations tribunal tasked with investigating the killing in 2005 of former Prime Minister Rafik Hariri, amid fears the country would again plunge into turmoil.

Torture, Ill-Treatment, and Prison Conditions

Lebanese law prohibits torture, but accountability for torture remains elusive. A number of detainees, especially suspected spies for Israel and armed Jihadists, told Human Rights Watch that their interrogators tortured them in a number of detention facilities, including the Ministry of Defense and the Information Branch of the Internal Security Forces. Lebanon has not yet established a national preventive mechanism to visit and monitor places of detention, as required under the Optional Protocol to the Convention against Torture (OPCAT), which it ratified in 2008.

Conditions in prisons remain poor, with overcrowding and lack of proper medical care a persistent problem. According to the Internal Security Forces, pretrial detainees represent around two-thirds of the total number of detainees.

Lebanon maintained its de facto moratorium on executions, but at least five death sentences were passed in 2010. Many political leaders called for the death penalty against persons convicted of spying for Israel. In July President Michel

Suleiman, who under Lebanese law must approve every death sentence, said that he would approve death penalties issued by military tribunals.

Freedom of Expression

Despite Lebanon's vibrant media, 2010 saw increased harassment of bloggers and journalists who criticize the army and certain high-ranking officials. In March Military Intelligence briefly detained and interrogated a blogger, Khodor Salemeh, for posting a series of articles critical of the army and the three heads of state. In June security forces detained Na`im Hanna, Antoine Ramia, and Shibel Kassab for posting comments critical of the president on Facebook. An investigative judge charged them with libel, defamation, and insulting the president, but released them on bail on July 2. In August Military Intelligence summoned Hassan Oleik, a journalist with *al-Akhbar* newspaper, for writing about an alleged conversation between Defense Minister Elias Murr and the country's army commander, Jean Kahwaji, concerning a suspected Israeli spy. They released him a few hours later. In August Military Intelligence also briefly detained Ismael Sheikh Hassan, an urban planner, over an article he published criticizing public authorities and the army for their handling of the reconstruction of the Nahr al-Bared refugee camp.

Refugees

The estimated 300,000 Palestinian refugees in Lebanon live in appalling social and economic conditions. In August Lebanon's parliament amended its labor law to facilitate the ability of Palestinian refugees to obtain work permits by exempting them from reciprocity requirements, eliminating work permit fees, and giving them limited social security benefits. However, the reform did nothing to remove restrictions that bar Palestinians from working in at least 25 professions requiring syndicate membership, including law, medicine, and engineering. It also leaves in place a work permit system that relies on employer cooperation, a system that has previously relegated most Palestinians to black market labor. Palestinian refugees are still subject to a discriminatory law introduced in 2001 preventing them from registering property.

Palestinians from the Nahr al-Bared refugee camp—destroyed in the 2007 battle between Lebanon's army and the armed Fatah al-Islam group—continue to live in dire conditions. Reconstruction efforts have been delayed, and UN Relief and Work Agency reported the first set of rebuilt houses will not be delivered before March 2011. The Lebanese army restricts movement to the camp by maintaining checkpoints around it.

According to government sources, the Ministry of Interior resumed issuing temporary identification papers to Palestinians in Lebanon who are without legal documentation as part of a plan to improve the legal status of at least 3,000 non-ID Palestinians who had previously lived in constant fear of arrest. The ministry had stopped the process in early 2009, citing fraudulent applications.

As of September 30 there were 9,768 non-Palestinian refugees and asylum-seekers registered with the United Nations High Commissioner for Refugees (UNHCR), more than 80 percent of them from Iraq. Since Lebanon has not ratified the 1951 Refugee Convention, it does not give legal effect to UNHCR's recognition of refugees and generally treats most as illegal immigrants subject to arrest. As of October 31, 54 recognized refugees or asylum seekers remained in detention solely for not holding proper residency papers.

Migrant Workers' Rights

Migrant domestic workers (MDW) face exploitation and abuse by employers, including excessive work hours, non-payment of wages, confinement in the workplace, and in some cases physical and sexual abuse. MDWs suing their employers for abuse face legal obstacles and risk imprisonment and deportation due to the restrictive visa system. In June the Ministry of Labor instituted a hotline to receive workers' complaints. MDWs continue to die in high numbers, with eight deaths in August alone. Most are classified as suicides.

Male migrant workers—mostly from Syria and Egypt—working in construction and other manual jobs face hazardous working conditions and are regular targets for robbery and violent attack. State authorities have not made any concerted effort to protect them or bring perpetrators to justice.

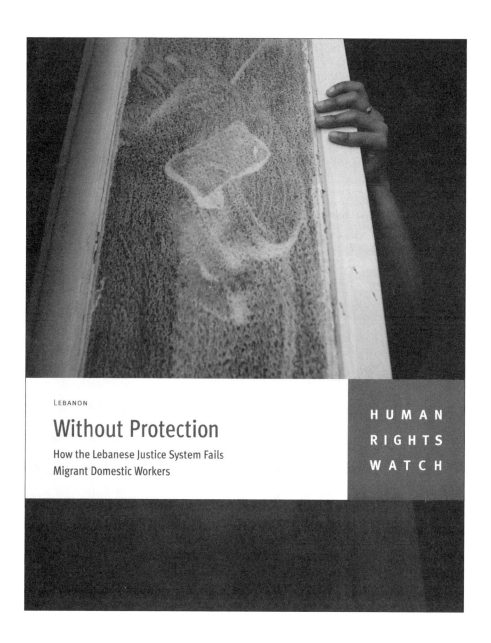

LEBANON

Without Protection

How the Lebanese Justice System Fails
Migrant Domestic Workers

HUMAN
RIGHTS
WATCH

Detention of Foreigners after their Sentence

According to the Internal Security Forces, around 13 percent of detainees in Lebanese prisons were foreigners who had finished serving their sentence. The group included asylum seekers and refugees who cannot safely return to their countries. Their ongoing detention is illegal. In September 2010 Lebanon's Council of Ministers adopted a decree with the stated purpose of reducing the number of foreigners detained beyond their sentence. However, the decree has not yet been implemented and will not address concerns about the detention of asylum seekers and refugees who do not hold proper residency papers.

Women's and Girls' Rights

Discriminatory provisions continue to exist in personal status laws, nationality laws, and penal laws relating to violence in the family. In May the Council of Ministers issued a decree expanding the right of children and husbands of Lebanese women to reside in Lebanon, but Lebanese women, unlike Lebanese men, still cannot pass pass their nationality to foreign husbands and children.

In April the Council of Ministers submitted to parliament a new bill that aims to criminalize domestic violence. The bill requires anyone who witnesses domestic violence to report it and obliges perpetrators to provide the plaintiff with alternative living arrangements, an allowance, and to pay medical expenses.

Legacy of Past Conflicts and Wars

Lebanon deposited its ratification of the Convention on Cluster Munitions with the UN on November 5, 2010. The submunition "duds" left behind by Israel's 2006 bombardment of southern Lebanon continue to harm civilians: according to the official Lebanon Mine Action Center, such duds have killed at least 45 and wounded more than 300 since 2006.

Despite a 2009 pledge to work to uncover the fate of the Lebanese and other nationals who "disappeared" during and after the 1975-1990 Lebanese civil war and to ratify the International Convention for the Protection of all Persons from Enforced Disappearances, the government took no steps on these issues in 2010.

An official joint Syrian-Lebanese committee established in May 2005 to investigate cases of Lebanese who "disappeared" at the hands of Syrian security forces has not published any findings at this writing.

Hariri Tribunal

Tension over the intention of the UN's international tribunal to try those responsible for killing former Prime Minister Hariri in 2005 and other politically motivated assassinations increased in anticipation of possible indictments that may implicate members of Hezbollah. Hezbollah called for a boycott of the tribunal, accusing it of being an "Israeli project."

Key International Actors

Multiple international and regional actors compete for influence in Lebanon. Regionally, Syria, Iran, and Saudi Arabia maintain a strong influence on Lebanese politics through their local allies.

France, the United States, and the European Union provide assistance for a wide range of programs, including armed forces training, torture prevention seminars, and civil society activities. However these countries have not fully used their leverage to push Lebanon to adopt concrete measures to improve its human rights record, such as investigating specific allegations of torture or adopting laws that respect the rights of refugees or migrant workers.

UN peacekeepers are still present in large numbers at Lebanon's volatile southern border with Israel.

LIBYA

Government control and repression of civil society remain the norm in Libya, with little progress made on promised human rights reforms. While releases of large numbers of Islamist prisoners continued, 2010 saw stagnation on key issues such as penal code reform, freedom of association, and accountability for the Abu Salim prison massacre in 1996.

Libya maintains harsh restrictions on freedom of assembly and expression, including penal code provisions that criminalize "insulting public officials" or "opposing the ideology of the Revolution," although there has been slightly more media debate in recent years, particularly online.

Arbitrary Detention and Prisoner Releases

An estimated 213 prisoners who have served their sentences or been acquitted by Libyan courts remain imprisoned under Internal Security Agency orders. The agency, under the jurisdiction of the General People's Committee for Public Security, controls the Ain Zara and Abu Salim prisons, where it holds political and "security" detainees. It has refused to carry out judicial orders to free these prisoners, despite calls from the secretary of justice for their release.

In March Libyan authorities released 214 prisoners, including 80 of a group of 330 detained despite the fact that courts had acquitted them and ordered their release. Some former prisoners have received compensation from the state for years of arbitrary detention. Others are still struggling to receive compensation, and many are banned from travelling outside Libya.

The 1996 Abu Salim Prison Massacre and Enforced Disappearances

The authorities have not made public any account of the June 1996 Abu Salim prison massacre in which 1,200 prisoners were killed, nor have they held anyone responsible. On September 6, 2009, the acting secretary of defense established a seven-judge investigation panel, headed by a former military tribunal judge, to conduct an investigation. The panel's final report was due in March 2010, but it

remains unpublished at this writing. Libyan authorities offered compensation of 200,000 dinars (US$162,000) to families who agree to relinquish all legal claims, but most of the victims' families in Benghazi, Libya's second-largest city, refused to accept compensation on those terms and continued to call for criminal accountability. In June families reported that local authorities and security officials were pressuring them to relinquish their compensation claims.

There are still dozens of unresolved disappearance cases in Libya, including those of Libyan opposition members Jaballa Hamed Matar and Izzat al-Megaryef, whom Egyptian security arrested in 1990 in Cairo. Their families later learned that Egypt had handed them over to Libyan security officials, who detained them in Abu Salim prison. Prominent Lebanese Shia cleric Imam Musa al-Sadr disappeared in Libya 32 years ago; his fate remains unknown.

Freedom of Expression, Association, and Assembly

While there was a gradual opening for greater debate and discussion in the media during the past five years, especially on the internet, 2010 saw a general regression in freedom of expression, which remains severely curtailed. In January the Libyan government blocked access to at least seven independent and opposition Libyan websites based abroad, including *Libya Al Youm*, *Al Manara*, and *Libya Al Mostakbal*. Journalists face harassment for expressing criticism, and lawsuits and criminal sanctions for defamation. In February security officers briefly arrested four journalists from the radio station *Good Evening Benghazi*, and authorities banned the program from airing. In November Internal Security officers arrested 20 journalists from the Libya Press agency for three days and suspended the publication of *Oea,* both established by Saif al-Islam al-Gaddafi, the Libyan leader's son.

In April the Libyan State Security Court acquitted dissident Jamal al-Haji of "insulting judicial authorities" and freed him after four months in prison. Al-Haji's arrest stemmed from his public complaint about the torture and inhumane conditions that he endured during two years as a political prisoner from 2007 to 2009, and the travel ban he has faced since his release. Article 178 of the penal code carries penalties up to life imprisonment for disseminating information considered to "tarnish [the country's] reputation or undermine confidence in it abroad."

Negative comments about Libyan leader Col. Mu`ammar al-Gaddafi are frequently punished, and self-censorship is rife.

Libya has no independent NGOs and Libyan laws severely restrict freedom of association. Law 71 bans any group activity opposing the ideology of the 1969 revolution, and the penal code imposes the death penalty on those who join such groups. The government has refused to allow independent journalists' and lawyers' organizations. The only organization able to criticize human rights violations publicly is the Human Rights Society of the Gaddafi Foundation, which is chaired by Saif al-Islam al-Gaddafi.

Demonstrations are also illegal, although those by families of victims of the Abu Salim prison killings continued in Benghazi in 2010. While the government allowed the demonstrations, some of the organizers faced harassment, intimidation, and arrest.

Treatment of Foreigners

Libya continues to abuse and mistreat non-Libyan migrants caught trying to leave the country by boat. Libya also refuses to recognize the presence of refugees in the country. In April Libyan Foreign Secretary Moussa Koussa said that Libya "does not have any refugees but only illegal migrants who break the laws." In July the government said that there were 3 million irregular migrants in Libya. A new law on "Illegal Migration" criminalizes trafficking of migrants, but does not provide protections for refugees.

On June 28 a group of detained Eritrean migrants tried to escape after Libyan officials allowed Eritrean embassy officials to take their photos and forced them to complete forms, raising fear of deportation. In response, Libyan authorities transported 245 detained Eritrean asylum seekers from Misrata to another detention center in al-Biraq, north of Sabha, in an apparent attempt to deport them. At least 11 of this group were Eritreans whom Italy had interdicted at sea and forced back to Libya without giving them an opportunity to claim asylum. After an international outcry, Libya released this group but did not give them any support or protection. They remain in Libya.

Libya has no asylum law, has not signed the 1951 Refugee Convention, and has no formal working agreement with the United Nations High Commissioner for Refugees (UNHCR). Although UNHCR had partial and ad hoc access to detained migrants for two years, in June Libya ordered UNHCR to close its office and expelled its representative, although it later allowed the agency to continue processing resettlement cases.

Rights of the Amazigh Minority

The Amazigh (Berbers), Libya's main cultural and linguistic minority, face discrimination and harassment by security officials. Libyan authorities do not allow schools to teach, or media to use, the Amazigh language. Libyan law also bans use of non-Arab Amazigh names on all official documentation. In January Colonel Gaddafi criticized Amazigh New Year celebrations as un-Islamic and not recognized by the state, saying they disrupted national unity; an Amazigh organization reported that at least two people had been arrested in connection with trying to organize celebrations. The Amazigh website *Libya Imal* was among those blocked by authorities in January. In August Internal Security officers arrested Amazigh activist Ali Abu al-Seoud and detained him incommunicado for eight days in connection with his online writing on Amazigh rights. They released him without charge.

Women's Rights

In January the General People's Committee adopted Law No. 24 of 2010 on the Provisions of Libyan Nationality, which permits the passing of Libyan nationality to children born to Libyan mothers and foreign fathers, but leaves the interpretation of the provision to implementing regulations that the committee has not yet issued.

The Libyan government continues to detain women and girls indefinitely without due process in "social rehabilitation" facilities for suspected transgression of moral codes. Many women and girls detained in these facilities have committed no crime, or have already served a sentence. Some are there only because they were raped, and are now ostracized for staining their family's "honor."

Key International Actors

In May member states elected Libya to a seat on the UN Human Rights Council. Libya's election was uncontested because the African Group of States presented the same number of candidates as there were vacancies for this election. In November Libya's human rights record came under review at the Council during Libya's first Universal Periodic Review. The government accepted 66 general recommendations but rejected 25 other concrete recommendations on revising penal code articles and publishing a list of the disappeared.

In October the European Union and Libya concluded an agreement on an agenda for migration cooperation, which made no mention of the lack of an asylum law or protection mechanisms in Libya. Negotiations over the EU-Libya Framework agreement resumed after Libya scrapped its ban on the entry of EU nationals.

In December 2009 Human Rights Watch released its "Truth and Justice Can't Wait" report at a news conference in Tripoli, the first time an independent human rights organization had been allowed to publicly criticize Libya's human rights record in the capital.

MOROCCO AND WESTERN SAHARA

In 2010 human rights conditions in Morocco were mixed, and in some aspects, decidedly poor. The government used repressive legislation and complaisant courts to punish and imprison peaceful opponents, especially those who violated taboos and laws against criticizing the king and the monarchy, questioning Morocco's claim over Western Sahara, or "denigrating" Islam.

The government particularly restricts rights in the restive Western Sahara region, over which Morocco claims sovereignty, and which it administers as part of its national territory. A Western Sahara independence movement based in exile, the Popular Front for the Liberation of Saguía al-Hamra and Río de Oro (the Polisario Front), demands a public referendum that includes the option of independence. Over the years the Moroccan authorities have imprisoned many peaceful advocates of this position while instead proposing autonomy under Moroccan sovereignty.

Terrorism and Counterterrorism

Hundreds of suspected Islamist extremists arrested in the aftermath of the Casablanca bombings of May 2003 remain in prison. Many were convicted in unfair trials after being held in secret detention and subjected to mistreatment and sometimes torture. Some were sentenced to death, a punishment that Morocco has not abolished even though it has not been carried out since 1993. Since further terrorist attacks in 2007, police have arrested hundreds more suspected militants, many of whom were convicted and imprisoned for belonging to a "terrorist network" or preparing to join "the jihad" in Iraq or elsewhere.

Intelligence agencies continued to interrogate terrorism suspects at an unacknowledged detention center at Temara, near Rabat, according to reports from detainees. Many suspects alleged that police tortured them under interrogation, while holding them in pre-charge custody for longer than the 12-day maximum the law provides for terrorism cases. For example, several men arrested in and around Casablanca in March and April for suspected al Qaeda links told Human Rights Watch that plainclothes agents who showed no warrants or identification arrested, blindfolded, and transported them to a secret location, which they

MOROCCO

"Stop Looking for Your Son"

Illegal Detentions under the Counterterrorism Law

HUMAN
RIGHTS
WATCH

believe was the Temara facility, and held and interrogated them for up to 36 days before transferring them to a regular police jail. Most said that they suffered torture. The government formally denied these allegations to Human Rights Watch and stated that the arrests and detentions in these cases were conducted according to the law.

In August tapes recorded by the United States CIA were made public showing that the US had in 2002 transported terrorism suspect Ramzi Benalshibh to Morocco for interrogation in a secret Moroccan-run facility, before flying him to Guantanamo. Moroccan authorities deny operating secret jails.

Confronting Past Abuses

Following the pioneering work Morocco's Equity and Reconciliation Commission (ERC) completed in 2005, the government acknowledged responsibility for "disappearances" and other grave abuses in the past, and compensated some 16,000 victims or their relatives. However, no Moroccan officials or security force members are known to have been prosecuted for rights violations committed during the period from 1956 to 1999 that the ERC investigated, and the government has yet to implement most of the institutional reforms the ERC recommended to safeguard against future abuses. In September the government said it would convert some notorious former secret prisons into memorials for the "preservation and rehabilitation of memory."

Police Conduct and the Criminal Justice System

Courts seldom provide fair trials in cases with political overtones. Judges routinely ignore requests for medical examinations from defendants who claim to have been tortured, refuse to summon exculpatory witnesses, and convict defendants on the basis of apparently coerced confessions. On July 16 the Rabat Court of Appeals upheld the 2009 conviction of all 35 defendants—in a trial known as the Belliraj case—on charges that included forming a terrorist network. The court maintained the life sentence imposed on alleged ringleader Abdelkader Belliraj while reducing the sentences for five codefendants who were political figures to 10 years in prison. As in the first trial the appeals court based the guilty verdicts almost entirely on the defendants' "confessions" to the police, even though most of the defendants had repudiated these statements in court. The court refused to investigate the defendants' allegations of torture, detention in secret jails, and the falsification of confessions.

The authorities jailed prominent nonviolent pro-independence Sahrawi activists Ali Salem Tamek, Brahim Dahane, and Ahmed Naciri after arresting them on October 8, 2009. Four other Sahrawi activists arrested at the same time were later released pending trial. The police arrested the seven upon their return from an unprecedented public visit with the Polisario leadership in the Sahrawi refugee camps near Tindouf, Algeria. A Casablanca judge initially referred the case against the seven to a military court on the grounds that the alleged offenses included harming "external state security" by "causing harm to Morocco's territorial integrity," but nearly one year later the military judge sent the case back to civilian court on the lesser charge of "harming [Morocco's] internal security." The trial opened on October 15 and was immediately postponed as three of the defendants entered their second year in provisional detention.

Sahrawi students Abdellah Daihani and Ali Toumi left prison in April after serving six months for "insulting state institutions." Their offense consisted of proclaiming that they recognized neither the Moroccan police nor the state during a political argument with other passengers on a train.

Freedoms of Association, Assembly, and Movement

Morocco boasts thousands of independent associations, but government officials arbitrarily impede the legalization of some organizations, undermining their freedom to operate. Groups affected include some that defend the rights of Sahrawis, Amazighs (Berbers), sub-Saharan immigrants, and unemployed university graduates, as well as charitable, cultural, and educational associations whose leadership includes members of Justice and Spirituality, a nationwide movement that advocates for an Islamic state and questions the king's spiritual authority.

The government, which does not recognize Justice and Spirituality as a legal association, tolerated many of its activities but prevented others. On June 28 the police arrested seven movement members in Fez after an ex-member claimed they had abducted and tortured him. According to the suspects, the police tortured them and forced them to sign confessions without reading them first. A medical examination conducted on one of the defendants noted that he had injuries that seemed to coincide with his period in police custody. The seven men are on trial for abduction and torture at this writing.

The government generally tolerates the work of the many human rights organizations active in Rabat and Casablanca, but individual activists sometimes paid a heavy price for whistle-blowing. Chekib el-Khayari, president of the Association for Human Rights in the Rif, has been serving a three-year term since February 2009 for "gravely insulting state institutions" and minor currency violations. The authorities arrested him after he accused certain Moroccan officials of complicity in narcotics trafficking. A Casablanca appeals court on November 24, 2009 confirmed the verdict.

Retired Col.-Maj. Kaddour Terhzaz, born in 1937, remains incarcerated after a military court convicted him in a one-day trial in November 2008 for disclosing "national defense secrets," solely because of a 2005 letter he had addressed to the king that criticized what he saw as Morocco's shabby treatment of pilots who had been held as prisoners of war by the Polisario.

Authorities generally do not hamper the activities of foreign human rights groups visiting Morocco. Surveillance is tighter in Western Sahara, although authorities in El-Ayoun eased the requirement they imposed in 2009 that foreigners notify them before visiting Sahrawi activists at home.

Sahrawi activists enjoyed more freedom to travel abroad than in 2009, with fewer reports of authorities confiscating or refusing to renew their passports or preventing them from boarding flights.

Most types of outdoor gatherings require authorization from the Interior Ministry, which can refuse permission if it deems them liable to "disturb the public order." Although many public protests run their course undisturbed, baton-wielding police have brutally broken up some demonstrations. Among the most frequent targets are the protests organized across the country by chapters of the National Association of Unemployed University Graduates. For example, on March 31, security forces charged and dispersed a sit-in by the association in Nador, injuring several and briefly detaining four of the organizers.

In early October several thousand Sahrawi residents of El-Ayoun, Western Sahara, erected a tent camp outside the city to dramatize a list of economic grievances. Authorities negotiated with camp leaders but early on November 8 ordered the protesters to leave and then dismantled their tent city by force, using mostly water cannons and tear gas. They encountered some violent resistance and there were casualties among the security forces and civilians. Sahrawis in the city of El Ayoun erupted in protest the same day, with further casualties on both sides, including scores of Sahrawi men and women whom the police beat brutally while in custody. At this writing Human Rights Watch is investigating these events.

Media Freedom

Morocco's independent print and online media investigate and criticize government officials and policies but face prosecution and harassment when they cross certain lines. The press law includes prison terms for "maliciously" spreading "false information" likely to disturb the public order or for speech that is defamatory, offensive to members of the royal family, or that undermines "Islam, the institution of the monarchy, or territorial integrity," that is, Morocco's claim on Western Sahara.

The independent, provocative Arabic daily *Akhbar al-Youm* was reborn as *Akhbar al-Youm al-Maghrebiya* after a court shut the newspaper down on October 30, 2009 for publishing a cartoon that depicted a cousin of King Mohammed VI in an allegedly disrespectful fashion. However, the narrow field of serious independent news media lost key publications in 2010 with the closures, for financial reasons, of *Nichan* and *Le Journal* weeklies and *al-Jarida al-Oula* daily. The latter two had in recent years been the object of numerous prosecutions, some of them politically motivated, for defamation and other offenses.

The king on June 12 pardoned the only journalist in prison during the first half of 2010, Driss Chahtane, editor of *al-Mish'al* weekly. Chahtane had served eight months of a one year sentence for "maliciously" publishing "false news" about the king's health.

Moroccan state television provides some room for investigative reporting but little for direct criticism of the government or for dissent on key issues. In May the

Ministry of Communication announced that foreign stations, which have a large viewership in Morocco, must obtain authorization before filming outside the capital. The ministry refused for the second straight year to accredit two local Al Jazeera correspondents without providing a reason and then, on October 29, announced the suspension of the channel's activities in Morocco on the grounds that the channel "seriously distorted Morocco's image and manifestly damaged its greater interests, most notably its territorial integrity," an apparent allusion to Western Sahara.

Religious and Cultural Freedoms

During 2010 Morocco summarily expelled over 100 Protestant foreign nationals among the several hundred living legally in the country. The authorities orally informed some that they had violated laws against proselytizing, but did not charge them before forcing them to leave. In other cases, the authorities told the persons their departures were "an urgent necessity for state or public security," a legal formulation that allows immediate expulsions without charges or due process.

The Interior Ministry issued a circular in April 2010 that made it easier for parents to register Amazigh (Berber) first names for their newborns. But civil registrars continued to reject Amazigh names in isolated cases, prompting calls from Amazigh activists for the ministry to ensure that all civil registrars heed the new circular.

Human Rights Violations by the Polisario

On September 21 the Polisario arrested Mostapha Selma Sidi Mouloud, a Sahrawi refugee residing in the Tindouf camps in Algeria, upon his return from Moroccan-controlled Western Sahara, where he had publicly announced his support for Morocco's proposal to maintain sovereignty over the region while granting it a measure of autonomy. The Polisario said they had arrested Selma for "espionage" and "treason," but on October 6 announced his release. At this writing he remains under Polisario auspices while the United Nations High Commissioner for Refugees work to resettle him in a place of his choosing.

Key International Actors

In 2008 the European Union gave Morocco "advanced status," placing it a notch above other members of the EU's "neighbourhood policy." Morocco is the biggest Middle Eastern beneficiary of EU aid after Palestine, with €580 million (approximately US$808 million) earmarked for 2011-2013.

France is Morocco's leading trade partner and source of public development aid and private investment. France increased its Overseas Development Assistance to €600 million for 2010-2012. France rarely publicly criticized Morocco's human rights practices and openly supported its autonomy plan for Western Sahara.

The US provides financial aid to Morocco, a close ally, including a five-year $697 million grant beginning in 2008 from the Millennium Challenge Corporation to reduce poverty and stimulate economic growth. On human rights, the US continued to publicly praise Morocco's reform efforts and advances made by women. The State Department's Counterterrorism Report for 2009 sent Morocco the wrong signal by favorably noting its convictions of alleged terrorists without mentioning the repeated fair-trial violations in such cases. Officials from the US embassy in Rabat told Human Rights Watch that they urged Morocco to reform its press code, provide due process to expatriate Christians facing expulsion, and apply its law on associations more consistently, including by recognizing Sahrawi human rights NGOs that currently lack legal status.

The UN Security Council in April 2010 renewed the mandate of the UN Mission for the Referendum in Western Sahara (MINURSO) for one year but once again declined to enlarge that mandate to include human rights observation and protection. Morocco opposes giving MINURSO such a mandate, whereas the Polisario says it supports it.

King Mohammed VI announced in 2008 that Morocco would lift its reservations to the Convention for the Elimination of All Forms of Discrimination against Women, but that has yet to happen at this writing. Morocco has not ratified the Rome Statute for the International Criminal Court or the Convention for the Protection of All Persons against Enforced Disappearances, although it helped to draft the latter.

SAUDI ARABIA

Human rights conditions remain poor in Saudi Arabia. King Abdullah has not ful-filled several specific reform promises; reforms to date have involved largely sym-bolic steps to improve the visibility of women and marginally expand freedom of expression.

Authorities continue to systematically suppress or fail to protect the rights of nine million Saudi women and girls, eight million foreign workers, and some two mil-lion Shia citizens. Each year thousands of people receive unfair trials or are sub-ject to arbitrary detention. Curbs on freedom of association, expression, and movement, as well as a pervasive lack of official accountability, remain serious concerns.

Women's and Girls' Rights

Saudi Arabia continues to treat women as legal minors, allowing male guardians to determine whether a woman may work, study, marry, travel, or undergo certain medical procedures. The government has not fulfilled its 2009 pledge to the United Nations Human Rights Council to dismantle the male guardianship sys-tem.

The Ministry of Interior since October 2009 has refused to issue a 43-year-old divorced woman cardiologist a new passport without male guardian approval. In 2010 the uncles and male guardians of a US-based adult woman with dual Saudi and US nationality did not allow her to obtain a Saudi passport. In May Nazia Quazi–the Indian father of 23-year-old dual Canadian and Indian national–finally permitted his daughter to leave Saudi Arabia after luring her to the kingdom in 2007 and keeping her there, as her guardian, against her will because he disap-proved of her fiance.

A medical doctor in her forties lost a court appeal to remove her father as her guardian after he refused to give her hand in marriage and confiscated her income. She lives in a women's shelter. The brothers of two unrelated women—one in Buraida, the other in Riyadh—acting as their guardians, forced their sisters to marry five men each, for money and against their wills. In January 2010 a court

SAUDI ARABIA

Looser Rein, Uncertain Gain

A Human Rights Assessment of Five Years
of King Abdullah's Reforms in Saudi Arabia

HUMAN
RIGHTS
WATCH

in Qasim province sentenced Sawsan Salim to 300 lashes and one-and-a-half years in prison for "appearing [in court] without a male guardian."

The Saudi Human Rights Commission did not respond to written requests from Human Rights Watch that it assist Nazia Quazi, Sawsan Salim, 'A'isha Ali, or the women in Buraida and Riyadh. The woman in Riyadh said she had contacted the commission but that it had failed to assist her.

Women and children who are victims of domestic violence face societal and governmental obstacles in obtaining redress. In September the appointed Shura Council that fulfills some functions of a parliament discussed a law aimed at better protecting children from violence. In March officials in the Family Protection Program said they had received 200 reports of child abuse in the previous six months.

Saudi Arabia strictly enforces gender segregation throughout the kingdom, including in work places, impeding women's full participation in public life. Women make up 14.4 percent of the workforce, triple the rate in 1992, a March 2010 study by Booz & Company found. Women's unemployment rate is four times that of men. Panda Supermarket in August reassigned 11 designated women cashiers after prominent cleric Yusuf al-Ahmad called for a boycott.

Women cannot work as judges or prosecutors. Promises by the Justice Ministry in February to draft a law allowing women lawyers to practice in court remained unmet.

The government has not yet set a minimum legal age for marriage, but in June issued new marriage contracts noting the bride's age. In January, a divorced father married off his 12-year-old daughter for 80,000 riyals (ca. US$21,300) because his ex-wife had gained custody, *Al-Riyadh* newspaper reported.

Migrant Worker Rights

8.3 million migrant workers legally reside in Saudi Arabia; an unknown number of other migrant workers are undocumented. They fill manual, clerical, and service jobs, constituting more than half the national workforce. Many suffer multiple abuses and labor exploitation, sometimes rising to slavery-like conditions. Saudi

Arabia did not bring any prosecutions under a 2009 anti-trafficking law against Saudis employing Nepali domestic workers trafficked from Kuwait.

Saudi Arabia made no progress reforming the restrictive *kafala* (sponsorship) system that ties migrant workers' residency permits to their employers; workers cannot change employers or exit the country without written consent from their initial employer or sponsor. The system fuels abuses such as employers confiscating passports, withholding wages, and forcing migrants to work against their will.

On Saudi National Day, September 23, the king announced a six-month amnesty for undocumented workers to return home without incurring immigration penalties.

In 2010, illegal strike actions by migrant workers increased, typically because of unpaid salaries. In May, 30 Nepalese cleaners were repatriated after striking in February over pay and lack of accommodation. They spent two months homeless and three weeks in deportation detention. Also in May workers at the Dhahran compound of Jadawel International—owned by Saudi Arabia's third richest man, Shaikh Muhammad bin Issa Al Jaber—went on strike over unpaid salaries and expired residency permits. Jadawel made a partial payment in August, but by September salary payments were again three months in arrears. In September workers at the Mecca metro went on strike, as did over 200 Filipino workers at Ansar hospital in Jeddah in June.

1.5 million migrant domestic workers remain excluded from the 2005 labor law. Although the Shura Council in July 2009 approved an annex to the law extending them limited labor protections, at this writing the government has not enacted it. Asian embassies report thousands of complaints each year from domestic workers forced to work 15-20 hours a day, seven days a week, and denied their salaries. Domestic workers frequently endure forced confinement; food deprivation; and severe psychological, physical, and sexual abuse. After returning home in August, a Sri Lankan domestic worker had dozens of metal nails extracted from her body that she claimed her Saudi employers had hammered into her as punishment for complaining about long working hours. In September a Filipina domestic worker was found dead with acid burns and stab wounds in her employers' home in Khobar.

Criminal Justice, Arbitrary Detention, Torture, and Ill-Treatment

Detainees, including children, are commonly the victims of systematic violations of due process and fair trial rights, including arbitrary arrest and torture and ill-treatment in detention. Saudi judges routinely sentence defendants to thousands of lashes.

Judges can order arrest and detention, including of children, at their discretion. Children can be tried and sentenced as adults if physical signs of puberty exist. It was unclear whether the law setting the age of majority at 18, passed by the Shura Council in 2008 but not yet enacted, would apply to criminal justice matters.

Authorities rarely inform suspects of the crime with which they are charged, or of the supporting evidence. Saudi Arabia has no penal code and prosecutors and judges largely define criminal offenses at their discretion. In April the Council of Senior Religious Scholars in principle approved codification of Sharia. During interrogation detainees are not assisted by lawyers; they face excessive pretrial delays and difficulty examining witnesses or presenting evidence at trial. The Shura Council in January approved, but the government at this writing has not enacted, a law to provide defendants with legal assistance free of charge.

In August a judge in Tabuk considered sentencing a man to be surgically paralyzed after convicting him of paralyzing another man in a fight two years earlier. In March a Medina court reaffirmed Lebanese television presenter Ali Sibat's death sentence for "witchcraft" based on his fortune-telling show broadcast from Lebanon. In September a Qatif court sentenced two high school pupils to six months in prison and 120 lashes for stealing exam questions.

Secret police detained without trial or access to lawyers, in many cases for years, around 2,000 persons suspected of sympathies or involvement with armed groups or for their peaceful political views. Muhammad al-'Utaibi and Khalid al-'Umair, two human rights activists arrested in January 2009 for trying to organize a peaceful Gaza solidarity demonstration, continued to be held in al-Ha'ir prison without trial beyond the six-month limit allowed under Saudi law and despite a prosecution order for their release. In Saudi Arabia, prosecutors under the Ministry of Interior issue arrest and detention warrants and orders for release.

On January 20, Saudi authorities informed the family of Jordanian professor Muhammad al-Nimarat that he had died in Abha secret police prison on November 27, 2009. Al-Nimarat remained in detention after he finished his two-year sentence in early 2009 for "issuing private religious rulings."

Prisoners and detainees in several facilities described inhumane conditions. Women twice rioted in Makka women's prison in 2010. Five Ethiopian detainees in Jizan deportation center died from alleged asphyxiation due to overcrowding in August, and Saudi websites in September published what they said were recent photos showing overcrowded communal cells in Riyadh's Malaz prison. In September a number of detainees in the Jeddah deportation center rioted and then escaped. Inmates in several prisons complained about ill-treatment and forced confessions extracted at police stations.

Freedom of Expression and Belief

Saudi authorities continue to brook little public criticism of officials or government policies in 2010. The Ministry of Culture and Information approves newspaper and television editors and heavily censors print and broadcast media. Internet critics crossing vague "red lines" face arrest.

Police in June arrested Sunni human rights activist Shaikh Mikhlif bin Dahham al-Shammari for "annoying others" with articles he wrote criticizing prominent Sunni clerics for their anti-Shia views. In August 2009, prosecutors charged Nasir al-Subai'i under unspecified articles of the Law against Cybercrimes with making allegedly libelous comments against the Saudi consul in Beijing. Al-Subai'i had written on his website about his ordeal trying to secure funding for his brother's medical care abroad.

In May Jamal Khashoggi, chief editor of the liberal *Al-Watan* newspaper, was sacked over articles questioning Saudi Arabia's religious ideology. A judge in October sentenced journalist Fahd al-Jukhaibid to prison and public lashes for a news article describing a public protest against electricity cuts in the northern town of Qubba. The books of Abdo Khal, a Saudi novelist and columnist, remain banned even after he won the International Prize for Arabic Fiction in March 2010.

A Ministry of Culture and Information spokesperson made conflicting statements regarding the requirement that blogs and news websites obtain a license under a proposed law regulating online expression.

Saudi Arabia does not tolerate public worship by adherents of religions other than Islam and systematically discriminates against its religious minorities, in particular Shia in the Eastern Province and around Media, and Ismailis (a distinct branch of Shiism) in Najran. Official discrimination against Shia encompasses religious practices, education, and the justice system. Government officials exclude Shia from certain public jobs and policy questions and publicly disparage their faith.

Authorities have kept Munir Al Jassas, a Saudi Shia human rights activist, in detention without trial since November 2009 and Muhammad Al Libad, a young Shia from 'Awwamiyya town, in detention since January 2010 for his alleged role in March 2009 sectarian disturbances there. Authorities in Ahsa' province continue to detain six Shia students arrested in January and February for publicly displaying religious banners during Ashura, a Shia religious holiday, in December 2009.

Key International Actors

Saudi Arabia is a key ally of the United States and the United Kingdom and both countries continued in 2010 to laud Saudi counterterrorism cooperation. US pressure for human rights improvements was imperceptible. In September the Pentagon proposed for Congressional approval a US$60 billion arms sale to Saudi Arabia, the biggest-ever US arms sale. It is unknown whether the UK made efforts through the Two Kingdoms Dialogue to promote human rights, but if so they had no tangible effect.

UN High Commissioner for Human Rights Navenathem Pillay, in a visit to the region in April, called on Saudi Arabia to improve women's rights; abolish the sponsorship system; address statelessness; and protect the rights to freedom of expression, assembly, and association. The Gulf Cooperation Council announced the establishment of a human rights committee in July 2010, but its mandate and working methods remain unclear at this writing. Other Gulf countries made no human rights demands of Saudi Arabia, and the kingdom joined others in supporting a crackdown in Bahrain on peaceful political dissidents and human rights activists ahead of elections there in October.

SYRIA

There was no significant change in Syrian human rights policy and practice in 2010. Authorities continued to broadly violate the civil and political rights of citizens, arresting political and human rights activists, censoring websites, detaining bloggers, and imposing travel bans.

Emergency rule, imposed in 1963, remains in effect and Syria's multiple security agencies continue to detain people without arrest warrants, holding them incommunicado for lengthy periods. The Supreme State Security Court (SSSC), an exceptional court with almost no procedural guarantees, regularly sentences Kurdish activists and Islamists to long prison terms.

A positive development in 2010 was the adoption in January of a new comprehensive anti-trafficking law.

Arrest and Trial of Political Activists

Twelve leaders of the Damascus Declaration, a prominent gathering of opposition groups, finished serving 30-month prison terms imposed in October 2008 for "weakening national sentiment." All were released except writer Ali al-`Abdallah, who is facing new charges of "spreading false information" and "spoil[ing] Syria's relations with another country" because of articles he wrote while in prison. His trial is still pending at this writing.

In February border police detained Ragheda Sa`id Hasan, a former political prisoner who was a member of the Communist Action Party. Three days later unidentified individuals confiscated a copy of a manuscript she wrote about her past detention from her apartment, as well as other political publications. She remains in detention.

The SSSC sentenced dozens of Kurdish political activists to prison in 2010, including many members of the PYD political party, which is affiliated with the Kurdistan Workers' Party (PKK). In April the SSSC sentenced four members of the Kurdish Yekiti Party—Yasha Wader, Dilghesh Mamo, Ahmad Darwish, and Nazmi Mohammad—to five years in prison on the charge of undertaking acts "to cut off

SYRIA

A Wasted Decade

Human Rights in Syria during Bashar al-Asad's
First Ten Years in Power

HUMAN
RIGHTS
WATCH

part of Syrian land." Three other prominent Yekiti members—Hassan Saleh, Muhammad Mustapha, and Ma`ruf Mulla Ahmad—face the same charges in their ongoing trial before the SSSC.

In June a military judge sentenced Mahmud Safo, a member of the Kurdish Left Party, to one year in prison for "inciting sectarian strife" and membership in an unlicensed organization.

Dr. Kamal al-Labwani, a physician and founder of the Democratic Liberal Gathering, who is serving a 15-year sentence for advocating peaceful reform, remains in prison.

Freedom of Expression and Civil Society Activism

Syria's press law provides the government with sweeping control over publications. The government has extended this control to online outlets. Internet censorship of political websites is pervasive and includes popular websites such as Blogger (Google's blogging engine), Facebook, and YouTube.

In December 2009 State Security detained Tal al-Mallohi, a 19-year-old student blogger, reportedly for a critical poem she wrote. At this writing the security services are holding her incommunicado and have not referred her to the judiciary.

In January blogger Karim `Arbaji was released by presidential pardon. The SSSC had sentenced him in 2009 to three years in prison for moderating a popular online youth forum, akhawia.net, which contained criticisms of the government.

In January security forces detained a journalist, Ali Taha, and a photographer, Ali Ahmad, who work for the satellite TV station Rotana, which mainly focuses on social life topics. They were released in February, without charge. In February security forces also released Ma`en `Akel, a journalist at the official newspaper *Thawra,* whom they had detained in November 2009 while he was investigating government corruption.

In March Military Intelligence in Aleppo detained `Abdel Hafez `Abdel Rahman, a board member of the unlicensed Kurdish human rights group MAF ("Right" in Kurdish), and along with another MAF board member, Nadera `Abdo. The security services released `Abdo and referred `Abdel Rahman to trial on charges of "undertaking acts to cut off part of Syrian land."A military judge released him on bail on September 1. His trial is ongoing at this writing.

In April authorities released on bail Ahmad Mustafa Ben Mohammad (known as Pir Rostom), a Kurdish political activist and writer, whom they detained in November 2009 for articles he wrote online.

In June a criminal court sentenced Muhannad al-Hasani, a human rights lawyer and president of the Syrian Human Rights Organization (Swasiah), to three years in prison for "weakening national sentiment" and "spreading false or exaggerated information" in connection with his monitoring of the SSSC. In May al-Hasani won the prestigious Martin Ennals Award for his work as a human rights defender.

In July a military tribunal sentenced Haytham al-Maleh, an 80-year-old prominent human rights lawyer and former judge, to three years in prison for "weakening national sentiment" and "spreading false information that weakens the nation's morale" after an opposition television station aired a phone interview with him in which he criticized Syrian authorities.

In June border security guards detained Kamal Sheikho, a member of Committees for the Defense of Democracy Freedoms and Human Rights in Syria (CDF). On August 23, security forces detained another CDF member, Isma`il `Abdi, a dual Syrian-German citizen who has lived in Germany since 1997 but was vacationing in Syria. A judge interrogated him in October on charges of "weakening national sentiment" and "membership in a prohibited group."

The government continues to prevent activists from traveling abroad, including Radeef Mustapha, head of the Kurdish Human Rights Committee.

All Syrian human rights groups remain unlicensed, as officials consistently deny their requests for registration.

Arbitrary Detention, "Disappearances," and Torture

Syria's multiple security services continue to detain people without arrest warrants and frequently refuse to disclose their whereabouts for weeks and sometimes months, in effect forcibly disappearing them. The fate of Nabil Khlioui, detained in 2008 from the region of Deir al-Zawr because of suspected ties to Islamists, remains unknown. The authorities have also kept silent about the fate of at least 20 Kurds detained since 2008 on suspicion of ties to a separatist Kurdish movement.

Human Rights Watch received numerous reports of ill-treatment and torture by security agencies. The United Nations Committee against Torture said in May that it was "deeply concerned about numerous, ongoing, and consistent allegations concerning the routine use of torture by law enforcement and investigative officials."

At least five detainees died in custody in 2010, with no serious investigations into the deaths by the authorities. In June security services returned the body of Muhammad Ali Rahman to his family. According to Syrian human rights activists, his corpse showed signs of torture. Syrian law provides Syrian security services with extensive immunity for acts of torture.

As in previous years, the government failed to acknowledge security force involvement in the "disappearance" of an estimated 17,000 persons, mostly Muslim Brotherhood members and other Syrian activists detained by the government in the late 1970s and early 1980s, as well as hundreds of Lebanese and Palestinians detained in Syria or abducted from Lebanon.

More than two years after security forces opened fire on rioting inmates in Sednaya prison, killing at least nine, the government has not released any information about the casualties. The authorities have not released Nizar Rastanawi, a prominent human rights activist who completed his four-year sentence in Sednaya on April 18, 2009, and there is no information about his well-being.

Discrimination and Repression against Kurds

Kurds, Syria's largest non-Arab ethnic minority, remain subject to systematic discrimination, including arbitrary denial of citizenship to an estimated 300,000 Syria-born Kurds. Authorities suppress expressions of Kurdish identity and prohibit the teaching of Kurdish in schools.

In March 2010, security forces shot at Kurds celebrating the Kurdish New Year in the northern town of Raqqa to disperse them, killing at least one. In July a military court sentenced nine Kurds alleged to have participated in the celebrations in Raqqa to four months for "inciting sectarian strife."

Women and Girls' Rights

Syria's constitution guarantees gender equality, and many women are active in public life, but personal status laws as well as the penal code contain provisions that discriminate against women and girls. The nationality law of 1969 denies Syrian women married to foreign spouses the right to pass on their citizenship to their children or spouses.

In January the government issued a comprehensive anti-trafficking law, Legislative Decree No. 3, which provides new grounds for prosecuting trafficking and protecting victims, and outlines a minimum punishment of seven years.

Syria amended its penal code in 2009 to require a minimum two-year sentence for so-called "honor" crimes; at least 10 honor crimes were documented by Syrian women's rights groups in 2010.

Migrant domestic workers, whose numbers have increased in Syria, reportedly face exploitation and abuse by employers. The government enacted two decrees regulating the work of recruiting agencies to better protect the workers, but enforcement mechanisms are still lacking.

Situation of Refugees Fleeing Iraq

Syria hosts more Iraqi refugees than any other country, with 210,000 registered with the UN High Commissioner for Refugees (UNHCR) at the beginning of 2010; the actual numbers are likely much higher. Syria gives Iraqi refugees, registered or not, access to public hospitals and schools, but prohibits them from working.

In February UNHCR closed the al-Tanf refugee camp—which is situated in the no man's land between Iraq and Syria and has hosted Palestinians from Iraq for nearly four years—and relocated the last of the refugees to the al-Hol camp inside

Syria. However, a more permanent solution is still needed for the more than 600 Palestinians in al-Hol camp.

Key International Actors

The international community's interactions with Syria have focused almost exclusively on its regional role. Key European Union and US officials have condemned the arrest and trials of prominent activists, but their interventions have had no impact on Syria's actions. In July both US Secretary of State Hillary Clinton and the EU High Representative Catherine Ashton publicly criticized Syria's detention and trial of Haytham al-Maleh, Muhanad al-Hasani, and Ali al-Abdallah. In September the European Parliament adopted a resolution condemning Syria's crackdown on human rights activists.

TUNISIA

The human rights situation remained dire in Tunisia, where President Zine el-Abidine Ben Ali and the ruling Democratic Constitutional Rally party (RCD) dominate political life.

The government frequently uses the threat of terrorism and religious extremism as a pretext to crack down on peaceful dissent, while state security agents use surveillance, arbitrary detention, and physical aggression to intimidate and persecute those whom the government deems to be a "threat." Independent journalists, human rights defenders, and union activists risk prosecution on trumped-up charges.

Activists often resort to the internet as a space to disseminate and access information when authorities deny them the physical space to do so. However, Tunisia aggressively blocks access to websites containing critical political and human rights information, and seems to be directly or indirectly involved in sabotaging the email accounts of persons known to engage in human rights or opposition political activity.

Criminalizing Contact between Tunisians and Foreign Entities

On June 15 the Chamber of Deputies, the lower house of parliament, amended article 61bis of the penal code to impose criminal penalties on persons who "directly or indirectly, have contacts with agents of a foreign country, foreign institution or organization in order to encourage them to affect the vital interests of Tunisia and its economic security." The amendment may threaten persons who furnish information about human rights in Tunisia to foreign governments and multi-lateral organizations, including the European Union and United Nations.

Justice and Human Rights Minister Lazhar Bououni told parliament on June 15 that "affecting the vital interests of Tunisia" includes "inciting foreign parties not to extend credit to Tunisia, not to invest in the country, to boycott tourism or to sabotage the efforts of Tunisia to obtain advanced partner status with the European Union." Parliament approved this provision on June 15 after Tunisian human rights defenders held a meeting with EU officials in Madrid in April in the context of EU-Tunisia negotiations over granting Tunisia advanced partner status.

Human Rights Defenders

Authorities have refused to grant legal recognition to every truly independent human rights organization that has applied over the past decade. After denying recognition, the authorities use the organization's "illegal" status to hamper its activities.

Human rights defenders and dissidents are subject to heavy surveillance, arbitrary travel bans, dismissal from work, interruptions in phone service, physical assaults, harassment of relatives, suspicious acts of vandalism and theft, and slander campaigns in the press. Members of unrecognized human rights organizations, such as the International Association in Support of Political Prisoners (AISPP) and the Tunisian Association to Combat Torture (ALTT), are regular targets for harassment by security forces. Plainclothes police harass lawyers who are members of these organizations and who take on politically sensitive cases. Radhia Nasraoui, a lawyer and spokesperson for the ALTT, reported that police regularly question her clients about what they have discussed with her in confidence, which scares away potential clients.

Prison authorities prevented Samir Ben Amor, a lawyer and secretary general of AISPP, from visiting his clients in prison between August 2009 and March 2010, even though he had court authorization for the visits.

Media Freedom

Domestic print and broadcast media do not provide critical coverage of government policies, apart from a few low-circulation magazines—such as the opposition weekly al-Mawkif—which are subject to occasional confiscation. Tunisia has licensed private radio and television stations, but none that have an independent editorial line. The government blocks access to certain domestic and international political or human rights websites featuring critical coverage of Tunisia.

On July 6, 2010, the Gafsa Appeals Court sentenced journalist Fahem Boukadous in an unfair trial to four years in prison for "participating in a criminal association with the intention of harming people and their property" and "spreading information liable to disrupt public order." The apparent motive behind his prosecution was his coverage in 2008 for El-Hiwar el Tounsi, an Italy-based satellite television channel, of demonstrations and social unrest in the Gafsa mining region that led to the prosecution of about 200 persons, many of whom reported torture and ill-treatment in detention. During the July 6 hearing the presiding judge refused to investigate Boukadous's allegations of torture and prevented defense lawyers from presenting their arguments in court. Police surrounded the courthouse and denied access to many journalists and local observers. Boukadous's wife said that he had not received adequate care in prison for his asthma and respiratory problems.

On April 27 authorities freed dissident journalist Taoufik Ben Brik from prison after he served his six-month sentence for assaulting a woman. Ben Brik was sentenced by the Court of First Instance in Tunis, the capital, following an unfair trial in which he was convicted solely on the basis of the alleged victim's testimony and a confession that Ben Brik claims was forged. The trial followed a pattern of prosecutions against journalists critical of the government on questionable criminal charges.

Counterterrorism Measures and Human Rights

Since 1991 there has been one deadly terrorist attack in Tunisia: an April 2002 truck bomb that targeted a synagogue on the island of Djerba, for which al-Qaeda claimed responsibility. Security forces have also clashed once with armed militants between December 2006 and January 2007 outside Tunis.

The 2003 Law in Support of "International Efforts to Fight Terrorism and the Repression of Money Laundering" contains a broad definition of terrorism that the United Nations Human Rights Committee criticized on March 28, 2008 for its "lack of precision." Authorities have charged many hundreds of men, and some minors, under the law. Nearly all of those convicted and imprisoned have been accused of planning to join jihadist groups abroad or inciting others to join, rather than of having planned or committed specific acts of violence. In July 2009

Tunisia's parliament adopted an amendment narrowing the law's definition of a terrorist act by restricting the extent to which "incitement to hatred" would meet the definition.

In January 2010 then-UN special rapporteur on the promotion and protection of human rights and fundamental freedoms while countering terrorism, Martin Scheinin, visited Tunisia and noted that "the most disturbing experience during my mission was the existence of serious discrepancies between the law and what was reported to me as happening in reality." He noted that "the frequent use of confessions as evidence in court without proper investigation into allegations of torture or other ill-treatment," and that there were a disproportionately low number of prosecutions or other clear findings related to torture, compared to the frequency of allegations.

Prosecution of Student Union Activists

Members of the General Union for Tunisian Students (UGET) have faced persecution for their union activities. On February 3 the Court of First Instance in Mahdia sentenced five UGET members to 20 months in prison on charges of aggression and destroying public property, despite lack of persuasive evidence of their guilt. The charges date to October 2007, when the students staged a two-day sit-in to protest what they saw as their arbitrary expulsion from the university for holding a demonstration. The students remain free pending their appeal, which has been postponed four times and at this writing is set for early January 2011.

Key International Actors

France is Tunisia's leading trade partner and its fourth-largest foreign investor. In April 2009 France concluded a nuclear energy cooperation deal and an €80 million (US$108 million) aid package for Tunisia. On July 16, 2010, French Foreign Ministry spokesperson Bernard Valéro noted France's commitment to freedom of expression and the press, and said that France was "monitoring the situation of Mr. [Fahem] Boukadous, in particular his prison conditions and his ability to access proper medical care." This statement was an exception to France's overall reluctance to publicly pressure Tunisia to improve its human rights record. On March 22, 2009, French Foreign Minister Bernard Kouchner acknowledged, "It's

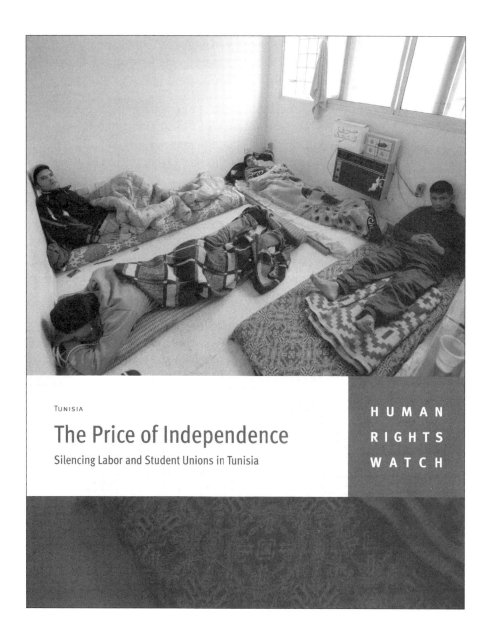

The Price of Independence

Silencing Labor and Student Unions in Tunisia

HUMAN
RIGHTS
WATCH

true that there are human rights abuses in Tunisia, journalists who are harassed, sometimes imprisoned, and a general policy of firmness." He then went on to praise Tunisia's economic and social achievements, notably regarding the status of women and the values of secularism.

The European Union-Tunisia Association Agreement remains in force, despite the government's human rights record. On May 11 the 8th session of the Tunisia-European Union Association Council took place in Brussels, Belgium. The two sides agreed to work on a roadmap to grant Tunisia "advanced status" with the EU.

At this writing, the United States 2011 Foreign Operations Appropriations bill would provide $15 million in Foreign Military Financing assistance to Tunisia. For the first time, the bill conditions $1 million of that sum on the Tunisian government making "significant efforts to respect due process and the rights of its citizens to peaceful expression and association and to provide access for its citizens to the internet."

While Tunisia allowed a visit during 2010 of the UN special rapporteur on counterterrorism (see above), at this writing it has not agreed to a request to visit from the special rapporteur on torture. The request, which has been pending since 1998, was renewed in November 2009.

United Arab Emirates

The human rights situation in the United Arab Emirates (UAE) worsened in 2010, particularly for migrant workers, as the construction slowdown in Dubai continued. Other pressing human rights issues include torture, restrictions on freedoms of expression and association, and violations of women's rights. Authorities continue to prevent peaceful demonstrations and to harass local human rights defenders.

Two prominent cases in 2010 highlighted ongoing concerns about the justice system: in January a court cleared a member of the royal family on torture charges despite video evidence against him; in March, 17 migrant workers in Sharjah were convicted of murder despite evidence their confessions were unreliable and the product of police torture. The latter decision remains on appeal at this writing.

Migrant Worker Rights

During six years of spectacular growth in the construction sector, mainly in Dubai, the UAE brought in hundreds of thousands of South Asian migrant workers. Immigration sponsorship laws grant employers extraordinary power over the lives of such workers. Workers do not have the right to organize or bargain collectively and face penalties for going on strike. The Labor Law of 1980 excludes from coverage domestic workers employed in private households. Although the law calls for a minimum wage, the Ministry of Labor has yet to adopt such a measure.

Across the country, abuses include unsafe work environments, squalid living conditions in labor camps, and the withholding of travel documents. Workers also complain of nonpayment of wages, despite a mandatory electronic payment system introduced in 2009, that requires companies to pay salaries directly into licensed banks to ensure timely payments without illegal deductions.

The financial crisis that began in late 2008 cost tens of thousands of workers their jobs. Trapped in camps lacking basics such as food and sanitation, many were unable to find new jobs or a way home. Other workers say that some employers forced them to accept reduced pay and benefits or face dismissal.

Hundreds of laid-off migrant workers in 2010 were stranded in labor camps without electricity or running water for months on end after their Dubai-based employers closed; some had to fight off rats while sleeping amidst garbage heaps.

In May hundreds of workers marched from their Sharjah labor camp to the Labor Ministry in Dubai demanding to be sent back home. The workers said they lived in squalor and their employer had not paid them in six months. That same week about 200 workers staged a sit-in at the Labor Ministry demanding unpaid wages. Police detained 95 Vietnamese workers who allegedly attempted to block the ministry's entry gates. In June three Asian workers suffocated to death in their labor accommodation in Dubai after inhaling carbon dioxide from a generator. In August a fire charred to death 11 sleeping workers. In September authorities finally began sending home 700 stranded workers from the al-Sajaa camp in Sharjah.

In February 2010 New York University committed publicly to requiring all companies building and operating its Abu Dhabi campus to reimburse workers for any recruiting or other employment-related fees that they had to pay. The new terms also bar companies from confiscating worker passports. In September the Guggenheim art museum followed suit, though its provisions do not require contractors to reimburse workers for fees paid. Neither institution publicly committed to independent, third-party monitoring of labor conditions or to collective bargaining and a minimum wage. At this writing Le Louvre Abu Dhabi has not made any specific public commitments.

Many female domestic workers in the UAE suffer unpaid wages, food deprivation, long working hours, forced confinement, and physical or sexual abuse. The Indonesian embassy registered a 24 percent increase in domestic worker exploitation incidents in Abu Dhabi in 2009 compared with 2008. In October 2010, makeshift shelters in Abu Dhabi and Dubai housed more than 300 runaway Filipina domestic workers. The standard contract for domestic workers introduced in April 2007 calls for "adequate breaks" but does not limit working hours or provide for a weekly rest day, overtime pay, or workers' compensation.

In October, two weeks after Kuwait announced plans to scrap its *kafala* (sponsorship) system, UAE's minister of labor said the UAE would not follow suit. However, the UAE government took some steps in 2010 to protect migrant workers. In March the Labor Ministry announced the creation of a new unit to identify and investigate potential labor trafficking cases. In May the Labor Ministry extended by an extra month the summer season midday break for individuals working outside in sweltering heat.

Torture and Suspicious Deaths

On January 10 an Emirati court cleared Sheikh Issa bin Zayed al Nahyan, a member of the UAE ruling family, of torture charges despite video footage that showed him abusing Afghan grain dealer Mohammed Shah Poor with whips, electric cattle prods, and wooden planks with protruding nails. The court convicted five co-defendants but accepted the sheikh's defense that he was under the influence of drugs, which diminished the responsibility for his actions. The public prosecutor did not appeal the ruling.

On March 29 a Sharjah court sentenced 17 Indian men to death for the murder of a Pakistani national during a brawl over control of the illicit alcohol trade. The 17 men alleged that police tortured them over nine days to obtain confessions. Lawyers for Human Rights International (LFHRI), an Indian group, said police beat the men with clubs, subjected them to electric shocks, deprived them of sleep, and forced them to stand on one leg for prolonged periods. As of October their appeal against their convictions continued.

In August 2010 criminal lawyer Abdul Hameed filed a public complaint with Dubai's public prosecutor urging an investigation into circumstances surrounding at least 20 suspicious deaths of inmates (19 Emiratis and one Afghan) in Dubai's central prison over the preceding two years. As of October, he had not received any response.

Freedom of Association and Expression

In 2010 the government subjected the Jurist Association, an NGO established in 1980 to promote the rule of law and raise professional standards, to mounting restrictions. The government did not permit association representatives to attend meetings abroad and cancelled symposiums that it deemed controversial at home. Members also complained of official pressure to quit the association.

Former association president Muhammad al-Mansoori, whom authorities have harassed for years, was dismissed from his position as a legal advisor to the government of Ras Al Khaimah in January after he gave a television interview in which he criticized restrictions on freedom of speech in the country. Authorities have refused to renew his passport since March 2008.

Police arrested at least four young activists after they attempted to organize a peaceful protest march on July 15 in response to increasing oil prices. Authorities fired one of the organizers from his government job and Dubai police held him in detention for a week for "inciting the nation against the government," even though the protest was cancelled. Another was imprisoned for more than a month and suspended from his work.

The government monitors press content and journalists routinely exercise self-censorship. Although Prime Minister Sheikh Muhammad stated in 2007 that journalists should not face prison "for reasons related to their work," a 1980 law still in force provides jail terms for journalists and suspension of publications that publish "materials that cause confusion among the public."

On February 7, authorities blocked access to the online discussion forum *UAE Hewar* (http://uaehewar.net/), a popular website that encourages debate on topics ranging from freedom of expression to political rights.

Women's Rights

Despite the existence of shelters and hotlines to help protect women, domestic violence remains a pervasive problem. The penal code gives men the legal right to discipline their wives and children, including through the use of physical violence. In October the Federal Supreme Court issued a ruling that upheld a husband's right to "chastise" his wife and children with physical abuse.

In January a Dubai court charged 23-year-old British woman and her fiance with having illegal sex and drinking outside permitted premises after the woman reported to police that a hotel employee had raped her. In June the Abu Dhabi criminal court sentenced an 18-year-old Emirati woman to a year in prison for illicit sex after she complained that six men gang-raped her a month earlier.

According to a survey conducted in January 2010 of 980 UAE residents, 55 percent of the female respondents said they would not report a sexual assault for fear of tarnishing their family's reputation, and 49 percent would not do so because society would judge them harshly.

The government made progress in law enforcement efforts against the trafficking of women and girls and successfully prosecuted several traffickers. In June the UAE announced it would establish two new shelters, in Ras Al Khaimah and Sharjah, for trafficked women and girls.

Key International Actors

In April United Nations High Commissioner for Human Rights Navanethem Pillay toured Gulf countries. During her UAE visit she criticized the sponsorship system "that leaves migrant workers vulnerable to exploitation in an unequal power relationship with their employers" and urged the creation of national human rights institutions that comply with international human rights standards.

In August the United States expressed disappointment at the UAE's planned cutoff of key BlackBerry services, noting that the ban would set a dangerous precedent in limiting freedom of information. In October the UAE government said it would not go ahead with the ban. The Telecommunications Regulatory Authority said Canadian manufacturer Research in Motion had brought its devices into line with strict local guidelines on security and encryption but authorities did not release terms of the agreement.

YEMEN

Yemen's human rights situation continued to deteriorate in 2010. Amid political unrest in the south, hundreds of arbitrary arrests and the use of lethal force against peaceful demonstrators undermined advances in the rule of law. Skirmishes tested a truce in the conflict with Huthi rebels in the north, and government ministries, the army, rebels, and "tribes" in various conflict affected northern areas obstructed humanitarian assistance. Accountability for laws of war violations remained lacking. Yemen intensified counterterrorism efforts against suspected al Qaeda members in the Arabian Peninsula (AQAP), but some attacks killed and injured civilians.

Friends of Yemen, a group of states and intergovernmental organizations established in January, failed to press for an end to human rights abuses as a condition for pledging financial and technical assistance.

Terrorism and Counterterrorism

The United States increased military assistance and cooperation with Yemen's government following the failed AQAP attempt in December 2009 to blow up an airliner en route to Detroit. AQAP conducted numerous deadly attacks in 2010, particularly on state intelligence and security officials on its list of 55 Yemenis targeted for assassination.

In June four AQAP gunmen attacked a post of the Political Security Organization (one of Yemen's several intelligence agencies) in Aden, killing at least 11 intelligence officers and soldiers, and freeing several suspected militants.

In a September bus ambush in San'a AQAP killed 14 senior officers who had recently completed a US counterterrorism intelligence course. In October militants in San'a fired a rocket-propelled grenade at a car carrying five British Embassy staff members, including the deputy ambassador, injuring three. In April a suicide bomber tried unsuccessfully to kill then British Ambassador Tim Torlot.

The US government revealed it had targeted Yemeni-American preacher Anwar al-Awlaqi for assassination based on his alleged links to AQAP plots. In November a

Yemeni court indicted Al-Awlaqi, who is hiding in Yemen, on terrorism-related charges and ordered his capture, dead or alive.

The US reportedly assisted Yemen in at least four airstrikes on alleged AQAP targets. One—a cruise missile attack on suspected AQAP members on December 17, 2009—resulted in at least 41 civilian deaths in the southern province of Abyan. The strike reportedly involved at least one cluster munition, a weapon that due to its indiscriminate nature poses unacceptable risk to civilians. Another US-assisted attack in central Marib province in May killed a deputy governor rather than the AQAP suspect, prompting the victim's tribesmen to attack strategic oil pipelines.

Yemen's government arrested scores of terrorism suspects on weak evidence and unlawfully detained many for weeks or months without charge, according to reputable Yemeni human rights activists. Concerns persisted that President Ali Abdullah Saleh used the counterterrorism campaign as an excuse to target members of Yemen's separatist Southern Movement and independent media.

For three weeks in August Yemeni security forces shelled suspected AQAP targets in Lawdar, a town in Abyan province that is home to separatists. Media reports said the three dozen victims included al Qaeda members and security forces, but that the attacks also damaged hundreds of homes and displaced tens of thousands of people. In September the government's three-day attack on suspected al Qaeda hideouts in Hawta, southern Shabwa province, displaced thousands more families.

Campaign against Southern Separatists

Security forces suppressed protests of the Southern Movement, establishing checkpoints on days of announced demonstrations and arresting suspected participants. On September 23, security forces arrested at least 12 Yemenis in Aden who were planning to demonstrate to draw attention to their grievances when the Friends of Yemen group of states met in New York to discuss aid to Yemen.

Deputy Interior Minister Salih al-Zawari said there were 245 southern protests in March, involving 200 acts of violence. A southern human rights report listed 13 dead, 31 wounded, and 61 arrested in separatists' clashes with government forces in May alone. In July police in Aden killed one man when they fired on a public funeral march for Ahmad Darwish, who allegedly died from torture in late June following his arrest after AQAP's attack on the Aden intelligence facility. Photographs appeared to show bruises covering Darwish's body. From May to July the army blockaded southern areas of al-Dhali', Lahj, and parts of Shabwa. Some Southern Movement activists erected road blocks and called for civil unrest, closing government offices, schools, and shops. In June the army repeatedly shelled al-Dhali' city center, leading to several civilian casualties.

Conflict in the North

On February 12, Huthi rebels and government forces in the northern Sa'da governorate agreed to a truce, ending six months of heavy fighting, which was the sixth round of violence since June 2004. In August both sides agreed to a 22-point plan to implement the truce, including releasing all prisoners. In June Yemeni NGOs presented a list of 249 persons they said the government had tried, or was trying, in connection with the Sa'da conflict, despite expectations under the truce that they would not face punishment. A further 86 remained detained without known charges. Despite the truce, skirmishes between Huthis and the army or army-backed tribal militias led to scores of civilian and fighter casualties.

As of mid-August the conflict had displaced just under 330,000 people, almost half of whom fled between August 2009 and February 2010. Only a few displaced persons went to official camps; more than 80 percent live with host families or in open spaces, schools, and mosques. Aid agencies reported struggling to reach them due to insecurity and access restrictions imposed by officials, local tribes, and rebels. By August over 16,000 displaced persons were known to have returned home.

Between November 2009 and January 2010 Saudi forces became a party to the armed conflict and prevented persons seeking refuge from crossing its border, forcing thousands back to Yemen, according to media reports.

Government forces and Huthi fighters recruited children for combat. Huthi fighters reportedly carried out summary executions and endangered civilians by firing from populated areas. Government forces reportedly conducted indiscriminate

All Quiet on the Northern Front?

Uninvestigated Laws of War Violations in Yemen's War
with Huthi Rebels

**HUMAN
RIGHTS
WATCH**

aerial bombardment in civilian-populated areas, including a crowded market in al-Talh on September 14, and a gathering of displaced persons in al-'Adi on September 16. Neither party took steps to investigate or address possible laws-of-war violations.

Freedom of Expression

On May 22—the 20th anniversary of the unification of North and South Yemen—President Saleh declared an amnesty that freed many, but not all, detainees and prisoners arrested for peaceful expression. Political Security continued to detain peaceful Southern Movement dissidents. On August 16, intelligence forces arrested Abd al-Ilah Haidar al-Shayi', a terrorism expert and journalist for the official Saba News Agency, accusing him of being an al Qaeda spokesperson based on his interviews with the group's members.

More than 16 journalists and peaceful activists received sentences ranging from fines to 10 years in prison in 2009 and 2010, mostly for airing grievances felt by many in the south of the country. The Specialized Criminal Court in March sentenced a professor of economic geography, Husain al-'Aqil, to three years in prison for publicly raising concerns about control of Yemen's oil wealth. After al-'Aqil's release in the May amnesty, Aden University in September "froze" his academic duties.

On May 24 the Press and Publication Court, established in 2009 to try journalists, sentenced Sami Ghalib, chief editor of the weekly *Al-Nida'*, and four colleagues to a suspended three-month prison term for "undermining the unity" of Yemen. The information minister banned newspapers, including *Al-Watani*, because of sympathetic coverage of southern protests. Some have managed to republish, others have been hauled to court or shut down.

In April Minister of Justice Ghazi al-Aghbari proposed amending the penal code by adding vague language that would criminalize "undermining established national principles." The proposals remained under parliamentary review at time of writing.

Women and Girls' Rights

Child marriages and forced marriages remain widespread, exposing young girls to domestic violence and maternal mortality, and truncating their education. Judges are not obliged to ensure girls' free consent before notarizing marriage contracts. In March a 12 or 13-year-old girl died from severe genital bleeding three days after her marriage. Amid opposition from Islamic conservatives, President Saleh has not yet signed into law a measure parliament passed in February 2009 setting the minimum age for marriage at 17.

Domestic violence and marital rape are not criminalized. A women's shelter opened in 2009 in San'a housing women fleeing from violence and former prisoners who have completed their sentences but are rejected by their families.

Despite some improvements, Yemen still has a high maternal mortality rate of 370 deaths per 100,000 live births. Approximately seven to eight women die each day from childbirth complications. More than 70 percent of women deliver at home.

Key International Actors

In August Qatar mediated between the government and Huthi rebels. The United Kingdom in January assembled the Friends of Yemen group, including key Gulf countries, the G8, and intergovernmental organizations. In March and September meetings, the group discussed financial assistance to Yemen, but failed to tie aid to ending the human rights abuses fueling Yemen's crises.

Donors contributed only 49 percent of the requested US$187 million under the United Nations 2010 Yemen Humanitarian Response Plan. Saudi Arabia, Qatar, and other Persian Gulf states provide substantial amounts of assistance to Yemen, including to tribal leaders, religious institutions, and the government. European Union states also gave humanitarian and development aid.

The US more than doubled its military assistance to Yemen to $150 million, as well as giving US$110 million in humanitarian and economic aid. The US publicly supported Yemen's unity, but urged peaceful resolution of its crises.

Costly and Unfair

Flaws in US Immigration Detention Policy

HUMAN
RIGHTS
WATCH

WORLD REPORT

2011

UNITED STATES

UNITED STATES

US citizens enjoy a broad range of civil liberties and have recourse to a strong system of independent federal and state courts, but continuing failures—notably in the criminal justice and immigration systems and in counterterrorism law and policy—mar its human rights record. Although the Obama administration has pledged to address many of these concerns, progress has been slow; in some areas it has been nonexistent.

There were positive developments in 2010, including a Supreme Court ruling abolishing the sentencing of children to life in prison without parole for non-homicide crimes; a new law that promises to reduce racial disparities in the sentencing of cocaine offenders; and a healthcare law promising health insurance to an estimated 32 million uninsured Americans.

All of these topics were examined in November 2010 during the first-ever Universal Periodic Review of the US at the United Nations Human Rights Council, part of a larger process in which the Council examines the human rights records of all 192 UN member states.

Extreme Criminal Punishments

The number of US states that impose the death penalty remained at 35 in 2010. At this writing 45 people have been executed in the US thus far in 2010; 52 were executed in 2009.

There are 2,574 youth offenders (persons under age 18 at the time they committed their offense) serving life without parole in US prisons. There are no known youth offenders serving the sentence anywhere else in the world. In a historic decision in June 2010, *Graham v. Florida*, the US Supreme Court ruled that the sentence cannot be imposed on youth offenders convicted of non-homicide crimes. While the ruling was a significant step forward, most youth offenders serving the sentence were convicted of homicide and were not affected by the ruling.

The Price of Freedom

Bail and Pretrial Detention of Low Income
Nonfelony Defendants in New York City

HUMAN
RIGHTS
WATCH

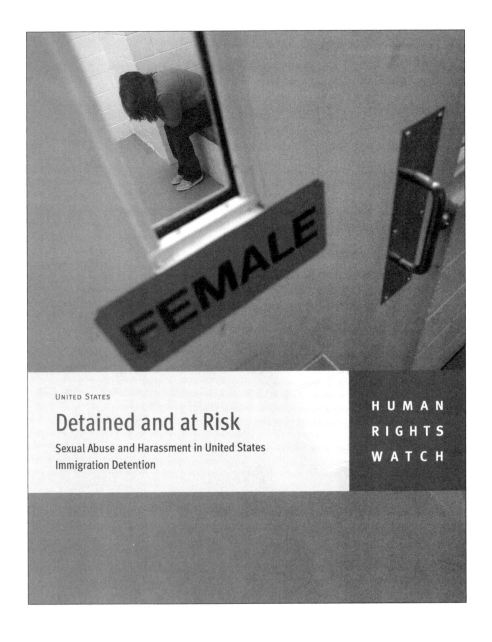

UNITED STATES

Detained and at Risk

Sexual Abuse and Harassment in United States
Immigration Detention

HUMAN
RIGHTS
WATCH

Prison Conditions

As of June 2009 the US continued to have both the largest incarcerated population (2,297,400, a decrease of 0.5 percent since December 2008) and the highest per capita incarceration rate in the world (748 inmates per 100,000 residents).

17 months after the National Prison Rape Elimination Commission delivered its proposals to eliminate prison rape to the Justice Department, Attorney General Eric Holder still had not promulgated final standards. Sexual violence, meanwhile, remains commonplace in US prisons. The Bureau of Justice Statistics (BJS) reported in August 2010 that 88,500 prison and jail inmates had experienced some form of sexual victimization between October 2008 and December 2009. According to a survey mandated by the Prison Rape Elimination Act and analyzed by the BJS, an estimated 12 percent of youth held in juvenile facilities reported that they had been sexually abused.

There were advances in treatment of women in US prisons. In August the Washington Department of Corrections, following a court order, began to address staff sexual misconduct against women prisoners, including through revamping complaint and investigation procedures, installing additional surveillance cameras, and increasing training. The number of states restricting the shackling of pregnant prisoners grew from six to ten with Colorado, Washington, Pennsylvania, and West Virginia joining New York, Illinois, California, Texas, Vermont, and New Mexico. But there were highly disturbing developments as well: in Colorado, for example, women inmates were subjected to degrading, routine, suspicionless searches requiring them to open their labia for inspection by guards.

In California legislation went into effect in January 2010 that is designed to reduce the prison population by, among other measures, giving more good time credits and diverting certain parole and probation violators from prison. Nevertheless, California has appealed to the US Supreme Court a federal court order requiring the state to reduce its prison population so that it can provide constitutionally adequate medical and mental health care to inmates.

Despite the large number of prisoners in the US with histories of substance use and addiction, evidence-based drug dependence treatment is rarely available to them. HIV and hepatitis prevalence among prisoners is significantly higher than in the non-incarcerated community, yet proven harm-reduction programs, such as condom availability and syringe exchange, remain rare. The 2010 Human Rights Watch and American Civil Liberties Union (ACLU) report, *Sentenced to Stigma*, documented the harmful impact on prisoners and their families of prison policies that mandate HIV testing, breach confidentiality, and promote stigma and discrimination.

Harsh US prison conditions were further exposed in July when the European Court of Human Rights temporarily halted the extradition of four terrorism suspects from the United Kingdom to the US due to concerns that their long-term incarceration in a US "supermax" prison would violate Article 3 of the European Convention on Human Rights, which prohibits "torture or... inhuman or degrading treatment or punishment."

Racial Disparities in the Criminal Justice System

The burden of incarceration falls disproportionately on members of racial and ethnic minorities, a disparity which cannot be accounted for solely by differences in criminal conduct: black non-Hispanic males are incarcerated at a rate more than six times that of white non-Hispanic males and 2.6 times that of Hispanic males. One in 10 black males aged 25-29 were in prison or jail in 2009; for Hispanic males the figure was 1 in 25; for white males only 1 in 64.

In August 2010 President Barack Obama signed the Fair Sentencing Act, which alters the federal government's historically far more punitive approach to crack versus powder cocaine offenders that has led to racial disparities in sentencing. While symbolically important, the act does little to address the overwhelming racial disparities in drug law enforcement: blacks constitute 33.6 percent of drug arrests, 44 percent of persons convicted of drug felonies in state court, and 37 percent of people sent to state prison on drug charges, even though they constitute only 13 percent of the US population and blacks and whites engage in drug offenses at equivalent rates.

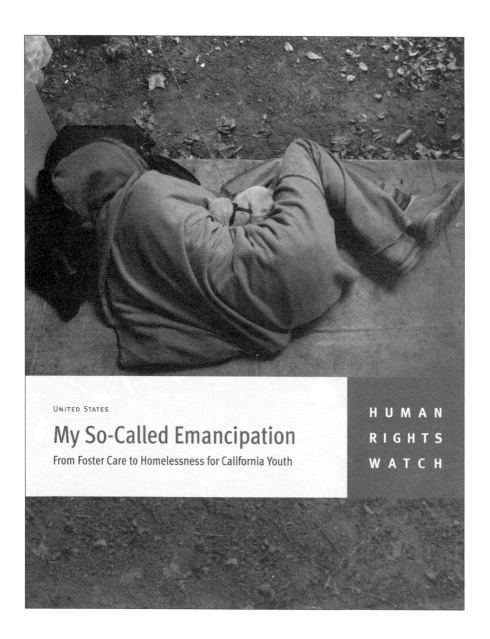

My So-Called Emancipation

From Foster Care to Homelessness for California Youth

HUMAN
RIGHTS
WATCH

UNITED STATES

Jailing Refugees

Arbitrary Detention of Refugees in the US Who Fail
to Adjust to Permanent Resident Status

**HUMAN
RIGHTS
WATCH**

Rights of Non-Citizens

There are some 38 million non-citizens living in the US, of whom approximately 12 million are undocumented. In 2009 US Immigration and Customs Enforcement (ICE) detained between 380,000 and 442,000 non-citizens in some 300 detention facilities, at an annual cost of US$1.7 billion.

In May 2010, reports surfaced that ICE was investigating allegations that a guard at a Texas immigration detention center had sexually assaulted several female detainees. This was the latest in a series of alleged sexual assaults, abuses, and episodes of harassment that have come to public attention since ICE was created in 2003.

In a July report, *Deportation by Default*, Human Rights Watch documented barriers facing persons with mental disabilities in immigration proceedings, including a lack of legal safeguards and numerous cases of prolonged detention.

ICE made useful proposals in 2010 for better addressing sexual abuse in immigration facilities and mistreatment of detainees with mental disabilities, but few have been implemented at this writing.

In late 2009 Human Rights Watch reported on the problem of extensive transfers of immigrant detainees between facilities across the US. More than 1.4 million detainee transfers occurred between 1999 and 2008, interfering with detainees' rights to access counsel, witnesses, and evidence. In July 2010 ICE announced the launch of an online detainee locator system—an important reform—but Congress has taken no steps to check ICE's expansive transfer power and ICE has failed to promulgate a promised policy to reduce transfers.

ICE also continues to have sweeping deportation powers. In June Assistant Secretary John Morton wrote of his desire to prioritize the deportation of "dangerous non-citizen criminals." If implemented, this would be an important reform—the largest numbers of deportations have been of non-violent and low-level offenders—but prospects for change in ICE practices remains unclear at this writing.

According to figures released in 2010 by the Center for Constitutional Rights and other groups, 79 percent of deportations under ICE's "Secure Communities" program were of nonviolent and low-level offenders. Human Rights Watch's own analysis of government data showed that three-quarters of non-citizens deported between 1997 and 2007 were nonviolent or low-level offenders. Under draconian laws passed in 1996, judges in many deportation cases are given no discretion to allow immigrants convicted of such minor offenses to remain in the US, regardless of their lawful presence in the country, status as a spouse or parent of a US citizen, economic contributions, or service in the US military.

Congressional efforts to overhaul the immigration system continued to flatline. No immigration reform bill moved in Congress, including the DREAM Act—designed to help immigrant children who grow up in the US—which was originally introduced in 2001. The current system has created a massive underground of persons who have lived undocumented in the US for many years. According to the Pew Hispanic Center, 5.9 million undocumented persons (53 percent of all undocumented persons) have lived in the US for more than 10 years, and 1.4 million have lived in the country for more than 20 years. A July 2010 Human Rights Watch report, *Tough, Fair, and Practical*, describes how lawmakers' failure to reform US immigration law violates basic human rights principles.

Individual US states continued to propose problematic immigration laws in 2010. An Arizona law, SB 1070, authorized police to interrogate anyone they reasonably suspect to be undocumented. In July a federal court enjoined enforcement of the most controversial sections of SB 1070, including "reasonable suspicion" interrogations, on grounds that federal immigration law preempts the Arizona statute and that lawfully-present aliens would be impermissibly burdened by the law. The court's decision is under appeal.

Labor Rights

US workers continue to face severe obstacles in forming and joining trade unions, and the US government is failing to meet its international obligation to protect their exercise of these rights. Human Rights Watch supported the Employee Free Choice Act, a modest legislative proposal to reduce some of these obstacles, but a Senate filibuster threat has blocked the bill for two years.

Fields of Peril

Child Labor in US Agriculture

HUMAN
RIGHTS
WATCH

Human Rights Watch's September 2010 report, *A Strange Case*, focused on violations of US workers' organizing and bargaining rights by European-based multinational corporations operating in the US. European firms that claim to comply with International Labor Organization core labor standards and other human rights laws too often violate these norms in their US operations, where labor laws offer substandard protections in key areas.

A May 2010 Human Rights Watch report, *Fields of Peril*, reported on the working conditions faced by hundreds of thousands of children who work on US farms. The 1938 Fair Labor Standards Act specifically exempts farmworker children from the minimum age and maximum hour requirements that apply to all other working children, exposing them to work at far younger ages, for far longer hours, and under far more hazardous conditions. Federal protections that do exist are often not enforced, and state child labor laws vary in strength and enforcement. As a result, child farmworkers, most of whom are Latino, often work 10 or more hours a day and risk pesticide poisoning, heat illness, injuries, and life-long disabilities. Many drop out of school and girls are sometimes subject to sexual harassment.

Health Policy

In March 2010 President Obama signed the Patient Protection and Affordable Care Act, which will provide health insurance to some 32 million uninsured Americans. However, the act's restrictions on how insurance companies may provide coverage for abortions are expected to impede abortion access.

In July 2010 the Obama administration issued the first National AIDS Strategy for the US. HIV infections in the US continue to rise at an alarming rate, particularly in minority communities, and many states continue to undermine both human rights and public health with abstinence-only restrictions on sex education, inadequate legal protections for HIV-positive persons, resistance to harm-reduction programs such as syringe exchange, and failure to fund HIV prevention and care.

Women's and Girls' Rights

Despite the Obama administration's stated support for ratification of the global women's rights treaty, the Convention on the Elimination of All Forms of

Discrimination against Women, neither the administration nor the Senate moved toward ratification. The US now stands as one of only seven nations that have not joined the treaty. A bill to enhance US efforts to combat violence against women globally gained momentum in 2010, but remained pending in Congress at this writing.

In the workplace, women continue to make 77 cents for every dollar earned by men. The US is one of only a handful of countries that have no guarantee of paid maternity leave and pregnancy discrimination claims have risen sharply. Women remain significantly underrepresented at all levels of government, including in the US Congress, where they constitute just over 17 percent of members.

Women experiencing violence in the US face barriers to safety and justice. Thousands of requests for emergency shelter and transitional housing from domestic violence survivors go unmet every year, with federal funding for such services falling short of targeted levels. In July Human Rights Watch released a report showing that up to 80 percent of rape kits (DNA evidence collected from a victim's body) in the state of Illinois may never have been tested. The state is attempting to address this problem: Governor Pat Quinn signed a bill contemporaneously with the release of the Human Rights Watch report requiring local law enforcement officials to send rape kit evidence for testing, making Illinois the first state in the nation to do so.

Discrimination Based on Sexual Orientation and Gender Identity

US law offers no protection against discrimination based on sexual orientation or gender identity. The Uniting American Families Act, which would allow same-sex relationships between a US citizen and a foreign national to be recognized for immigration purposes, did not advance in Congress. The Defense of Marriage Act (DOMA), which prohibits the federal government from recognizing the relationships formed by same-sex couples, remains in force.

There have been steps at the state level to better protect the rights of lesbian, gay, bisexual, and transgender people. A federal district court in Massachusetts declared unconstitutional the DOMA provision that prohibits the federal government from recognizing same-sex marriages valid in other jurisdictions. Separate district courts in California ruled that the California constitutional amendment barring same-sex couples from marrying (Proposition 8) and the federal policy barring lesbian, gay, and bisexual people from serving openly in the military (Don't Ask Don't Tell) violate the US Constitution.

A move in Congress in May to repeal Don't Ask Don't Tell remains pending at this writing. The Employment Non-Discrimination Act—a bill that would prohibit discrimination in employment based on sexual orientation or gender identity at the federal level—is also pending before Congress.

Counterterrorism

Despite overwhelming evidence that senior Bush administration officials approved illegal interrogation methods involving torture and other ill-treatment, the Obama administration has yet to pursue prosecutions of any high-level officials or to establish a commission of inquiry. In January the Justice Department's Office of Professional Responsibility released a report concluding that top lawyers in the Bush-era Office of Legal Counsel did not violate legal ethics rules when they wrote memos authorizing so-called enhanced interrogation techniques, but rather "exercised poor judgment."

Although Attorney General Eric Holder appointed a federal prosecutor in 2009 to review post-9/11 interrogation practices, the prosecutor has yet to issue a report and, by all indications, the investigation is unlikely to examine the responsibility of senior officials who set the policies in place and authorized the abuses. The Obama administration's continued invocation of an overly broad understanding of the "state secrets" privilege was accepted by several courts, cutting off another possible avenue for redress for victims of torture and other abuses.

In transferring counterterrorism detainees abroad, the Obama administration said that it would continue to rely on "diplomatic assurances": non-binding and often unreliable promises from the receiving country that detainees would be treated humanely. In July the Obama administration transferred a detainee from Guantanamo to his native Algeria on the basis of such assurances, despite his

UNITED STATES

Counterterrorism
and Human Rights

A Report Card on President Obama's First Year

HUMAN
RIGHTS
WATCH

UNITED STATES

"I Used to Think the Law Would Protect Me"

Illinois's Failure to Test Rape Kits

HUMAN
RIGHTS
WATCH

claims that he would face torture or ill-treatment by the Algerian government or non-state actors.

The Obama administration missed its self-imposed deadline to shut down Guantanamo and failed to provide any real indication of when the facility would actually be closed. Although the administration did not seek to enact preventive detention legislation, it continues to hold suspects without charge at Guantanamo based on wartime detention authority. In May the administration announced its plans to continue to hold indefinitely at least 48 detainees who have already been in US custody for approximately eight years. Following an attempted attack on a US jetliner in December 2009 by a Nigerian man who allegedly trained with al Qaeda in Yemen, the administration stopped transferring detainees to Yemen, leaving 57 Yemeni detainees whose transfers had been approved stuck at Guantanamo indefinitely.

The political uproar that followed Attorney General Holder's announcement in November 2009 that Khalid Sheikh Mohammed and four other "high-value" detainees would be tried in federal criminal court led the administration to recon-sider its decision. At this writing no decision has been made as to where and how they would be tried.

Meanwhile the administration pursued other cases in military commissions, including the prosecution of Ibrahim al Qosi, a Sudanese man who pled guilty but whose sentence was kept secret. The Obama administration also pursued the military commission prosecution of child soldier Omar Khadr, even though Khadr was only 15 years old when he was captured, and he was charged with an offense not considered to be a war crime. Despite some improvements to the military commissions, they continue to lack the basic guarantees of fairness found in US federal courts, allow certain evidence obtained coercively, discriminate against non-citizens, and are used to prosecute people for conduct that has never before been considered a violation of the laws of war, raising serious retroactivity concerns.

ASIA AND THE MIDDLE EAST

Slow Reform

Protection of Migrant Domestic Workers in Asia
and the Middle East

HUMAN
RIGHTS
WATCH

WORLD REPORT

2011

2010
HUMAN RIGHTS WATCH
PUBLICATIONS

By Country

Afghanistan
The "Ten-Dollar Talib" and Women's Rights: Afghan Women and the Risks of Reintegration and Reconciliation, July 2010, 65pp.

Angola
Transparency and Accountability in Angola, April 2010, 31pp.

Argentina
Illusions of Care: Lack of Accountability for Reproductive Rights in Argentina, August 2010, 52pp.

Azerbaijan
Beaten, Blacklisted, and Behind Bars: The Vanishing Space for Freedom of Expression in Azerbaijan, October 2010, 94pp.

Bahrain
Slow Reform: Protection of Migrant Domestic Workers in Asia and the Middle East, April 2010, 26pp.

Torture Redux: The Revival of Physical Coercion during Interrogations in Bahrain, February 2010, 89pp.

Bangladesh
"Trigger Happy": Excessive Use of Force by Indian Troops at the Bangladesh Border, December 2010, 81pp.

Burma
"I Want to Help My Own People": State Control and Civil Society in Burma after Cyclone Nargis, April 2010, 102pp.

Burundi
Closing Doors?: The Narrowing of Democratic Space in Burundi, November 2010, 69pp.

"We'll Tie You Up and Shoot You": Lack of Accountability for Political Violence in Burundi, May 2010, 47pp.

Mob Justice in Burundi: Official Complicity and Impunity, March 2010, 105pp.

Cambodia

Off the Streets: Arbitrary Detention and Other Abuses against Sex Workers in Cambodia, July 2010, 76pp.

"Skin on the Cable": The Illegal Arrest, Arbitrary Detention and Torture of People Who Use Drugs in Cambodia, January 2010, 93pp.

Cameroon

Criminalizing Identities: Rights Abuses in Cameroon based on Sexual Orientation and Gender Identity, November 2010, 62pp.

China

"I Saw It with My Own Eyes": Abuses by Chinese Security Forces in Tibet, 2008-2010, July 2010, 73pp.

"Where Darkness Knows No Limits": Incarceration, Ill-Treatment and Forced Labor as Drug Rehabilitation in China, January 2010, 37pp.

Colombia

Paramilitaries' Heirs: The New Face of Violence in Colombia, February 2010, 122pp.

Cote d'Ivoire

Afraid and Forgotten: Lawlessness, Rape, and Impunity in Western Côte d'Ivoire, October 2010, 72pp.

Croatia

"Once You Enter, You Never Leave": Deinstitutionalization of Persons with Intellectual or Mental Disabilities in Croatia, September 2010, 74pp.

Democratic Republic of Congo

Tackling Impunity in Congo: Meaningful Follow-up to the UN Mapping Report, October 2010, 16pp.

Always on the Run: The Vicious Cycle of Displacement in Eastern Congo, September 2010, 88pp.

Trail of Death: LRA Atrocities in Northeastern Congo, March 2010, 67pp.

"You Will Be Punished": Attacks on Civilians in Eastern Congo, December 2009, 183pp.

Egypt

Elections in Egypt: State of Permanent Emergency Incompatible with Free and Fair Vote, November 2010, 24pp.

Ethiopia

Development without Freedom: How Aid Underwrites Repression in Ethiopia, October 2010, 105pp.

"One Hundred Ways of Putting Pressure": Violations of Freedom of Expression and Association in Ethiopia, March 2010, 59pp.

France

"No Questions Asked": Intelligence Cooperation with Countries that Torture, June 2010, 62pp.

Germany

"No Questions Asked": Intelligence Cooperation with Countries that Torture, June 2010, 62pp.

Guinea

Bloody Monday: The September 28 Massacre and Rapes by Security Forces in Guinea, December 2009, 108pp.

Honduras

After the Coup: Ongoing Violence, Intimidation, and Impunity in Honduras, December 2010, 79pp.

India

Dignity on Trial: India's Need for Sound Standards for Conducting and Interpreting Forensic Examinations of Rape Survivors, September 2010, 54pp.

Back to the Future: India's 2008 Counterterrorism Laws, July 2010, 20pp.

Indonesia

Policing Morality: Abuses in the Application of Sharia in Aceh, Indonesia, December 2010, 10pp.

Prosecuting Political Aspiration: Indonesia's Political Prisoners, June 2010, 43pp.

Turning Critics into Criminals: The Human Rights Consequences of Criminal Defamation Law in Indonesia, May 2010, 91pp.

"Unkept Promise": Failure to End Military Business Activity in Indonesia, January 2010, 20pp.

Iran

Iran: Abuses against LGBT People, December 2010, 77pp.

The Islamic Republic at 31: Post-election Abuses Show Serious Human Rights Crisis, February 2010, 19pp.

Iraq

"They Took Me and Told Me Nothing": Female Genital Mutilation in Iraqi Kurdistan, June 2010, 80pp.

Ireland

A State of Isolation: Access to Abortion for Women in Ireland, January 2010, 57pp.

Israel and the Occupied Territories

"I Lost Everything": Israel's Unlawful Destruction of Property during Operation Cast Lead, May 2010, 116pp.

Turning a Blind Eye: Impunity for Laws-of-War Violations during the Gaza War, April 2010, 62pp.

Jordan

Slow Reform: Protection of Migrant Domestic Workers in Asia and the Middle East, April 2010, 26pp.

Stateless Again: Palestinian-Origin Jordanians Deprived of their Nationality, February 2010, 60pp.

Kazakhstan

"Hellish Work": Exploitation of Migrant Tobacco Workers in Kazakhstan, July 2010, 115pp.

Kenya

Needless Pain: Government Failure to Provide Palliative Care for Children in Kenya, September 2010, 78pp.

"I Am Not Dead, But I Am Not Living": Barriers to Fistula Prevention and Treatment in Kenya, July 2010, 82pp.

"Welcome to Kenya": Police Abuse of Somali Refugees, June 2010, 99pp.

Kosovo
Rights Displaced: Forced Returns of Roma, Ashkali and Egyptians from Western Europe
to Kosovo, October 2010, 77pp.

Kuwait
Walls at Every Turn: Abuse of Migrant Domestic Workers through Kuwait's Sponsorship System,
October 2010, 97pp.

Slow Reform: Protection of Migrant Domestic Workers in Asia and the Middle East,
April 2010, 26pp.

Kyrgyistan
"Where is the Justice?": Interethnic Violence in Southern Kyrgyzstan and its Aftermath,
August 2010, 91pp.

Lebanon
Without Protection: How the Lebanese Justice System Fails Migrant Domestic Workers,
September 2010, 54pp.

Slow Reform: Protection of Migrant Domestic Workers in Asia and the Middle East,
April 2010, 26pp.

Libya
Libya: Silencing Civil Society: Draft Association Law Fails to Protect Freedom of Association,
December 2010, 18pp.

Malaysia
Slow Reform: Protection of Migrant Domestic Workers in Asia and the Middle East,
April 2010, 26pp.

Morocco

Morocco: "Stop Looking for Your Son": Illegal Detentions under the
Counterterrorism Law, October 2010, 56pp.

Nigeria
"Everyone's in on the Game": Corruption and Human Rights Abuses by the Nigeria Police Force,
August 2010, 102pp.

Pakistan

Their Future is at Stake: Attacks on Teachers and Schools in Pakistan's Balochistan Province, December 2010, 40pp.

Philippines

"They Own the People": The Ampatuans, State-Backed Militias, November 2010, 96pp.

Rwanda

Genocide, War Crimes and Crimes Against Humanity: A Digest of the Case Law of the International Criminal Tribunal for Rwanda, January 2010, 500pp.

São Tomé e Príncipe

An Uncertain Future: Oil Contracts and Stalled Reform in São Tomé e Príncipe, August 2010, 23pp.

Saudi Arabia

Looser Rein, Uncertain Gain: A Human Rights Assessment of Five Years of King Abdullah's Reforms in Saudi Arabia, September 2010, 52pp.

Slow Reform: Protection of Migrant Domestic Workers in Asia and the Middle East, April 2010, 26pp.

Senegal

Fear for Life: Violence against Gay Men and Men Perceived as Gay in Senegal, November 2010, 95pp.

"Off the Backs of the Children": Forced Begging and Other Abuses against Talibés in Senegal, April 2010, 114pp.

Singapore

Slow Reform: Protection of Migrant Domestic Workers in Asia and the Middle East, April 2010, 26pp.

Somalia

Harsh War, Harsh Peace: Abuses by al-Shabaab, the Transitional Federal Government, and AMISOM in Somalia, April 2010, 62pp.

Spain

Eternal Emergency: No End to Unaccompanied Migrant Children's Institutionalization in Canary Islands Emergency Centers, June 2010, 40pp.

Sri Lanka

Legal Limbo: The Uncertain Fate of Detained LTTE Suspects in Sri Lanka, February 2010, 30pp.

Sudan

Democracy on Hold: Rights Violations in the April 2010 Sudan Elections, June 2010, 32pp.

Syria

A Wasted Decade: Human Rights in Syria during Bashar al-Asad's First Ten Years in Power, July 2010, 35pp.

Thailand

"Targets of Both Sides": Violence against Students, Teachers, and Schools in Thailand's Southern Border Provinces, September 2010, 111pp.

From the Tiger to the Crocodile: Abuse of Migrant Workers in Thailand, February 2010, 124pp.

Tunisia

The Price of Independence: Silencing Labor and Student Unions in Tunisia, October 2010, 62pp.

Repression of Former Political Prisoners in Tunisia: "A Larger Prison", March 2010, 42pp.

Turkey

Protesting as a Terrorist Offense: The Arbitrary Use of Terrorism Laws to Prosecute and Incarcerate Demonstrators in Turkey, November 2010, 74pp.

Uganda

"As if We Weren't Human": Discrimination and Violence against Women with Disabilities in Northern Uganda, August 2010, 73pp.

A Media Minefield: Increased Threats to Freedom of Expression in Uganda, May 2010, 60pp.

Making Kampala Count: Advancing the Global Fight against Impunity at the ICC Review Conference, May 2010, 102pp.

United Arab Emirates

Slow Reform: Protection of Migrant Domestic Workers in Asia and the Middle East, April 2010, 26pp.

United Kingdom

Without Suspicion: Stop and Search under the Terrorism Act 2000, July 2010, 64pp.

"No Questions Asked": Intelligence Cooperation with Countries that Torture, June 2010, 62pp.

Fast-Tracked Unfairness: Detention and Denial of Women Asylum Seekers in the UK, February 2010, 69pp.

United States

The Price of Freedom: Bail, Pretrial Detention, and Nonfelony Defendants in New York City, December 2010, 75pp.

A Strange Case: Violations of Workers' Freedom of Association in the United States by European Multinational Corporations, September 2010, 130pp.

Detained and at Risk: Sexual Abuse and Harassment in United States Immigration Detention, August 2010, 24pp.

Deportation by Default: Mental Disability, Unfair Hearings, and Indefinite Detention in the US Immigration System, July 2010, 98pp.

"I Used to Think the Law Would Protect Me": Illinois's Failure to Test Rape Kits, July 2010, 42pp.

"Tough, Fair, and Practical": A Human Rights Framework for Immigration Reform in the United States, July 2010, 24pp.

Costly and Unfair: Flaws in US Immigration Detention Policy, May 2010, 11pp.

Fields of Peril: Child Labor in US Agriculture, May 2010, 99pp.

My So-Called Emancipation: From Foster Care to Homelessness for California Youth, May 2010, 70pp.

Sentenced to Stigma: Segregation of HIV-Positive Prisoners in Alabama and South Carolina, April 2010, 45pp.

Jailing Refugees: Arbitrary Detention of Refugees in the US Who Fail to Adjust to Permanent Resident Status, December 2009, 40pp.

Yemen

All Quiet on the Northern Front?: Uninvestigated Laws of War Violations in Yemen's War with Huthi Rebels, April 2010, 54pp.

Hostile Shores: Abuse and Refoulement of Asylum Seekers and Refugees in Yemen, December 2009, 53pp.

In the Name of Unity: The Yemeni Government's Brutal Response to Southern Movement Protests, December 2009, 73pp.

Zambia

Unjust and Unhealthy: HIV, TB, and Abuse in Zambian Prisons, April 2010, 135pp.

Zimbabwe

Deliberate Chaos: Ongoing Human Rights Abuses in the Marange Diamond Fields of Zimbabwe, June 2010, 16pp.

Sleight of Hand: Repression of the Media and the Illusion of Reform in Zimbabwe, April 2010, 26pp.

Making Kampala Count

Advancing the Global Fight against Impunity
at the ICC Review Conference

**HUMAN
RIGHTS
WATCH**

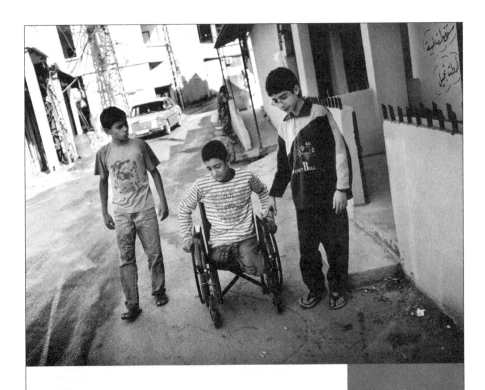

Meeting the Challenge

Protecting Civilians through the Convention
on Cluster Munitions

HUMAN
RIGHTS
WATCH

BY THEME

Arms Issues

Meeting the Challenge: Protecting Civilians through the Convention on Cluster Munitions, November 2010, 224pp.

Business and Human Rights Issues

A Strange Case: Violations of Workers' Freedom of Association in the United States by European Multinational Corporations, September 2010, 130pp.

An Uncertain Future: Oil Contracts and Stalled Reform in São Tomé e Príncipe, August 2010, 23pp.

"Hellish Work": Exploitation of Migrant Tobacco Workers in Kazakhstan, July 2010, 115pp.

Deliberate Chaos: Ongoing Human Rights Abuses in the Marange Diamond Fields of Zimbabwe, June 2010, 16pp.

Transparency and Accountability in Angola, April 2010, 31pp.

"Unkept Promise": Failure to End Military Business Activity in Indonesia, January 2010, 20pp.

Children's Rights Issues

Their Future is at Stake: Attacks on Teachers and Schools in Pakistan's Balochistan Province, December 2010, 40pp.

Needless Pain: Government Failure to Provide Palliative Care for Children in Kenya, September 2010, 78pp.

"Targets of Both Sides": Violence against Students, Teachers, and Schools in Thailand's Southern Border Provinces, September 2010, 111pp.

"Hellish Work": Exploitation of Migrant Tobacco Workers in Kazakhstan, July 2010, 115pp.

"Tough, Fair, and Practical": A Human Rights Framework for Immigration Reform in the United States, July 2010, 24pp.

Eternal Emergency: No End to Unaccompanied Migrant Children's Institutionalization in Canary Islands Emergency Centers, June 2010, 40pp.

Fields of Peril: Child Labor in US Agriculture, May 2010, 99pp.

"I Lost Everything": Israel's Unlawful Destruction of Property during Operation Cast Lead, May 2010, 116pp.

My So-Called Emancipation: From Foster Care to Homelessness for California Youth, May 2010, 70pp.

"Off the Backs of the Children: Forced Begging and Other Abuses against Talibés in Senegal, April 2010, 114pp.

"Skin on the Cable": The Illegal Arrest, Arbitrary Detention and Torture of People Who Use Drugs in Cambodia, January 2010, 93pp.

Disability Rights Issues

"Once You Enter, You Never Leave": Deinstitutionalization of Persons with Intellectual or Mental Disabilities in Croatia, September 2010, 74pp.

"As if We Weren't Human": Discrimination and Violence against Women with Disabilities in Northern Uganda, August 2010, 73pp.

Deportation by Default: Mental Disability, Unfair Hearings, and Indefinite Detention in the US Immigration System, July 2010, 98pp.

Health and Human Rights Issues

Development without Freedom: How Aid Underwrites Repression in Ethiopia, October 2010, 105pp.

Needless Pain: Government Failure to Provide Palliative Care for Children in Kenya, September 2010, 78pp.

Illusions of Care: Lack of Accountability for Reproductive Rights in Argentina, August 2010, 52pp.

"I Am Not Dead, But I Am Not Living": Barriers to Fistula Prevention and Treatment in Kenya, July 2010, 82pp.

"I Used to Think the Law Would Protect Me": Illinois's Failure to Test Rape Kits, July 2010, 42pp.

Unaccountable: Addressing Reproductive Health Care Gaps, May 2010, 10pp.

Sentenced to Stigma: Segregation of HIV-Positive Prisoners in Alabama and South Carolina, April 2010, 45pp.

Unjust and Unhealthy: HIV, TB, and Abuse in Zambian Prisons, April 2010, 135pp.

"Skin on the Cable": The Illegal Arrest, Arbitrary Detention and Torture of People Who Use Drugs in Cambodia, January 2010, 93pp.

"Where Darkness Knows No Limits": Incarceration, Ill-Treatment and Forced Labor as Drug Rehabilitation in China, January 2010, 37pp.

International Justice Issues

Memorandum for the Ninth Session of the International Criminal Court Assembly of States Parties, November 2010, 37pp.

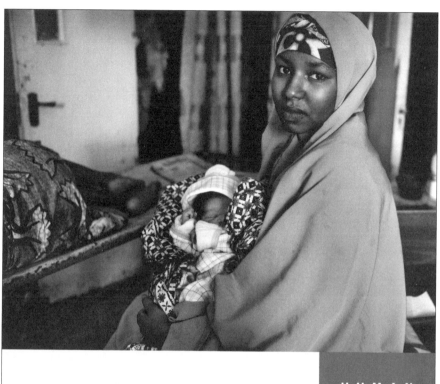

Unaccountable

Addressing Reproductive Health Care Gaps

HUMAN RIGHTS WATCH

GENOCIDE, WAR CRIMES
AND CRIMES
AGAINST HUMANITY

H U M A N
R I G H T S
W A T C H

A Digest of the Case Law of the
International Criminal Tribunal for Rwanda

Tackling Impunity in Congo: Meaningful Follow-up to the UN Mapping Report, October 2010, 16pp.

Making Kampala Count: Advancing the Global Fight against Impunity at the ICC Review Conference, May 2010, 102pp.

Genocide, War Crimes and Crimes Against Humanity: A Digest of the Case Law of the International Criminal Tribunal for Rwanda, January 2010, 500pp.

LGBT Rights Issues

Criminalizing Identities: Rights Abuses in Cameroon based on Sexual Orientation and Gender Identity, November 2010, 62pp.

Fear for Life: Violence against Gay Men and Men Perceived as Gay in Senegal, November 2010, 95pp.

"Tough, Fair, and Practical": A Human Rights Framework for Immigration Reform in the United States, July 2010, 24pp.

Migrant Worker Issues

Ukraine: Buffeted in the Borderland: The Treatment of Asylum Seekers and Migrants in Ukraine, December 2010, 123pp.

Walls at Every Turn: Abuse of Migrant Domestic Workers through Kuwait's Sponsorship System, October 2010, 97pp.

Without Protection: How the Lebanese Justice System Fails Migrant Domestic Workers, September 2010, 54pp.

Deportation by Default: Mental Disability, Unfair Hearings, and Indefinite Detention in the US Immigration System, July 2010, 98pp.

"Hellish Work": Exploitation of Migrant Tobacco Workers in Kazakhstan, July 2010, 115pp.

"Tough, Fair, and Practical": A Human Rights Framework for Immigration Reform in the United States, July 2010, 24pp.

Eternal Emergency: No End to Unaccompanied Migrant Children's Institutionalization in Canary Islands Emergency Centers, June 2010, 40pp.

Fields of Peril: Child Labor in US Agriculture, May 2010, 99pp.

"Off the Backs of the Children: Forced Begging and Other Abuses against Talibés in Senegal, April 2010, 114pp.

Slow Reform: Protection of Migrant Domestic Workers in Asia and the Middle East, April 2010, 26pp.

Unjust and Unhealthy: HIV, TB, and Abuse in Zambian Prisons, April 2010, 135pp.

From the Tiger to the Crocodile: Abuse of Migrant Workers in Thailand, February 2010, 124pp.

Refugees/Displaced Persons Issues

Rights Displaced: Forced Returns of Roma, Ashkali and Egyptians from Western Europe to Kosovo, October 2010, 77pp.

Always on the Run: The Vicious Cycle of Displacement in Eastern Congo, September 2010, 88pp.

"Where is the Justice?": Interethnic Violence in Southern Kyrgyzstan and its Aftermath, August 2010, 91pp.

"Tough, Fair, and Practical": A Human Rights Framework for Immigration Reform in the United States, July 2010, 24pp.

"Welcome to Kenya": Police Abuse of Somali Refugees, June 2010, 94pp.

Costly and Unfair: Flaws in US Immigration Detention Policy, May 2010, 11pp.

Fast-Tracked Unfairness: Detention and Denial of Women Asylum Seekers in the UK, February 2010, 69pp.

Terrorism and Counterterrorism Issues

Protesting as a Terrorist Offense: The Arbitrary Use of Terrorism Laws to Prosecute and Incarcerate Demonstrators in Turkey, November 2010, 74pp.

Morocco: "Stop Looking for Your Son": Illegal Detentions under the Counterterrorism Law, October 2010, 56pp.

Back to the Future: India's 2008 Counterterrorism Laws, July 2010, 20pp.

Without Suspicion: Stop and Search under the Terrorism Act 2000, July 2010, 64pp.

"No Questions Asked": Intelligence Cooperation with Countries that Torture, June 2010, 62pp.

Harsh War, Harsh Peace: Abuses by al-Shabaab, the Transitional Federal Government, and AMI-SOM in Somalia, April 2010, 62pp.

Women's Rights Issues

Policing Morality: Abuses in the Application of Sharia in Aceh, Indonesia, December 2010, 10pp.

Criminalizing Identities: Rights Abuses in Cameroon based on Sexual Orientation and Gender Identity, November 2010, 62pp.

Afraid and Forgotten: Lawlessness, Rape, and Impunity in Western Côte d'Ivoire, October 2010, 72pp.

SENEGAL

Fear for Life

Violence against Gay Men and Men Perceived
as Gay in Senegal

**H U M A N
R I G H T S
W A T C H**

Dignity on Trial: India's Need for Sound Standards for Conducting and Interpreting Forensic Examinations of Rape Survivors, September 2010, 54pp.

Detained and at Risk: Sexual Abuse and Harassment in United States Immigration Detention, August 2010, 24pp.

Illusions of Care: Lack of Accountability for Reproductive Rights in Argentina, August 2010, 52pp.

"I Am Not Dead, But I Am Not Living": Barriers to Fistula Prevention and Treatment in Kenya, July 2010, 82pp.

"I Used to Think the Law Would Protect Me": Illinois's Failure to Test Rape Kits, July 2010, 42pp.

The "Ten-Dollar Talib" and Women's Rights: Afghan Women and the Risks of Reintegration and Reconciliation, July 2010, 65pp.

"Tough, Fair, and Practical": A Human Rights Framework for Immigration Reform in the United States, July 2010, 24pp.

"They Took Me and Told Me Nothing": Female Genital Mutilation in Iraqi Kurdistan, June 2010, 80pp.

"Welcome to Kenya": Police Abuse of Somali Refugees, June 2010, 94pp.

Unaccountable: Addressing Reproductive Health Care Gaps, May 2010, 10pp.

Slow Reform: Protection of Migrant Domestic Workers in Asia and the Middle East, April 2010, 26pp.

Fast-Tracked Unfairness: Detention and Denial of Women Asylum Seekers in the UK, February 2010, 69pp.

A State of Isolation: Access to Abortion for Women in Ireland, January 2010, 57pp.

All reports can be accessed online and ordered at www.hrw.org/en/publications.